Indian Education

A Developmental Discourse

Editors
Marmar Mukhopadhyay
Madhu Parhar

Educational Technology and Management Academy, Gurgaon

SHIPRA

Rs. 1250; US$ 62.50

ISBN: 978-81-7541-780-9

First Published in India in 2015

Indian Education: A Developmental Discourse

Published by:
SHIPRA PUBLICATIONS
LG 18-19, Pankaj Central Market, I.P. Ext.
Patparganj, Delhi-110092
Tel: 91-11-2223 5152, 2223 6152
E-mail: info@shiprapublication.com
www.shiprapublication.com

Preface

Documenting developments in Indian education was initiated to commemorate 50 years of Indian independence. Beginning in 1997, we published Indian Education: Development since Independence in 1999. The first publication caught the imagination of researchers, students of education and policy makers at the highest level alike. There may be several reasons. Firstly, there is no well documented account of post independence developments in education. Secondly, the book presented developments in every department of education under one umbrella. Thirdly, instead of one-person view, the book carried specialist views and assessments in the concerned areas making the book authentic. Also, the book brought in multiple view points because it adopted 'symposia format'. Encouraged by the success, we brought out an updated but substantially different version, Education in India: Dynamics of Development in 2007 because there were many developments in ten years.

Now we have entered into the second decade of the 21st century. We are encouraged to analyse the Indian education from within the system. Accordingly, we present Indian Education: A Developmental Discourse to our readers. The format of this book is different from the earlier ones. The book contains six major themes. Under each theme, there are few chapters authored by experts in the field. Each chapter carries the assessment and viewpoint of the concerned author(s), and not necessarily those of the editors.

In the first chapter, author takes a comprehensive helicopter view of educational developments focusing on achievements, missing targets, and 'miles to go'. Elementary Education comprises three chapters. One chapter examines the status, growth, policies, special schemes and interventions. Two other chapters examine Right to Education Act implemented in 2009, especially from the angle of challenge of achieving equity and equality in elementary education. Next section on secondary education comprises again three chapters. First chapter brings in a detailed account of policies, plans, achievements, schemes, etc. in secondary education. This is followed by two chapters; one, a critique on secondary education and two on scientific techniques of student assessment. Higher Education has faced multiple challenges since independence. Following the same pattern, first chapter in higher education brings in an authentic analysis of developments of higher education. Second chapter provides a global perspective on higher education. Third chapter under this section is on Open and Distance Higher Education. Teacher education is critically positioned for quality improvement in education. Under this theme, there are two chapters. One provides a glimpse of ongoing reforms and needed reforms; the other is a critique on National Curricular Framework for Teacher Education, 2010 an instrument of reforms in teacher education. Inclusion refers not only to children with special needs but it is inclusion of marginalised groups. The theme on Education for Inclusion brings in four chapters one each on adult education in India after Independence, education of persons with disabilities, women's education, and empowerment of junior youth. There is a chapter on ICT in Education covering status, innovations in ICT as well as concerns about under utilization of ICT in education. The book closes with a chapter – a case study of educational reform initiatives in Gujarat.

This book is not a mere description of educational developments, but a critical developmental discourse at the hands of some of the most authentic scholars in the field. I am grateful to all the contributing authors for their patience allowing us time enough to bring this book to fruition. I thank Ms. Gopa Biswas for lending her editing hand in the manuscript. I am equally thankful to Mr. D. Kumar of Shipra Publications for undertaking this publication project. I am equally thankful to Sri Sabyasachi Panja for the beautiful cover design of this book.

I cannot thank my co-editor. But I feel fortunate enough to edit this book with Prof. Marmar Mukhopadhyay. His support, patience and encouragement were most helpful in this task.

We hope that this book too will find favour with readers who have either an abiding interest in education, or need to understand how Indian education has evolved to give shape to the future of education, hence India.

November 5, 2014 **Madhu Parhar**
ETMA: Gurgaon

Contents

1

Indian Education

Where have we Arrived? Where are we to Go?[1]

Marmar Mukhopadhyay

Most unmistakable conclusion about Indian education is its massive growth moving steadfastly towards equity through increasing access, almost from rubbles of 1947 to making of the castle in 2020's. From 19 per cent literacy in 1951 it stands not only at 74 per cent but also is the home of second largest literate population in the world. Indian elementary education is simply massive; there is no country in the world that feeds more than 120 million children every day in the school (mid-day meal); there are not many countries of India's comparable economic development where Right to Education is a right. Secondary education, thus far neglected is catching up. Higher education with 20 per cent GER steadily moving towards targeted 30 per cent by 2020, makes it the third largest higher education system in the world. Though there are not many high quality institutions of higher education in India, by default due to demographic advantage, Indian top-end graduates ably compete with their peers from the developed countries. To quote, Philip Altbach, "*India has not done bad at all*".

Quality education for all (at least many) is the biggest casualty in this otherwise encouraging and optimistic scenario. Plotting equity and quality on a linear sequence as a policy is largely responsible for this equity-quality imbalance. System failed to recognise that in the scheme of educational development, quality is the necessary condition for achieving equity. Poor quality education is like filling a bucket (equity) with a hole at the bottom (drop out, unemployability, poor thinking skills, etc.). Hence, the other conclusion about Indian Education is: *it could have done better*.

India stands at the crossroads of political transition, if not transformation. Dutta (2014) termed it as end of Nehruvian Republic in his article from Nehru to Modi. New government, although elected in Republicans style is essentially shaping up as presidential form of government. It is keenly looking to reshape new educational policies. Next only to Sri P.V. Narasimha Rao, Sri Narendra Modi has serious interest in education[2]. This is the right time to stop, pause, and do a comprehensive diagnosis of educational developments in India. Appreciating all that has happened with brow ha ha! is self-fulfilling prophecy; but negating all the developments that happened despite the inheritance of a hugely illiterate population in dire poverty, a few schools and colleges strewn here and there in the vast land of India with all 12 religions of the world co-existing, linguistic and cultural diversity, and above all poor economic resources will also be cynical neglect of truth. At this juncture, we need to carry out an impartial scientific diagnosis of educational development to answer questions like where did we want to reach at the dawn of independence? Where have we arrived? What is the gap between our destination and point of arrival? Did we miss important opportunities? How should we ensure that we cover up the accumulated gap in the journey in the shortest possible time and at minimum cost?

Educational policies are political statements on education. With the paradigm shift in political ambiance and style of governance, there is a need to enact a new policy on education. Education is the foundation of development in all other sectors, be it infrastructure, health, defence, industry, external affairs, and what not; it does not require any fresh argument. It's time enough for a fresh policy on education. Last National Policy on Education was enacted in 1986, before economic liberalization. Lot of changes have happened in India and the world that warrants a new policy. Educational Technology and Management Academy (ETMA) articulated the need for a fresh policy in its International Conference in 2011.

My agenda in this chapter is to flag issues that should help us carry on a collective diagnosis of Indian education.

Starting Point

If we want to measure the distance that we were supposed to cover during the last 60 years, we need to find a landmark at the starting point. There is no better landmark than constitutional dictum (Article 45) that 'state shall endeavour to provide free and compulsory education upto the age of 14 within first 10 years [from the date of adoption of Indian Constitution in 1951]. The fathers of Indian Constitution left a big gap; instead of making state accountable by saying 'shall provide', it chose softer option of making state responsible only to 'endeavour to provide'. The difference is between commitments to making efforts versus performance accountability. The Indian state took it easy; Indian education lost out to other sectors. Later, the 'wisdom of politics' further mutilated the provision by restating the age of free and compulsory education from 6 to 14 thereby excluding children in the age group 0 to 6, especially when age of 3 to 6 is extremely important for preparation to schooling.

If we take this landmark (article 45) literally, by 1961, every child in the age group of at least 6 to 14 would have been in schools. People born after 1961, would now be 55-year-old. If every child would have gone to school, India would not have any illiterate person in the country, leave alone carrying the burden of defame of hosting the largest number of illiterates in the world. Further, by extrapolating transition rates from primary to elementary to secondary education, it can be assumed that more than 80 per cent children and adolescents of the concerned age group would have been participating in high and higher secondary education causing universal secondary education. The government policy states to move 'towards universal secondary education' as late as in 2010. With universal secondary education (80% participation rate), Indian higher education would have been equal to the OECD countries in terms of the rate of participation — anything between 40 to 50 per cent of the concerned age-group. It has not happened. We missed the bus right at the first five-year plan. We got so used to missing the buses (targets), India took missing the buses as normal. We could never make a turnaround. The accumulated gaps and deficiencies kept on increasing.

Because we did not succeed in education, our growth in agriculture, business and industry, health and in all walks of life became slow. India lost out. Lost out not only to the developed countries, but also lost out to many other developing countries, like China, Brazil, Russia, Indonesia, and in certain areas even to Sri Lanka and Bangladesh.

In this chapter, I'll scan Indian educational scenario from elementary to higher and technical education. This book carries several chapters that are authentic in terms of describing the present status of education at different levels by some of the distinguished scholar-authors. They literally describe where we have arrived. For brevity and avoiding repetition, I'll only flag in this chapter a few issues that need to be considered for framing India's future policy on education.

Adult Education

Adult education in India has been equated with adult literacy. Hence, compared to the global connotation of adult education, Indian connotation is extremely narrow. Irrespective of the literacy, challenge is information management that substantially influences quality of life in the modern world. When information transfer and management is largely picking up through the electronic and social media, the relevance of conventional literacy is an important question.

Examples are mobile based information and education of farmers, pregnant and lactating mothers, teachers and students, and many more. Nonetheless, importance of everybody being able to read and write cannot be underestimated. As mentioned in the introduction, if education for all children upto the age of 14 was implemented by 1961, India would not have any adult illiterate at all, now. If India was a literate India, adult education could have come out of its limited connotation of adult literacy; it could have taken up the mantle of adult and continuing education.

There is a very detailed discourse on adult education by an outstanding international scholar of the order of Prof. H.S. Bhola in this book (Chapter 13). I would restrict myself to flagging a few issues especially how we missed opportunities. Adult education had a very stunted growth as a movement in India. Indian Adult Education Association provided leadership and some of the most outstanding contributors were Satyen Moitra, Mushtaq Ahmad and others.

Adult education took the shape of a movement, and positively shook up the country in the early 1990s under the leadership of late Sri Anil Bordia, then Union Education Secretary, and his worthy comrade of indomitable spirit, Dr. Lakshmidhar Mishra, then Joint Secretary in the Ministry of Human Resource Development and Director-General of National Literacy Mission. Once this team moved out due to either retirement or transfer/promotion, the scheme came to the conventional hands. The movement lost its momentum, and continued in the usual ritualistic manner. During the peak period of the movement, government of India set up a specialised institute, Indian Adult Education Institute, with the primary objective of building grounded research base to support adult education movement. Probably, this also intended to fill the gap created due to the closure of the UNESCO Institute, then in Iran. The Indian Institute of Adult education was winded up and merged back into the Directorate of Adult Education, a subordinate office of the Ministry of HRD, Department of School Education and Literacy. India lost a major opportunity of positioning it globally in the field of adult education. Government needs to protect national policies, programmes and institutions from the whims and fancies of successive bureaucracy.

Elementary Education

In the chapter 2 on elementary education, Mehta and Chugh have provided a detailed account of developments in elementary education in India since independence. The expansion of facilities and enrolment, in other words access and equity, is phenomenal.

Primary education got a push from the 1990 Jomtien Conference where almost all the country heads put their minds together under the banner of the

International Organisations especially the UN organisations to create a literate world. This was designated as EFA (Education For All) movement. India was one of the signatories to the Jomtien resolution. As this EFA movement picked up, India hosted E-9 summit in 1993 where all the nine high population countries met in the presence of UN organisations, multilateral and bilateral organisations. This movement gathered momentum to set up Millennium Development Goals for 2015. Hence, the otherwise neglected primary education sector got some momentum with international pressure and also with international funding from the World Bank, UN organisations, European Union, and other bilateral agencies like DFID and others. This, however, did not happen at the same level in secondary education.

From the policy perspectives, we need to flag a few major issues. First and foremost is setting deadlines that successive governments never meant. The first deadline of universal elementary education in 1961 was violated. Every five-year plan, every policy statement has reiterated its intention without actually meaning it. To the extent, the constitutional directive of free and compulsory education up to age of 14 was mutilated on both sides. Education of children between 0 to 6 years was excluded; on the other end, the concept of free and compulsory education was reduced to primary education until grade 5 (UPE). With every five-year plan, the target was shifted so much so that India is still to fulfil its constitutional obligation of universal elementary education, leave alone its international commitment to Millennium Development Goals that is just one year away (2015). Government enacted RTE in 2009 inspiring a fresh hope to move towards universal elementary education with free and compulsory components being mandatory. Adequacy of funds and effective management are two major challenges.

Governments of India appointed several commissions and committees on secondary and higher education but left the most complicated domain of elementary education to the wisdom of politicians and bureaucrats. This is another indication of governmental apathy, if not policy deficit, with respect to universal elementary education.

This contention of policy deficit gets further strengthened by the fact that the approach to development has been rather concessional. If the primary school had one room, it was given one more room; if it had one teacher, it was given another teacher. From the angle of strategic planning, it is essentially concessional approach. There is no norm of primary schooling, the way it is there in secondary education (affiliating clauses). Compare it with the report on Universal Secondary Education that provides fairly clear list of norms of secondary schooling. Till today, we have not developed a norm for primary schooling. It may not be possible for fulfilling the norms immediately, but it provides a roadmap towards which it should move. Right to Education Act of 2009, once again, indicates the first commitment to infrastructure norms.

Further, the concept of teacher student ratio is far too outdated and nonworking. As the population growth rate reduces, number of students per school is reducing in many states. The current formula of teacher-student ratio will increasingly result into more and more one or two teachers in four or five class schools; and hence, multigrade teaching affecting the quality of instruction. Every class needs a teacher, preferably with at least one on leave reserve so that no class goes without a teacher. Second outdated planning parameter is the school distance. The distance of 0.5 km or 1 km was fixed when the road conditions and transport systems were not developed. There is a sea change even in rural areas in both road conditions as well as rural transport systems. Because of change in the village road conditions, it requires much less of energy today to walk a kilometre or two than what we required when we were village students some five decades ago[3]. In metropolitan cities and urban areas, children travel 10 to 30 km for a good school in school bus or a public transport. In urban areas, good schooling wins the bargain over distance; in rural areas it is the reverse — bad school is good enough if it is within 1 km. In 2013, we did a study on Punjab Education 2030. Our study indicated that Punjab population will get stabilised by 2016-17. This implies that Punjab will not have enough students to fill the schools. In 2014, unconfirmed information is that more than 12,500 places are going vacant in the schools in Union Territory of Chandigarh. Elementary schools in Kerala, educationally most advanced state in the country, is steadily shrinking. There is a need to reconsider and reconstruct the planning process of elementary education.

Mehta and Chugh have already pointed out several problems like inter grade rate of transition of students; rate of completion of elementary education; average years of schooling for completing eight years of elementary education, ratio between primary and elementary schools and many such other serious issues. The most serious among the various issues is the regional disparity — the disparity in the growth and development of elementary education in different states. The DISE database provides a comprehensive picture every year. With a composite index it ranks states in terms of its performance in elementary education. Whether Kerala, Tamil Nadu, Puducherry and such states keep on interchanging the top position is not as important as Bihar constantly figuring at the lowest end; West Bengal, Jharkhand, Odisha figuring consistently among the last four or five states. Issue is not ranking; issue is the lack of performance of the state systems that actually affects and deprives children from right quality of education in these states. So far, India has been comfortably moving forward with such wide regional disparity although from time to time there have been expressions of concern. However, one doesn't come across any kind of strategic plan to overcome this serious deficiency to bring in some kind of comparability among the states in terms of progress in elementary education across the country. With the new agenda of development for all, policies and programmes need to be put in place to reduce, if not eradicate, regional disparities in elementary education.

Successive governments have consistently increased budgetary allocation for universalization of elementary education. The performance in utilisation of budget is far more prominent in civil works, compared to other heads like school facilities, teaching-learning material, teacher training and all that goes into development of the intrinsic aspect of quality management. Despite huge expenditure, there is a gross mismatch between expenditure and quality of civil works. This is equally true although not at the same level, about expenditures on teaching-learning material, teacher training, etc. Obviously, there's a huge amount of leakage during the passage of funds from the top end to the implementing end. This is largely because of lack of monitoring and social accountability.

The net result is the accumulated learning deficiency among the students in the government schools. Quality is the casualty. Large numbers of private schools have mushroomed in the rural areas all over the country. These private schools are actually attracting students from the government funded schools. The reason is lack of faith and trust in government run schools by the parents. There are good number of studies on shadow financing and schooling by certain international institutions (Bray 2009, ADB 2012). Such studies indicate that a huge percentage of students take private tuition to complement school education. The private tuition adds further financial burden on the parents. Most of the private tutors are actually school teachers. By extrapolation, a teacher in the school is not trusted, but he/she is trusted as a home-tutor. This serious dichotomy needs immediate attention.

There are enough evidences globally as well as in India that supervised schools perform better than unsupervised ones. In majority of the states, school supervision has become more of a history. The supervisory staffs have not increased proportionately to the increase in the number of schools and teachers. Over and above, the supervisory staffs remain busy in day-to-day administration of managing large number of primary schools and elementary schools under their jurisdiction, and continuously providing data to their superiors in the district and the state. There has been no effort to overcome this deficiency. Howrah Rural Teachers' Forum successfully experimented with a model of peer supervision by retired but reputed primary school teachers (Mukhopadhyay, 2013). This model, in a modified version, has been adopted by Government of Gujarat.

With the change of the government at the centre, India stands at the crossroads. The new government can choose to continue with incremental changes backed by 'learned helplessness'. Alternatively, it can create a completely new paradigm, a new approach to universalization of elementary education in a time bound manner. It will be wiser to appoint a committee of strategic consultants to examine and create a strategic plan to achieve universalization of elementary education in a time bound manner.

Secondary Education

Secondary education has been the most neglected sector among all the levels of education. We have elaborated this thesis in a chapter later in this book. Politics of/in education is a significant factor in this neglect. Both primary education and higher education have significant political implications in terms of electoral benefits for the political candidates. This is not true so far as secondary education is concerned.

The neglect of secondary education has all along been argued under the garb of 'state's responsibility'. States already spend more than 22 per cent of their annual budget in education, compared to central spending of less than 4 per cent. The state budget is consumed largely on staff salary leaving marginal amount of money for maintenance and upkeep. Hardly, there is 'any resource left for innovation and modernisation. The regional disparity in secondary education can is largely because it is left to the states with marginal central involvement and commitment.

In the pattern of RTE, what was needed was a policy towards Universalization of Secondary education. Constitution of a CABE Committee on Universalization of Secondary Education in 2005 was a major step forward. The report was adopted by the full bench of the CABE[4]. In 2010, Government of India decided to move towards universal secondary education. Government of India formulated Rashtriya Madhyamik Siksha Abhiyan (RMSA) to move forward in mission mode in expanding and improving quality of secondary education. RMSA received allocation of Rs. 39,000 crore, unprecedented allocation to secondary education in independent India. However, as it is common with all other sectors and schemes, actual release of the fund was far less than allocation on paper. But RMSA took shorter time to take off compared to SSA, primarily because of the experience gained in mission mode implementation of schemes and programmes under SSA itself.

The welcome expansion of secondary education and support with RMSA resulted in to some unusual development. The quality of secondary schools did not change, as we experienced in case of primary education despite several years of SSA intervention. Majority of the parents did not have education enough to support their children academically at home. Result was mushrooming of private tuition which has been studied by several international agencies and scholars under the titles of shadow financing and shadow schooling (Bray 2009 and Asian Development Bank 2012). Although such studies put the extent of shadow schooling, namely private tuition, at about 70 per cent, our own micro-level studies in certain rural areas indicate that more than 97 per cent students take private tuition to survive and perform in the school. In many states, unfortunately it has become not only a fashion but also a point of prestige. After the declaration of the results of the state board of education, the toppers in the board results are show cased in the television proudly announce that they had 6 to 8 private tutors.

As we move towards USE, significant question today is the rate of participation and rate of completion of secondary schooling in India. On an average, out of 100 children admitted in standard 1, only about 38 reach 10th standard. 62 per cent students get lost between standard one and 10. By extrapolating pass percentage of 63.36 per cent (COBSE, 2005) in the 10th board examination, only about 24 per cent students finally succeed to get a school final/maturation certificate. Thus, 76 per cent students get lost on the way. If we call this as system effectiveness index, it is miserable. There is a huge regional disparity. 57 per cent students admitted in grade 1 in Kerala, completes high school graduation; on the other extreme is Bihar where the completion rate is less than 10 per cent. This must change, and there is a hope.

Secondary education stands at a very important and crucial juncture. On one hand, it provides the teaching manpower to the primary education; on the other, it is the secondary school graduates who form the constituency for higher education. A qualitatively weak secondary education will burn the national ambition of development on both ends. It will provide poor teachers to primary schools affecting the quality of primary education; and it will provide poor quality students to higher education. Higher education system will be handicapped when it makes serious effort of quality improvement of the large mass of undergraduate education. Government needs to take a fresh look and dynamically different policies to change secondary education, specially improve quality with increasing access and equity.

Higher and Technical Education

There are frequent lamentations from some important quarters that none of the Indian universities figure in top 100 or 200 universities in the world. It seems to have developed as an obsession. As a response to this challenge, India has decided to set up 15 "World Class Universities" though the coinage has no locus standi in professional literature. The only way to give respectability to this coinage is to imply world ranking universities as the World Class Universities. New government also came up with the proposal of setting up high profile institutes like more IITs and IIMs with little realization that IITs and IIMs are not made out of buildings and infrastructures. Their brand value is due to quality of teachers and students. The policies of the UPA government now reinforced by NDA government need careful examination. It is necessary for Indian policy makers to examine how important it is to rank in the Top 100 universities in the world; and also differentiate between 'nutritious Bharat' versus 'shining India'; international prestige versus substance. Accordingly, we need to create strategic plan to achieve the policy goals.

In world ranking of universities, overwhelming emphasis, and weightages, in all the three Ranking Systems, namely, THES, SJTU and QS is on quality of research, often at the level of Nobel Prizes, Field Medals, and citations. Implications are heavily upon high quality doctoral and postdoctoral research. Careful analysis indicates that undergraduate programmes of IITs and IIMs are one of the best in the world; hence graduates are on demand globally. But that's not true when it comes to postgraduate and doctoral programmes and faculty research (Mitra 2007). That all Indians who won Nobel Prizes in science and social science in recent years won it from one of the western universities indicate two things: (a) India has the talent for original research at the highest level, but (b) Indian higher education institutions are ill equipped to support such talent—finance, facilities, incentives and ecosystems. Level of facility, finance, incentives and ecosystem for such frontline research is of a different magnitude altogether. Indian policy making system need to understand the dimensions of the kind of universities that can produce Nobel laureates. Indian universities and institutions are nowhere near that level of research to claim ranking.

But more realistically, figuring in Top 100/200 universities can be a prestige issue for India, but far removed from what India needs. This is a case of 'excellent icing on a bad cake', if we consider cake as the undergraduate programme.

Substance

India hosts world's third largest higher education system, her score on GER is 20 per cent. There was a huge gain in the recent years, especially the last five years of UPA regime. Now that higher education is demand driven levered by social aspiration, improvement in economic capability, India will achieve 30 per cent GER even before 2020. Great strides, indeed. Government must recognise that almost 87.4 per cent higher education students are in undergraduate programmes. Hence, only realistic equation is to equate quality of higher education with quality of undergraduate education. For, postgraduate and graduate programmes stand on the shoulder of undergraduate programmes.

Quality of undergraduate programme is abysmally low. Less than 3 per cent graduates who take Central Teacher Eligibility Test succeed; equivalent percentage of postgraduates and doctorates succeed in State Eligibility Test for College Teaching. Further, India's middle level employment is occupied by graduates; poor graduation leads to poor performance in employment market affecting economic growth.

Central institutions support education of only 2.6 per cent higher education students; 38.6 per cent by state institutions and almost 58.9 per cent by private institutions (2011-12) (FICCI, 2012). Private institutions have sharply changed the equation of participation but also added burden to the parents without any assured quality. The state colleges and universities that actually carry the national burden of equity and access in higher education are in a state of utter deprivation. Staff rooms are like railway platforms where teachers are expected to spend five hours every day, library budget is not enough to buy 20 books by any established Indian and international author; laboratories are more of an apology; student amenities are in despicable condition. My studies indicate unbearable contrast between state institutions and central institutions. Quality education in such deprived condition can only be accidental.

Technical education has witnessed massive expansion in equal degree. The expansion can be credited largely to the private initiative and enterprise. Reasons of such phenomenal expansion through private initiative is tremendous aspiration and enthusiasm among young people of India, financial capabilities of the parents, and government policy of maintaining bottle necks in technical and engineering education by creating too few institutions to match the demand. The prestigious IITs admit hardly one among 100 candidates; the second level institutes, namely NIIT (former RECs) admit, at best two or three out of 100 candidates. But, private initiatives have their own dynamics. It was largely a response to market demands inspired by business opportunities in education. As a result, exceptions apart, quality of education and institutional values are the casualties. There emerged the paradox—coexistence of vacancies in engineering jobs and large number of unemployed engineering graduates.

Studies by NASSCOM on employability of IT graduates widely publicised and disseminated by print media (e.g. Economic Times, April 7, 2011) and Aspiring Minds, 2010, 2013 indicate poor employability skills among large mass of Indian graduates. During the economic recession in Europe in the early 2000's, several studies were commissioned to figure out the way out to resurrect economy. Almost all studies converged on employability skill as the key to economic regeneration and national economic growth. Western Universities have a clearly defined set of skills called 'Generic Graduate Skills', one component of employability skill, other being mental skills of research and higher studies. Despite high unemployment and low employability skills among graduates, Indian universities have no such concept or programme. Policy initiative needs to focus on developing generic graduate skills and employability skills.

Less than 20 per cent students (18% to be precise) enrolled in science, compared to 37 per cent in Arts and Humanities, 17 per cent in Commerce; 6 per cent in medicine/nursing/pharmacy, in 2012-13[5] This is an issue of equity and provision of science education. Less than 50 per cent undergraduate colleges offer science courses compelling students, especially girls who cannot travel long distances for a variety of reasons, to give up the ambition of science education and concede to 'whatever is available in the college nearby'. This iniquitous provision of science education adds further to unemployment.

One of the important policies of the UPA government was to create a central empire through setting up central universities, apparently to create quality institutions. Hidden agenda was to create a set of institutions that can be under direct control of the central government, and associated 'politics' of higher education. As of 2012, 63.9 per cent colleges are private colleges, 35.6 per cent are state institutions and only 0.5 per cent is central institutions. These high cost, less than necessary, central institutions cost the state colleges and universities dearly. The comparative allocations for central universities and RUSA for all higher education institutions in the country provides a meaningful glimpse in this case. Allocation for the few Central Universities is Rs. 40,000 crores compared to Rs.25,000 crores for RUSA. According to available information, only about Rs.5000 crores (20%) of the fund allocated to RUSA has been spent during the first 3 years of the 12th FYP. Instead of draining money in the central institutions that cannot even spend, it is necessary to rationalise and substantially enhance support to state colleges and universities;

There is a wide gap between budgetary allocation and actual release of funds. The 11th FYP plan allocation was raised to Rs.84,000 Crores; but only 46 per cent was actually released and spent. There is a need to reduce the gap between allocation and actual release.

Way Forward

If Indian higher education is to shine in future, focus must be on improvement of undergraduate education, especially in the state colleges. Private institutions have significantly reduced the financial burden of the government. Following the recommendations of the Yashpal Committee, new government should reorient its policies to provide project based development support to private institutions, a practice that is quite common in the USA. Participation in undergraduate science education needs to be significantly boosted. That would necessitate creating facilities for science education, especially in rural colleges.

There are about 36000 colleges (and 659 universities) for little above 2.03 crore students giving an average per college enrolment of little more than 550. Hence, there are enough colleges. Lateral expansion of underprovided colleges and universities may be politically sound, but educationally unsound. The need is to augment quality by reorienting policies and redefining funding parameters.

Curricular reforms are another area that needs immediate attention. Despite huge student migration and mobility, universities are yet to introduce multi-cultural curriculum and campus diversity programmes. These are necessary. As boundaries of conventional disciplines are melting down, need is to introduce inter-disciplinary and multi-disciplinary courses and programmes. Universities and colleges need to reconstruct curriculum to cultivate employability skills and generic graduate skills.

Teacher welfare has unfortunately been equated with salary enhancement. Concept must be expanded and rationalised to ensure minimum facilities at work places like a dedicated works space/station, a laptop with internet connectivity, adequate provision of books in the library; large research grants for teacher to be able to work on problems of significance.

There is a need for a complete fresh look at policies and practices in higher education moving away from elitism of quality for few to ensuring equity with quality. Quality as a competitor of equity and access is a wrong perception. Reality is different; as mentioned earlier, equity without quality is like trying to fill a bucket with a hole at the bottom. Depriving undergraduate programmes in state and private institutions for the central institutions will be a case of expensive face wash in empty stomach.

Conclusion

Indian education at all levels has experienced tremendous expansion enhancing both access and equity at all levels. The benefits of the expansion is largely neutralised or reduced due to drop out, non-completion of courses and larger number of years in completion of courses almost at every level; but most significantly due to poor quality of education. In fact, poor quality is the common denominator across all sectors and levels of education.

There has been a serious imbalance of emphasis, and policy perspectives, at different levels of education. Inter-structural linkages among various levels of education are critically important for development of all sectors. Prof. Armaity Desai (Former Chairperson of UGC) dealt with this issues elaborately (Desai, 2009). Somehow this has been missed out. Plans are largely isolated and sector specific, often competing with each other especially for resource allocation as if primary and elementary, secondary, higher and professional education stand independent of each other.

There have been some policy gaps. More seriously, there have been policies without the sensitivity to people's aspiration and the larger perspective of human development (not the narrow band manpower planning). If we compare the momentum of the adult education in the 1990s, and the SSA in the early 2000, there seems to be some laxity or missing sense of urgency for implementing the government programmes and schemes, even those that were supposed to be implemented in mission mode. At this point of time when Indian education has arrived at a threshold for the big new breakthrough, it needs strategic planning for each sector plotted in a holistic composition and implemented with a sense of urgency to fit into the ambience being created by the new government at the centre.

Notes

1. This assessment draws also from my experience of being personally involved in many of the development matters in education for nearly two decades since 1985 when I actively engaged myself and/or have been eye witness as official member of CABE, SSA Governing Council, Working Committees of the Planning Commission. Hence, my narratives and comments are based on my experience and involvement.
2. I had the privilege of being eyewitness to a few events in Gujarat.
3. In Udang in Howrah District where village roads remained underwater for almost four months in a year.
4. Please see note at the end of the chapter. For, it is a unique case where a national policy (USE) emerged out of the initiatives of few academicians of an educational institution.
5. http://www.ugc.ac.in/pdfnews/6805988_HEglance2013.pdf.
6. Universalization of Secondary Education—Case of Emergence of a Policy: The need for universal secondary education was voiced for the first time in the conference, *Focus Secondary Education*[6], from the platform of NIEPA in 2001 (for details see Mukhopadhyay, 2001). There were serious reservations in some important quarters about desirability, feasibility and time-maturity of the concept, universal secondary education, when universal primary education was still a distant dream.

   Our arguments were different from manpower approach emanating from our experiences at the grassroots. Our first argument was, parents do not send their children to school for literacy (expected effect of primary or even elementary education). Children are sent to school to get a qualifying education (X and XII) that opens their doors to higher education and to white collar jobs, and thereby change the quality of life. This is the aspiration of large mass of rural people and urban poor who have been deprived for centuries. In other words, there is a demand for education that is also corroborated by certain studies, e.g. PROBE Report. And, government of an independent welfare state is obliged to provide educational facilities to all till they reach at least X, preferably XII.

   Our corroborative argument was: more people have not only the urge for education but also the capacity to spend on education especially complimenting and supplementing schooling with private tuition in absence of 'home support' due to poor educational base of the parents and elder siblings. This financial capacity was largely due to economic growth and early stages of financial inclusion.

   Another important argument that we put forward was from global experience. School education—9 or 10 or 12 years of education—is one compact unit, and not assimilation of three or four levels like primary, elementary, secondary and higher secondary. This four tier classification is for academic purposes and not for structural purposes of flushing out—drop out or push out—at different levels allowing a majority of them relapsing into illiteracy. Universalization of primary, elementary and secondary education has not been on a timeline in the history of nations. Without the provision of secondary education for every child admitted in grade 1 is either a social concessionism or a wasteful adventure. Concept has to be necessarily universalization of school education.

Other side of the argument was from societal need to develop educated manpower for sustainable economic growth. Secondary education is the single largest source of skilled and unskilled manpower in the organized sector. Further, secondary school graduates are the catchment area for higher education and also for teacher-force for primary education. For India's sustainable economic growth as well as development in higher education, a robust universal secondary education is necessary.

Furthermore, as India is ambitioning to place itself at par with the global leaders with research in science and technology, e.g. space research, defence research and development, research and technology in electronics and ICT, it is necessary to develop educational structures, processes and quality at the globally comparable level. While India is likely to miss the MDG goals in 2015, universalization of secondary education need not wait for UEE or achievement of MDG.

Fortunately, political will was indicating a positive shift in favour of expansion of secondary education during the X FYP. The main challenges for universalizing secondary education were articulated in a paper (Mukhopadhyay, 2004). This paper was discussed during the preparation of the tenth plan. This paper (Mukhopadhyay, 2004) also flagged the likely impact of success in SSA on demand for secondary education. Three alternative scenarios were built with 50 per cent, 75 per cent and 100 per cent successes in SSA. The optimum scenario of 75 per cent indicated that about 11 million more children will demand places in secondary education by 2010. In our assessment, existing system will not be able to accommodate so many additional students. Further, given the Indian ambition for taking on the global competitiveness, lateral expansion of the present pattern of secondary education will also be qualitatively inadequate. We drew the attention of the then Education Secretary to our assessment. Responding to our contentions, he asked for a presentation of our theses to the officials in the Ministry of Human Resource Development. Compared to our experience in 2001, this paper was well received.

CABE appointed a committee on Universal Secondary Education in 2005 chaired by Minister for Education, Government of Rajasthan; our paper mentioned above was shared with the members of the Committee. Though I was not a member of the committee, I was called upon for 'an interaction' on our paper with the Committee. After the initial discussion, I was asked to chair the subcommittee for drafting the report on Universal Secondary Education". The document was approved by the CABE in its meeting held in 2005. The story of USE will remain incomplete without the mention of inspiration and substance provided by Late Prof. Tapas Majumdar. Indeed, a new chapter in secondary education has been added (CABE, 2005).

The CABE report reiterates the mission of quality as the hall mark of universal secondary education. Importantly, the document proposed reconceptualization of secondary education as education of the adolescents for nurturing multiple intelligence to bring to surface the full potential of the students. Accordingly, it suggests flexible curriculum offering-interest and capability based choices supported by constructivist approach to learning. For the first time, this document specified 'norm of schooling'. Though the actual norms were seriously debated from the angle of feasibility, what is important is the acceptance of the concept of a norm of schooling. This seemingly influenced setting up institutional infrastructure norms in the RTE.

The document also recommended projection of enrolment of students as well as requirement of additional teachers, classrooms and finance at the state and district levels; National level projection to be treated only as indicative. Since the mission is to provide quality secondary education, the document recommends not appointing para teachers as softer option. Among many other important policy propositions is the training of the heads of schools and use of open learning institutions for extending facilities of secondary education.

The document was approved in July, 2005 by the CABE. The Government of India, Ministry of Human Resource Development initiated planning of secondary education on the basis of this report, particularly as a preparation for the 11th plan.

2

Elementary Education in India

Status, Progress and Prospects

Arun C. Mehta and *Sunita Chugh*

Education has become an article of faith and it has been increasingly being realized that the key to human development squarely depend upon the investment in education. Economic development and empowerment of people especially the marginalized can only be possible if education can reach to nook and corner of society. Economists long since have advocated that the investment in education has the highest return and the development of human capital is essential for achieving better living standards and an equitable world. In fact, it was this realization that pitch education into the core of millennium development goals. The importance of basic education in transforming human lives was the force that led to the movement of 'Education for All' and Universalization of Elementary Education. The Delor's Commission's report (Learning the Treasure within, UNESCO, 1996) that emphasized on 'lifelong learning' addressed the issue of continuous skills development through education in order to face the challenges of globalization. The Millennium Development Goals Report (2012) mentioned that poverty of nations is related to as much lack of resources as it is to their lack of access to knowledge. It actually denotes to the education's ability in equipping learners with and competency necessary to respond to various challenges.

Education is coming to occupy an ever larger place in people's lives as its role among the forces at work in modern society increases. Basic education is more than an end in itself. It is the foundation for lifelong learning and human development on which countries may build, systematically, further levels and types of education and training. Elementary education empowers and equips individuals with analytical capabilities, instills confidence and fortifies them with determination to achieve goal-setting competencies. It, therefore, plays a pivotal role in improving the socioeconomic condition of the nation. For any country to grow, it is imperative that it has in place a strong elementary school driven education system.

The value of education so highly extolled in the classical tradition and literature of India too has its resonance in the policy documents and planning of the post-independent India. The Constitutional commitment under the directive principles of state policy guided much of post-independent India's approach towards educational development and found solid legal status in the form of the Right of Children to Free and Compulsory Education Act in 2009. However, much before things took a concrete shape educational development at least the elementary level meant increasing access to schools, creating infrastructure, setting of educational goals and emphasizing on enrolment. The most crucial dimension that was missing in these schemes of things was the comprehensive policy to include access, retention and quality in one whole. Without the necessary policy framework to unite and activate all these dimensions together it was impossible to improve the overall educational scenario in multicultural and diverse social setting of India.

These years of piecemeal approach to educational development primarily based on the assumption of 'tickle down' theory has had its success in terms of structural growth and at times qualitative change is some clusters but it was largely fragmented and uneven. For example, in the case of poor, segregated, marginalized populations where education becomes a third or fourth priority much after food, clothing, shelter and health, this approach had little or no meaning. In fact, on the contrary these spasmodic and sporadic educational interventions further marginalized and excluded children of disadvantaged sections such as Scheduled Caste, Scheduled Tribes and Minorities etc. in the era of stiff competition and better learning outcomes from the advantageous sections. The inherent structures of inequality and discrimination have their own forces to deprive these marginalized sections from the fruits of education and skills which in turn could allow them to overcome the difficulties and free them from the vicious cycle of poverty, illiteracy and deprivation. Now the challenge is to ensure equal access and provision to all sections of society in general and children from marginalized sections in particular essentially in the context of RTE 2009. The present paper makes an effort to map these dimensions.

It is generally claimed that since independence India has shown a deep commitment towards the achievement of Universalisation of Elementary Education and has strived hard to provide equal opportunity to all at the secondary and higher secondary level of education. The Constitutional obligation compounded with various policies and programmmes in implementing the commitment undoubtedly depict the efforts and seriousness of the government. However, despite all these efforts in making education accessible to all sections of society, certain groups of individuals and communities have remained outside the ambit of education. The basic issue is that with the considerable growth in the number of educational institutions and teachers, is the access to quality education available to all the children? Are the children able to complete elementary cycle of education and if not what are the reasons responsible for this? What special measures have been taken by the government to address the equity issue and improve the educational status of Scheduled Caste, Scheduled Tribes, girls and minorities? What kind of administrative and management reforms have been introduced to revitalize the school system? Does the additional support and funds provided by the Central government by launching centrally sponsored schemes have helped to achieve the target of UEE?

In the above context, the present paper focuses on the status and progress of elementary education in terms of access, enrolment and teacher since 1950s and also presents the future challenges to meet the target of UEE in the light of recently passed Right to Free and Compulsory Education Act, 2009.

Policy Framework for UEE

To fulfill the constitutional commitment, various commissions and committees have been constituted by the Government of India from time to time, which determine the educational priorities and accordingly formulate the policies. While some of the committees concentrated on specific education sector or a specific focused group, a comprehensive review of education was taken by the Education Commission in 1964 which culminated into National Policy on Education, 1968. In order to achieve the goal of equalization of educational opportunity, and bring national consciousness for social and national integration, NPE 1968 advocated for 'Common School System (CSS)' that would serve all sections of the society living in a common neighborhood. The CSS implies that all the children should be entitled to comparable quality of schooling irrespective of socio-economic background. NPE, 1968 reiterated free and compulsory education for all children upto the age of 14 years. For improving the quality of education, it recommended that school complexes need to be established. Each upper primary school should be integrally related to ten primary schools that exist in its neighborhood.

National Policy on Education (1986)

By mid 1980s it was realized that the desired progress had not been achieved in education sector and the need was felt to revitalize the education therefore National Policy on Education was (NPE) formulated and adopted in 1986 followed by another document known as 'Programme of Action' (POA) which focused on details of the implementation of this policy. The NPE, 1986 emphasized a cardinal principle that education is a unique investment in the present and the future, therefore all the children be given an equal opportunity to receive quality education. It focused on the National System of Education, removal of disparities and to equalize opportunity by attending to the specific needs of those who have been denied equality so far. The NPE, and its Programme of Action emphasized on decentralization of education by restructuring the planning and management of education. It put a new thrust on elementary education emphasizing on two aspects (i) universal enrolment and retention of children upto 14 years, and (ii) a substantial improvement in the quality of education.

Special Programmes and Schemes towards UEE

Sustained efforts are being made to fulfill the educational goal set by the Constitution and the priorities defined by the NPE. This is evident from the number of programmes and schemes launched at the national as well as state level to achieve the target of Universalisation of Elementary Education (UEE). This endeavour got further impetus due to the developments at the international level. The world declaration on Education for All in 1990 at Jomtien and at Dakar in 2000 brought to the centre stage the need for viewing elementary education as a fundamental right of citizens. The Dakar framework set six major 'Education for All (EFA)' goals and proposed twelve strategies. Beginning from early childhood and extending throughout life, the declaration emphasized high quality educational opportunities to all and these opportunities must neither exclude nor discriminate any child on the basis of sex, caste or religion. Concomitant to the international resolutions and commitments, Indian Government launched several state-specific/district specific programmes to reduce the regional, spatial, social and gender disparities. During 1980s and 1990s a large number of educational projects were initiated to improve the access and quality in educationally backward areas in different parts of the country e.g. Andhra Pradesh Basic Education Project (1983), Shiksha Karmi Project in Rajasthan (1987), Bihar Education Project (1991), Lok Jumbish in Rajasthan (1992) and Uttar Pradesh Basic Education Project (1993). All these projects emphasized on the local level planning and involvement of community in reducing the gender disparities, improving access, enrolment and retention, the prerequisites for achieving the target of UEE.

The experiences gained from the state level projects led to the launching of District Primary Education Project (DPEP) in 1994 with the objective of providing access of primary schooling facilities to all children thereby reducing gender gap in enrolments and dropouts and improving learning achievement. It was initiated in 42 districts spread over 7 states and later spread to 285 districts in 18 states. The DPEP emphasized on need-based and area-specific planning so that each district could concentrate on its weak areas. The programme components included construction of classrooms and new schools, opening of Alternative Schooling centers, appointment of new teachers etc. The DPEP attempted to promote decentralized management with the involvement of Panchayati Raj Institutions (PRIs), grassroots functionaries, Village Education Committees and the Community.

Sarva Shiksha Abhiyan (SSA)

Although compulsory education from Grade I to Grade VIII was envisaged as one integrated unit in the Constitution of India, yet in practice it had been segregated into two distinct stages of primary and upper primary. For the first time in 2001, the SSA was initiated nation-wide emphasizing on achievement of UEE by 2010. SSA is an integrated, comprehensive scheme to achieve UEE in partnership with the state governments, the local self governments, the community and the civil society. While quality still remains an area of concern, the SSA has been able to improve the schooling facilities and boost the enrolment, retention and reduce dropout of females as well as of various socially disadvantaged groups.

Against this background, the ensuing section discusses the progress and growth in access to schooling facilities, number of schools, teachers and students at elementary level of education over a period of time.

Universal Access and Enrolment

Universal access in the Indian context implies that primary schooling facilities are available within 1 km. of each and every habitation where as upper primary schooling facilities are available within 3 kms of every habitation. It is reported in the 7th All India Educational Survey conducted by NCERT (2002) that 87 per cent of habitations were having primary schools within 1 km., whereas 78 per cent of habitations were having upper primary schools within 3 km. Data from Annual Report (2008-09) of Ministry of Human Resource Development reveal that across the country 99 per cent of the households has schooling facilities within 1km and 93 per cent to an upper primary school. It implies that universal access at the primary level has almost been achieved whereas access at the upper primary level has considerably improved but it further needs to be extended. Ensuring universal access to all the habitations and population is being addressed through progressive expansion of educational institutions with a special focus on the unserved/underserved areas.

Access to Educational Facilities

Accessibility of a school in the neighbourhood or within the walking distance is the minimum requirement for the child to regularly attend the school. Access not only connotes the availability of physical facilities but also overcoming the economic and social obstacles. As per the national norms, habitations having a population of 300 or more and not having primary school within a walking distance of 1 km, are eligible for opening of formal primary schools and similarly habitations having population more than 500 and not having upper primary schools within a walking distance of 3 km, are eligible for opening of formal upper primary schools. Further relaxation has been made in the case of difficult/hilly terrain and areas with ethnic minority population. Table 2.1 reveals the progress made in this direction.

Table 2.1: Habitations/Coverage (percentage) by Primary Schools / Upper Primary Schools/Sections

Particulars	*6th Survey 1993*	*7th Survey 2002*
% of habitations served by primary schools/ sections within 1 km	85.36	86.96
% of rural population served by primary schools/sections within 1 km	93.76	98.53
% of habitations served by Upper Primary schools/ sections within 3 km	76.15	78.11
% of rural population served by Upper Primary schools/sections within 3 km	85.00	86.14

Source: NCERT All India Educational Surveys, (Various Years).

As per the All India Educational Survey conducted by the NCERT, the number of having a primary school/section within a radius of one kilometer improved from 85 to 87 per cent between 1993 and 2002. This implies that nearly 13 per cent of rural villages/habitations do not have a primary school within a radius of 1 km. In absolute terms, as many as 1,60,549 villages/ habitations (total rural habitations are 12,31,391) do not have a primary school within a radius of 1 km. in 2002-03.

Though, access to upper primary schooling has improved over the years, yet the number of villages/habitations not having upper primary schools within the village/habitation continues to be large. Around 78 per cent of habitations had upper primary schools within the radius of 3 km in 2002-03. NSSO data shows that the access to schooling facilities has improved significantly in both rural and urban areas as depicted in Table 2.2.

Data from the above table reveal though access to upper primary level of education has increased over the years, yet it continues to be a problem in some parts of rural India. This clearly suggests that the states, indeed, need to open new schools in all villages/habitations that are not served or served only by schools located at far away places. Particularly, the expansion of upper

Table 2.2: Availability of Schooling Facility

Sector	*Level*	*Distance to Nearest School*					
		D < 1km	*1km < 2km*	*2km < 3km*	*3km < 5km*	*D > 5km*	*Total*
Rural	Primary	91.7	6.5	1.2	0.2	0.1	100
	Middle	61.6	17.1	12.2	5.8	3.1	100
Urban	Primary	92.3	6.7	0.9	0.1	0.0	100
	Middle	82.5	14.1	2.5	0.7	0.2	100

Source: NSSO 64th round.

primary stage and also secondary stage needs to be given a new impetus to achieve universal access and enrolment.

Growth in Educational Institutions

The growth of primary and upper primary schools has been estimated for different points of time based on increase in the educational institutions over the period of time. The growth of upper primary schools in India is influenced by the expansion of primary education and growth in the completion of primary education by the children. The number of primary schools in India increased from 2,09,671 in 1950-51 to 748547 in 2010-11 an increase of more than three and a half times. The upper primary schools have grown around 33 times during the same period. The number of upper primary schools has gone up from 13,596 to 447600 between 1950-51 and 2010-11. There has been an increase of 79855 schools in the years 2010-11 from the preceding year which could be due to the implementation of RTE 2009.

Table 2.3: Growth of Educational Institutions: Primary and Upper Primary

Year	*Primary*	*Upper Primary*
1950-51	209671	13596
1960-61	330399	49663
1970-71	408378	90621
1980-81	494503	118555
1990-91	560935	151456
1995-96	593410	174145
1999-2000	641695	198004
2003-04	712239	262286
2004-05	767520	274731
2005-06	772568	288493
2006-07	784852	305584
2007-08	787827	325174
2009-10	823162	367745
2010-11	748547	447600
Increase (times) since 1950-51	3.6	32.9

Source: (MHRD) Selected Educational Statistics, New Delhi.

Type of School Management

Government is the main provider of education at the elementary level, though the share of private sector has been steadily increasing over the years. Around 83 per cent of the primary schools in 2010-11 are managed by the Government and local bodies put together and around 7.3 per cent are run by the private management. However at the same time the share of government at the upper primary level accounted for 77.3 per cent whereas around 13 per cent were managed by the private sector.

Table 2.4: Percentage Share of Primary Schools under Different Managements

Year	*Govt.*	*Local Body*	*Govt.+ Local Body*	*Private Aided*	*Private unaided*
1973-74	50.88	42.47	93.34	5.01	1.64
1978-79	38.96	55.03	93.99	4.42	1.59
1986-87	41.37	51.71	93.08	4.34	2.57
1993-94	44.63	47.47	92.10	3.78	4.12
1996-97	47.78	43.88	91.66	3.34	5.00
2001-02	47.45	43.47	90.92	3.07	6.01
2002-03	55.77	32.98	88.75	3.63	7.63
2003-04	42.60	48.08	90.68	2.85	6.48
2004-05	43.33	46.87	90.20	2.55	7.24
2005-06	42.60	46.51	89.11	3.09	7.79
2006-07	44.21	44.96	89.17	3.08	7.75
2007-08	58.25	28.48	86.73	5.76	7.51
2009-10	62.85	22.96	85.81	6.57	7.62
2010-11	54.8	29.0	83.8	8.9	7.3

Source: Selected Educational Statistics, MHRD, New Delhi.

Table 2.4a: Percentage Share of Upper Primary Schools under Different Management

Year	*Govt.*	*Local Body*	*Govt.+ Local Body*	*Private Aided*	*Private unaided*
1973-74	50.71	26.86	77.57	17.75	4.67
1978-79	40.31	38.13	78.44	16.90	4.66
1986-87	42.79	32.33	75.12	16.30	8.58
1993-94	45.94	33.51	79.45	9.53	11.02
1996-97	46.41	29.13	75.54	10.25	14.20
2001-02	47.36	29.05	76.41	7.81	15.77
2002-03	45.37	27.19	72.56	7.37	20.07
2003-04	39.75	32.56	72.31	6.68	21.01
2004-05	42.96	29.24	72.20	6.41	21.39
2005-06	43.17	28.80	71.97	6.14	21.88
2006-07	44.02	27.05	71.07	6.65	22.28
2007-08	55.78	17.82	73.60	9.30	17.10
2009-10	57.32	15.79	72.11	10.68	16.21
2010-11	60.8	16.5	77.3	9.9	12.7

Figures in Tables 2.4a make it clear that the share of government and government aided has increased considerably in 2010-11 from the 2006-07 which could be due to the new schools being opened in the unserved/ underserved areas.

Improvement in Infrastructure Facilities

School-wise information collected through District Information Systems for Education (DISE, for various years) reveals that around 3.6 per cent of the primary schools and 6.5 per cent of upper primary schools were without school building in 2006-07 which have slightly increased to 5.8 per cent and 7.1 per cent respectively for primary and upper primary level in 2007-08. But in case of toilets, 46.3 per cent of primary schools and 41.9 per cent of all schools did not have any toilet in 2006-07 that have decreased to 37.2 per cent and 33.2 per cent in 2008-09. Research indicates that the availability of toilet especially for girls help to boost the enrolment and retention in the school. Similarly there has been improvement in respect of other physical facilities like boundary walls, drinking water, electricity, computers and separate toilets for girls at both primary and upper primary levels during 2006-07 and 2009-10. However, in many of the institutions, though the infrastructural facilities are available but the information is not available on whether the toilets or taps, computers and electricity provisions are in working condition or not. The micro level studies suggest that in large number of institutions they are not found to be in working conditions. Table 2.5 presents details on the non-availability of physical infrastructure.

Table 2.5: Schools without Basic Infrastructural Facilities

	Primary					*All Schools*				
% without the facility of	2006-07	2007-08	2008-09	2009-10	2010-11	2006-07	2007-08	2008-09	2009-10	2010-11
Building	3.6	5.8				6.5	7.1			
Toilets	46.3	41.4	37.2			41.9	37.3	33.2		
Boundary walls	58.0	57.2				50.8	49.8	49.0	48.5	
Drinking Water	17.6	15.8	14.7			15.1	13.2	12.2		
Electricity	78.6	78.6	76.4	72.3		69.5	72.4	64.4	61.1	
Computers	93.5	94.0	94.2	93.5		85.4	70.6	71.7	66.6	
Separate Toilet for Girls	65.9	58.0	55.6	49.1		47.7	49.5	47.4	41.2	

Source: Analytical Report, 2004-05, 2005-06, 2006-07 & 2007-08, DISE, NUEPA, New Delhi.

Quantitative Expansion in Enrolment at Elementary Level

Increased schooling facilities and growing awareness among the communities have created tremendous demand for elementary education. The enrolment in elementary education in absolute numbers has increased steadily since independence but it increased enormously during 1980s. This trend has continued well into early 1990s. Figures in the table below suggest that the absolute increase in enrolment at elementary education has been in the range of 25-30 lakhs per annum with the exception of a few peak as well as low years. During 1999-2000 through 2010-11, enrolment in the elementary education increased substantially, more with respect to the upper primary stage. Both in primary as well as upper primary stages, proportionate increase in girls' enrolment were higher than boys'.

Table 2.6: Growth in Enrolment at Primary and Upper Primary Levels

(Figures in million)

Year	*Primary*			*Upper Primary*		
	Boys	*Gxirls*	*Total*	*Boys*	*Girls*	*Total*
1950-51	13.8	5.4	19.2	2.6	0.5	3.1
1960-61	23.6	11.4	35.0	5.1	1.6	6.7
1970-71	35.7	21.3	57.0	9.4	3.9	13.3
1980-81	45.3	28.5	73.8	13.9	6.8	20.7
1990-91	57.0	40.4	97.4	21.5	12.5	34.0
1995-96	60.9	46.2	107.1	22.7	14.8	37.5
1999-2000	64.1	49.5	113.6	24.3	17.0	41.3
2000-01	64.0	49.8	113.8	25.3	17.5	42.8
2001-02	63.6	50.3	113.9	26.1	18.7	44.8
2002-03	65.1	57.3	122.4	26.3	20.6	46.9
2003-04	68.4	59.9	128.3	27.2	21.5	48.7
2004-05	69.7	61.1	130.8	28.5	22.7	51.2
2005-06	70.4	61.6	132.0	29.0	23.4	52.4
2006-07	71.1	62.6	133.7	29.9	24.6	54.5
2007-08	71.1	64.4	135.5	31.1	26.2	57.3
2009-10	70.8	64.8	135.6	31.8	27.6	59.4
2010-11	70.4	64.8	135.3	32.8	29.2	62.0
Growth (times) since 1950-51	5.0	12.0	7.0	12.6	58.4	20.0

Source: (MHRD) Selected Educational Statistics (Various years), Govt. of India, New Delhi.

Gross Enrolment Ratio (GER)

A perusal of the GER over a period of time reveals that the same, irrespective of boys and girls, has improved consistently. At primary stage, starting with 42.6 in 1950-51, it improved to 113.9 per cent in 2007-08, to 115.4 per cent in 2010-11. For upper primary, the same was as low as 12.7 per cent in 1950-51 this improved to 78.1 per cent in 2007-08, to 85.5 per cent in 2010-11. The GER of girls in 1960-61 was as low as 41.4 per cent and that of boys 82.6 per cent, thus showing a differential of about 40 per cent. At the upper primary level it was 11.3 per cent for girls and 33.2 per cent for boys, depicting a differential of about 22 per cent. In 2010-11, GER for girls at primary level was 116.7 per cent whereas for boys it was 115.4 per cent, showing the differential of 1.3 per cent in favour of girls. At the upper primary level it was 87.7 per cent for boys and 83.1 per cent for girls, with a differential of 4.6 per cent. Table 2.7 depicts the improvement in GER both for boys and girls at the primary and upper primary levels.

The figures make it clear that GER has tremendously improved for girls which indicate increasing participation of girls in elementary education. However, the GER does not represent the true picture of participation levels of corresponding age groups in education as they include the overage and underage children. Therefore GER provides estimation of the participation level of children in the relevant grades irrespective of age. Besides it is claimed that teachers often inflate the data on enrolment to avoid transfers and protect their placement (*see* Table 2.8).

Growth in Number of Teachers

The quality of education is predominantly related to the availability of teachers as well as competence of teachers both in the subject as well as in classroom interaction. As far as the availability of teachers is concerned, the number of teachers has grown significantly especially since 2000-01. The teachers account for more than 10 per cent of the government employees in India. The growth in the number of teachers has not kept pace with the growth in enrolment resulting in progressively higher Pupil-Teacher Ratio (PTR). The PTR has increased from 24 to 43 at primary level and from 20 to 33 at upper primary level between 1950-51 and 2010-11. As per RTE 2009 norms, high PTRs at both the levels needs to be further improved especially at the primary level of education (*see* Table 2.9).

Inclusive Approach to UEE

Educational progress is uneven and varied among different social groups. A large chunk of population of socially disadvantaged groups has remained excluded from formal education for a long time and a sizeable proportion of their population is still educationally backward. These groups include SCs, STs and Muslim minority comprising 37 per cent of the total population of the country.

The concern for empowerment of these groups through elementary education stems from Constitutional commitments and policy directives. Article 46 of the Constitution of India clearly outlines that, the state shall "*promote with special care the education and economic interests of the weaker sections of the society, and in particular of SC, ST and girls.*" The National Policy on Education (1968) called for strenuous efforts to correct regional

Table 2.7: GER at Primary, Upper Primary and Elementary Level in India

	Primary				*Upper Primary*				*Elementary*			
	Boys	*Girls*	*Total*	*Gender Parity Index*	*Boys*	*Girls*	*Total*	*Gender Parity Index*	*Boys*	*Girls*	*Total*	*Gender Parity Index*
1950-51	60.6	24.8	42.6	0.41	20.6	4.6	12.7	0.22	46.4	17.7	32.1	0.38
1960-61	82.6	41.4	62.4	0.50	33.2	11.3	22.5	0.34	65.2	30.9	48.7	0.47
1970-71	95.5	60.5	78.6	0.63	46.3	20.8	33.4	0.45	75.5	44.4	61.9	0.59
1980-81	95.8	64.1	80.5	0.67	54.3	28.6	41.9	0.53	82.2	52.1	67.5	0.63
1990-91	94.8	71.9	83.8	0.75	76.6	47.0	62.1	0.61	100	70.8	86	0.71
1995-96	97.1	79.4	88.6	0.82	67.8	49.8	59.3	0.73	86.9	69.4	78.5	0.80
2000-01	104.9	85.9	95.7	0.82	66.7	49.9	58.6	0.75	90.3	72.4	81.6	0.80
2003-04	100.6	95.6	98.2	0.95	66.8	57.6	62.4	0.86	87.9	81.4	84.8	0.93
2004-05	110.7	104.7	107.8	0.95	74.8	65.8	70.5	0.88	97.6	90.6	94.2	0.93
2005-06	112.6	105.8	109.4	0.94	75.4	66.5	71.15	0.88	98.50	91.05	94.92	0.92
2006-07	114.6	108.0	111.4	0.94	77.6	69.6	73.78	0.90	100.4	93.5	97.1	0.93
2007-08	115.3	112.6	113.9	0.98	81.5	74.4	78.06	0.91	102.4	98.0	100.3	0.96
2009-10	115.6	115.4	115.5	1.00	84.5	78.3	81.5	0.93	103.8	101.1	102.5	0.97
2010-11	115.4	116.7	116.0	1.01	87.7	83.1	85.5	0.95	104.9	103.7	104.3	0.99

Source: (MHRD) Selected Educational Statistics (Various years) and DISE, 2007-08, NUEPA, New Delhi.

Table 2.8: Net Enrolment ratio at All India Level

	GER at Primary Level	*NER at Primary Level*
2005-06	103.77	84.53
2006-07	110.86	92.75
2007-08	113.94	95.92
2008-09	115.31	98.59
2009-10	115.47	NA
2010-11	116.0	NA

Source: Elementary Education in India: Progress towards UEE, Analytical Report 2008-09, NUEPA

Table 2.9: Teachers and Pupil-Teacher Ratio (PTR)

Year	*Primary Level*		*Upper Primary*	
	Teachers (in 000)	*Pupil Teacher Ratio (PTR)*	*Teachers (in 000)*	*Pupil Teacher Ratio (PTR)*
1950-51	538	24	86	20
1960-61	742	36	345	31
1970-71	1060	39	638	32
1980-81	1363	38	851	33
1990-91	1616	43	1073	37
1995-96	1734	43	1182	37
2000-01	1896	43	1326	38
2003-04	2097	45	1592	35
2004-05	2161	46	1589	35
2005-06	2184	46	1671	34
2006-07	2323	44	1717	34
2007-08	2315	47	1780	35
2009-10	2480	42	1912	34
2010-11	2100	43	1887	33
Increase (times)	4.3		20.7	

Source: (MHRD) Selected Educational Statistics (Various years).

imbalances and inter-group disparities in education. Reinforcing the 1968 resolutions, the National Policy on Education, 1986 and Programme of Action, 1992 laid emphasis on the removal of disparities and equalization of educational opportunity by attending to the specific needs of those who have been denied equality so far. Both the policies have dealt with the educational needs of the SC, ST and Muslim minorities in great details.

Based on the Constitutional commitments and policy directives, planned efforts have been made since independence to promote educational development in equitable manner. The government is the main provider of education and other welfare inputs for the SC, ST and Muslim minorities. They have been identified as special focus groups in a large number of centrally-sponsored educational programmes including SSA. These programmes provide for development of context specific strategies and interventions for education of these groups. SSA has identified and targeted geographical areas in districts and blocks with predominance of SC, ST and Muslim minority population for allocation of funds and school infrastructure to promote education of these groups. In order to increase literacy and education among the SCs and STs, students from these groups are provided incentives like stipends, scholarships, free tuition, monetary aid for books, stationery and free accommodation in hostels. Efforts to extend the educational facilities to SCs, STs and Muslim minorities have been further strengthened since 1990s following the renewed focus on UEE. The DPEP and SSA laid a lot of stress on equity besides laying special focus on districts with large population of SCs, STs and Muslim. Consequently, there has been a good deal of improvement in educational condition of the socially disadvantaged groups. With the adoption of protective discrimination policy participation of children of SCs at primary level has increased from 11.0 million in 1980-81 to 27.1 million in 2010-11. During the same period, ST enrolment at primary level has increased from 4.66 million to 14.8 million. It is worthwhile to note that at primary level, the enrolment of SCs and STs has grown at much higher pace by 2.7 and 3.2 times compared to 1.8 times increase in the enrolment of all categories between 1980-81 and 2010-11. It is observed that SC and ST enrolment has registered higher growth rate at upper primary level than the primary. SC enrolment at upper primary level has increased from 2.22 million in 2000-01 to 11.2 million in 2010-11 and for STs, it increased from 0.74 to 5.4 million during the same period. The figures (Figs. 2.1 to 2.4) below depict the trends in enrolment for SC and ST children.

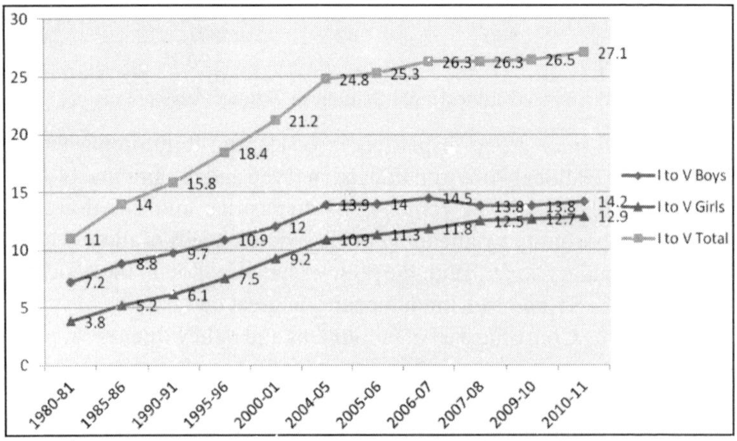

Fig. 2.1: Enrolment of SC Student at the Primary Stage of Education (I-V)

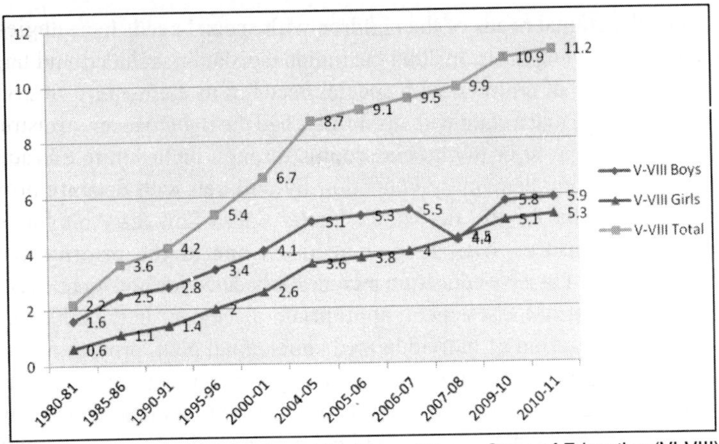

Fig. 2.2: Enrolment of SC Student at the Upper Primary Stage of Education (VI-VIII)

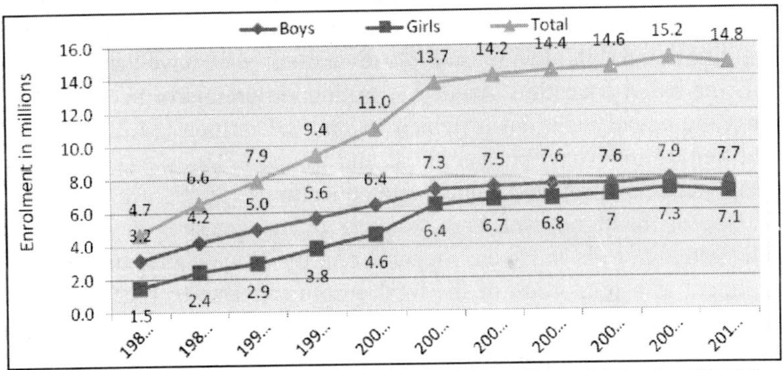

Fig. 2.3: Enrolment of SC Student at the Upper Primary Stage of Education (VI-VIII)

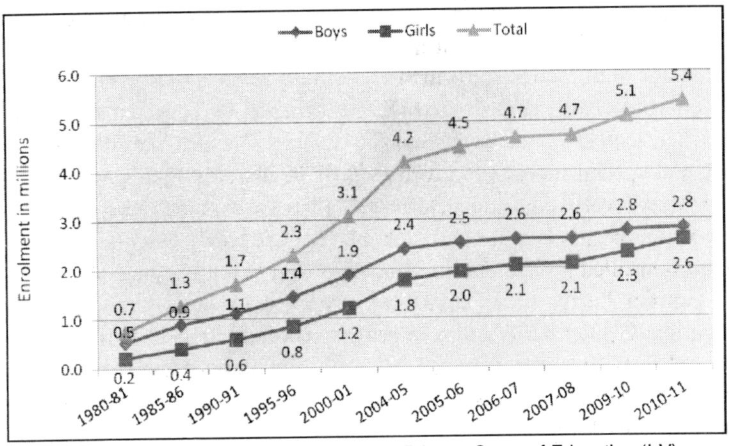

Fig. 2.4: Enrolment of ST Student at the Primary Stage of Education (I-V)

The educational needs of the children with special needs have also been provided due and emphasis. In 2005 the Indian legislation included a provision for the education of children with special needs in its elementary education policy, stipulating that a child with disabilities had the right to receive schooling within regular private or public classrooms through inclusion in education. This access to free elementary education by children with disabilities was mandated in India for the first time. Under Sarva Shiksha Abhiyan also education of children with special needs is one of the priority areas. Interventions for inclusive education include early detection and identification, functional and formal assessment, appropriate placement in the educational institution, preparation of individualized educational plan, provision of aids and appliances, teacher training, resource support, removal of architectural barrier. Amendment in the RTE Act has been made to include children with disabilities within the meaning of child belonging to disadvantaged group. It mentions that child with disability shall have the right to pursue free and compulsory education in the same manner in which children with 'severe disabilities' and a child with 'multiple diversities' shall have the right to opt for home based education. Around 3 million children have been identified across the country and out of which around 2.3 million (81.25% of those identified) children have been enrolled, and around 77 thousand children with special needs are provided homebound education.

One of the significant ways to bring inclusiveness is to increase the participation of girls and to ensure gender parity which is measured by girls' enrolment as a proportion of the total enrolment. Due to special schemes launched and the special incentives given to girls the enrolment of all girls even of the disadvantaged groups has increased steadily. In 2000-01, around 43.7 per cent of the students enrolled in primary classes (I-V) were girls which increased to 50.3 per cent in 2010-11. For upper primary the girls' enrolment increased from 39.26 per cent in 2000-01 to 48.7 per cent in 2010-11. The percentage of SC and ST girls at upper primary level is 47.1 per cent and 47.8 per cent respectively compared to 47.9 per cent and 48.3 per cent at the primary level. The increase could be attributed to various schemes like NPEGEL under SSA and special incentives given to girls to increase their participation at elementary level of education. Despite the increase over the years, considerable proportion of girls is still out of school. It is extremely essential to bring all the non-enrolled girls under the education fold to realize the goal of UEE.

Gender Parity Index measures progress towards gender equity in education. Gender parity Index at primary level in 2010-11 is reported to be 1.0 and 0.91 at upper primary level for the same period. However the interventions still need to be augmented to bring the absolute gender parity at upper primary level.

The framework for implementation of SSA acknowledges the need for special measures to improve the educational status of children belonging to Muslim communities. Various initiatives have been undertaken to increase the participation of children belonging to Muslim communities such as 121 districts with high Muslim population have been identified for targeted interventions under SSA. Around 1470 new primary schools and 445 upper primary schools have been opened in these identified areas and 45,541 new classrooms have been constructed. 32,728 new teachers have been recruited in the schools during 2011-12 (Education for All, status and Trends, MHRD, 2012). With these interventions there has been reduction of out of school Muslim children from 2.1 million in 2005-06 to 1.1 million in 2008-09 from 9.97 per cent to 7.67 per cent of the Muslim population of children in the age group 6-14 years (SRI-IMRB Survey, 2009).

Trends in Dropout

The dropout is one of the perennial problems inflicting Indian education system across all levels and this condition is more acute at the elementary stage till now. Many children who enter schools are unable to complete even the primary level of education and multiple factors are responsible for the children to drop out of the school. Risk factors begin to add up even before students get enrolled in the school which includes: poverty, low educational level of parents, the weak family structure, pattern of sibling, and the lack of pre-school experiences. Family background and domestic problems create an environment which negatively affects the value of education. Further, students could drop out as a result of a multitude of school factors such as uncongenial atmosphere, poor comprehension, absenteeism, attitude and behaviour of the teachers, and failure or repetition in the same grade, etc. It is important to carefully design the preventive measures and intervention strategies that could be adopted in order to help all young dropouts. SSA specifies reduction of dropout rate by 5 percentage point each year as a benchmark outcome indicator. By adopting special measures like no detention upto elementary level, remedial teaching, bridge courses etc. the dropout rates have reduced considerably over the years but still remain significantly high (*see* Table 2.7).

The dropout rate for general category children decreased from 64.9 per cent in 1960-61 to 27 per cent in 2010-11 at primary level. The corresponding figure for elementary classes is 78.3 per cent for 1960-61 which decreased to around 40.6 per cent in 2010-11.

The reduction in dropout rate is quite significant at primary classes for SCs and STs-from 50.4 per cent for SCs and 62.5 per cent for STs in 1990-91 to 26.7 per cent for SCs and 35.6 per cent for STs in 2010-11. The dropout rate for SC at the elementary level reduced from 50.4 per cent in 1990-91 to

Table 2.7: Dropout Rates at Primary and Elementary Levels

Year	*Classes I-V*			*Classes I-VIII*		
	Boys	*Girls*	*Total*	*Boys*	*Girls*	*Total*
1960-61	61.7	70.9	64.9	75.0	85.0	78.3
1970-71	64.5	70.9	67.0	74.6	83.4	77.9
1980-81	56.2	62.5	58.7	68.0	79.4	72.7
1990-91	40.1	46.0	42.6	59.1	65.1	60.9
1995-96	41.4	43.0	42.1	56.6	61.7	58.8
2000-01	39.7	41.9	40.7	50.3	57.7	53.7
2002-03	35.9	33.7	34.9	52.3	53.5	52.8
2003-04	33.7	28.6	31.5	51.9	52.9	52.3
2004-05	31.8	25.4	29.0	50.5	51.3	50.8
2005-06	28.7	21.8	25.7	48.7	49.0	48.8
2006-07	24.6	26.8	25.6	46.4	45.2	45.9
2007-08	25.7	24.4	25.1	43.7	41.3	42.7
2009-10	30.25	27.25	28.86	40.59	44.39	42.39
2010-11	28.7	25.1	27.0	40.3	41.0	40.6

Source: Selected Educational Statistics for various years.

52.5 per cent in 2007-08 and for ST from 78.6 per cent in 1990-91 to 62.5 per cent during the same period.

At elementary level of education the dropout rate in 2006-07 for boys of General category is 43.7 per cent and it is encouraging to observe that the dropout rate for girls is less than those of the boys, though still it is quite high with 41.3 percent. More than 50 per cent of SC boys as well as girls (53.6% for boys and 55% girls) dropout at elementary education. Dropout rate remains to be the highest for children belonging to ST communities with 62.6 per cent for boys and 62.3 per cent for girls. The issue of dropout is related to the quality in education and educational reforms at the schools as well as system level are being tried out to improve the quality of education (*see* Figs. 2.5 and 2.6).

Aforesaid analysis reveals that despite the significant progress achieved, all the children were not having equal opportunities to quality basic education. Considering the significance of basic education for the national development and individual growth, a movement towards making elementary education a fundamental right began in mid 1990s and resulted into the landmark Bill of Right to Free and Compulsory Education Act, 2009. The Act marks a new phase in the history of education for children to meet the challenges of the 21st century.

RTE: Right of Children to Free and Compulsory Education: Access with Equity and Quality

Following the enactment of Right to Education Act 2009, the elementary education consisting of 8 years of schooling has become a fundamental right

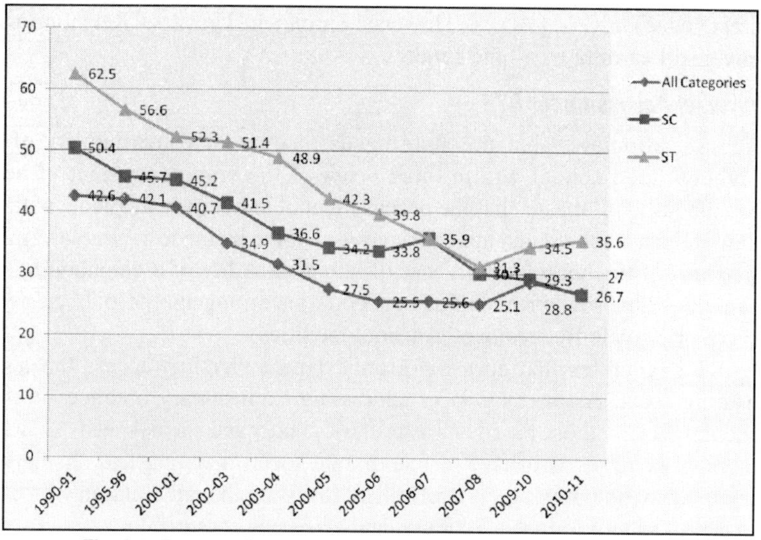

Fig. 2.5: Drop-out Rates at Primary Level: All Categories, SC and ST

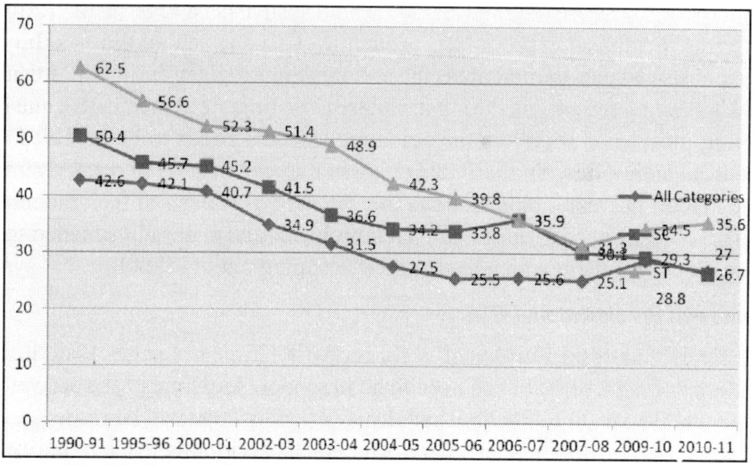

Fig. 2.6: Drop-out Rates at Elementary Level: All Categories, SC and ST

for all children aged six to 14. The enactment of Act is expected to bring fundamental shift in making public policies relating to education particularly of elementary education. The act makes it incumbent on Government to provide free and compulsory education to all children of 6-14 years of age; ensure compulsory admission, attendance and completion of elementary education by every child of the age of six to fourteen years. Equality, Equity and Quality are the fundamental principles of RTE Act 2009. The spirit behind the mandate is the attainment of Universalisation of Elementary Education which has four components: Universal Access, Universal Enrolment, Universal Retention and Universal Learning by all the children.

Universal Access under RTE

RTE Act stipulates that the state needs to guarantee availability of a neighbourhood school within three years of the commencement of act. 'Neighbourhood' means that the primary school to be made available within 1 km of the household and upper primary school to be made available within three kms of the household. In case of non availability of a neighbourhood school the State shall provide free transportation arrangements to the nearest school or provide free residential school/facilities.

RTE reiterates that access not only denote physical access but also ensuring social access by way of addressing exclusionary practices in the school, specially those based on caste, class, gender and special needs. School mapping exercises will have to incorporate social mapping and should be undertaken with community involvement to ensure that all children who can not access school for social, cultural and economic reasons.

Emphasising on the 'Right based Approach', RTE reinforces that the systemic reforms are required and the school system need to be made flexible in terms of admission procedure, academic cycle and school timings. It has been observed that in rural areas the children are irregular during the sowing and harvesting season and the urban children also migrate to their native village during this period therefore the academic calendar needs to be prepared by the local authorities. Similarly the children may not be able to reach on time due to their peculiar circumstances like fetching of water and fuel, therefore the school may need to understand their problems and make adjustment rather than punishing them which lead to their dropping out of school.

Universal Enrolment and RTE

As far as Universal Enrolment is concerned RTE clearly states that all the children of 6-14 years of age need to be in school. Any time of the academic year, a child can go to a school and demand that his/her right be respected. It also makes education free in order to give equal opportunity to all the children to attend school and the expenses should not become a hindrance in pursuing or completing elementary education. The act also mentions that each child is given age appropriate education which implies that children will be enrolled in the class that corresponds to their age. For example if nine year old has not been to school or dropped out earlier, he/she will be enrolled in class IV. To enable the 9 year to cope in class IV 'special training/ bridge course' will be provided on the premises to bring the child upto the age appropriate level.

Universal Retention and RTE

The Act also ensures that the State should facilitate the completion of elementary education and clearly directs that no child shall be held back, expelled or required to pass a board examination until completion. The Act specifically addresses equity issue and requires the appropriate government and every local authority to " ensure that the child belonging to disadvantaged groups are not discriminated against and prevented from pursuing and completing elementary education on any grounds." Various practices followed by the school like separate seating arrangements in the classroom, calling them by different names, discriminatory attitude of teachers etc makes it difficult for Scheduled Caste, Scheduled Tribes and Minority students to complete the elementary levels of education. It forbids capitation fee/screening procedure for child or parents. It strictly prohibits physical punishment and mental harassment of children.

RTE suggests number of strategies at the local level like pre service orientation of teachers, curricular reforms, to be practiced to make the schools inclusive for all the children.

Equitable Quality

RTE stipulates that each child is entitled to quality education and not only insists on adequate infrastructure, teaching aids, number of teachers but also on the processes and the classroom interaction. For the successful completion of the elementary education the Act lays down the norms and standards relating to, *inter alia*, Pupil Teacher Ratios (PTR), infrastructure including school building, learning equipment, school working days, teacher working hours etc. School infrastructure (where there is a problem) is to be improved in three years, else recognition is cancelled.

In respect to school building the Act states that it should be safe, having drinking water facility, separate toilet facility for girls and boys, kitchen for Mid day meal and playground secured by boundary wall. As per DISE data (2009-10) around 92 per cent of the schools were having drinking water facility and only around 31 per cent boys' schools were having toilets and around 59 per cent girls' schools were having toilet facility. Therefore the huge funds are required to build the toilets, additional rooms in those schools which do not have adequate infrastructure.

For effective teaching-learning to take place, the teacher needs to have manageable children and the Act specifies that teacher-student ratio of 1:30 at primary level and 1:35 at the upper primary level to be met within a given time frame. The primary school must function for 200 days and upper primary school to function for 250 days. The teachers are required to work for 45 hours a week.

To regulate the adequacy of teachers in each school, the Act clearly directs rational deployment of teachers by ensuring that the specified pupil teacher ratio is maintained for each school, rather than as an average for the State or District or Block. It lays down strict criteria for the qualification of teachers. School teachers will need adequate professional degree within five years or else will lose job.

To Make Learning Effective

RTE rests the onus of ensuring learning on the State whereas earlier this burden was often placed on the child and the children were accordingly categorized as 'brilliant' or 'slow learner'. It provides for development of curriculum in consonance with the values enshrined in the Constitution, and which would ensure the all-round development of the child, building on the child's knowledge, potentiality and talent.

Equity and RTE

Protecting the rights of the socially disadvantaged groups as is enshrined in our Constitution it directs the State that the children belonging to weaker section or to disadvantaged groups are not discriminated against and prevented from pursuing and completing elementary education on any grounds. Moreover, the specific needs and predicaments of the traditionally excluded categories-the SC, ST, Muslim minority and other disadvantaged groups should be understood and school should be made accessible to these children. Seeking the cooperation and partnership of the private sector in fulfilling the target of UEE, the Act mandates unaided private schools to reserve upto 25 per cent of the seats for students from weaker sections. The Act clearly prohibits donation or capitation fee on admission; and interviewing the child or parents as part of the screening process.

Decentralized Management and RTE

Besides focus on equity, efficiency and quality improvement the RTE stress on the decentralisation and has many provisions for ensuring accountability through decentralisation including the creation of School Management Committees (SMC) empowered to make plans and monitor school-level expenditures. SMCs comprising local authority officials, parents, guardians and teachers will prepare the School Development Plans. RTE also mandates the inclusion of 50 per cent women and parents of disadvantaged children. Parents will comprise three fourth of its members with special representation from those belonging to weaker and deprived section and remaining twenty five per cent would be from amongst the elected members of the local authority, teachers and local educationist. SMCs would be responsible to monitor the working of the school, prepare school development plan, and monitor the utilization of grants. Other major functions of the SMCs are to ensure the enrolment and continued attendance of all children from the neighbourhood in the school; monitor the maintenance of the norms and standards like adequate physical infrastructure and number of teachers in the school; identify the needs of school; monitor the implementation of the Mid-day Meal in the school. Such community participation will be crucial to ensuring a child friendly "whole school" environment.

The school Development Plan will provide details related to the estimates of class-wise enrolment for each year; requirement over the three year period of the number of additional teachers, physical requirement of additional infrastructure and equipment, entitlements of children such as free text books and uniform. It appears that the expectations from the SMCs are too high considering the fact that the parents in the governments' school may not be well informed and too occupied to participate actively and efficiently.

Teachers at the Center Stage

Recognising teachers as the backbone of the education system the Act lays down duties and responsibilities of teachers in specific terms to ensure quality education to all children. The Act clearly prohibits physical punishment, expulsion or detention of a child and deployment of teachers for non-educational purposes other than census or election duty and disaster relief. The teacher has the duty to transact and complete the curriculum, regularly assess the learning level of each child, provide supplementary instruction if required and apprise every parent/guardian about the progress of learning and development of the child. Teachers are prohibited from giving private tuitions.

Responsibility of the Centre, State and Local Authority

The Act also specifies that the Central Government and the State Government shall have concurrent responsibility for providing funds for carrying out the provisions of Act. The Central Government shall provide to the State Government as grants-in-aid of revenues, in consultation with the State Government.

The Act not only defines the responsibilities of State but also that of the local governments. They must maintain records of children up to the age of fourteen years residing within their jurisdiction, to ensure admission of children of migrant families, monitor functioning of schools within their jurisdiction and decide the academic calendar.

Monitoring of the Implementation of RTE Act

The Government is taking necessary steps to implement the Act. The National

Commission for the Protection of Child Rights (NCPCR), the State Commissions for Protection of Child Rights shall in addition to the functions already assigned also (a) Examine and review the safeguards for rights provided by or under this Act and recommend measures for their effective implementation; (b) inquire into complaints relating to child's right to free and compulsory education; (c) Take necessary steps as provided under sections 15 and 24 of the said Commissions for Protection of Child Rights Act.

Proper implementation of the Act calls for collective efforts on the part of the Center, State Governments, schools, teachers and civil society to ensure every child of 6-14 years of age in school. Besides the enactment of RTE Act, since independence number of initiatives have been undertaken to achieve the target of UEE; few of them are discussed below.

Key Interventions in Elementary Education Sector

Education being a concurrent subject since 1976, Central government has launched various centrally sponsored schemes to enhance the access, enrolment and retention of children in the school.

National Programme of Nutritional Support to Primary Education

National Programme of Nutritional Support to Primary Education [commonly known as the Mid-Day Meal Scheme] was launched as a centrally-sponsored Scheme on 15th August 1995. Its objective was to boost "universalisation of primary education by increasing enrolment, retention and attendance and simultaneously impacting on nutrition of students in primary classes". Apart from enhancing school attendance and child nutrition, mid-day meals have an important social value and foster bondage and equality. As children of diverse background eat together a common meal, it tends to break caste barrier and class inequality. Moreover, at the household, the boys are given preference therefore girls are more affected by hunger. Mid-day meal can improve the educational and nutritional status of the girl child.

The programme originally covered children of primary stage (Classes I to V) in government, local body and government-aided schools, and was extended in October, 2002, to cover children studying in Education Guarantee Scheme (EGS) and Alternative & Innovative Education (AIE) Centers also. The programme was extended to upper primary education level from 2008-09 onwards.

Kasturba Gandhi Balika Vidyalaya (KGBV)

The KGBVs was launched in July 2004 for setting up of 750 residential schools with boarding facilities at upper primary level for girls, predominantly belonging to the SCs, STs, OBCs, and minorities in Educationally Backward Blocks (EBBs) characterized by low female literacy rate and high gender gap in literacy. A minimum of 75 per cent of the enrolment in KGBVs was reserved for girls from the target groups and the remaining 25 per cent was open for girls belonging to the Below Poverty Line (BPL) category.

National Programme for Education of Girls at Elementary Level (NPEGEL)

NPEGEL is an integral but distinct component of SSA was launched in 2003 in educationally backward blocks. NPGEL is aimed at enhancing the education of underprivileged and marginalized girls at elementary level through intense community mobilization, development of model schools in clusters, gender sensitization of teachers, preparation of gender sensitive learning materials, early childhood care and education facilities and provision of need based incentives like escorts, stationery material, work books and uniforms.

Teacher Education

The centrally-sponsored scheme of Teacher Education was launched in 1987-88 as a follow up of the recommendations of the NPE, 1986. It aimed at creating an institutional infrastructure to provide academic and technical resource support for continuous education and training of school teachers. District Institutes of Education and Training (DIET) set up under the scheme provide academic resource support to formal and non formal elementary school teachers, Colleges of Teacher Education (CTEs) and Institutes of Advanced Studies in Education (ASEs) have been given the responsibility of organizing pre-service and in-service training of secondary school teachers.

District Information System for Education (DISE)

NUEPA has created a comprehensive database on elementary education in India known as District Information System for Education (DISE) which covers both primary and upper primary schools/sections of all the districts of the country. It is providing vital information related to school infrastructural facilities, enrollment of children in the schools as well as on teachers profile. In the current year 2008-09 12, 85,576 schools imparting elementary education across 633 districts are covered under DISE.

For the last four years, NUEPA has been computing educational development Index (EDI) which is largely based on the data collected through DISE. A set of 21 indicators have been used in computing EDI which are re-grouped into four sets of sub-groups namely; Access, infrastructure, teachers and outcome indicators. This index helps to determine the status of schools in different states and what kind of further improvements are required.

Emerging Issues and Challenges

Indian education system has made significant improvement in increasing access and narrowing social and gender disparities especially at the elementary level of education. In spite of enormous progress, still large inequalities exist among different regions and social groups, which needs to be addressed. There is also the challenge of bringing the last 6-7 per cent children who are "hard to reach" into the fold of education. The issue of quality of primary and elementary education and enhancement of learning levels of students still persists and has to be addressed squarely. Bridging gender and social gaps in educational attainments and reducing inter-State, inter-district and inter-block disparities also pose a serious challenge. The biggest challenge is the implementation of right to Compulsory and Free Education Act.

Bridging the Disparities: Regional, Social and Gender

It is worthwhile to mention that notwithstanding the success of SSA, large variation is observed across the states and union territories in terms of accessibility to schooling facilities, participation rates, retention rate and dropout rates. Issue of universalisation of elementary education has to be seen in disaggregated terms. Huge disparities not only exist among the districts but also with regard to various socio-economic groups. Children belonging to Scheduled castes, Scheduled tribes and minorities are lagging behind as far as enrolment in schools are concerned which needs to be addressed especially in the context of Right to Education Act. Though the participation of the girls has increased over the years but still the gender disparities is one of the major areas of concern which needs the attention of educational planners and administrators.

Improving Quality in Education

Research and survey findings indicate that around 30 per cent children completing primary education are not able to achieve the competencies equivalent to Grade II. Children from poor socio economic background generally do not have academic support from their families, thus are primarily dependent on the school and teacher for learning. Poor infrastructural facilities, uncongenial atmosphere and low motivation of the teachers tend to create disinterest in students leading to their dropping out of school even without completing the primary education cycle. Therefore the biggest challenge is to improve the quality in education in order to enable children to retain in school and complete the elementary education cycle as well as to achieve competency level corresponding to their grade. Improving quality in education denotes improving the basic physical infrastructure facilities, teacher competence, classroom interaction and processes, revising the curriculum in such a way as it relates to child's experiences. This must be accompanied by a clear definition and accurate assessment of learning outcomes.

Decentralized Planning and Management in Operation

Over the last few years there has been shift towards decentralization and the effort is being made to involve the local bodies such as Village Education Committees/ward committees, School Management Committees, Parent-Teacher Association and Community in the planning and implementation of elementary education programmes. Though in most of the states and blocks these structures have been put in place but their functioning is still in question. The challenge is to strengthen these institutions and provide them the financial and administrative powers to help them to discharge their functions more effectively.

Addressing Imbalances and Inequities in Teacher Provision

Though there has been an impressive increase in the number of primary and upper primary school teachers in India in the last two decades, the imbalance in teacher allocation between states, districts and within districts, between rural and urban areas continues to be a major concern. Large number of school still remains single teacher school.

Implementation of RTE 2009 at the Ground Level

Making education a fundamental right is surely a step in right direction to address the anomalies and disparities of elementary education in India. It gives legislative framework through which we can question and improve the education system. Nevertheless the proper implementation, monitoring and evaluation of improving quality of government schools, enhanced public-private participation, enhancement of access and adequate quality of education to all children is a big challenge that needs to be addressed. Availability of sufficient number of teacher in each school is another major challenge.

Mobilizing resources and funds to implement the RTE Act is another big challenge. Major portion of the allocations are earmarked for the Sarva Shiksha Abhiyan (SSA) which is according to the Government, the main vehicle to implement the RTE Act. Government allocation to the SSA has increased by only 10.53 per cent, the majority of which comes from the 2 per cent education cess on central taxes. The allocation in 2011-12 is Rs. 20999.28 crores over last year allocation of Rs. 18999.10 crores at the revised estimated stage. The allocations for SSA from other sources other than Education cess have gone down from Rs. 7769.10 crore (Revised estimate 2010-11) to Rs. 7096.15 crore (Budget estimate 2011-12). Insufficient budget therefore remains one of the biggest hurdles to proper implementation of the Act.

The School Management Committees are entrusted with large number of responsibilities but are not given sufficient administrative and financial powers therefore they may not be able to function efficiently. Capacity building of SMC members, teachers, planners is a huge task that needs to be undertaken for the proper implementation of the RTE.

Conclusion

In conclusion a few policy options need to be considered:

- Government shall focus on achieving universal access with greater emphasis on expansion of upper primary schools so that on the one hand, the norm of each habitation having upper primary school within 3 km. is achieved and the national norm of ratio of 2:1 for primary and upper primary schools is achieved.
- Transfer of plan and non-plan resources through planning and finance commission and also design of central and centrally-sponsored schemes must address the needs of these educationally backward states.
- Children from the disadvantaged and socially backward groups need special attention. Children of these groups are out of school due to demand driven factors like poverty, low educational attainment of the parents, large family size as well as supply related constraints like poor accessibility to schooling facilities, overcrowding in the school, low motivation of teachers, poor teaching etc. Hence, the provision of physical facilities may not automatically address the social and economic constraints faced by disadvantaged sections belonging to SC, ST and Muslim minority groups in attending the school. These children may also be provided monthly stipend, free uniform and free stationery items to overcome their financial constraints.
- The focus on the most vulnerable groups of children who are still out of school would require partnership with NGOs and a commitment to a rights-based, equity oriented approach.
- Teachers are the pillars of any education system and they can play a major role in the qualitative improvement of schools there by facilitating bridging of disparities between social groups. They need to actively participate in the enrolment drives and be continuously monitoring the activities of the child to avoid their exclusion.
- Equally important is improving the quality in education especially of the government schools. This involves improvement of infrastructure facilities as well as the teaching learning process in the schools. More focus need to be given on individualized attention to each child and use of appropriate materials and methods for teaching children with special needs or children who come from a different language background.
- The NCF 2005 and the syllabus prepared by NCERT should become the guiding document for States and UTs to work on revising their curricula and syllabi.

3

The Right of Children to Free and Compulsory Education (RTE) Act, 2009

A Step Towards Right Direction

Sumanjeet Singh

Knowledge is power and education is a tool to acquire it. Education is undoubtedly one of the most important factors that impact the growth and development of future course of country's people as a whole. Globally, the role of education in facilitating social and economic development is well recognized. But, the importance of education is most evident in developing countries. There, it is a means to alleviate poverty and engineer social change by empowering women, safeguarding children from exploitation, controlling population growth, promoting human rights and democracy. It reduces social and economic disparity, allowing progress to be equally shared. Studies indicate that educated people are in a better position to contribute more positively to society and even towards the planet, as they understand the implications of their choices and actions. Therefore, education is recognized as one of the best financial investments States can make; and globally it is acknowledged that access to good quality elementary education, at minimum, must be treated as a fundamental right (Ramachandran *et al.,* 2003). During the World Education Forum held in Dakar, Senegal in 2000, the right to education was strongly re-affirmed through the Education for All (EFA) goals. According to the UNESCO's '*Education for All Global Monitoring Report 2010*', about 135 countries (Dhar, 2010) have constitutional provisions for free[1] and non-discriminatory education for all. In India, the Right to Education received considerable impetus[2] during the last decade as a result of the concerted efforts of many groups and agencies that made determined efforts to ensure that all children in India receive at least minimum of education irrespective of their socio-economic status and their ability to pay for education in a situation of continuous impoverishment and erosion of basic needs (Aradhya and Kashyap, 2006). Finally, sixty-three years after independence, India enforced a historic the Right of Children to Free and Compulsory Education (henceforth RTE) Act that promises freedom from illiteracy for this vast and diverse country. The RTE guarantees every Indian child the most basic fundamental right[3] '*the right to education*'. The Act-with its latest amendment[4]—that became operationalized on 1 April, 2010[5] guarantees every child in the 6-14 age groups[6] up to class 8, both free and compulsory education. The enactment of Act is a step in the right direction (Jha and Parvati, 2010) and a matter of national importance. The Act seeks to achieve 10 broad objectives such as free and compulsory education, quality education, focus on social responsibility and the obligations of teachers and de-bureaucratization of admissions. Its implementation will directly benefit close to 1 crore children who do not go to schools at present. These children, who have either dropped out from schools or have never been to any educational institution, will be enrolled in schools.

Remarkable Provisions in Right to Education Act

The RTE Act has many remarkable provisions. The Act is not just about taking children to school. This is the Act that speaks about the physical infrastructure, teacher-pupil ratio, qualification of teachers and many other concerned matters. The RTE Act makes it obligatory on part of the State governments and local bodies to ensure that every child in age group of 6–14 years[7] get 8 years of elementary education in a school[8] in the vicinity/neighborhood[9]. This means that such child does not have to pay a single penny as regards books, uniforms etc. It shall be the duty of every parent or guardian to admit or cause to be admitted his or her child or ward, as the case may be, to an elementary education in the neighborhood school. No child shall be denied admission for want of documents[10]; no child shall be turned away if the admission cycle in the school is over and no child shall be asked to take an admission test. It is also mentioned that no child admitted in a school shall be held back in any class or expelled from school till the completion of elementary education. No child shall be required to pass any Board examination till completion of elementary education. No child shall be subjected to physical punishment or mental harassment. Children with disabilities[11] will also be educated in the mainstream schools[12]. All the private schools shall be required to enroll children from weaker sections and disadvantaged communities in their incoming class to the extent of 25 per cent of their enrolment, by simple random selection. No seats in quota can be left vacant. However, the reservation for weaker section will not be implemented from this year as the admission season is almost over. It will be implemented from 2011-12. These children will be treated on par with all other children in the school and subsidized by the State at the rate of average per learner costs in the government schools (unless the per costs in the private school are lower). All schools will have to prescribe to the norms and standards laid out in the Act (Table 3.1) and no school that does not fulfill these standards within 3 years will be allowed to function.

Table 3.1: Schedule Outlining Norms and Standards for a School

No.	*Item*	*Norms and Standard*
1.	Number of Teachers For Class I-VI For Class VI-VIII	 30:1 35:1 At least three subjects teachers (VI-VIII)
2.	Building	• 1 classroom for every teacher and an office cum store cum Head teacher's room • Barrier Free Access • Separate toilets for boys and girls • Safe and adequate drinking water facility • 1kitchen for mid day meal • Playground and boundary wall
3.	Minimum working days in an academic year/hours	• 200 working days (for class I-V)/800 instructional hours • 220 working days (for VI-VIII)/1000 instructional hours
4.	Minimum number of working hours per week for the teacher	45 teaching including preparation hours
5.	Teaching Learning Equipment	Shall be provided to each class
6.	Library	Shall be provided to each class
7.	Play, material, games, sports equipment	Shall to provided to each class

Source: The Right of Children to Free and Compulsory Education Act, 2009; pp. 12-13.

All private schools will have to apply for recognition, failing which they will be penalized to the tune of Rs. 1 lakh and if they still continue to function will be liable to pay Rs. 10,000 per day as fine. The government will evolve some mechanism to help marginalized schools comply with the provisions of the Act. Any person possessing minimum qualifications[13], as laid down by an academic authority, authorized by the Central Government, by notification, shall be eligible for appointment of teacher. It is also important to note that no teacher shall engage himself or herself in private tuition or private teaching activity. There is requirement of a teacher student ratio[14] of 1:30 at each of these schools that ought to be met within a given time frame. Unaided and private schools shall ensure that children from weaker sections and disadvantaged groups shall not be segregated from the other children in the classrooms nor shall their classes be held at places and timings different from the classes held for the other children. The Centre and States have agreed to share the financial burden in the ratio of 55:45, while the Finance Commission has given Rs. 25,000 crore to the States for implementation of the Act. The Centre approved an outlay of Rs. 15,000 crore for 2010-2011. The Central government may issue such guidelines to the appropriate Government or, as the case may be, the local authority, as it deems fit for the purpose of implementation of this Act.

Challenges before Right to Education Act

The RTE Act is an essential step towards improving each child's accessibility to secondary and higher education, bringing India closer to achieving national educational development goals, as well as the Millennium Development Goals (MDG) and education for all (EFA). Highlighting the importance of RTE Act, UNESCO Director-General said that "without India, world can not reach the MDG of having every child complete primary education by 2015. It is expected that the Act will propel to even greater heights of prosperity and productivity for all guaranteeing children their right to a quality education and a brighter future. But the RTE Act, that promises to provide compulsory and free elementary education to all childern of India, is set to face many challenges in its implementation. The first hurdle is shortage of funds. In the first year, the Act is likely to face a shortage of Rs. 7,000 crore (Rs. 70 billion). The RTE will have a funding system similar to the Sarva Shiksha Abhiyan[15] (SSA) which is already being carried out successfully in the country.[16] The Central and State funding pattern for the scheme will be 55:45. However, for executing the scheme in all the eight North Eastern States the Central government will be responsible for the 90 per cent of the cost of the scheme. So, if all the States cooperate with the Centre, the scheme will have about Rs. 27,000 crore (Rs. 270 billion) including the Rs. 15,000 crore (Rs. 150 billion) with the HRD ministry but with a shortage of Rs. 7,000 crore (Rs. 70 billion) the scheme will require an estimated sum of nearly Rs. 34,000 crore (Rs. 340 billion) for a period of five years (Kulkarani, 2010). States like Orissa, UP and Bihar have already conveyed the message that they require fund for implementation of the Act to HRD ministry in their respective States. The Orissa government has also demanded that the State should be considered as a special category like States in north east. Chief Minister of Uttar Pradesh, Mayawati also said that *"It would be difficult for the State to arrange Rs. 8,000 crore considering its present financial condition*". Karnataka, Madhya Pradesh and Gujarat have also expressed reservations about the huge financial burden the path breaking legislation will entail for them.

The second challenge is related with infrastructure. The Act will monitor the infrastructure in schools including the number of classrooms, separate toilets for boys and girls, facility of drinking water, kitchen for mid-day meal, playground and barrier free access for physically challenged students. But, thousands of schools still do not have required infrastructure. Infrastructure facilities range from inadequate to dismal (Table 3.2). In a survey conducted by National University of Educational Planning and Administration (NUEPA), has found that almost half of the recognized elementary schools in the country do not have separate toilets for girls. District Information Systems for Education Report (2008-09) on elementary education in India gives a bleak picture of the 1.29 million government and private school covered, over 60 per cent did not have electricity, 46.4 did not have toilets for girls and almost 50 per cent did not have boundary walls to ensure the safety of the students. For example, Uttar Pradesh needs to construct 100,000 rooms to satisfy the norms laid down by the RTE Act (Sahoo, 2010). This goes out to prove and depict the sorry state that our schools are in and going to be a challenge to provide the requisite infrastructure that the Act expects.

Table 3.2: Conditions of Private and Public Schools in India

Infrastructure for teaching	*Government*	*Private*
Per cent teacher present in school	87.6	89.4
Per cent of teacher trained	85.9	43.8
Per cent teacher with college degree	43.7	64.4
Per cent student present in school	86.9	91.9
Some subject taught in English	26.8	51.1
English Instruction begins in 1st standard	53.2	88.2
Toilet facility	60.9	78.3
Chairs/desk for all students	29.2	63.5
Blackboard in all classrooms	95.4	98.1
Computer available for students	5.9	29.2
School has fans	28.4	63.3
Kitchen for cooked meals	41.3	10.8
Cook employed by school	74.9	11.1
Any teaching material on the wall	77.3	78.9
Children's work on the wall	67.6	73.9

Source: Human Development Survey, 2008 by NCEAR.

The third important problem with the implementation of the Act is related with accountability aspect of schools defined by the Act. In most private and public schools the accountability among the teaching staff is lacking. The ultimate victims of this malpractice are the innocent students who would like to excel in life. To ensure the culture of accountability, the Act requires that all schools, except those that are unaided, constitute school management committee[17] (SMC). But, the Act is not clear why unaided schools are left out of purview of accountability with regard to the provisions contained in

Section 21.1 and disclaimers that are provided. Section 37[18] of the Act also maintains that legal proceedings against such actions of the government can not be initiated in the event that these have been undertaken in good faith and best interests of children. Rather than pursuing an objective vision, the Act is ridden with loopholes.

The fourth biggest challenge in implementation of Right to Education Act is massive shortage of qualified teachers. Both the government and private schools lack many thousands teachers. But major shortages of teachers are in government schools–especially schools situated in rural areas and semi-urban areas. There are a number of untrained teachers in the states that ranges from 10-40 per cent of the total strength. This problem is mainly related to private schools as in the government schools teachers are appointed as per the government rules. The Annual Survey of Education Report (2009) says half of India's children in Class V can not read a class II level text book and fewer still can do basic mathematics. A major cause for this is the lack of trained teachers (Table 3.3).

Table 3.3: Shortage of Teachers in Various Indian States

States	*No. of Positions in Schools*	*Vacancies*	*% Vacancies*
Uttar Pradesh	298,602	111,850*	37.4
Bihar	300,000	104,500	34.8
West Bengal	N/A**	60,000	—
Rajasthan	250,000	56,000	22.4
Maharashtra	561,910	29,551	5.2
Karnataka	309,631	12,803	4.1
Haryana	39,627	11,000	27.7
Andhra Pradesh	300,000	11,000	3.7
Chhattisgarh	80,000	7,000	8.25
Gujarat	182,000	6,200	3.4
Jammu & Kashmir	28,652	1,099	3.8

Source: The Survey of Education Report, 2009 (Sahoo, 2010);
* the government did not share the figure;
** some of these have been filed by temporary para-teachers appointed on contract).

The average student-to-teacher ratio in a classroom at present stands at 50:1, and as the act envisages that this ratio should be 30:1, it implies that at least 12 lakh more trained teachers will be required within six months of notification of the Act. However, inadequate staff is only part of the problem. A 2005 World Bank Report said 25 per cent of teachers were absent from schools and only half of those present taught anything. Added to this, there are hundreds of students in some classes and there is a huge gap between the training imparted to teachers and what they practice on ground. In the absence of competent teachers who are considered the pillar of education, it would be next to impossible for the Act to realistically achieve its goals.

The fifth, the RTE Act is to be implemented through Public Private Partnership (PPP). It implies that the private sector will be encouraged to start primary and middle schools in non served areas and they will have to admit wards of the weaker sections up to at least 25 per cent of their total intake in each class in the case of unaided schools and up to the percentage of annual recurring grant-in-aid to their annual expenditure in the case of aided schools. This arrangement raised a question that at one hand the Act aims at removing bipolarity in education and on the other hand it is feared that interfering in the functioning of private schools will have an adverse effect on the quality of education. These institutes claim to have brought some semblance of order to the education system in our country (Nitst, 2010).

The sixth, Section 4 of the Act prescribes that a child must be admitted to a class appropriate to his age. This would mean that if a child aged nine years approaches a private, unaided school to get admission, the management would be bound to admit him to the appropriate class, in this case Class V or VI, irrespective of the fact he had no formal education in the past. This raises a very serious question whether the purpose of the Act is really to educate children or merely produce certificate holders.

Added to these challenges, the Act has many other limitations. The RTE Act is highly criticized primarily for setting an age limit of 6 to 14[19] years for the beneficiaries. The Act ensures compulsory admission, attendances and completion of elementary education by every child in the age group of 6-14 years. But, early childhood care and development (3-6 years) is currently left out of the RTE Act. This group is critical for brain development and sets the foundation for sound learning in later years. It is difficult to understand the logic of not including the child between age group 3-5 when more than 50 per cent of children, five years old, are enrolled on regular basis. Another problem with the Act is continuation of the traditional emphasis on inputs without adequate attentions to outcomes. If a child goes to school for two years, four years, six years or even eight years, what should his/her learning achievement be? If some basic minimum learning is not achieved, should it not be considered a violation of the child's right to education (Nitst, 2010). Last but not the least is the tough task of bringing together children from varying economic and social backgrounds on the same platform. It would indeed be challenging for the teachers to maintain equilibrium and create an environment for them to blend together.

Suggestions for Successful Implementation of RTE Act

The plight of millions of children and adults with no access to basic education in today's *"knowledge society"* calls for sweeping measures to guarantee education for all. The RTE Act gave new impetus to an international movement for achievement of education for all. Despite many limitations, the Act has many remarkable provisions. However, the success of the Act will depend on the exact implementation of these provisions. In fact, it is the first step taken by the Government of India, but more needs to be done to achieve its objectives. There are some suggestions towards successful implementation of RTE Act.

- First, as Stated above, there is acute shortage of trained and qualified teachers and without qualified trained teachers it is almost impossible to equip the children with knowledge. It is therefore absolutely critical that the government makes clear budgetary provisions to appoint new teachers and impart training to them to make them capable of delivering the knowledge needed in 21st century.
- Second, the RTE Act can only become real when it gives all the children, be it the 3-6 age group or out of school children, equal opportunity to realize their fundamental right. It is therefore, important for the government to pay more focused attention to pre-school education (which is currently grossly neglected) and to primary education by enhancing financial as well as academic resource to create good quality schools accessible to all children (Ramachandaran, 2009).
- Third, to attract and retain children of poor families in the schools it is not possible through compulsion alone, nor is it a question of opening of schools in the neighborhood. The children of these families remain uneducated because of the mere accident of their birth in such families. They must not be allowed to suffer for no fault of theirs. They have the right to be educated like many others. The State has to take some initiatives in this direction. Schooling may be provided when the children are freed from domestic duties or paid or unpaid work through the night schools, mobile schools and the like. This will involve no cultural break and no cost to the family. Involvement of NGOs and teacher entrepreneurs would be necessary in such conditions (Mehta and Kapoor, 2010).
- Fourth, convergence of various schemes with the right to education is needed. All families with working children should be covered under below poverty line (BPL), the houseless families whose children have no address should be provided with housing; the children of migrants' labourers should be admitted in boarding schools and so on. Similarly convergence could be in terms of creating infrastructure as well. For instance, NREGA should be used to create schools, play grounds, etc. The specialized agencies like Sports Council or art schools need to be linked with the efforts.

- Fifth, the current provisions of the Child Labour (Prohibition and Regulations) Act, 1986 are inconsistent with the RTE Act. When the Child Labour (Prohibition and Regulations) Act, 1986 allows a child to be hired and taken for work during school hours, the right to education cannot be ensured. The Child Labour (Prohibition and Regulations) Act, 1986 should be amended to ban any kind of work up to 14 years[20] of age. Under Chapter VII entitled Miscellaneous, a new section be added to remove these inconsistencies. It should be specifically mentioned in this section that 'provisions of this Act shall override the provisions of any other Act that are inconsistent with this RTE Act'. The Child Labour (Prohibition and Regulations) Act, 1986 should be specifically mentioned in this section as a reference.
- Sixth, schools to which children of the underprivileged have access are run by the State or local authorities. The curriculum and teaching methodologies in these schools stand obsolete and outdated, with the emphasis being on rote-learning and merely developing reading and writing skills instead of holistic education. Lack of vocational training and non-availability of such courses renders students with barely any employable skills at the end of their schooling (Shubhi, 2009). By and large, these have a poor record of performance and there is no mechanism specified for ensuring quality education. The present Act is also silent in this regard. Therefore, there is dire need of specified mechanism for ensuring quality education. It is suggested that in Chapter 2 a new section should be added: '*Special provisions for first generation learners*'. The section should specify special tuitions, counseling and care of the children whose parents are illiterates and know nothing about education.

Further, the Act has made only three penal provisions with regard to charging of capitation fee (Sec. 13(2), running an unrecognized school (Sec. 18(5) and running of derecognized school (Sec. 19(5). There is no general penal clause for violation of the provisions of the Act. There are several important provisions which do not specify penalty for violation. For instance, if a non-aided school does not fill-in 25 per cent free seats; no penal action has been specified. There should be a general penal provision that should penalize any one who violates any provision of the Act save the provisions made in specific sections. This penal provision should be included in Chapter VI. The penalty clauses should include monetary, derecognition of a school and imprisonment. There should be a minimum monetary penalty specified. Last but not the least, private schools have been given the freedom to form their own management committees, however, there are no rules and guidelines regarding community participation in the management of private schools. Therefore, a set of guidelines needs to be developed by the government so that the communities are included.

Conclusion

No doubt, Right to Education Act is a path breaking step towards the universalisation of education. With the new Act operational, India has joined the over 135 countries which have legal guarantees to provide free and compulsory education to children and some 20 nations, including Afghanistan, China and Switzerland, providing free education for eight years. The Act envisages providing free and compulsory education to all children to equip them with knowledge, skills and value to make them accountable and enlightened citizens of India. It is expected that an estimated 1 crore children, who have either dropped out of schools or have never been to any educational institution, will get elementary education as it will be binding on the part of local and State Governments to ensure that all children in the 6 to 14 years age group get schooling. The Act is also being lauded for providing a platform to *"reach the unreached,"* as it contains specific provisions for disadvantaged groups, such as child labourers, migrant children, children with special needs, or those who have a disadvantage owing to social, cultural, economical, geographical, linguistic, gender or such other factor. Thus, the goals are indeed commendable. But, to realize them is a huge challenge. The sheer size of out of school children is the biggest one. Shortage of qualified teachers, poor infrastructure in schools, requirement of new schools, and finances are the other big challenges. Further, evidence suggests that most well meaning and well defined legislations fail to make significant change without proper implementation. Successful implementation of RTE Act requires proper planning and awareness at grassroots level. For this, there is strong need to generate awareness among the various stakeholders responsible for its implementation. Schools also need to be made aware of provisions of the 25 per cent reservations, the role of SMCs and the requirements under the schedule. This can be done through mass awareness programme. Further, rigorous efforts should be made to implement this Act in rural areas where more than 70 per cent child labour work in agriculture where access to school is severely limited and non availability of trained and qualified teacher make the situation worse. Last but not the least, there is strong need to address some issues which are very critical for the success of RTE Act, but has not been addressed adequately. The Act does not address the issue of under-funding. It has no financial memorandum. The Act sets no deadline for universalization of education. Most importantly, some norms are mentioned in the Act, but only as items as they are qualified by the phrase *"as the government may determine."* The Act has already been enacted. When will the government determine norms or does it simply mean that these norms will not be justice-able and may never be determined. Unless all the above mentioned issues and challenges are dealt with, the basic objective of RTE can not be achieved.

Acknowledgements: While bearing full responsibiltiy for any error and inadequacy, the author would like to thank *Prof. L.N. Dahiya, Prof. S.D. Vashistha* (M.D. University, Rohtak, India) and *Sudhanshu Kumar (IGIDR, Mumbai, India)* for enlightening conversations and suggestions on the draft version of the paper.

Notes

1. However, the report says that despite the legal guarantee of free education, primary school fees continue to be charged in some countries.
2. 86th Amendment Act (2002) via Article 21A (Part III) seeks to make free and compulsory education a Fundamental Right for all children in the age group 6-14 years. A first draft of the legislation envisaged in the above Article, viz., Free and Compulsory Education for Children Bill, 2003, was prepared and posted on this website in October, 2003, inviting comments and suggestions from the public at large. Subsequently, taking into account the suggestions received on this draft, a revised draft of the Bill entitled Free and Compulsory Education Bill, 2004, was prepared and posted on the http://education.nic.in website. The CABE (Central Advisory Board of Education) committee drafted the 'Right to Education' Bill and submitted to the Ministry of HRD. MHRD sent it to NAC where Mrs. Sonia Gandhi is the Chairperson. NAC sent the Bill to PM for his observation. The rough draft of the bill was composed in the year 2005. It received much opposition due to its mandatory provision to provide 25 per cent reservation for disadvantaged children in private schools. In 2006, the finance committee and planning commission rejected the Bill citing the lack of funds and a Model bill was sent to States for the making necessary arrangements. On July 2008, HRD minister circulated another draft of the bill. August 2008, Union Cabinet referred the Right to Education Bill to Group of Ministers; constitute to look into operationalizsation the Fundamental Right to Education. Union Cabinet cleared a revised draft of the bill and sent it to the Cabinet in October 2008. The Right to Children to Free and Compulsory Education Bill was introduced in the Rajya Sabha and made available to the public. In month of February 2009, the Standing Committee released its Report of Recommendations and placed it before both the houses of parliament in session. But, parliament ended the budget session without passing the bill. On July 20, 2009, bill was passed in the Rajya Sabha with the minor changes to the draft bill 2008 and finally on August 4, 2009 bill was passed by Lok Sabha.
3. RTE has been a part of the directive principles of the State Policy under Article 45 of the Constitution, which is part of Chapter 4 of the Constitution. And rights in Chapter 4 are not enforceable. For the first time in the history of India we

have made this right enforceable by putting it in Chapter 3 of the Constitution as Article 21. This entitles children to have the right to education enforced as a fundamental right.

4. The 86th Constitutional Amendment making education a fundamental right was passed by the Parliament in 2002.
5. The bill was approved by the cabinet on 2nd July 2009. Rajya Sabha passed the bill on 20th July 2009 and the Lok Sabha on 4th August 2009. It received the Presidential assent and was notified as law on 3rd September 2009 as The Children's Right to Free and Compulsory Education Act. The Law came into effect in the whole of India except the State Jammu and Kashmir from April 2010, the first time in the history of India a law was brought into force by a speech by the Prime Minister.
6. At present, there are nearly 22 crore children in the relevant age group. However, 4.6 per cent of these children (nearly 92 lakh) are out of school, a ministry official said.
7. Where a child above six years of age has not been admitted in any school or though admitted, could not complete his or her elementary education, then, he or she shall be admitted in a class appropriate to his or her age. Provided further that a child so admitted to elementary education shall be entitled to free education till completion of elementary education even after 14 years.
8. The school management committee or the local authority will identify the drop-outs or out of school children above six years of age and admit them in classes appropriate to their age after giving special training.
9. This is similar to the model in United States. This would imply that the State government and local authorities will establish primary schools within the walking distance of maximum 1 km of the neighborhood. In case of children for class VI to VIII, the School should be within a walking distance of the three km of the neighborhood.
10. On one hand, it is argued that the Act stipulates free education to children in the age group of 6 to 14 years, while at the same time Section 14 prevents schools to insist upon producing an age proof.
11. The existing Act refers to the Children as defined under the Person with Disabilities (Equal Opportunities, Protection and Full Participation) Act, 1996. The amendment will treat children with disabilities as defined in the National Trust for Welfare of Persons with Autism, Cerebral Palsy, Mental Retardation and Multiple Disabilities Act, 1999.
12. India was one of the first countries to ratify the UN Convention on Rights of Persons with Disabilities, in October 2007, which says: *"State parties shall ensure that persons with disability are not excluded from the general education system on the basis of disability and that children with disabilities are not excluded from free and compulsory primary education or from secondary education on the basis of disability."*
13. Where a State does not have adequate institutions offering course or training teacher education, or teacher possessing minimum qualification as laid down under the Act are not available in sufficient numbers, the Central Government may, if it deems necessary, by notification, relax the minimum qualification

required for the appointment as a teacher, for such period, not exceeding five years, as may be specified in that notification.

14. For the purpose of maintaining teacher student ratio, no teacher posted in a school shall be made to serve in any other school or office or deployed for any non-educational purpose.
15. The financial assistance under the programme of Sarva Shiksha Abhiyan (SSA) was 85:15 sharing arrangement during the IX Plan, 75:25 sharing arrangement during the X Plan, and 50:50 sharing thereafter between the Central government and State governments. The revised funding pattern between the Central Government and States/UTs shall be in the ratio of 65:35 for the first two years of the XI Plan i.e. 2007-08 and 2008-09; 60:40 for the third year i.e. 2009-10; 55:45 for the fourth year i.e. 2010-11; and 50:50 thereafter i.e. from 2011-12 onwards. For the 8 North-Eastern States, the fund sharing pattern between Centre and States shall be 90:10 under the programme with the Centre's share resourced from the 10 per cent earmarked funds for the NE Region in the SSA's Central Budget.
16. Sarva Shiksha Abhiyan is Government of India's flagship programme for achievement of Universalization of Elementary Education (UEE) in a time bound manner, as mandated by 86th amendment to the Constitution of India making free and compulsory Education to the Children of 6-14 years age group, a Fundamental Right.
17. The school management committee will perform the four functions: (1) monitor working of school; (2) prepare and recommend school development plan; (3) monitor the utilization of the grants received from the appropriate government or local authority or any other source; and (4) perform such other functions as may be prescribed.
18. No suit of legal proceeding shall lie against the Central Government, the State Government, the National Commission for Protection of Child Rights, the State Commission for Protection of Child Rights, the Local Authority, the School Management Committee or any person, in respect of anything which is in good faith or intended to be done, in pursuance of this Act, or any rules or order made thereunder.
19. The RTE Act has also created a unique problem for the State like Kerala. The issue is of minimum age limit for the children to be admitted to the first standard. For one, the Right to Education Act advocates the age limit to be fixed at six years. However, under the present situation, the minimum age for first standard admissions in the State is five years. The problem is that it would mean there would not be many takers for admissions to the first standard in the next academic year. This is mainly because most of the children who six years were admitted to schools this academic year and will be in the second standard the next academic year. The result will be that a large chunk of teachers will become excess.
20. According to the civil society organizations, approximately 40 million kids are engaged in child labour in the country, although official estimates are much less. There are close to 13 million children in India under 14 years of age who are at present engaged in child labour, according to the 2001 census. This is an anomaly in a country where education is a constitutionally guaranteed right.

4

Right to Elementary Education

Focus on Equity and Equality

Snehlata Verma and *S.K. Das*

Right of Children to Free and Compulsory Education in India is a boon for Indian Children and will help them to acquire primary education to become an independent decision maker lifelong and which will further build strong foundation for India's future.

The right to education has been universally recognized since the Universal Declaration of Human Rights in 1948 (though referred to by the ILO as early as the 1920s) and has since been enshrined in various international conventions, national constitutions and development plans. However, while the vast majority of countries have signed up to, and ratified, international conventions (such as the UN Convention on the Rights of the Child) far fewer have integrated these rights into their national constitutions or provided the legislative and administrative frameworks to ensure that these rights are realized in practice. In some cases the right exists along with the assumption that the user should pay for this right, undermining the very concept of a right. In others, the right exists in theory but there is no capacity to implement this right in practice. Inevitably, a lack of government support for the right to education hits the poorest hardest. Today, the right to education is still denied to millions around the world.

The right to education is an enabling right. Education creates the voice through which rights can be claimed and protected. If people have access to education they can develop the skills, capacity and confidence to secure other rights. Education inculcates among people the ability to access information and develop the communication skills and confidence to speak in a variety of forums, and the ability to negotiate with a wide range of planners and administrators.

In 1950, the Constitution of India articulated its commitment to education under the Directive Principles of State Policy, a set of articles meant to serve as guidelines while framing laws and policies, but not enforceable in any court. Then in 2002, in the wake of a number of landmark Supreme Court judgments on the issue and vigorous civil society campaigning, the 86th Constitutional Amendment made education a fundamental right of all children in the age-group of 6-14. In the same year, the Government circulated a draft Right to Education bill, which went through several alterations thereafter, until the most recent version of it, upon receiving approval from the Union Cabinet, was introduced in the Rajya Sabha in December 2008. Thus, it has taken 55 years from Independence to make education a fundamental right of children and a further 6 years for the Right to Education Bill to be introduced in Parliament.

The Right of children to Free and Compulsory Education Act has come into force from April 1, 2010. This is a historic day for the people of India as from this day the right to education has been accorded the same legal status as the right to life as provided by Article 21A of the Indian Constitution. Every child in the age group of 6-14 years will be provided 8 years of elementary education in an age appropriate classroom in the vicinity of his/her neighbourhood. Indian Education System has shown improvement in the recent decade as per the percentage of enrollment in the schools.

The RTE Act is a comprehensive piece of legislation which includes provisions related to schools, teachers, curriculum, evaluation, access and diversification of responsibilities of various stakeholders. Key features of the Act include:

- Every child from 6 to 14 years of age has a right to free and compulsory education in a neighborhood school till completion of elementary education;
- Private schools must take in a quarter of their class strength from 'weaker sections and disadvantaged groups sponsored by the Government.
- All schools except private unaided schools are to be managed by School Management Committees with 75 per cent parents and guardians as members
- All schools except government schools are required to be recognized by meeting specified norms and standards within 3 years to avoid closure.

Emerging Issues

The RTE Act has been criticized by a diverse array of voices, including *some of the best educationist and economists*. The crucial hurdles are inputs and outcomes, school recognition, school management committees and teachers.

The Act is input-focused rather than output oriented. Even though better school facilities, books, uniforms and better qualified teachers are important, their significance in the Act has been overestimated in the light of inefficient, corrupt and unaccountable institutions of education provision. The Act unfairly penalizes private unrecognized schools for their payment of market wages for teachers rather than elevated civil service wages. It also penalizes private schools for lacking the infrastructural facilities defined under the Act. These schools, which are extremely cost efficient, operate mostly in rural areas or urban slums, and provide essential educational services to the poor. A better alternative would have been to find mechanisms through which public resources could have been infused into these schools. The exemption from these same recognition requirements for government schools is a case of double standards —with the public sector being exempted from the same requirements.

By the Act, School Management Committees (SMCs) will constitute mostly parents and will be responsible for planning and managing the functions of government and aided schools. SMCs will help increase the accountability of government schools, but SMCs for government schools need to be entrusted with powers for evaluation of teacher competencies and students learning assessment. Payment of some compensation to members of SMCs could help increase their participation for the same.

Teachers are the sole arbitrator of the curriculum and need to be paid market-driven compensation. But the government has gone too far by requiring high teacher salaries. These wages are clearly out of tune, when compared with the market wage of a teacher, for most schools across the country. A better mechanism would have involved schools being allowed to design their own teacher salary packages and having autonomy to manage teachers. In the RTE Act, proper disciplinary channels for teachers have not been defined. Such disciplinary action is must as there are problems of teachers being absent from schools at any juncture and almost half of those who are present are not engaged in teaching activity. School Management Committees need to be strengthened to take disciplinary action at the local level. Performance based pay scales need to be considered as a way to improve teaching.

The Act and the Rules require all private schools (whether aided or not) to reserve at least 25 per cent of their seats for economically weaker and socially disadvantaged sections in the entry level class. These students will not pay tuition fees. Private schools will receive reimbursements from the government calculated on the basis of per-child expenditure in government schools. Greater clarity for successful implementation is needed on identification of weaker and disadvantaged sections, selection of these students for entry level class, procedure of conducting admission by neighbourhood or by entire village/town/city, issue of the supply-demand gaps in neighbourhood, mechanism for reimbursement to private schools, procedure to monitor the whole process, the type of external vigilance/social audit would be allowed/encouraged on the process, alternatives to shift the schools in higher classes. Moreover, the method for calculation of per child reimbursement expenditure will yield an inadequate resource flow to private schools. Private schools will end up charging more to the 75 per cent of students—who are paying tuitions—to make space for the 25 per cent of students they are forced to take. This will drive up tuition fees for private schools while government schools continue to be taxpayer funded and essentially free.

Critical Concerns

We travelled a lot to attend schools in the past. But when different schemes came into existence; we have primary schools within one kilometer which is more easily accessible to children. There are still various portions in the country where we lack access to schools for children and they remain without education due to non-availability of schools nearby. We have about eight million children who are still not enrolled in schools and lack the right to education in various states.

The government of India shared its first model of Right to Education Act with all state governments, a few of which still oppose this Act due to multiple reasons. It is really a challenging job to convince all the stakeholders, especially the state governments, and provide sufficient resources and funds to the state governments to implement RTE. Families and communities need to play a vital role to translate RTE into a reality.

RTE states that all children between ages of 6 to 14 will have the right to free and compulsory elementary education. There will be no cost on uniforms, textbooks, midday meals, transportation, or school fees. For better implementation of RTE, central and state governments should join hands for financial expenditure to assure that every child get a quality education. Any expenditure that prevents a child from accessing school have to be taken care of by the State which shall have the responsibility of enrollment, retention as well as completion of 8 years of schooling by the child. No child shall be denied admission due to lack of documents or if the admission cycle in the school is over and no child shall be asked to appear in an admission test.

Children with disabilities will be educated in the mainstream schools. All schools will have to adhere to norms and standards laid out in the Act and the schools that do not fulfill these standards within 3 years will not be allowed to function. All private schools will have to apply for recognition, failing which they will be penalized. Norms and standards of teacher qualification and training are also being laid down by an academic authority. Teachers in all schools will have to subscribe to these norms within 5 years.

The quality of education provided by the government system remains in question. While it remains the largest provider of elementary education (about 80% of all recognized schools), it suffers from shortages of teachers, infrastructural gaps and several habitations continue to lack schools altogether. There are also frequent allegations of government schools dealing with absenteeism, mismanagement and appointments of teachers based on political considerations and conveniences. Teachers training will be the most vital challenge for Indian government to make RTE a success. The systems need an army of teachers who can implement this act and create enough enthusiasm so that they may take active role to educate their children. UNICEF is playing a vital role with the government to provide basic education to Indian children.

Children attending the private schools are at an advantage thus discriminating against the weaker sections who are forced to go to government schools. Furthermore, the system has been criticized as catering to the elites who are able to afford school fees in a country where large number of families live in absolute poverty. The act has been criticized as discriminatory for not addressing these issues. The act has been criticized for being hastily-drafted. Many of the ideas are continuing the policies of Sarva Shiksha Abhiyan and District Primary Education Programme of the '90s, both of which set up a number of schools in rural areas and have not been known for effectiveness. It is rather a fraud on our children as it gives neither free nor compulsory education. In fact, it only legitimizes the present multi-layered, inferior quality school education system where discrimination will continue to prevail.

The RTE Act has been passed. But does that mean that the policy process is now impervious to change? Even today, much can be achieved through a sustained engagement with this problem. Even though state rules are likely to be in compliance with the model rules, these rules are still to be drafted by state level authorities keeping in mind contextual requirements. Advocacy on the flaws of the central arrangements, and partnerships with state education departments, could yield improvements in some states.

Examples of critical changes which state governments should consider is to strengthen School Managing Committees with greater disciplinary power over teachers and responsibility of students learning assessment, greater autonomy for schools to decide teacher salaries and increased clarity in the implementation strategy for 25 per cent reservations. If even a few states are able to break away from the flaws of the central arrangements, this would yield benefits from better policies.

Since unrecognized schools could face closure in view of prescribed recognition standards within three years, ways have to be found to support such schools to improve their facilities by resource support and providing linkages with financial institutions. Moreover, by instituting proper rating mechanisms wherein schools can be rated on the basis of infrastructure, learning achievements and other quality indicators, constructive competition can be ensured.

Most well-meaning legislations fail to make significant changes without proper awareness and grassroots pressure. Schools need to be made aware of provisions of the 25 per cent reservations, the role of SMCs and the requirements under the schedule. This can be undertaken through mass awareness programmes as well as ensuring proper understanding by stakeholders responsible for its implementation.

Finally, along with ensuring implementation of the RTE Act which enhance focussed reforms in government schools and regulation for private schools, we need to broaden our vision so as to create an environment conducive to spontaneous private involvement. The contemporary regulatory restrictions in the education sector discourage philanthropists from opening more schools.

Input Prerogative

Since its launch in 2001, SSA has enriched resources for India's elementary education. Long before the Fundamental Right to Education became part of the Constitution, SSA has been striving to fulfill that right of the children in the age group of 6-14. The SSA funds have been used basically to add infrastructure, new schools, class rooms, and resource centers, to recruit and train manpower and to provide incentives to students to come to schools.

There is no doubt that SSA has been very successful in increasing the number of schools, classrooms and teachers in the state education system. There is a need to explore the status of education system expanded by SSA. SSA claims to lay a special thrust on making education at the elementary level useful and relevant for children by improving the curriculum, child-centered activities and effective teaching-learning strategies. However the number of private schools that serves the poor, not the upper classes, has been steadily growing.

SSA thus reflects the mindset that when you fail, do more of the same as if increase in the magnitude would convert the failure into success. If the existing several lakhs of schools cannot provide meaningful education, then add one more lakh and hope that now they all would provide good education. Common sense suggests that if the current schools are not delivering what is expected of them, then our attention, efforts and resources should be first spent on improving them and not on adding more of the failing schools.

Expansion turns failure into success is supposed to be the key factor of educational planning as evident from the recent announcement by the Government of hiring of two lakh more teachers. The question which need to be answered are whether the current lakhs of teachers are imparting quality education or does the Government believe that the failure of these existing teachers would be compensated by increasing their number? This is the mindset of the educational planners and administrators who frame the policy far away from the ground realities. If the teachers are not teaching, hire more of them, If the textbooks are uninspiring, add or delete more pages from the same, If the curriculum seems irrelevant to the students real life, revise it more frequently; if more and more students fail in the annual exam, announce 'no-retention policy, promote all students to the next class. Expansion is the key word to convert failures into successes.

Grant managerial and financial autonomy to schools, principals and teachers. The government schools are minutely controlled by education departments. The schools have hardly any autonomy to manage their affairs. They are closest to their customers and they have the necessary freedom to adjust their functioning so that they are better able to meet the changing needs of students and parents. The principals should be education leaders and role models not just older bureaucrats. They and their teachers must be empowered and given the freedom that their private school counterparts enjoy.

While funding government schools *focus should be on student*. It is very common that government schools with same number of students get widely different funding from the state. This inequity in funding is unjust. This mode of funding must be changed and the state should fund schools based on the number of students they have. Obviously, it would not be a simple multiplication but would require a somewhat complex formula. The formula would have to take into account the fixed cost, variable cost per child, location of the school, composition of the student and other pertinent factors.

The current model of imparting education to the poor is based on the government initiative to give grants to government schools and the schools then provide free education to the children. This system of financing education has created a situation where government schools have become the only junction for the education of poor. The problem of government schools is that it don't deliver good education and are less responsive and accountable to their customers. We must break this trend by changing the way we finance education of the poor. Instead of giving grants to schools, the money should be given to poor parents, through a school voucher. The parent would take the voucher and go to any school of their choice. Schools will collect the vouchers, deposit in a bank, and the government transfers the equivalent money into school's bank account. School vouchers are a special scholarship that empowers the poor with choice that the rich enjoy.

Quality of government schools should set a benchmark for all to emulate: Private schools have to meet stringent standards set by the government to be recognised. However, the government exempts itself from such standards. The implicit rationale seems to be that it would be too much of a financial burden to require all government schools to fulfill the same standards that the private recognised schools are expected to meet. Now largely the children of the poor go to government schools. This means that the government worries about the education quality of the children of the rich by requiring private schools to meet its standards but feels that the poor should be grateful that they at least have a school to go to. This inequity must end and government schools must meet the same standards of quality. Every government school should be required to follow the same application process for recognition as private schools and must be formally recognised by the education department. It would be even better if government schools actually excel and become role model for private schools to emulate.

Link government school grants to performance: The government funding is very uneven, across states, across urban and rural areas and even within a given urban or rural area. These expenditure estimates are based on the number of students that are enrolled in government schools. For anyone concerned about disparities in education, the first task should be to bring about some rationality to the funding of government schools by the government. These disparities are not in compliance with the constitutional right to equal treatment of all citizens. The fundamental right to education has little meaning when the government itself treats its young citizens so unevenly.

At present there is no relation between the performance of government schools and teachers with the grant and salaries they receive. There is no incentive for better performance, whether student learning achievements are good or bad, the schools and teachers get the same funds. It is critical to link the grant amount to performance. One way to start the process is to link increments in the grant to schools as well as to teacher salaries to performance. The current grant amount can continue but tomorrow's increment could be tied to their performance.

Keep the worst performing government schools on learning achievement contracts: Select a group of worst performing government schools and hand them to other interested and qualified parties to manage them. There are many ways to identify such parties. One could be through tenders, based not on the amount of money the parties would charge, but the degree of improvements they promise in student learning. The government can promise to pay the same amount per child to the new managers as it currently spends. The parties then compete on the degree and type of progress they promise to achieve every year during the period of the contract.

Establish independent organisation as evaluation agencies: Except for board examinations, there is no objective information to judge the quality of schools in India. We need to develop more meaningful systems of evaluation, other than annual exams, and implement them at regular intervals. These evaluations should be made public so that parents can make informed decisions.

Keeping into consideration the size and diversity of the education market in India, we require competing independent agencies to perform this task.

The implementation of Right of Children to Free and Compulsory Education Act, 2009 means 25 per cent of all recognized private schools must admit poor and marginalized students between the age of 6 and 14 and government will pay for their tuition. Though not consciously designed as a school voucher programme, this is nothing short of a revolution in school choice and a recognition of reality. Indian parents are already moving to both registered and unregistered private schools, which provide a far better education than their public-school counterparts.

The 2009 Annual Status of Education Report conducted by a New Delhi based nonprofit organization, shows that more than half of fifth-grade public-school students can't read at a basic second-grade level. Private-school students have a 41 per cent reading advantage in English over their public-school peers. These differences in learning outcomes are not surprising since 25 per cent of public-school teachers are absent on any given day and half of those present don't do any teaching.

There will be serious problem with the implementation of the innovative school-voucher programme. It mandates that private schools will have to admit 25 per cent of their students from economically and socially disadvantaged groups such as scheduled castes, scheduled tribes and other groups as determined by state governments. The mandate also raises a constitutional issue—can government force private schools to take students chosen by it? How would schools resist further government controls when taxpayers pay for one-fourth of their students? Then there is the question of regulation, a common problem in Indian education system. According to the new law, all private schools must obtain official government recognition within three years or be closedown. Schools must have a certain size of land plot, playground, library, teacher qualifications and salaries. Private schools for the rich would have little difficulty in meeting these norms. It's impossible to demand that a slum school be earthquake resistant when all the houses and buildings in the slum can barely stand up to heavy rains and winds.

The salaries of teachers in private unaided schools are four to seven times lower than those of government schools. Requiring these budget schools to pay government-scale salaries would be an impossible expectation. They would have to raise tuition fees substantially or close down; either way, the poor would lose the one option they have to escape attending failing government schools. Thus the Act opens the door to private schools for some of the poor but closes the door for the rest of the poor by shutting down budget private schools. It's hard to pin down just how many of these schools would be affected. The policy says the poor can attend private schools supported by state but not on their own.

A graded recognition system which evaluates and rates schools through independent agencies could be the way out of this contradiction. Such a rating system could involve various tiers based on facilities, teacher performance and student learning outcomes. Broader standards focused on outcomes as much as on inputs would help keep many efficient budget schools within the purview of recognition. It would also enhance competition around quality by providing incentives to schools to acquire higher ratings and assist parents in choosing more suitable schools. The new Act has put India's school system on a higher trajectory, but the future of millions rests on the compatibility between planning and implementation of Right to Education.

Conclusion

Right to Education Act is a revolutionary policy development that can change the face of basic education in India. However, policies are only as good as the way they are implemented. During the last about five years, since its enactment in 2009, many issues have not been sorted out yet. Major issues are states' capability and willingness to fund such a massive project; also, magnitude of central funding to states. Private schools have a significant share of service in educating Indian children. They still remained either outside the framework of government policies or they come to the gagging rules of government. Success of RTE will depend upon how government machinery reorient itself to facilitate the cause of basic education for all rather than obstinately following self-laid protocols.

5

Secondary Education

Policies, Strategies and Development Challenges

K. Biswal

> "... (.) It is obvious that there can be no intelligent decision without acquaintance with facts. With the growing condensation of space and time, relations between countries and peoples are becoming continually closer. Modern democracy therefore demands that the people at large must have knowledge not only about their own country but also of the world in general. It is largely the function of secondary education to meet this demand of democracy. ..."
>
> —*Humayun Kabir* (January, 1955, p. 194)

The Context

Education, the fulcrum of sustainable development, holds the key to 'social inclusion'. It is one of the necessary conditions for advancing quality of life and freedom. In other words, universal access to quality knowledge and skills ensures that everybody has an equal opportunity to play a full part in work and society. It, thus, is essential for integrating the marginalized and vulnerable groups to the development process. Promoting equity and active citizenship through a well developed education and training system, therefore, need to occupy the centre-stage of development agenda in every society.

However, even when the benefits of education are obvious, it has yet to acquire the required weightages in the development agenda of several nations, including India. In the 1960s, while education was recognized as a strong explanatory variable of differential levels of socio-economic development of nations, the low income countries, however, realized the same much latter, in the 1980s, when there was some visible policy shifts towards increasing investment in education. International commitments—in the early 1990s, particularly for EFA, and at the dawn of the 21st century, for MDGs—rather than domestic development policy concerns, made education, mainly primary education, to figure prominently in the priority list of reform programmes of these countries. Since then, many developing nations, including India, have been following a sort of truncated education development agenda leaving relatively little space for policy-planning and resources for expansion of the post-compulsory levels of education, mainly the middle segment of the education chain—i.e. secondary and higher secondary levels of education[1].

In recent years, while stakeholders continue debating the nature and functions of secondary education,[2] the need for its development has become apparent with the changing context of schooling. Besides its contributions to formation of active citizens (Secondary Education Commission, 1953; Kabir, 1955; Alvarez, 2000; Lewin and Caillods, 2001; Briseid and Caillods, 2004; World Bank, 2003, 2009), secondary education plays a critical role in addressing the emerging human development concerns in countries engaged in building knowledge societies for staying connected to the globalization process[3]. For several decades, it has been argued in the literature that secondary education needs to be expanded both as a response to increased social demand and as a feeder cadre for higher education, giving little emphasis on its other important functions, including its role in the 'social capital' formation. It is also argued that investment in secondary education yields considerable social and economic returns making it crucial for national development (World Bank, 1993, 2005, 2009; Tilak, 2001; Mukhopadhyay, 2007; Alain and Tan, 1996; Lewin and Caillods, 2001; Duraisamy, 2002; Lewin, 2006, 2008). It, however, continues to be the most neglected segment of school education in developing countries, including India.

In countries like India prominently following a service-led growth model and striving hard to survive the global competition, it is being increasingly recognized that secondary education, which has remained 'sandwiched' so far, is the most critical segment of the education chain. Apart from the bottom-up pressure (i.e. arising from the growth of primary schooling) and the top-down pressure (as the source of potential intakes for higher education) for its expansion, there is a need to pay greater attention to secondary education as it caters to the needs of the most important segment of the population—i.e. *adolescents and youth*, the source of the future human and social capital of a nation. While examining trends in secondary education across industrialized nations, Briseid and Caillods (2004. p. 17) rightly argue that:

> "Dealing with adolescents at a very critical moment of their lives, education has an important mission: to provide youths with the necessary knowledge and skills to live in an advanced technological society; to prepare them for the world of work but also for further learning; and to foster social cohesion and transmit the cultural and

ethical values necessary for active participation in a democratic society."

Preparing youth for life, advancing science education and learning to learn and communicate effectively in the global village are considered additional forces affecting secondary education across the globe. In fact, at this level, two main functions of education (i.e. individual and social) converge (Alvarez, 2000). At the individual level, secondary education empowers, prepares youth for life—viz., personal development, preparation for the labour market, training for higher cognitive functioning; and as part of its social function, advances 'human and social capital' for nation building, redistributes income and wealth and alleviates income poverty. Its development, therefore, can greatly contribute towards acquiring global competitiveness and achieving the MDGs.[4] In fact, it is argued that, 'investing in youth will provide the longest and most effective dividend towards meeting the Millennium Development Goals by building the social capital needed to foster pragmatic development' (UN, 2005).

In the context of emerging challenges of human development worldwide (viz., HIV/AIDS; conflicts; environment degradation and climate change; increasing inequality within and between nations caused by the de-bordering process; pressure to acquire and maintain competitive edge through innovation/ advancing science education and/or capacity to adopt new technology and learning to learn through global communication networks), it is, indeed, crucial to invest in secondary education.

In the Indian context, balanced development of education is critical for nation building. Education is also one of the important components of the inclusive development model of the emerging Indian democracy, which was well articulated even in the 1960s in the report of the Education Commission (1963-64). However, the current Indian setting no doubt reflects the socio-economic consequences of the distortions in the development model envisaged in the early years of freedom—i.e. we have grown visibly, yet remain far away from having a developed society. Some of the following stylized facts describe the Indian setting calling for renewed attention to development of education. There are around 125.4 million youth illiterates (age group 15-24) in the world (UNESCO, 2010), and 99.5 per cent of them (124.8 million) live in the developing world. More than half of the world's youth illiterates (51.8%) are found in South Asia, and India's share in the total youth illiterates of South Asia is around 62 per cent. In fact, India alone is home to a little less than one-thirds (40.4 million; 32.2%) of the world's youth illiterates (see Table 5.1A).

There is wide spread income poverty and socio-economic inequality in India.[5] More than one-thirds of the country's population (34%) is living on

Table 5.1A: Key Demographic and Economic Development Indicators in Select Countries

Country	*Average annual growth rate (%), age 0-4 popula-tion*	*GNP per capita (PPP) 2 (US$)*	*Populatio n living on less than US$1 per day 3(%)*	*Share of income or expendi-ture (%), the richest 20%*	*Youth literacy rate (15-24), total (%)*	*Number of youth illiterates (000)*
	2005-10	**2007**	**1990-05**	**1992-05**	**2000-07**	**2000-07**
Brazil	0.0	9270	8.0	61	98.0	766
Bangladesh	–0.3	1330	41.0	43.0	72	8965
China	–1.0	5420	10.0	52.0	99.0	1639
Columbia	1.3	8260	7.0	63.0	98.0	176
Eritrea	–0.1	780	—	39.0	86.0	138
France	–0.3	33850	—	40.0	—	—
India	–0.1	2740	34.0	45.0	82.0	40412
Indonesia	–0.6	3570	8.0	43.0	97.0	1431
Iran	3.0	10840	—	50.0	97.0	589
Italy	–0.1	30190	—	42.0	100.0	7
Japan	–1.4	34750	—	36.0	—	—
Korea	–1.8	24840	—	38.0	—	—
Pakistan	1.9	2540	17.0	40.0	69.0	11151
Philippines	0.4	3710	15.0	51.0	94.0	975
Russia	1.1	14330	—	47.0	100.0	71
Sri Lanka	–1.1	4200	6.0	48.0	97.0	90
Thailand	0.0	7880		49.0	98.0	181
United Kingdom	1.0	—	—	44.0	—	—
United States	0.8	45840	—	46.0	—	—
Vietnam	0.0	2530	—	44.0	94.0	1105
World	0.5	9947	—	—	89.0	125401
Developed Countries	0.2	—	—	—	100.0	451
Developing countries	0.5	—	—	—	87.0	124807
South and West Asia	0.3	—	—	—	80.0	65013

Source: UNESCO, EFA GMR, 2010.

Notes: 1. Demographic indicators are from the UN Population Division estimates, revision 2006 (UNDP, 2007).

2. World Bank, 2009.

3. UNDP, 2001. Data are for the most recent year available during the period specified.

— Data not available.

less than US$ 1 per day as compared to a smaller proportion of population found in the similar situation in other BRIC and Asia-Pacific countries and South Asian neighbours—viz., Brazil (8%), China (10%), Indonesia (8%), the Philippines (15%), Sri Lanka (6%) and Pakistan (17%).[6] The inequalities in the distribution of income and wealth are evident from the fact that the share of the top population quintile (richest 20%) in the total income/ expenditure is around 45 per cent. In fact, 28 per cent of the rural population[7] in the country is in the lowest wealth quintile[8] (NFHS III, 2007). It may be noted that household wealth heavily influences school attendance in India (Lewin, 2008). This is partly reflected in the key education development indicators. For example, in the family of 128 nations, India ranks 105th in terms of EFA Development Index (EFADI), which is relatively lower compared to that of several other developing countries—viz., Indonesia (65th), the Philippines (85th) and Brazil (88th) (see Table 5.1B).

In a country like India where one in every 10 children in the age group 6-10 is out of school; only around two-thirds of the grade I cohort survive to the last grade of the primary cycle; around 84 per cent of primary graduates transit to upper primary level; participation rate in upper primary level is relatively much lower (GER 71%); and the pubic current expenditure per pupil at the primary and secondary levels (as % of GNP per capita) is 9.0 and 16.7 respectively (see Table 5.1C), it would be interesting to examine the growth trends and development approaches in the secondary education sub-sector. As greater economic growth and social equity are associated with balanced public educational investment (World Bank, 1993, 2005; Wood and Mayer, 1999), the study of secondary education reform policies, approaches and programmes in India would not only help identify the development direction but also provide clues for future policy planning.

It is in this context that the paper makes an attempt to assess the current status of secondary education (with focus on general secondary education); briefly review the related policies, approaches and programmes; and reflect on development concerns and challenges with the basic objective of initiating the discourse on the theme of the conference, which focuses on the 'positive developments' in the education sector, perhaps caught in the 'reform turmoil', in search of future directions. The paper has five parts. As is clear by now, the first provides the context and rationale for expansion of secondary education. The second attempts to identify growth trends and assess the current status of secondary education in India. The third briefly reviews the related development policies since the colonial period. The fourth looks into the current reform agenda, approach and programmes, mostly focusing on the interventions of the central government. The final while concluding highlights major development challenges and also briefly reflects on the development directions.

Growth Trends and Current Status

Historical forces have largely influenced the policy-planning processes[9] and growth trends in education, both in developed and low income countries. Initially, secondary education was considered a subsidiary to tertiary education as its primary function was to prepare pupils for higher studies. As such, by and large, it evolved as an elite system facilitating local processes for 'elite

Table 5.1B: Key School Education Development Indicators in Select Countries

Country	*Compulsory education (Age group)*	*Duration of primary education*	*EFA Development Index (EFADI) rank (according to level of EDI out of 128 countries)*	*NER in primary education, total (%)*	*Survival rate to last grade in primary education, total (school year ending in 2006) (%)*	*Transition from primary to secondary general education, total (school year ending in 2006) (%)*	*GER in secondary education, total, 2007 (%)*		*NER in secondary education (lower + upper secondary education), total, 2007 (%)*
	2009	*2009*	*2007*	*2007*	*2006*	*2006*	*Lower secondary*	*Upper secondary*	*2007*
(1)	(2)	(3)	(4)	(5)	(6)	(7)	(7)	(8)	(9)
Brazil	7-14	4	88	93	76	82	108	90	77
Bangladesh	6-10	5	112	87	84y	97y	60	30	41
China	6-14	5	...	...	...	...	96	60	70
Columbia	5-15	5	...	87	88	99	94	68	67
Eritrea	7-14	5	124	41	60	77	43	18	25
France	6-16	5	7	99	...	100	111	117	98
India	6-14	5	105	89*	66y	84y	71	42	...
Indonesia	7-15	6	65	95	95	99	90	57	68
Iran	6-10	5	...	94	...	83	86y	77y	77y
Italy	6-18	5	5	99	100	100	108	88	85
Japan	6-15	6	2	100	...	...	101	101	98

(Contd.)

(1)	(2)	(3)	(4)	(5)	(6)	(7)	(7)	(8)	(9)
Korea	6-15	6	21	98	97	99	101	95	97
Pakistan	5-9	5	117	80	70	76	68	32	42
Philippines	6-12	6	85	91	73	98	87	73	61
Russia	6-15	4	...	...	95	...	82	88	...
Sri Lanka	5-14	5	...	66*	93y	97y	45	23	32
Thailand	6-16	6	...	95	...	87	101	67	81
United Kingdom	5-16	6	9	97	...	...	98	97	91
United States	6-17	6	...	92	95	...	100	89	88
Vietnam	6-14	5	...	...	92	93y	...	...	...
World	...	...	...	87		93	78	54	59
Developed Countries	...	...	...	96		99	102	99	90
Developing Countries	...	...	...	86		88	75	48	54
South and West Asia	...	...	...	86		84	67	39	46

Source: Ibid.

Note: (y) Data are for the school year ending in 2005.

Table 5.1C: Key School Education Development Indicators in Select Countries

Country	*Pupil/Teacher Ratio (PTR) in secondary education, 2007*		*Total public expenditure on education, 2007*		*Public current expenditure on primary education, 2007*		*Public current expenditure on secondary education, 2007*	
	Lower secondary	*Upper secondary*	*As % of GNP*	*As % of total govt. expenditure*	*As % of GNP*	*Per pupil as % of GNP per capita*	*As % of GNP*	*Per pupil as % of GNP per capita*
(1)	(2)	(3)	(4)	(5)	(6)	(7)	(8)	(9)
Brazil	20	17	5.2z	16.2z	1.6z	1.6z 15.0y	2.2z	13.0y
Bangladesh	29	21	2.4	15.8	0.9	8.5	0.9	13.6
China (in 1999 1.9/13.0)	16	16	...	.	...	...	...	...
Columbia	...	...	5.1	12.6	1.9	16.1	1.3	12.9
Eritrea	57	40	2.4z	...	0.8z	9.7z	0.2z	5.1z
France	13	11	5.6z	10.6z	1.0z	16.0z	2.4z	24.1z
India	...	...	3.2y	...	1.2y	9.0y	1.4y	16.7y
Indonesia	14	12	3.6	17.5	...	...	...	...
Iran	19	19	5.6	19.5	1.4	14.1	2.3	10.7y
Italy	9	11	4.8	9.7z	1.1z	24.1z	2.1z	26.7z
Japan	14	11	3.4z	9.5z	...	...	...	...
Korea	20	16	4.4y	15.3y	1.4y	16.2y	1.6y	20.2y
Pakistan	...	...	2.8	11.2	...	...	...	...
Philippines	39	25	2.3y	15.2y	1.2y	7.6y	0.6y	7.9y
Russia	...	4	...	12.9	...	...	...	...
Sri Lanka	19	...	...	...	...	...	...	...
Thailand	20	23	4	20.9	...	...	...	...

(*Contd.*)

(1)	(2)	(3)	(4)	(5)	(6)	(7)	(8)	(9)
United Kingdom	16	14	5.4y	12.5y	1.3y	16.8y	1.8y	18.3y
United States	14	15	5.7z	14.8z	...	...	...	...
Vietnam	20	26	...	...	...	...	...	...
World	...	...	4.9	15	1.4	13.7	1.6	19.5
Developed Countries	...	...	5.3	12.4	1.1	17.8	2.1	22.3
Developing Countries	...	...	4.5	...	1.6	12.5	1.3	17.3
South and West Asia	...	...	3.8	15.8	1.3	11.4	1.4	13.6

Source: Ibid.

Notes: (z) Data are for 2006; (y) data are for 2005.

formation' and catering to the needs of the socially and the economically privileged[10] (Briseid and Caillods, 2004; Chaudhary, 2007). The mid-twentieth century, however, marked the beginning of a new era in secondary education. By the 1960s and 1970s, secondary education was more linked to primary education than to tertiary education. Around this time, secondary education also underwent structural changes in several countries.[11] Such developments changed the basic approach towards public provisioning of secondary education in these countries calling for a significant role of the government in its massification (Briseid and Caillods, 2004).

Interestingly, world-wide trends show that the expansion of secondary education is a much more recent phenomenon. Secondary education actually began to expand in developed societies only after the World War II. In fact, barring a few nations,[12] the expansion of general secondary education is yet to happen at the desired pace, more so in many developing societies, including India. The growth of secondary education in India, however, shows unique trends. During the period starting from 1850 to 1919 when the colonial government completely transferred the education authority to elected Indian Ministers at the provincial level, there was an undue emphasis (compared to primary education) on expansion of secondary schools and colleges (Ghosh, 2000; Chaudhary, 2007). Indian social structure and local factors (in terms of ethnic fragmentation/caste structure) played a pivotal role in the provisioning of both primary and secondary schooling during this period. It is argued that the number of public primary schools was lower in districts with higher levels of caste and religion diversity. In such districts, traditional elites preferred developing secondary schools (Chaudhary, 2007).

After the Wood's Despatch (1884) and with the introduction of the new system of education in India by the British Crown that largely replaced the indigenous network of schools[13] and the implementation of the 'grant-in-aid' policy, the secondary schooling provisions expanded relatively faster as many indigenous schools acquired the status of 'aided schools'.[14] After 1919, policies of the provincial governments largely influenced the pattern of growth of secondary schooling provisions. In fact, in 1948, India had around 12,500 secondary schools of all grades in its major states (which included lower secondary stage/UPS) enrolled in them a little less than 3 million children. Even after favourable expansion policies of the colonial government, the number of high and higher secondary schools in India was around 4000 in 1948 with an enrolment of about 1.8 million (Kabir, 1955).

In free India, the network of educational institutions has expanded remarkably during the past six decades. The growth rate of secondary level institutions during this period has remained much lower compared to that of middle and primary levels (see flatter trend lines in Chart 5.1). Between 1950/51 and 2007/08, while the number of primary level institutions increased by almost four fold from 209.7 thousand to 787.8 thousand, the number of the middle level institutions went up by twenty-four fold from 13.6 thousand to 325.2 thousand, and the secondary level institutions by more than twenty-three fold, from 7416 to 173.0 thousand.[15] It may, however, be noted that the growth rates of middle and secondary level institutions seem to be relatively very high during the period primarily because of their small base (see Chart 5.1). The number of teachers at the secondary level (Grades IX-XII) also increased from 127 thousand in 1950/51 to 2126.88 thousand in 2007/08. The Pupil-Teacher Ratio (PTR) at the secondary and higher secondary stages taken together (Grades IX-XII), however, increased from 21 in 1950/51 to 33 in 2005/06. In 2007/08, PTR was 33 at the secondary stage (Grades IX-X) and 37 at the higher secondary level (XI-XII).

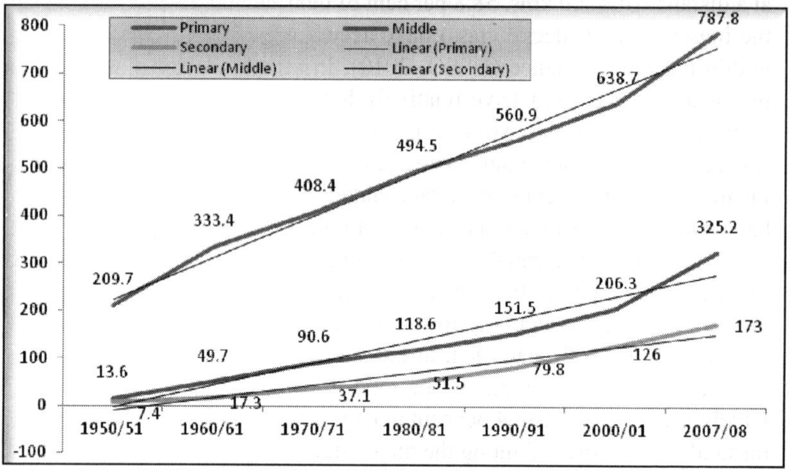

Source: Selected Educational Statistics, various years.

Note: $ Includes high/higher secondary/intermediate/pre-university/junior college/pre-degree level institutions.

Chart 5.1: Growth of primary, middle and secondary level institutions in India since 1950/51 (in '000)

Not only has the expansion happened in the country in terms of the number of institutions, but also in terms of the spatial distribution of the schooling provisions at secondary and higher secondary levels. Some eight years back, more than 73 per cent of habitations in the country had access to secondary schooling provisions at a maximum walking distance of ≤ 5.0 kms; and more than 62 per cent of habitations had access to higher secondary schooling provisions at a maximum walking distance of ≤ 8.0 kms (7th AIES, 2002, see Table 5.2A). More than four-fifths of the population in the country had physical access to secondary schooling provisions at a maximum distance of ≤ 5.0

kms from their habitations in 2002; and around 69 per cent of them had physical access to higher secondary schooling provisions at a maximum distance of ≤ 8.0 kms. Now, according to the NSS 64th Round (2007/08), 82.9 per cent of rural households and 99 per cent of urban households have access to secondary schooling provisions up to a distance of 5.0 kms.[16]

What is more interesting to note is that compared to the poor households, the rich have access to all types of schooling provisions much closer to their residence, particularly in rural areas. The availability of middle and secondary level schooling provisions in close proximity of households is relatively less for lower decile classes of the monthly per capita expenditure[17] (MPCE). For example, in rural India, while 38.8 per cent of poor households (belonging to the lowest MPCE decile class) have access to secondary schooling provisions at a distance of < 2.0 kms, 58.8 per cent of the rich households (belonging to the highest MPCE decile class) have access to secondary schools/sections within the same distance (NSSO, 2010). In other words, even in terms of physical distance, poor have relatively low access to secondary schooling facilities in rural India. Moreover, with 34.6 per cent of private un-aided institutions at the secondary stage and 34.4 per cent of private un-aided institutions at the higher secondary stage[18] (SSE, 2007/08), the poor may have a hard time to access secondary schooling facilities in the country.

The issue of differential access to secondary schooling provisions becomes further compounded as the private un-aided sector plays a significant role in providing access, particularly in some of the economically backward states. It is evident from the fact that, at the sub-national level, the proportion of private un-aided institutions in the total institutions at the secondary stage widely varies between 88.4 per cent in Uttar Pradesh and none in West Bengal (around 2% in Bihar). Among the major states, the proportion of private un-aided institutions in the total number of institutions at the higher secondary stage varies between around 70 per cent in Andhra Pradesh and 4.5 per cent in Bihar.[19]

At the macro level, thus, physical access to schooling provisions[20] (as per the distance norm) at the secondary and higher secondary levels seems to be very encouraging, which, in fact, hides the story of large variations across states in India, and within states, across districts and sub-district level units. Large regional variations in physical access to secondary and higher secondary schooling provisions are clear from the fact that, still in some nine states and UTs (A&N Islands, Manipur, Meghalaya, Chhattisgarh, Madhya Pradesh, Jharkhand, Mizoram, Nagaland, Arunachal Pradesh)[21], more than 40 per cent of habitations have physical access to secondary schooling provisions at a distance of >5.0 kms; and in 20 states and UTs, nearly the same proportion of habitations have access to higher secondary schooling provisions beyond 8.0 kms (see Chart 5.2, Tables 5.2A and 5.2B).

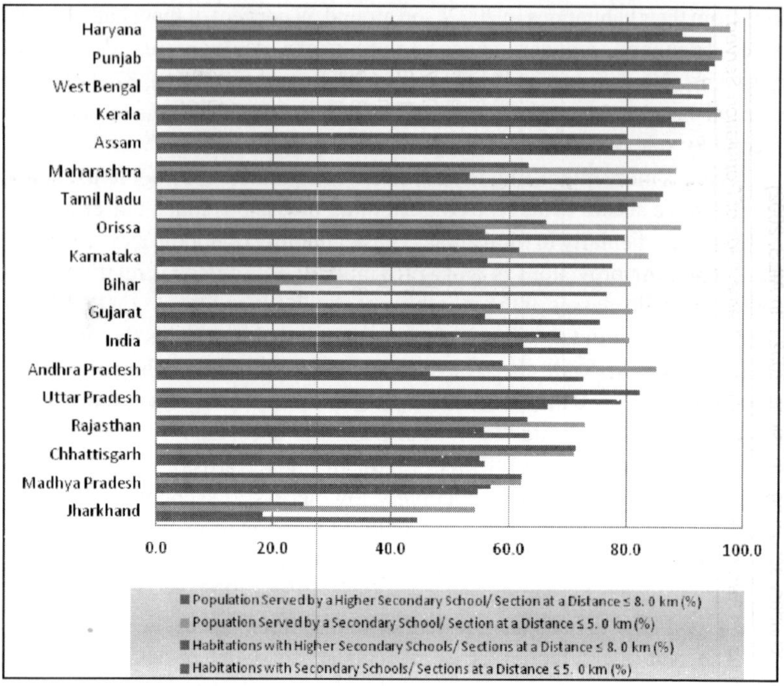

Source: Table 5.2A, Annex I.

Chart 5.2: Physical access to secondary and higher secondary schooling provisions in select states[22], 2002

At the all-India level, on an average, 10 secondary schools/sections and 5 higher secondary schools/sections were available per lakh population in 2007/08 (see Table 5.3A, Annex I). At the sub-national level, the size of this indicator varied between 3 secondary schools/sections per lakh population in Bihar and Delhi to 53 in Mizoram. However, major states like Uttar Pradesh (04), West Bengal (05), Tamil Nadu (05) and Madhya Pradesh (07) had less than 10 secondary schools/sections per lakh population in 2007/08. Although a crude indicator of access, availability of secondary and higher secondary schooling provisions per lakh population provides important clues about the potential size (in terms of enrolment) of secondary and higher secondary level institutions, particularly in rural areas. Given the fact that the share of the relevant secondary school age child population (14-15 years) in the total population is around 4 per cent in most states, a secondary school/section per 10,000 persons at the macro level limits its potential size to less than 450 particularly in rural areas, which can well be called a small school. Similarly, the potential size of a higher secondary school/section would be less than 1000, assuming full participation of the relevant age group at this level of education.

Table 5.2A: Physical access to secondary and higher secondary schooling provisions, 2002 (7th AIES, 2002)

Sl. No.	State/UT	Total Habitations	Number of Habitations		Percentage of Habitations		Percentage of Population Served	
			With Secondary Schools/ Sections at a Distance ? 5. 0 km	With Higher Secondary Schools/ Sections at a Distance ? 8. 0 km	With Secondary Schools/ Sections at a Distance ? 5. 0 km	With Higher Secondary Schools/ Sections at a Distance ? 8. 0 km	By a Secondary School/ Section at a Distance ? 5. 0 km	By a Higher Secondary School/ Section at a Distance ? 8. 0 km
(1)	(2)	(3)	(4)	(5)	(6)	(7)	(8)	(9)
1.	Andhra Pradesh	66431	48162	30997	72.5	46.7	85.03	58.78
2.	Arunachal Pradesh	4204	1048	819	24.9	19.5	46.28	36.72
3.	Assam	65818	57582	50899	87.5	77.3	89.23	79.93
4.	Bihar	72668	55580	15327	76.5	21.1	80.52	30.67
5.	Chhattisgarh	37491	20914	20650	55.8	55.1	70.91	71.26
6.	Goa	706	630	437	89.2	61.9	95.91	80.8
7.	Gujarat	31281	23566	17451	75.3	55.8	80.98	58.52
8.	Haryana	8583	8088	7671	94.2	89.4	97.53	93.85
9.	Himachal Pradesh	35718	27788	23410	77.8	65.5	87.17	78.96
10.	Jammu and Kashmir	20792	15573	12052	74.9	58.0	83.68	69.01
11.	Jharkhand	50007	22282	9164	44.6	18.3	54.25	25.31
12.	Karnataka	51533	39924	28974	77.5	56.2	83.63	61.61
13.	Kerala	6592	5923	5769	89.9	87.5	96	95.27
14.	Madhya Pradesh	83949	45850	47778	54.6	56.9	62.03	62.05
15.	Maharashtra	77298	62523	41113	80.9	53.2	88.43	63.17
16.	Manipur	3858	2263	1903	58.7	49.3	75.99	63.14
17.	Meghalaya	7245	4157	1920	57.4	26.5	65.61	33.16
18.	Mizoram	744	301	47	40.5	6.3	65.74	9.74
19.	Nagaland	1224	445	147	36.4	12.0	45.48	14.92
20.	Orissa	83427	66370	46633	79.6	55.9	89.3	66.15

(*Contd.*)

(1)	(2)	(3)	(4)	(5)	(6)	(7)	(8)	(9)
21.	Punjab	14623	13736	13895	93.9	95.0	96.27	96.25
22.	Rajasthan	80461	50909	44843	63.3	55.7	72.86	63.07
23.	Sikkim	1383	1022	840	73.9	60.7	80.45	66.95
24.	Tamil Nadu	53577	42873	43818	80.0	81.8	85.57	86.03
25.	Tripura	7538	6432	6251	85.3	82.9	90.65	88.31
26.	Uttar Pradesh	201606	133915	159396	66.4	79.1	71.07	82.33
27.	Uttaranchal	25495	20616	21125	80.9	82.9	83.78	86.66
28.	West Bengal	113635	105473	99572	92.8	87.6	93.98	89.07
29.	A and N Islands	673	398	387	59.1	57.5	83.19	79.47
30.	Chandigarh	39	39	39	100.0	100.0	100	100
31.	D and N Haveli	460	308	261	67.0	56.7	75.49	67.48
32.	Daman and Diu	82	82	82	100.0	100.0	100	100
33.	Delhi	187	187	187	100.0	100.0	100	100
34.	Lakshadweep	7	6	2	85.7	28.6	99.25	47.83
35.	Puducherry	186	183	182	98.4	97.8	98.64	98.44
36.	**India**	**1209521**	**885148**	**754041**	**73.2**	**62.3**	**80.43**	**68.51**

Table 5.2B: Grouping of states/union territories according to the level of physical access to secondary and higher secondary schooling provisions, 2002 (7th AIES)

	Percentage of Habitations having Physical Access to Secondary/Hr. Secondary Schooling Provisions, 2002				*Percentage of Population Served by Secondary/Hr. Secondary Schooling Provisions, 2002*			
	≥ 80	70-80	60-70	< 60	≥ 90	80-90	70-80	< 70
(1)	(2)	(3)	(4)	(5)	(6)	(7)	(8)	(9)
Access to Secondary Schooling Provisions (Distance >5.0 km)	Chandigarh, Daman and Diu, Delhi, Puducherry, Haryana, Punjab, West Bengal, Kerala, Goa, Assam, Lakshadweep, Tripura, Maharashtra, Uttaranchal, Tamil Nadu	Orissa, Himachal Pradesh, Karnataka, Bihar, Gujarat, J&K, Sikkim, Andhra Pradesh	D & N Haveli, Uttar Pradesh, Rajasthan	A&N Islands, Manipur, Meghalaya, Chhattisgarh, MP, Jharkhand, Mizoram, Nagaland, Arunachal Pradesh	Chandigarh, Daman & Diu, Delhi, Lakshadweep, Puducherry, Haryana, Punjab, Kerala, Goa, West Bengal, Tripura	Orissa, Assam, Maharashtra, Tamil Nadu, Andhra Pradesh, Uttaranchal, J&K, Karnataka, A&N Islands, Gujarat, Bihar, Sikkim	Manipur, D&N Haveli, Rajasthan, Uttar Pradesh, Chhattisgarh	Mizoram, Meghalaya, MP, Jharkhand, Arunachal Pradesh, Nagaland

(*Contd.*)

(1)	(2)	(3)	(4)	(5)	(6)	(7)	(8)	(9)
Access to Higher Secondary Schooling Provisions (Distance >8.0 km)	Chandigarh, Daman and Diu, Delhi, Puducherry, Haryana, Punjab, West Bengal, Kerala, Tripura, Uttaranchal, Tamil Nadu	Uttar Pradesh, Assam	Himachal Pradesh, Goa, Sikkim	J&K, A&N Islands, MP, D&N Haveli, Karnataka, Orissa, Gujarat, Rajasthan, Chhattisgarh, Maharashtra, Manipur, Andhra Pradesh, Lakshadweep, Meghalaya, Bihar, Arunachal Pradesh, Jharkhand, Nagaland, Mizoram	Chandigarh, Daman and Diu, Delhi, Puducherry, Haryana, Punjab, Kerala,	West Bengal, Tripura, Uttaranchal, Tamil Nadu, Uttar Pradesh, Goa	Assam, A&N Islands, Himachal Pradesh, Chhattisgarh	J&K, D&N Haveli, Sikkim, Orissa, Maharashtra, Manipur, Rajasthan, MP, Karnataka, Andhra Pradesh, Gujarat, Lakshadweep, Arunachal Pradesh, Meghalaya, Bihar, Jharkhand, Nagaland, Mizoram

Source: Based on the analysis of the 7th AIES data, 2002.

Table 5.3A: Relevant secondary school age projected child population and availability of schooling provisions in states and union territories, 2007

State/UT	Total Population, 2001	Share in the Total Population of India, 2001	Share of SC Population, 2001	Share of ST Population, 2001	Projected Total Population, 2007 ('000)	Projected Child Population (Boys + Girls) by Age Group, 2007 (in '000)		Share of Projected Total Child Population (14-15 age group) to Projected Total Child Population (14-15 age group) of India	Number of Secondary Schools/Sections, 2007-08	Number of Hr. Secondary Schools/Sections, 2007-08	Availability of Secondary Schools/Sections per Lakh Population, 2007	Availability of Hr. Secondary Schools/Sections per Lakh Population, 2007
						14-15	16-17					
(1)	(2)	(3)	(4)	(5)	(6)	(7)	(8)	(9)	(10)	(11)	(12)	(13)
Andhra Pradesh	76210007	7.4	16.9	6.6	81554	3330	3403	6.9	16937	4032	21	5
Assam	26655528	2.6	6.9	12.4	29053	1315	1304	2.7	5072	748	17	3
Bihar	82998509	8.1	15.7	0.9	92208	4503	4333	9.3	2951	795	3	1
Chhattisgarh	20833803	2.0	11.6	31.8	22933	1004	992	2.1	2042	2148	9	9
Gujarat	50671017	4.9	7.1	14.8	55809	2239	2256	4.6	5523	2805	10	5
Haryana	21144564	2.1	19.4	0.0	23743	1042	1061	2.1	3420	2675	14	11
Jharkhand	26945829	2.6	11.8	26.3	29745	1409	1384	2.9	1429	225	5	1
Karnataka	52850562	5.1	16.2	6.6	56909	2280	2343	4.7	11835	3426	21	6
Kerala	31841374	3.1	9.8	1.1	33535	1100	1122	2.3	3145	2380	9	7
Madhya Pradesh	60348023	5.9	15.2	20.3	67569	3050	3004	6.3	4997	4675	7	7
Maharashtra	96878627	9.4	10.2	8.9	106386	4236	4330	8.7	15762	4575	15	4
Orissa	36804660	3.6	16.5	22.1	39276	1632	1645	3.4	7434	1088	19	3
Punjab	24358999	2.4	28.9	0.0	26391	1056	1072	2.2	2330	1780	9	7
Rajasthan	56507188	5.5	17.2	12.6	63407	2967	2897	6.1	8309	5358	13	8
Tamil Nadu	62405679	6.1	19.0	1.0	65629	2272	2336	4.7	2990	4582	5	7
Uttar Pradesh	166197921	16.2	21.2	0.1	186755	8912	8750	18.4	7518	8000	4	4
West Bengal	80176197	7.8	23.0	5.5	86125	3597	3644	7.4	4686	3954	5	5
INDIA	1028610328	100.0	16.2	8.2	1128520	48529	48559	100.0	113824	59166	10	5

Source: SES, various years.

An encouraging macro level scenario of physical access to secondary and higher secondary schooling provisions coupled with large variations at the sub-national levels directs our attention to the distortions in the policy planning with regard to expansion of school networks, often due to political and local factors. Such a pattern of growth of schooling provisions has serious policy implications in terms of ensuring minimum standards in schooling provisions and the capacity of the country to finance the same. Eventually, secondary education becomes very costly (both in terms of private costs and public subsidy) making it unaffordable. The point to be underlined here is that development policies and programmes that promote a secondary school network dominated by small schools/sections and largely influenced by political and local factors would over a period become unsustainable in terms of maintaining standards and equity in provisions, processes and outcomes.

Participation in secondary education also shows encouraging trends in free India. From 1.5 million in 1950/51, the total enrolment in secondary and higher secondary stage has gone up almost thirty times to 44.48 million in 2007/08 (see Chart 5.3). It can be seen in Chart 5.3 that the trend line showing growth trends in the enrolment at primary level is much steeper compared to that of the middle and secondary levels, thereby implying relatively slow growth of enrolment at the secondary and higher secondary levels. It may be underlined that, at the all India level, during the period 2000/01 to 2007/08, the average annual growth rate of enrolment at secondary and higher secondary stage was highest (7.06%) compared to that of the middle (4.23%) and primary stages (2.52%). Such a trend in the growth of enrolment at the national level, indeed, hides large variations across regions, gender and social categories in participation in secondary and higher secondary education.

At the all India level, the Gross Enrolment Ratio (GER), which shows total enrolment in secondary stage (Grades IX-XII) as a percentage of total population in the relevant age-group also increased steadily from 19.3 in 1990/91 to 44.81 per cent in 2007/08. It may be noted that the GER figures for secondary stage (Grades IX-X) and higher secondary (Grades XI-XII) stages were not available separately till 2004/05 making it difficult to study their growth trends. In 2004/04, the GER at secondary stage (Grades IX-X) was 51.65 per cent in 2004.05 in India, which increased to 58.15 per cent (50.87% in rural areas) in 2007/08; only around 7 percentage point improvement during this period. Similarly, the GER at the higher secondary stage (Grades XI-XII) was 27.82 per cent in 2004/05 India, which increased to 33.48 per cent (19.22% in rural areas) in 2007/08, only around 6 percentage point improvement in its size (see Table 5.4A). At the secondary level (Grades IX-X), the GER was 52.47 per cent for Scheduled Castes and 43.27 per cent for Scheduled Tribes in 2007/08. At the higher secondary level (Grades XI-XII), the GER was 27.91 per cent for SCs and 20.33 for STs (SSE, 2007/08).

Table 5.4A: GER Trends at Secondary and Higher Secondary Levels, 2004/05 to 2007/08

State/UT	GER at Secondary Level, Classes IX-X (Age Group 14-16)				Average Percentage Point Change in GER at Secondary Level, 2004/05 - 2007/08	GER at Hr. Secondary Level, Classes XI-XII (Age Group 16-18)				Average Percentage Point Change in GER at Hr. Secondary Level, 2004/05 - 2007/08
	2004/05	2005/06	2006/07	2007/08		2004/05	2005/06	2006/07	2007/08	
Andhra Pradesh	53.09	56.72	58.70	61.21	2.7	42.17	41.17	40.80	42.04	-0.04
Assam	49.41	49.36	48.61	44.14	–1.8	14.38	14.30	14.38	10.67	-1.24
Bihar	22.47	22.67	24.42	28.08	1.9	9.82	8.92	11.19	11.40	0.53
Chhattisgarh	43.93	38.94	44.29	45.71	0.6	30.38	23.78	23.04	23.31	-2.36
Gujarat	55.30	53.49	54.69	57.64	0.8	21.78	25.51	27.75	27.71	1.98
Haryana	52.94	52.43	56.35	60.02	2.4	34.16	32.04	35.62	42.11	2.65
Jharkhand	26.49	27.39	26.07	29.75	1.1	2.45	3.20	3.48	6.86	1.47
Karnataka	59.03	57.11	65.73	68.09	3.0	33.85	33.45	38.10	41.32	2.49
Kerala	93.19	93.30	92.93	92.54	-0.2	27.85	36.67	51.80	47.99	6.71
Madhya Pradesh	45.66	48.01	52.95	59.61	4.7	25.33	26.91	31.02	35.41	3.36
Maharashtra	68.91	70.49	69.56	69.41	0.2	42.32	43.25	41.75	43.82	0.50
Orissa	53.73	53.37	52.74	53.77	0.0	32.92	32.19	30.56	22.77	-3.38
Punjab	51.47	49.77	48.95	46.95	-1.5	27.87	29.95	31.06	32.04	1.39
Rajasthan	43.91	45.89	48.61	54.04	3.4	21.59	22.25	22.26	24.49	0.97
Tamil Nadu	80.66	82.62	86.72	90.79	3.4	43.87	45.40	48.59	53.74	3.29
Uttar Pradesh	48.92	48.77	48.60	64.27	5.1	22.93	22.45	22.00	41.23	6.10
West Bengal	41.46	44.66	44.55	47.91	2.2	21.07	26.23	24.25	27.21	2.05
India	**51.65**	**52.19**	**53.27**	**58.15**	2.2	**27.82**	**28.47**	**28.96**	**33.48**	1.89

Source: Selected Educational Statistics (various years) and Statistics of School Education, 2007/08.

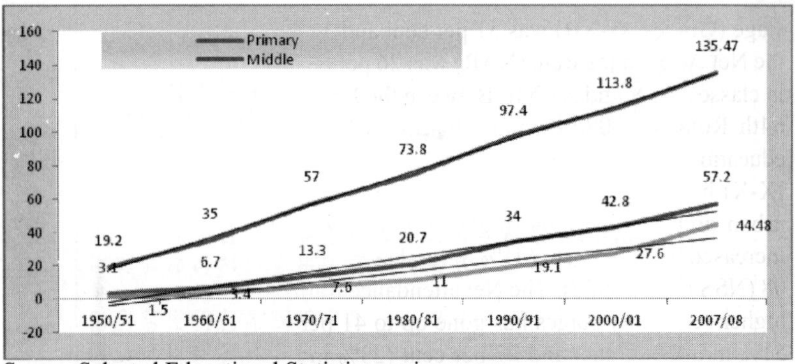

Source: Selected Educational Statistics, various years.
Note: $ Includes enrolments in high/higher secondary/intermediate/pre-university/ junior college/pre-degree level.

Chart 5.3: Growth of Primary, Middle and Secondary Level Enrolment in India Since 1950/5 (in millions)

Apart from variations by gender and social categories, the size of the GER varies greatly across states and union territories. In 2007/08, the GER at secondary stage (Grades IX-X) was less than the national average in 15 states and union territories including several north-eastern states, Bihar, Jharkhand, J&K, Chhattisgarh, Punjab, West Bengal, Orissa, Rajasthan and Gujarat. Except Rajasthan, West Bengal, Meghalaya, and to some extent, Bihar, none of the states in the group had made any significant progress in participation in secondary education. Mostly, educationally backward states in the Hindi-belt like Uttar Pradesh, Bihar, Rajasthan and Madhya Pradesh, which are home to around 38 per cent of the county's population, have been found performing poorly in terms of both development and performance indices[23] at the secondary level (Rani, 2007). Among the major states, only Tamil Nadu and Kerala had relatively higher level of participation in secondary education with a GER of more than 75 per cent in 2007/08.

Similarly, at the higher secondary stage (Grades XI-XII), the GER in 17 states and UTs was lower than that of the country average, which included some the major states—Bihar, Orissa, West Bengal, Jharkhand, Chhattisgarh, Rajasthan, Gujarat and Punjab. Among the major states, only Kerala and Tamil Nadu had GER more than 45 per cent at the higher secondary stage in 2007-08. During 2004/05 and 2007/08, only a few major states—Kerala, Uttar Pradesh, Madhya Pradesh, Tamil Nadu, West Bengal and Haryana—had improved their GER at this level by, on an average, more than 2 percentage points per annum (see Table 5.4A, Annex I).

According to NSS 52nd Round (NSSO, 1998), the Gross Attendance Ratio (GAR) at the secondary stage (Grades IX-X) and higher secondary stage (Grades XI-XII) was 51 per cent and 32 per cent respectively. Further, the Net Attendance Rate (NAR) was 26 per cent and 15 per cent respectively in classes IX-X and XI-XII. Between the NSS 52nd Round (1995/96) and the 64th Round (2007/08), participation in secondary and higher secondary education has improved significantly. The GAR at the secondary stage (Grades IX-X) has improved to 70 per cent (66% in rural areas and 85 per cent in urban areas), and at the higher secondary stage (Grades XI-XII), it has increased to 48 per cent (41% in rural areas and 65% in urban areas) in 2007/08 (NSS 64th Round). The Net attendance Ratio (NER) at the secondary and higher secondary stages has gone up to 41 per cent (38% in rural areas and 51% in urban areas) and 27 per cent (23% in rural areas and 40% in urban areas) respectively in 2007/08 (see Chart 5.4). However, the level of participation at various stages of school education varies significantly across socio-economic groups. At the secondary level, while only 34 persons per 1000 population (ages 5-29) in the lowest MPCE decile class participate in secondary education, it increases to 89 persons for the highest MPCE decile class (NSS 64th Round). Similarly, only 12 persons out of 1000 population (ages 5-29) in the lowest MPCE decile class attend higher secondary institutions, and the number goes up significantly to 80 for the highest MPCE decile class. In other words, poverty hurts visiöly when it comes to participation in post-compulsory levels of school education, particularly at the higher secondary stage.

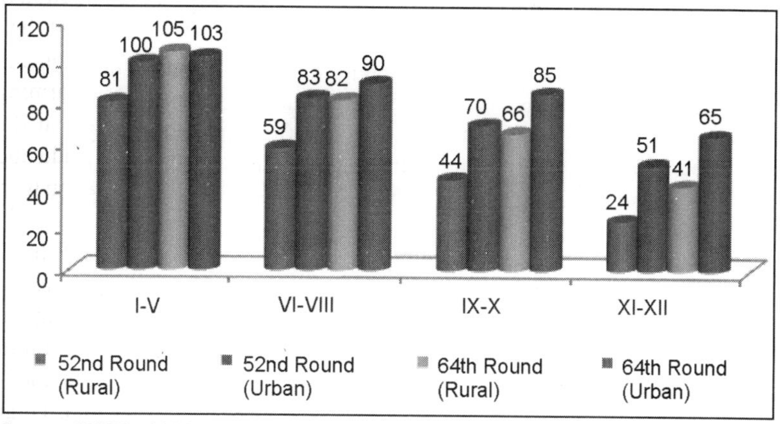

Source: NSSO, 2010.

Chart 5.4: Gross Attendance Ratios (GAR) at various stages of school education in 1995/96 (NSS 52nd Round) and 2007/08 (NSS 64th Round)

Even after visible progress in secondary education, regional, gender and social disparity in access and participation continue to be a major concern. Although the share of girls in the total enrolment at the secondary and higher secondary (grades IX-XII) stages has increased substantially from 13.3 per cent in 1950/51 to 42 per cent in 2005/06, there still exists wide gap in the participation of boys and girls. In fact in 1950/51, only 16 girls per 100 boys were enrolled in classes IX-X, which increased to 73 in 2005/06 and 77 in 2007/08. Interestingly, more or less the same level of gender disparity in participation in secondary education (Grades IX-X) is seen among other social categories. In 2007/08, 76 SC girls/100 boys and 70 ST girls/100 boys participated in secondary classes IX-X. Over the years, the gender parity indices, both at the secondary and higher secondary stages have also improved significantly. In 2007/08, the Gender Parity Index (GPI) in participation was 0.84 and 0.85 respectively at the secondary (Grades IX-X) and higher secondary (Grades XI-XII) stages (SSE, 2007/08).

Relative to other social categories, the participation rate of SCs and STs in secondary and higher secondary education continues to be lower. In 2007/08 at the secondary stage, the GER for SCs and STs was 52.64 per cent and 43.27 per cent respectively. It was 27.91 per cent for SCs and 20.33 per cent for STs at the higher secondary stage (SSE, 2007/08). According to the NSS 64th Round, among the SCs, 55 per 1000 persons in the age group 5-29 were attending secondary classes IX-X, while only 27 persons were attending higher secondary classes. This figure was as high as 73 and 48 respectively at secondary and higher secondary stages for general category of the population. Similarly, in 2007/08 among the STs, only 46 per 1000 persons in the same age group were attending secondary classes and 22 were attending higher secondary classes (NSSO, 2010).

During the last six decades, development of school education has happened mostly in terms of country-wide expansion of school networks and participation rates at all levels. High wastage (low internal efficiency) and low levels of learning achievement still plague the school system. The dropout rate[24] in Classes I-X continues to as high as 56.71 per cent (56.55% for boys and 57.33% for girls). In other words, only around 43 out of every 100 grade I cohort survive up to grade X (SSE, 2007/08). Moreover, the dropout rates of 68.42 per cent for SCs and 76.87 for STs in Classes I-X indicate huge wastage in school education in India.

If we consider the findings of the NSS 64th Round (2007/08), household level data still reveals high dropouts from secondary and higher secondary stages. Out of all education discontinued persons in the age group 5-29, around 25 per cent were found enrolled in classes IX-X but not attending in 2007/08. In other words, these persons dropped out when they were enrolled in classes IX-X. Similarly, 11.2 per cent of all education-discontinued persons in the age group 5-29 were enrolled but not attending higher secondary classes in 2007/08 (see Chart 5.5). This is an important proxy indicator of low efficiency of the school system in the country. The repetition rates at the secondary and

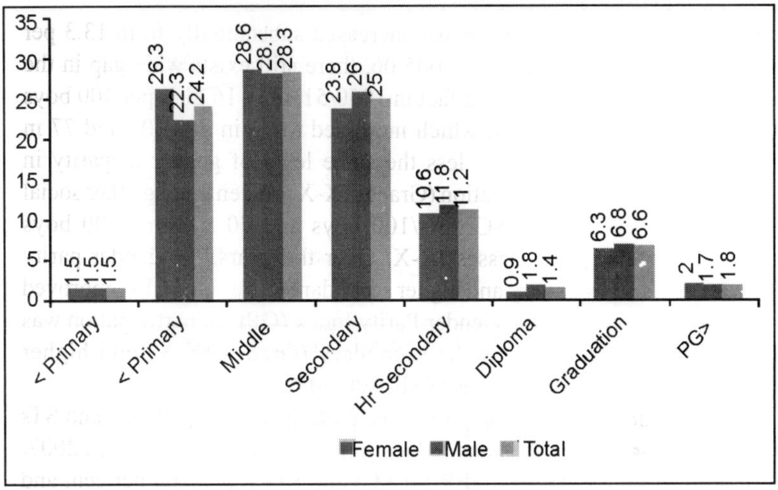

Source: NSSO, 2010.

Chart 5.5: Percentage distribution by level of last enrolment of persons aged 5-29 enrolled in the past but currently not attending (rural+ urban), India (NSS 64th Round)

higher secondary stages are found to be somehow lower at 5.5 per cent and 3.5 per cent respectively (NSSO, 2010).

As has been mentioned earlier, education sector has always received relatively less weightage in terms of its share in the total public expenditure. In absolute terms, the public expenditure on education by education and other departments has increased from 644.6 million in 1950/51, which increased to 1864985.85 million (BE) in 2008/09. In relative terms, public expenditure on education has never crossed 15 per cent of the total public expenditure during the last six decades (see Chart 5.6). As a percentage of GDP, public expenditure on education has never crossed 4 per cent, except for 1999/00 and 2000/01. In 2008/9, the budgeted public expenditure on education was as low as 3.78 per cent of its GDP. Further, while elementary education takes away more than half of the education budget (i.e. 52.13% in 2008/09, BE), the share of public expenditure on secondary education in the total public expenditure on education continues to be as low as 29.34 per cent (2008/09, BE); almost no increase since 2005/06 (BE), when its share was 28.79 per cent.

The imbalance in the pattern of public expenditure within the school education sector in India is clearly visible. While India spends around 62 per cent of its planned education budget on elementary education, secondary education receives only about 16 per cent of this budget (2008/09, BE). In fact, the share of secondary education in the total planned expenditure on education was around 11 per cent (in 2005/06) prior to the launch of several

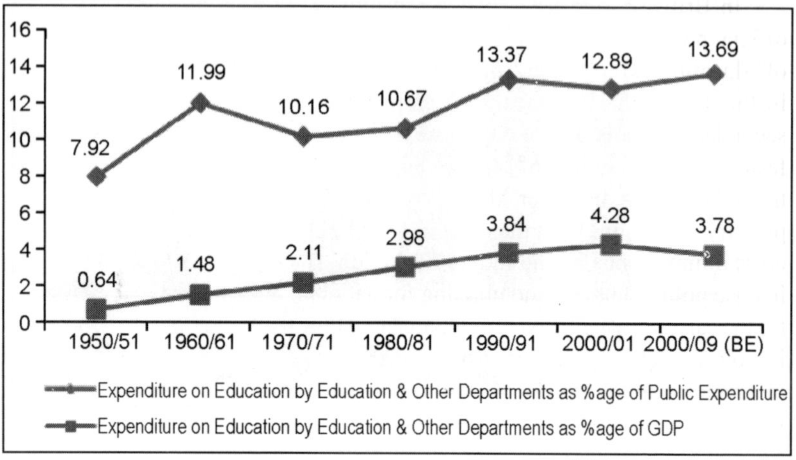

Source: Analysis of Budgeted Expenditure on Education, various years.

Chart 5.6: Trends in Public Expenditure on Education in India, 1950/51 to 2008/09

centrally sponsored development programmes like the Rashtriya Madhyamik Shiksha Abhiyan (RMSA) in April 2009. However, the matter of concern is that, over the years, there is an increase in the private costs of post-compulsory levels of education while the public subsidy at this level school education has remained more or less stagnant. For example, the average annual per capita expenditure on secondary/higher secondary education was Rs. 1577 in 1995/96 (NSS 52nd Round), which increased to Rs. 4351 in 2007/08 (NSS 64th Round). In rural India in 2007/08, the poorest households (in the bottom MPCE decile) were spending on an average Rs. 1623 per pupil per annum at the secondary/higher secondary stage compared to the average annual per capita private expenditure of Rs. 5517 by the richest households (in the top MPCE decile).

Development Policy

In the Indian setting, capturing comprehensively the education development policy shifts at the macro level since independence is a difficult task in the absence of relevant information, particularly at the state level as many of them do not have even the sector specific policy documents. Further, quite a number of development policy shifts do not sit in the policy documents as these are primarily associated with implementation of state and/or centrally sponsored development programmes/schemes. Currently, documentation and policy analysis in education by sub-sector, in fact, themselves are development concerns in India. This section, therefore, attempts to provide an overview of the changing secondary education development policies as found in the reports of various commissions and national education policy documents.

In British India, the Wood's Education Despatch (1854) was the first official policy document of the Colonial Government for public provisioning of education that promoted growth of secondary education.[25] Subsequently, in the second half of the 19th century, the network of English-medium secondary schools and colleges, mostly private aided, expanded relatively faster compared to that of primary education. Towards the late 19th century the policy focus, however, shifted to include issues relating to expansion of primary education. With the recognition of primary education as a subject of critical importance by the Indian Education Commission Report (1883) and intense political unrest and uprising for nationalism among educated Indians (in the early 20th century), the Colonial Government was compelled to review its policy of quantitative expansion and private support for schooling in favour of greater state involvement. In other words, during this period, the policy focus shifted from quantitative expansion to quality improvement of secondary education with greater state control. The policies of promoting aided secondary schools and colleges were abandoned in favour of expansion of the network of government schools.

After independence, the first step towards improving policy planning for development of secondary education was the setting up of the Secondary Education Commission in 1952 (also known as the Mudaliar Commission). The primary objective of the Commission was to diagnose the growth pattern and suggest measures for reorganization and improvement of secondary education. The Commission's major recommendation was to develop a 3-year national system of secondary education after 8-years of elementary education (8 + 3 system of school education) to make it a complete stage. The Commission also recommended for the reconstruction of the syllabus to provide a wider and more balanced course and adopt mother tongue as the medium of instruction (Kabir, 1955). Some of the other important recommendations of the Commission included introduction of craft work in school curriculum, making provisions for increased co-curricular activities, greater emphasis on activity-based teaching-learning, improving school libraries & Laboratories and examination reforms, and establishment of multi-purpose schools with diversified courses as model schools.

After nearly one-and-a-half decade of the Mudaliar Commission, the Kothari Commission (1964-66), while articulating goals and objectives at all stages of education in the context of national development priorities, recommended for a 4-year secondary education system and discontinuing the practice of 'streaming' up to Grade X. It may be noted that, ten years after the Commission submitted its report; education was placed in the Concurrent List making States and the Centre responsible for its development. This changed the policy context for development of secondary education.[26] The National Policy on Education (NPE), 1986 subsequently reiterated the views of the Education Commission to implement a 4-year secondary education system across States and UTs.[27] The NPE (1986) emphasized on improving equitable access to secondary education for improving enrolment of girls, SCs and STs, particularly in science, commerce and vocational streams (Para 5.13 of the NPE, 1986). The NPE and the Programme of Action (POA), 1992 while recognizing secondary education as a critical instrument for social change, called for its planned expansion. The NPE, 1986 (as modified in 1992) specifically laid emphasis again on increasing access to secondary education with particular focus on participation of girls, SCs and STs; increased autonomy of Boards of Secondary Education to enhance their ability to improve quality; introduction of ICT in school curriculum for coping with the globalization process; renewed emphasis on work ethos and values of a humane and composite culture in the curricula; and vocationalization through specialized institutions or through the refashioning of secondary education to meet the manpower requirements of the growing Indian economy (Para 5.13 to 5.15).

Even with explicit policy emphasis on central support for expansion and quality improvement of secondary education, the Centre, however, has played a minimal role in the expansion of the secondary education during the last six decades. As education was a State Subject prior to 1976, the relative economic status of states shaped the pattern of growth of secondary education resulting in wide regional variations reflected in the structure of school education, management, infrastructure facilities, teacher deployment, quality of learning achievements, etc. The Central Government's support for development of this segment of school education has been indirect and limited to technical support through apex level bodies and implementation of a few centrally sponsored schemes. Besides, the Central Government directly supports secondary education by running some 1500 Kendriya Vidyalayas (KVs) and Navodaya Vidyalays (NVs) that contribute to around 2 per cent of the total enrolment in the sub-sector.[28]

Keeping in view the changing development context and as a logical extension of the policy of Universal Elementary Education (UEE), the Central Government shifted its policy emphasis, to some extent, towards development of secondary education during the Tenth Five-Year Plan. The Working Group on Secondary Education for the Tenth Five-Year Plan (2002-07) suggested the Central Government providing support to states in areas of access, equity, quality improvement, ICT, inclusive education, and vocational education. Further, in 2005, the Central Advisory Board of Education (CABE)[29] accordingly emphasized on providing high quality secondary education to all Indian adolescents, girls and boys, up to the age of 16 by 2015 and up to 18 by 2020 (i.e. universalization of secondary and higher secondary education). The CABE Committee on Universalization of Secondary Education[30] (USE) recommended that each state should develop norms for USE keeping in view the common national parameters as well as the state specific parameters. States should also develop their medium-term Perspective Plans for USE; go for decentralization as the main approach to planning and implementation of USE; and invest in public school system with specified norms and standards as that of the KVs for enhancing its effectiveness. The Committee also emphasized that vocational education and training should become a major national programme in the mission mode and be structurally and administratively placed outside the school system. Accordingly, the targets for USE as spelled out by the CABE Committee included: (i) universal participation by 2015; (ii) universal retention by 2020; (iii) mastery learning by more than 60 per cent learners by 2020; and (iv) universal higher secondary education (Grades XI-XII) by 2020.

Current Reform Agenda and Development Interventions

The recommendations of the CABE Committee (2005) largely shaped the development priorities in secondary education during the Eleventh Plan period (2007-2012). The 11th Plan, therefore, targeted to: (i) achieve universal access (to secondary schooling provisions within 5 kms, and higher secondary schooling provisions within a distance of 5-8 kms of every habitation); (ii) raise GER at secondary stage to 75 per cent by 2011/12; (iii) reduce substantially gender, social and regional disparities in enrolment, dropout and retention rates; (iv) improve Teacher-Pupil Ratio (TPR) at the secondary stage to about 25, and ensure availability of trained subject and other teachers by 2011/12; and (vi) introduce ICT at secondary and higher secondary schools.

The broad secondary education development strategies envisaged (at the macro level) during the 11th Plan included: (i) restructuring of the school system (5+3+2+2) and expansion of the secondary school network/physical access by upgrading the existing schooling provisions and establishing new institutions/sections including high quality model schools at the CD Block level to serve as benchmark for excellence in secondary schooling; (ii) promoting Public-Private Partnership (PPP) to leverage private investment in the expansion of secondary schooling provisions; (iii) ensuring quality secondary education with focus on Science, Mathematics and English; (iv) promoting inclusiveness in secondary education through demand-side financing strategies; (v) introducing ICT @ government and aided schools; (vi) adopting the National Curriculum Framework, 2005; and (vii) undertaking institutional reforms in school management. Implicitly, the development policy during the 11th Plan emphasized more on the supply of schooling provisions and ensuing equity in participation rather than the quality improvement and governance components. Moreover the plan gave little emphasis on expansion and quality improvement of higher secondary education.

Currently, several secondary education development schemes and programmes, including the recently launched Rashtriya Madhyamik Shiksha Abhiyan (RMSA), are being implemented in the country to achieve the 11th Plan targets. The RMSA has been launched since April 2009 with the basic developmental objectives of universalizing access to and improving quality of secondary education (Grades IX-X) in the country. In other words, the RMSA aims at making secondary education of good quality accessible and affordable to all young persons. Specifically, the RMSA aims at: (i) maintaining standards in secondary education by making schools confirm to the prescribed norms related to physical facilities, staff and academic matters (rationalizing facilities, staff and TLM across secondary schools as per norms); (ii) universalizing physical access to all young persons (taking a distance norm of 5.0 kms at secondary and 7.0 kms at higher secondary stages); (iii) improving participation and retention in secondary education (75% GER at secondary stage by 2013/14, 100% GER by 2016/17, and universal retention by 2020); (iv) overcoming barriers to secondary schooling due to gender, socio-economic status, disability and other disadvantaged circumstances (improving equity and delivery of secondary education); and (v) enhancing intellectual, social and cultural learning in secondary schooling—i.e. improving quality of learning outcomes (a very ambiguous objective in the absence of benchmarks in the quality of secondary schooling, often measured in terms of pass percentage in board examination).

Unlike the centrally-sponsored schemes, the RMSA has been designed as a country-wide reform programme (more or less in line with the reform programme in elementary education sub-sector, i.e. the Sarva Shiksha Abhiyan) to be implemented in partnership with states (primarily in terms of resource sharing; whereas strategic management responsibilities of secondary education continues to stay with states). As such, it adopts a 'sector-wide approach' rather than a 'functional approach' (generally followed in implementing the centrally sponsored schemes) to development of secondary education, calling for 'convergence of all on-going interventions' in the sub-sector. However, it may be underlined that, although in principle, the RMSA envisages to cover all government and aided institutions at secondary and higher secondary stages, its coverage is limited to only government managed secondary schools/sections during the 11th Plan period. Similarly, the on-going centrally sponsored schemes in secondary education have not been subsumed in the RMSA during this period. It is expected that, during the 12th Plan period, convergence will happen in the RMSA, and its coverage would increase to include the aided secondary level institutions and institutions at the higher secondary stage. Like the SSA, the RMSA is also envisaged to adopt a decentralized institutional framework for its implementation. Evidence based participatory planning and management at the district and institutional levels, therefore, are considered 'critical for its success. The unique feature of the RMSA relates to its focus on mainstreaming (in terms of institutional arrangements for its implementation) from the day one to ensure greater level of sustainability.

The broad development strategies of the RMSA primarily focuses on improving access, quality, equity, school effectiveness and governance, including support services.[31] However, in practice, the development path followed during the 11th Plan puts too much emphasis on improving physical access to and facilities in secondary schools/sections, filling in gaps in the infrastructure and staff in the existing secondary schools/sections (only government managed) so as to make them confirm to norms and standards. In practice, there is, in fact, little emphasis on quality improvement and school effectiveness interventions. So much so that, even, innovations in secondary schooling are envisaged to be promoted beyond the RMSA framework, primarily through involvement of NGOs and private sector research and resource institutions. In a way, in the initial years, the effort is to ensure standards in government managed secondary schooling provisions.

However, the important quality improvement interventions envisaged in the programme, among others, include curriculum revision and examination reforms; teacher upgradation and rationalization of subject teacher deployment; capacity building of the SMDC, including the leadership development programme for school heads; strengthening classroom-based support and supervision; promotion of life skills and adolescent education; strengthening guidance and counseling at the school level; and establishing Learning Resource Centre, with library, ICT support and link with EDUSAT. The RMSA offers a strategic opportunity in secondary education to improve access, equity, quality, accountability and ability to measure learning outcomes through standardization of curriculum and examinations across states. With all its good development intentions and as it is into just the second year of its implementation, the RMSA is yet to be concretized as a reform programme in secondary education, mainly in terms of its strategic management.

Apart from the RMSA, the prominent on-going centrally sponsored schemes in secondary education relate to establishment of model schools and strengthening of boarding and hostel facilities for girl students, ICT @ schools, inclusive education, incentives to girls and national merit-cum-means scholarship to improve participation and retention, vocationalization of secondary education, improving deployment of language teachers and adolescence education.[32] It is important to note here that, in the absence of any holistic approach to the development of secondary education, the centrally sponsored schemes are hardly integrated into the State Plan and these schemes operate as stand alones with little indication of state ownership.

Development Challenges and the Way Forward

A run through the above discussions makes it very clear by now that secondary education as a critical segment of the school education sub-sector has never been properly positioned[33] in the policy-planning process in India since independence. While in British India, secondary education was promoted through favourable colonial development policies and community initiatives, it was equally neglected in free India because of relatively high political commitment for compulsory level of education and higher & professional education. Moreover, even though there has been visible quantitative expansion of secondary education (mainly as a response to increased voluntary social demand), the sub-sector is yet to align itself to the changing context of schooling. In fact, little thinking has gone into developing secondary education to discharge effectively its social and individual functions; rather all these years, the focus has been on its growth as an extension of elementary education. As such, like in several other developing economies, secondary education in India faces a number of development challenges.

The development challenges facing secondary education can be broadly grouped into two categories—(i) those that sit at the systems level; and (ii) the rest that are related either to individual functions of secondary education or to strategic management of the sub-sector specific reform programmes (i.e. challenges relating to implementation of development initiatives), excluding those that are exogenous. In this section, while highlighting some of the systems level challenges in secondary education, the attempt is to identify key challenges relating to implementation of major reform programmes like the RMSA, which are of immediate concern for improving strategic management of the sub-sector. The systems level challenges are generally more dynamic in nature that try to deal with development issues related to aligning secondary education to larger socio-economic needs of society, which, among others, include issues such as:

(i) What is the appropriate secondary schooling model (in terms of its objectives and functions), particularly in ever changing national and global settings? How to diversify secondary education to accommodate the growing social demand for quality schooling?

(ii) How to have expanded access while maintaining quality and equity? In other words, what are the limits of trade-off between quality, quantity and equity in developing secondary education?

(iii) What are the implications of uniform provisioning and mixed market providers (private participation) in terms of coverage and equity?

(iv) What should be the appropriate curriculum and evaluation system to prepare pupils simultaneously for workplace, pursuing higher education, and preparing for life? What kind of secondary curriculum would lead to high level of relevance and external efficiency?

(v) What should be the mode of financing secondary education that is sustainable and affordable? Given the investment priorities in other development sectors in a developing country like India, where to get funds to finance secondary education development initiatives?

These issues continue to be debated in national and international development forums, that generally results mostly in development rhetoric (i.e. statements dense with 'should', "need to be', etc.) leaving individual countries to man their schooling by designing reform programmes considered appropriate, given its socio-political and economic contexts. Such systems level secondary education development dialogue, in fact, started much earlier in India immediately after independence, when the Secondary Education Commission (1952-53) had foreseen patterns of growing interdependence among nations, which became subsequently a reality in the late 20th century. While the quest for effective schooling models is on, developing countries like India have remained more or less inefficient both in terms of articulating 'appropriate sustainable change' in secondary education (i.e. designing reform programmes) and in generating the right kind of political and key stakeholder support for its translation into actions.

Several factors have contributed to the inappropriate design and ineffective implementation of education reform programmes in India. First, besides political factors (i.e. how secondary education figures in the political agenda?), 'comprehensive profiling of the secondary education sub-sector' is, perhaps, the starting point for articulating change. How much do we know our secondary schools? Surprisingly, one comes across very little evidence based information about what affects secondary schooling in terms of inputs, processes, outputs and outcomes? Lack of data and information is the critical development constraint in secondary education in India. Although, in recent years, efforts are being made (as part of RMSA and NUEPA initiative) to institutionalize the Secondary Education Management Information System (SEMIS) at the sub-national levels, it is yet to feed effectively into the planning and management processes of secondary education. Absence of proper monitoring and feedback mechanisms coupled with thin research in the sub-sector limits the knowledge of secondary education in the country.

Second, lack of related data and information has resulted in designing 'over ambitious reform programmes' such as the RMSA, and very often, fragmented centrally-sponsored schemes in secondary education. How a reform programme is designed has important bearing for its success and sustainability? Although, the RMSA has been designed taking into account the recommendations of the CABE, which itself, in the absence of appropriate data, emphasized relatively more on accommodating increased demand for secondary school places[34] due to the success of the SSA and maintaining the minimum standards in schooling provisions. It may also be underlined that whether or not to achieve a higher level of expansion of secondary education (higher access rate) is largely conditioned by the growth pattern of elementary education. Projecting the success of the SSA is, therefore, critical in estimating social demand for secondary schooling. Even with increased participation in secondary education in recent years, there still exists a large gap between grade VIII and grade IX enrolment[35] (see Chart 5.7). At the all India level, while the promotion rate from grade IX to X seems to be very high (more than 95%), there has always been substantial transition loss (around 10-15% without adjusting for repeaters in grades VIII and IX) between elementary and secondary stages (see Chart 5.8). It, of course, varies greatly across regions and social categories. Besides, the poor internal efficiency of the elementary education sets the limits of expansion of secondary education.

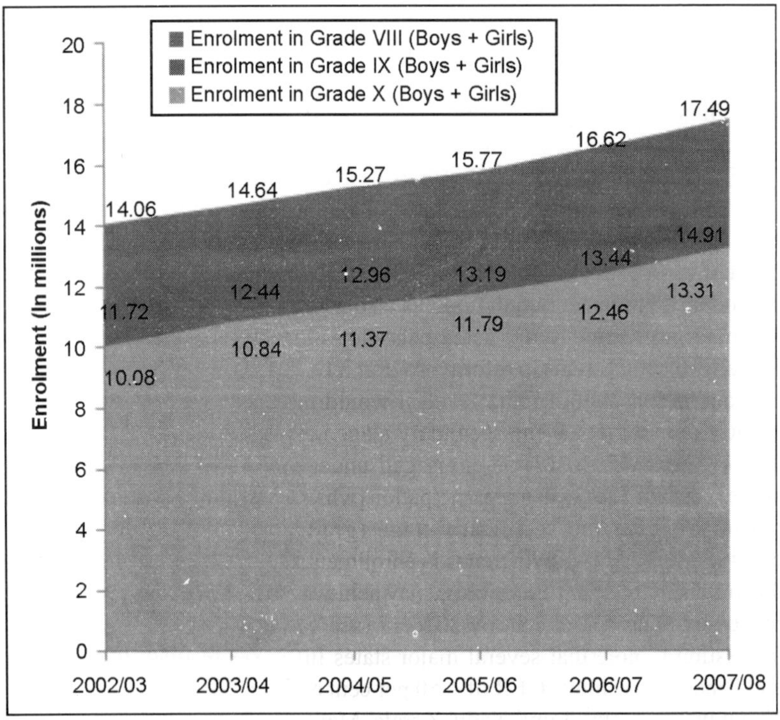

Source: SES, various years.

Chart 5.7: Growth of Enrolment in Grades VIII, IX and X in India (In millions)

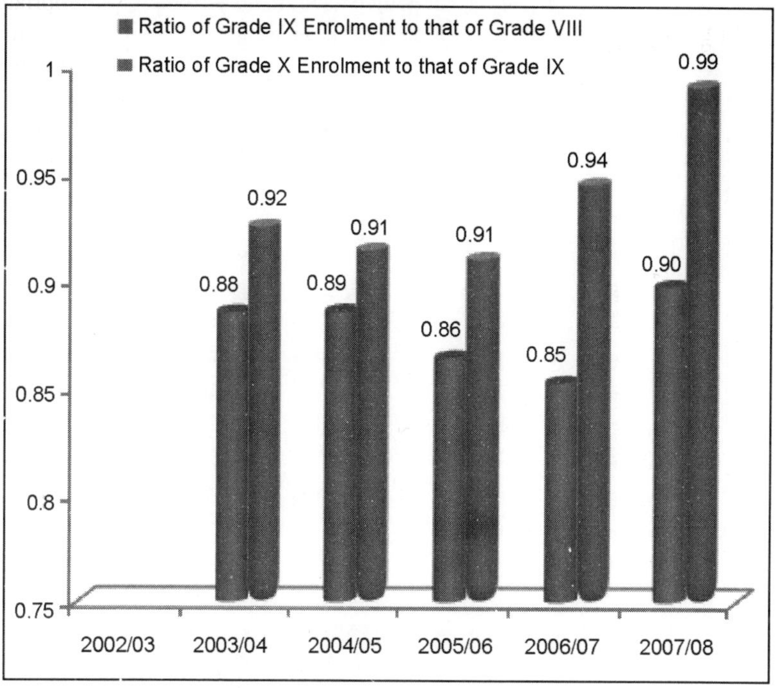

Source: Estimated on the basis of the SES data, various years.

Chart 5.8: Ratio of Grade IX Enrolment to VIII and Grade X to IX in India

During the tenth plan period (2002-2007), increase in the relevant secondary school age population has also pulled down the size of the GER, the indicator mainly used to set targets and assess progress in participation in RMSA. High ambitions in reform programmes are evident, for example, from the fact that, at the all India level, it would not be possible to achieve the participation targets at the secondary stage (i.e. 75% GER by 2013/14 and 100% GER by 2016/17) as envisaged under the RMSA. Assuming some success of the SSA in raising participation [which would have already impacted participation at the secondary stage (grades IX-X) by 2002/05], and considering that the growth trends in enrollment at secondary stage since 2004/05 continues into the future, India may achieve a GER of around 69 per cent by 2013/14 and 76 per cent by 2016/17 (see Table 5.4B, Annex I). It is also interesting to note that several major states like Assam, Jharkhand, Punjab and Bihar may achieve GER of < 50 per cent at the secondary stage by 2016/17. Only Karnataka, Tamil Nadu, Kerala, Madhya Pradesh and Uttar Pradesh may achieve a GER of >90 per cent at the secondary stage by 2016/17 (see Table 5.4B, Annex I).[36]

Table 5.4B: Linear growth trends of GER at secondary level in the coming years if the present trend (from 2004/05 to 2007/08) continues

State/ UT	*GER at Secondary Level, Classes IX-X (Age Group 14-16)*				*Projected Size of the GER at the Secondary Level, Classes IX-X, if the Growth Trends of the Past Four Years Continues*												
	2004/ 05	*2005/ 06*	*2006/ 07*	*2007/ 08*	*2008/ 09*	*2009/ 10*	*2010/ 11*	*2011/ 12*	*2012/ 13*	*2013/ 14*	*2014/ 15*	*2015/ 16*	*2016/ 17*	*2017/ 18*	*2018/ 19*	*2019/ 20*	*2020/ 21*
Andhra Pradesh	53.09	56.72	58.70	61.21	64.02	66.65	69.28	71.92	74.55	77.19	79.82	82.45	85.09	87.72	90.36	92.99	95.62
Assam	49.41	49.36	48.61	44.14	43.74	42.08	40.43	38.77	37.12	35.46	33.80	32.15	30.49	28.84	27.18	25.52	23.87
Bihar	22.47	22.67	24.42	28.08	29.06	30.91	32.77	34.63	36.49	38.35	40.20	42.06	43.92	45.78	47.64	49.49	51.35
Chhattisgarh	43.93	38.94	44.29	45.71	45.89	46.96	48.03	49.10	50.17	51.24	52.30	53.37	54.44	55.51	56.58	57.65	58.72
Gujarat	55.30	53.49	54.69	57.64	57.34	58.16	58.98	59.80	60.62	61.45	62.27	63.09	63.91	64.73	65.56	66.38	67.20
Haryana	52.94	52.43	56.35	60.02	61.73	64.24	66.76	69.27	71.79	74.31	76.82	79.34	81.85	84.37	86.89	89.40	91.92
Jharkhand	26.49	27.39	26.07	29.75	29.54	30.39	31.23	32.08	32.92	33.77	34.62	35.46	36.31	37.15	38.00	38.85	39.69
Karnataka	59.03	57.11	65.73	68.09	71.44	75.02	78.60	82.18	85.76	89.34	92.92	96.50	100.08	103.66	107.24	110.82	114.40
Kerala	93.19	93.30	92.93	92.54	92.41	92.18	91.95	91.71	91.48	91.25	91.02	90.79	90.55	90.32	90.09	89.86	89.63
Madhya Pradesh	45.66	48.01	52.95	59.61	63.26	67.93	72.61	77.29	81.97	86.65	91.33	96.01	100.69	105.37	110.05	114.72	119.40
Maharashtra	68.91	70.49	69.56	69.41	69.74	69.79	69.85	69.91	69.96	70.02	70.08	70.13	70.19	70.25	70.31	70.36	70.42
Orissa	53.73	53.37	52.74	53.77	53.28	53.22	53.17	53.12	53.07	53.02	52.97	52.92	52.87	52.82	52.77	52.71	52.66
Punjab	51.47	49.77	48.95	46.95	45.69	44.25	42.81	41.38	39.94	38.50	37.06	35.62	34.19	32.75	31.31	29.87	28.43
Rajasthan	43.91	45.89	48.61	54.04	56.39	59.70	63.01	66.32	69.63	72.95	76.26	79.57	82.88	86.19	89.50	92.81	96.12
Tamil Nadu	80.66	82.62	86.72	90.79	93.32	97.27	100.72	104.17	107.62	111.07	114.51	117.96	121.41	124.86	128.31	131.76	135.21
Uttar Pradesh	48.92	48.77	48.60	64.27	64.11	68.70	73.29	77.87	82.46	87.05	91.64	96.23	100.81	105.40	109.99	114.58	119.17
West Bengal	41.46	44.66	44.55	47.91	49.46	51.38	53.30	55.23	57.15	59.08	61.00	62.92	64.85	66.77	68.70	70.62	72.54
India	**51.65**	**52.19**	**53.27**	**58.15**	**58.96**	**61.02**	**63.08**	**65.13**	**67.19**	**69.25**	**71.31**	**73.37**	**75.42**	**77.48**	**79.54**	**81.60**	**83.66**

Source: Based on SES, various years.

Table 5.4C: Linear growth trends of GER at higher secondary level in the coming years if the present trend (from 2004/05 to 2007/08) continues

State/UT	*GER at Hr. Secondary Level, Classes XI-XII (Age Group 16-18)*				*Projected Size of the GER at the Higher Secondary Level, Classes XI-XII, if the Growth Trends of the Past Four Years Continues*												
	2004/05	*2005/06*	*2006/07*	*2007/08*	*2008/09*	*2009/10*	*2010/11*	*2011/12*	*2012/13*	*2013/14*	*2014/15*	*2015/16*	*2016/17*	*2017/18*	*2018/19*	*2019/20*	*2020/21*
Andhra Pradesh	42.17	41.17	40.80	42.04	41.36	41.28	41.20	41.13	41.05	40.98	40.90	40.82	40.75	40.67	40.60	40.52	40.44
Assam	14.38	14.30	14.38	10.67	10.67	10.67	10.67	10.67	10.67	10.67	10.67	10.67	10.67	10.67	10.67	10.67	10.67
Bihar	9.82	8.92	11.19	11.40	12.09	12.79	13.49	14.19	14.89	15.59	16.29	16.99	17.69	18.39	19.10	19.80	20.50
Chhattisgarh	30.38	23.78	23.04	23.31	23.31	23.31	23.31	23.31	23.31	23.31	23.31	23.31	23.31	23.31	23.31	23.31	23.31
Goa	41.79	40.23	40.10	44.12	43.28	43.96	44.65	45.33	46.02	46.71	47.39	48.08	48.76	49.45	50.14	50.82	51.51
Gujarat	21.78	25.51	27.75	27.71	30.70	32.70	34.70	36.70	38.71	40.71	42.71	44.72	46.72	48.72	50.73	52.73	54.73
Haryana	34.16	32.04	35.62	42.11	42.84	45.58	48.33	51.07	53.81	56.56	59.30	62.04	64.78	67.53	70.27	73.01	75.76
Jharkhand	2.45	3.20	3.48	6.86	7.38	8.73	10.08	11.43	12.78	14.13	15.48	16.83	18.18	19.53	20.89	22.24	23.59
Karnataka	33.85	33.45	38.10	41.32	43.45	46.15	48.86	51.56	54.27	56.98	59.68	62.39	65.09	67.80	70.51	73.21	75.92
Kerala	27.85	36.67	51.80	47.99	59.97	67.52	75.08	82.63	90.19	97.74	105.30	112.85	112.85	112.85	112.85	112.85	112.85
Madhya Pradesh	25.33	26.91	31.02	35.41	38.26	41.69	45.13	48.56	52.00	55.43	58.87	62.30	65.74	69.17	72.61	76.04	79.48
Maharashtra	42.32	43.25	41.75	43.82	43.54	43.84	44.14	44.44	44.74	45.04	45.34	45.64	45.94	46.24	46.54	46.84	47.14
Orissa	32.92	32.19	30.56	22.77	22.77	22.77	22.77	22.77	22.77	22.77	22.77	22.77	22.77	22.77	22.77	22.77	22.77
Punjab	27.87	29.95	31.06	32.04	33.64	35.00	36.36	37.72	39.08	40.45	41.81	43.17	44.53	45.89	47.26	48.62	49.98
Rajasthan	21.59	22.25	22.26	24.49	24.83	25.70	26.57	27.44	28.31	29.18	30.05	30.92	31.79	32.66	33.54	34.41	35.28
Tamil Nadu	43.87	45.40	48.59	53.74	56.10	59.38	62.66	65.94	69.22	72.50	75.78	79.06	82.34	85.62	88.90	92.18	95.46
Uttar Pradesh	22.93	22.45	22.00	41.23	40.77	46.21	51.66	57.10	62.55	67.99	73.44	78.88	84.33	89.77	95.22	100.66	106.11
West Bengal	21.07	26.23	24.25	27.21	28.80	30.44	32.09	33.73	35.38	37.02	38.66	40.31	41.95	43.60	45.24	46.88	48.53
India	**27.82**	**28.47**	**28.96**	**33.48**	**34.05**	**35.80**	**37.54**	**39.29**	**41.04**	**42.79**	**44.53**	**46.28**	**48.03**	**49.77**	**51.52**	**53.27**	**55.01**

Source: Ibid.

Table 5.5: Categorization of States and UTs according to Growth Trends in Class VIII Enrolment, 2001-2004

State/UT	*Total Enrolment in Grade VIII*							*Linear Growth Trends: Average Annual Growth Rate (%)*		
	2001/02	2002/03	2003/04	2004/05	2005/06	2006/07	2007/08	2001/02-2005/06	2005/06-2007/08	2001/02-2007/08
(1)	(2)	(3)	(4)	(5)	(6)	(7)	(8)	(9)	(10)	(11)
Group I: Negative Growth Rate (2001-2007)										
Kerala	605813	586041	573682	554921	543831	534802	533926	-2.7	-0.9	-2.1
Mizoram	15868	16024	15719	16366	16544	16434	15519	1.0	-3.1	-0.4
A & N Islands	6867	6961	6816	7050	7384	7606	6813	1.8	-3.9	-0.1
Goa	25097	25834	25442	25714	25363	25092	24968	0.3	-0.8	-0.1
Group II: Growth Rate < 2%										
Maharashtra	1662922	1815110	1815409	1844510	1928972	1885411	1687215	3.8	-6.5	0.2
J & K	154397	165259	136350	150856	162028	162028	162028	1.2	0.0	0.8
Tamil Nadu	1138596	1056333	1111760	1169045	1143584	1166641	1196248	0.1	2.3	0.8
Puducherry	20331	21145	21679	21707	21743	21735	21875	1.7	0.3	1.2
Punjab	302129	324740	314196	315329	321858	325269	330688	1.6	1.4	1.5
Orissa	450000	444635	450744	461345	479071	495957	502144	1.6	2.4	1.8
Assam	357520	326126	374471	376523	383872	384020	400312	1.8	2.1	1.9
Group III: Growth Rate between 2-4%										
Haryana	333203	374466	367950	407298	408276	440751	379846	5.2	-3.5	2.2
Delhi	234957	252282	248676	212449	251345	242028	269408	1.7	3.5	2.3
Chandigarh	12398	13754	12494	12089	11491	12978	14291	-1.9	11.5	2.4
Manipur	40651	40651	42580	43984	45391	47041	47084	2.8	1.8	2.5

(*Contd.*)

(1)	(2)	(3)	(4)	(5)	(6)	(7)	(8)	(9)	(10)	(11)
Rajasthan	962990	730408	832939	918062	965658	1104038	1133317	0.1	8.3	2.8
Himachal Pradesh	130025	146157	143165	144197	146683	142156	153228	3.1	2.2	2.8
Daman & Diu	2413	2826	2804	2612	2889	2930	2940	4.6	0.9	3.3
Uttaranchal	146039	157634	167333	171084	173321	174094	178983	4.4	1.6	3.4
West Bengal	890731	952149	1063759	1034824	1051671	1092435	1102356	4.2	2.4	3.6
Gujarat	689304	756445	739896	760165	777225	817206	856043	3.0	4.9	3.7
Karnataka	745283	798440	777092	810096	841061	895204	926178	3.1	4.9	3.7
Group IV: Growth Rate between 4-6%										
Lakshadweep	1298	1741	1631	1426	1440	1661	1661	2.6	7.4	4.2
Tripura	42546	46394	50050	50319	54442	56212	55865	6.4	1.3	4.6
Sikkim	7217	8512	7585	8621	9806	9031	9488	8.0	-1.6	4.7
India	**13170216**	**14059195**	**14641856**	**15266907**	**15766769**	**16622436**	**17495128**	**4.6**	**5.3**	**4.8**
Andhra Pradesh	829056	901755	1000339	1066846	1087713	1122443	1173320	7.0	3.9	6.0
Arunachal Pradesh	16060	18093	16023	16784	18854	19532	22733	4.1	9.8	6.0
Group V: Growth Rate >6%										
Chhattisgarh	294515	326550	348404	367988	325791	410610	422069	2.6	13.8	6.2
Nagaland	18451	18960	24864	27448	30191	30191	29323	13.1	-1.4	8.0
Jharkhand	227379	200004	251313	268223	284641	318621	378482	5.8	15.3	8.9
D & N Haveli	2800	3366	3661	3530	4003	4093	4686	9.3	8.2	9.0
Madhya Pradesh	809009	953253	994887	1154025	1293693	1464833	1422932	12.5	4.9	9.9
Bihar	568195	554046	564511	651050	702319	885527	1002562	5.4	19.5	9.9
Meghalaya	23547	29150	30074	37626	39034	43429	43598	13.5	5.7	10.8
Uttar Pradesh	1402609	1983951	2103558	2152795	2205581	2260397	2982999	12.0	16.3	13.4

Source: Selected Educational Statistics, various years.

Third, low level of 'readiness to take off' in terms of pre-reform/project activities has invariably affected planning and implementation of education reform programmes in general and secondary education development programmes in particular. Whatever may be the reasons, India has always invested little time and resources for creating an enabling environment—particularly, in terms of awareness building, information generation through research and consultation, stakeholder participation, capacity building and institutional and management reforms[37]—for adopting and managing education reform programmes such as the RMSA. In the absence of a threshold level of related capacity, stakeholder participation in education reform programmes generally remain limited, and the 'proximate forums' such as PRIs, ULBs, SMDCs, VECs, PTAs, etc. engaged in educational development are captured by local elites. Even after two years of implementation of the RMSA, states are not ready with the required capacity to plan and mange the programme, particularly at the district and the sub-district levels. Many states have not put together the norms, standards and procedures that would guide them in planning and monitoring the RMSA interventions. They have also not made any substantial investment in awareness and capacity building of personnel, institutions and local governments and making related institutional arrangements for strategic management. As information enhances the power and professional authority of policy-makers, planners and administrators; capacity building becomes a precedence requirement for development. If there is no capacity, especially at the sub-national and institutional levels, there is no development. As long as this dimension of education reform programmes is neglected, programmes like RMSA can hardly make any difference in improving secondary education in the country.

Fourth, 'decentralization' as a policy strategy has been considered a panacea for decades in designing and implementing education development programmes. In other words, almost all education reform programmes, including the RMSA, view the 'bottom-up' approach to planning and management as key to their success. In such a decentralized development model, the unit at the bottom of the educational hierarchy (in most cases, the school) is envisaged to play a critical role in designing and implementing reforms (like the RMSA) in terms of administrative, fiscal and curricular decisions. In other words, the bottom-up approach creates space for schools to act as key decision-makers rather than mainly agents of others decisions. In practice, however, the implementation of the bottom-up approach in education reform programmes has faltered in India. This has happened primarily because of too much emphasis by policy-makers and administrators at the top of the educational hierarchy on demonstrating 'efficiency' rather than 'effectiveness' of reform interventions. Simply putting, the secondary education reform programmes, including the RMSA, have not made enough provisions in their programme designs (in terms of policy and institutional arrangements) to facilitate school-wide reform.

What changes need to be brought about at the central level to enable school decision-making? Policy-makers and development planners have hardly designed education reform programmes taking into account this concern. It is, in fact, difficult to find the kind of 'up' in the 'bottom-up approach' that promote school improvement.[38] In major reform programmes such as the RMSA, issues of quality and equity are generally addressed through macro level interventions such as rationalization of schooling inputs, improvements in teacher quality, curriculum and examination reforms, improved support services, and demand-side financing strategies such as scholarship schemes, incentives to socio-economically disadvantaged groups like free uniforms, textbooks, transport allowances, etc, which often do not demonstrate desired results. School effectiveness interventions (based on whole school reform experiences) may certainly prove critical in supplementing macro strategies and interventions in dealing with issues of equity and quality.

It is a fact that socio-economically disadvantaged groups receive relatively less pedagogical support at home, which needs to be compensated at the school level, Moreover, improving school-wide leadership through school improvement planning is essential for addressing quality related issues including pedagogical practices and school-based support and evaluation systems. In short, the school is the most appropriate unit for identifying what works and what does not in terms of promoting governance, pedagogy, support services, evaluation of learning achievements, professional commitment and authority, leadership to manage and sustain change and communication with key stakeholders. The school, however, needs support in terms the enabling institutional environment, capacity and funds to undertake school improving activities. Creating space for school improvement in policy planning and programme design (viz., the RMSA) and making adequate budgetary provisions for this intervention are considered important development challenges in secondary education.

Fifth, the education reform programmes in the country assign too much weightage to resource allocation (mostly within their rigid frameworks) as compared to the resource utilization aspects. It is evident from the huge spillovers in annual budgets of states under the RMSA. Resources allocated under the education reform programmes like the RMSA are tied funds giving little scope for reallocation at the sub-national and institutional levels thereby limiting innovations and best practices. District Secondary Education Plan is viewed as an instrument for resource allocation rather than a strategic development document. The criteria for resource allocation often do not take into account the priority areas of development and the capacity of individual states to absorb the allocated resources. Such a strategy has affected both efficiency and effectiveness of investments in secondary education. Moreover, education reform programmes have generally gone for creating monitoring and reporting systems that focus on 'compliance' rather than identification of achievements and failures. In other words, designing appropriate monitoring and feedback systems that celebrate failures along with successes of the reform interventions is a development challenge in secondary education sub-sector in India.

Besides, at the functional level, critical areas of reform in secondary education relate to teacher management (i.e. deployment, teacher education, working conditions, and incentives); better school infrastructure; textbooks and teaching material; progressive technology and examination reforms; and school based management and leadership development (IADB, 2000; World Bank, 2009; Lewin, 2008; Briseid and Caillods, 2004). In addition, developed country strategies to improve secondary education such as: emphasis on continuity from grade I to XII rather than maintaining distinctly separate cycles of school education; retaining as many children as possible in the school system for as long as possible; combination of school and enterprise based training at the upper secondary level; emphasis on transversal competencies or general skills in curricula—i.e. communication, problem solving, reasoning, ability to learn and motivation; emphasis on new subject areas such as ICT, citizenship, health, sustainable development, human rights, etc; emphasis on differentiation to meet the learning needs of individual students; developing team teaching; stronger emphasis on project work; giving schools more autonomy and space for pedagogical innovations and good practices; giving high priority to teacher development; emphasis on school-based support system to provide pedagogical help to teachers; emphasis on delegation and wider accountability of schools on outcomes; and allocating relatively large resources for secondary education provide important clues for designing reform programmes in India.

Conclusion

To conclude, reforming secondary and higher secondary education in India from hitherto an elite system to an inclusive one is a huge challenge. It can only be addressed through improved political will, policy focus, strategic management ensuring continuity in change at the school level, and an increased budgetary allocation.

ANNEX I

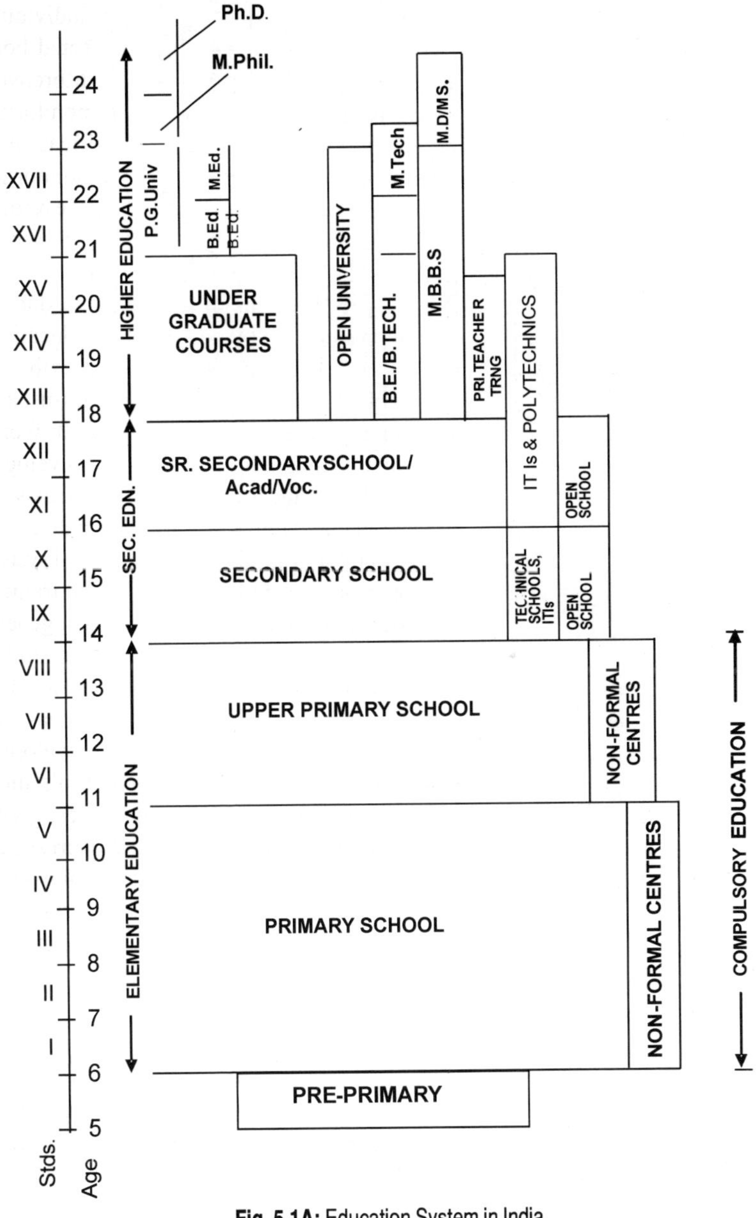

Fig. 5.1A: Education System in India

Level/ Stage of Education	*Grades*	*State/UT*
Primary	1-5	Andhra Pradesh, Arunachal Pradesh, Bihar, Chhattisgarh, Haryana, Himachal Pradesh, Jammu & Kashmir, Karnataka, Jharkhand, Madhya Pradesh, Manipur, Orissa, Punjab, Rajasthan, Sikkim, Tamil Nadu, Tripura, Uttar Pradesh, Uttaranchal, A & N Islands, Chandigarh, Delhi, and Pondicherry
	1-4	Assam Goa, Gujarat, Kerala, Maharashtra, Meghalaya, Mizoram, Nagaland, West Bengal, D&N Haveli, Daman & Diu and Lakshadweep,
Upper Primary	6-8	Arunachal Pradesh, Bihar, Chhattisgarh, Haryana, Himachal Pradesh, Jammu & Kashmir, Jharkhand, Madhya Pradesh, Manipur, Punjab, Rajasthan, Sikkim, Tamil Nadu, Tripura, Uttar Pradesh, Uttaranchal, A & N Islands, Chandigarh, Delhi and Pondicherry
	5-8	Nagaland, West Bengal
	5-7	Assam, Goa, Gujarat, Kerala, Maharashtra, Meghalaya, Mizoram, D&N Haveli, Daman & Diu and Lakshadweep
	6-7	Andhra Pradesh, Karnataka, Orissa
Secondary/ High School	9-10	Arunachal Pradesh, Bihar, Chhattisgarh, Haryana, Himachal Pradesh, Jammu & Kashmir, Jharkhand, Madhya Pradesh, Manipur, Nagaland, Punjab, Rajasthan, Sikkim, Tamil Nadu, Tripura, Uttar Pradesh, Uttaranchal, West Bengal, A & N Islands, Chandigarh, Delhi and Pondicherry
	8-10	Andhra Pradesh, Assam, Goa, Gujarat Karnataka, Kerala, Maharashtra, Meghalaya, Mizoram, Orissa, D&N Haveli, Daman & Diu, Lakshadweep
Higher Secondary/ Junior Colleges	11-12	Andhra Pradesh, Arunachal Pradesh, Assam, Bihar, Chhattisgarh, Goa, Gujarat, Haryana, Himachal Pradesh, Jammu & Kashmir, Karnataka, Kerala, Jharkhand, Madhya Pradesh, Maharashtra, Manipur, Meghalaya, Mizoram, Nagaland, Orissa, Punjab, Rajasthan, Sikkim, Tamil Nadu, Tripura, Uttar Pradesh, Uttaranchal, West Bengal, A&N Islands, Chandigarh, D&N Haveli, Daman & Diu, Delhi, Lakshadweep and Pondicherry
Higher Secondary Classes attached to Degree Colleges	11-12	Andhra Pradesh, Assam, Bihar, Chhattisgarh, Goa, Haryana, Himachal Pradesh, Karnataka, Jharkhand, Maharashtra, Manipur, Meghalaya, Mizoram, Nagaland, Orissa, Punjab, West Bengal, Chandigarh

Fig. 5.1B: Educational Pattern in States and UTs

Notes

1. In India, the secondary stage consists of grades IX and X (relevant ages 14-15) and higher secondary stage consists of grades XI and XII (relevant ages 16-17) (see Figure 1, Annex I). In this paper, both stages have been referred to as secondary education (grades IX to XII, relevant ages 14-17).
2. In India, the same debate has been on since the early 1950s as is clear from the writings of the then Secretary to the Ministry of Education, GOI, Dr. Humayun Kabir that, "Qualitatively, secondary education has suffered from the lack of a clear definition of objectives and scope. Treated either as mere a continuation of primary education or only a preparation for higher education, it cannot at present be regarded as a definite stage making the end of formal education of a specified standard (.) .... Planned to cater only for those who have an intellectual bent of mind, even its emphasis on intellect is one-sided: it tends to test memory at the cost of reasoning and judgment. ...it is modeled primarily to serve the needs of urban life" (January, 1955, p. 195).
3. The 'globalization' phenomenon has compressed time and space. It has resulted in 'new circuits of exchange' of capital, people, goods and knowledge. There is global shift in manufacturing, division of labour, and integration of labour markets creating novel global institutions that increasingly influence the development policies of nations. Pressures resulting from globalization also affect cultural and social values. New forms of inequalities have emerged. Economic issues have dominated the de-bordering process; there is conflict between economic primacy and social values. 'Staying connected' to the globalization process has become a major challenge for many developing nations. In the globalization context, one of the major challenges for education is to discover new ways of 'knowing' so as to make nations effectively participate in the globalization process, while ensuring equitable economic and socio-cultural diversity. There is, indeed, the need for changing the role of the school from an institution of knowledge generation and transmission to an institution, which can respond effectively to the skill requirements of the future world, i.e. making pupils communicate effectively in terms of culture, technology and language.
4. While all the Millennium Development Goals (MDGs) are related to youth, Goals 1, 3, 5, 6 and 8 directly affect the development of youth. In fact, development of youth can increase their engagement in poverty reduction (MDG 1); enable them to act as peer educators and teachers for achieving UPE (MDG 2); support them, particularly young women, to help themselves (MDG 3); enable them to participate in health care programmes to reduce child mortality (MDG 4); make them aware of the reproductive and sexual heath for improving maternal health (MDG 5); engage them in combating HIV/AIDS (MDG 6) and ensuring environmental sustainability (MDG 7); and promote their employability, entrepreneurship and capacity to use ICT for promoting global partnership for development (MDG 8).
5. If we consider the composite measure of poverty (as measured by the new international Multi-dimensional Poverty Index developed by the Oxford Poverty and Human Development Initiative for the UNDP's HDR 2010), about 645 million people or 55 per cent of India's population is poor. The MPI is made up

of ten indicators of education, health and standard of living achievement levels. The ten indicators relates to: years of schooling and child enrollment (education); child mortality and nutrition (health); and electricity, flooring, drinking water, sanitation, cooking fuel and assets (standard of living). Each education and health indicator has a 1/6 weight, each standard of living indicator a 1/18 weight (Shrinivasan, 2010).

6. EFA Global Monitoring Report 2010.
7. The share of rural households and population in India is around 72 per cent and 74 per cent respectively (NSS 64th Round, 2007/08). According to the 64th Round of the NSS (2007/08), the literacy rate in India (population aged 7 years and above) is 71.7 per cent (67% in rural areas and 84.3 per cent in urban areas. The literacy rate ranges from 58 per cent in Bihar to 94 per cent in Kerala.
8. In the NFHS III, the wealth index has been constructed by combining information on 33 household assets and housing characteristics such as ownership of consumer items, type of dwelling, source of water, and availability of electricity into a single wealth index. The household population is divided into five equal groups of 20 per cent each (quintiles) at the national level from 1 (lowest, poorest) to 5 (highest, wealthiest).
9. These include mainly institutional structures, choice of providers, curriculum decisions, teacher recruitments, evaluation systems, certification and financing. Further, it is often argued that, in the developed world and in some of its colonies, public education systems were established from 'top to bottom'—i.e. the foundation of universities came first in the beginning of the 12th century followed by the secondary schools in 15th and 16th centuries, and finally, the public primary schools in the 19th century.
10. Towards the end of the 16th century, secondary schools in Europe and USA were promoting mental discipline of pupils, giving little attention to practical application of knowledge in vocational settings aimed at preparing an elite group of persons trained and educated in liberal arts and prepared to assume leadership roles in any sphere. The curriculum at the secondary stage was dominated by the needs of the socially and economically privileged rather than by the needs of the masses (Briseid and Caillods, 2004). In British India, the East India Company and the subsequent colonial policies in the 19th century promoted new public schools of western learning to serve the higher classes of society with the hope that the educated elites would promote schooling among the rural masses, which later on came to be known as the 'downward filtration theory' (Chaudhary, 2007). In fact, it is argued that, as a by-product of colonization, the European model of education was exported to a large portion of the less developed world. The colonial educational policies are believed to have been largely affecting the human capital formation in these countries even after independence (Foster, 1966; Clignet, 1968). In fact, the present system of secondary education in India can still be called Macaulayian given the selection process and the curricular emphasis for preparing pupils for white collar urban jobs.
11. Towards the late 1980s and in 1990s, the lower secondary stage became part of compulsory basic education in many OECD countries.
12. For example, in East Asian countries, secondary education received greater

attention from 1945 on, with significant increase in public investments for its quantitative and qualitative expansion. Countries like Japan, Korea, Singapore, the Philippines, Malaysia and Thailand, which invested more on secondary education, has now been reaping high dividends because of the resultant broadening of the human capital base.

13. The 'indigenous system of schools' in British India consisted of mainly two types of institutions – i.e. elite religious schools and local elementary schools.
14. The indigenous schools which did not receive grant-in-aid from the colonial government came to be known as 'private un-aided schools'. Provinces of British India responded differently to the colonial government's grant-in-aid policy – viz., aided schools became more common in Bengal province. Some argue that, during the early 1860s, a new system of schooling emerged in India with government universities, a network of affiliated colleges and a number of primary and secondary schools, both aided and un-aided. It was during Lord Curzon's tenure (1899-1905) emphasis was laid on qualitative improvements in schooling and greater state control. The former policies of promoting aided secondary schools and colleges were abandoned in favour of instituting government schools as role models for aided schools.
15. According to SEMIS 2009/10, the total of secondary and higher secondary schools in he country is around 189 thousand (NUEPA, December 2010).
16. Around 92 per cent of both rural and urban households have access to primary schooling provisions at a distance of < 1.0 km; and 91.1 per cent of rural households and 99.1 per cent of urban households have access to middle level schooling provisions at a distance of < 3.0 km (NSS 64th Round).
17. It is the sum total of monetary values of all the items (i.e. goods and services) consumed by the household on domestic account during the reference period. Monthly per capita expenditure (MPCE) is the household consumer expenditure over a period of 30 days divided by household size (NSSO, 2010).
18. At the primary and middle levels, the share of the private un-aided institutions is 17.1 per cent and 7.5 per cent respectively (SSE, 2007/08). In 1973/74, the share of the private unaided institutions in the total institutions at the secondary and higher secondary stage was just 5.59 per cent . Over the years since 1973/74, the relative share of private unaided institutions at the secondary and higher secondary stage declined steadily to 28.87 per cent in 2005/06. In 2007/08, the share of aided institutions in the total institutions at the secondary stage was 26.11 per cent ; and it was 30.27 per cent at the higher secondary stage. According to the NSS 64th Round (2007/08), nearly 18 per cent of secondary and higher secondary level enrolment was in private un-aided institutions.
19. It seems that states like West Bengal and Bihar have not furnished complete data on private un-aided institutions at the secondary and higher secondary levels as one would expect their presence, at least, in urban areas.
20. It may be noted that, in this paper, the analysis of the physical access to secondary and higher secondary schooling provisions does not take into account varying infrastructure, teaching-learning and related facilities (i.e. deviations from the laid down standards) existing across individual institutions, which are essential elements of access to schooling in any society.

21. Partly, may be because of the geophysical features of some of these states and UTs.
22. These 17 states and union territories share more than 94 per cent of the country's population (Census, 2001).
23. Following the methodology of the UNDP, Rani has constructed the 'secondary education development index' using three indicators – i.e. institutions, teachers and enrolment; and the 'educational performance index' has been constructed using four indicators – i.e. (i) transition rate from upper primary to secondary, (ii) cumulative dropout rate from Grades I-X, (iii) per cent age of students appeared in the secondary board examination to the enrolment, and (iv) per cent age of passouts (in the appeared students).
24. The Apparent Cohort Method has been used to estimate the dropout rate in SSE, 2007/08, which is relatively crude.
25. For example, in 1916/17, India had a larger share of population enrolled in secondary schools as compared to France and Japan (Chaudhary, 2007).
26. It is, however, interesting to note that, unlike elementary and higher education, the respective responsibilities of the Centre and States are not clearly defined for secondary education. This has seriously constrained the development of secondary education in the country.
27. The fist official policy document, the National Policy on Education (1968), emphasized more on increasing access to secondary education, including increasing facilities for technical and vocational education at this stage. Moreover, even after a little over two decades of policy emphasis for a uniform system of 12 years of schooling (8+2+2), 7 + 3 + 2 system of school education continues in several states (see Figure 1B, Annex I).
28. Besides, the Central Government has committed to set up 6,000 model secondary schools during the eleventh five year plan (2007-12). It proposes to set up another 500 NVs, 500 more KVs, 2500 schools in KV template in educationally backward areas and another 2,500 schools in Public-Private Partnership (PPP) mode.
29. The CABE constituted two committees on secondary education: (i) CABE Committee on Universalization of Secondary Education; and (ii) CABE Committee on Girls' Education and Common School System in 2004, which submitted their reports in June 2005.
30. It is pertinent to mention here that, for the first time, 'universal secondary education' (USE) as an emerging development agenda was articulated and debated at NIEPA in a national conference organized by Professor Marmar Mukhopadhyay in 2001. The conference not only provided alternative secondary education development paths (in terms of development scenarios) but also provided important inputs to the Tenth Plan formulation process and the CABE Committee on Secondary Education (2005). In a way, historically, the USE movement in the country began at NIEPA in 2001.
31. For details, see the *Framework for Implementation of the Rashtriya Madhyamik Shiksha Abhiyan* (RMSA), Department of School Education and Literacy, MHRD, GOI, 2009.
32. It may be noted that not much information is currently available about the development interventions being pursued by states in secondary education.

33. Positioning secondary and higher secondary education in a country simply means assigning priority to these sub-sectors in the policy planning process and determining the optimum size of these sub-sectors through strategic planning for increasing access and relevance.
34. Assuming 75 per cent success in the SSA, the CABE Committee had projected that the total enrolment in grades IX-X would increase to 28 million in 2007/08 and 34.20 million at the end of the 11th plan period (2011/12). In 2007/08, the actual enrolment in grades IX-X (including the repeaters) in India was 28.22 million (SSE, 2007-08).
35. Several major states like Kerala, Maharashtra, Tamil Nadu, Punjab, Haryana and West Bengal have registered ether negative or low growth of grade VIII enrolment during 2005/6 and 2007/08 (see Table 5.5, Annex I).
36. The large size of the projected GER at the secondary stage in Madhya Pradesh and Uttar Pradesh is because of low base and large change during the first four years starting from 2004/05.
37. The general understanding of the scope of 'capacity development' and the strategies to scale up the related interventions have been narrowly conceived in various reform programmes in India. Broadly, capacity development is seen as a *process* by which individuals, groups, organizations and societies create, enhance and maintain their capacities over time (Caillods and Grauwe (2006). It refers to organizational and technical abilities, relationships and values that enable countries, organizations, groups and individuals at all levels of society to carry out functions effectively and achieve their development objectives. It has human resource, organizational and institutional dimensions.
38. School improvement, school wide or whole school or comprehensive school reform calls for to develop and implement their own improvement plans mainly focusing on identifying learning potentials and barriers to learning and creating enabling environment for effective pedagogy as well as staying connected to its external environment.

6

Secondary Education

From Neglect to Universalization

Marmar Mukhopadhyay and *Sweta Singh*

After almost six decades of neglect and deprivation. There seems to be some hope for secondary education. There is a paradigm shift in the focus on secondary education with the constitution of the CABE Committee on Universalization of Secondary Education in 2005 and subsequent centrally sponsored scheme Rashtriya Madhyamik Siksha Abhiyan (RMSA) (National Secondary Education Mission) in the pattern of Sarva Siksha Abhiyan (SSA) in elementary education. RMSA was formulated for implementing universalization of secondary education in mission mode. There was also a dramatic shift in central funding of secondary education from a usual about Rs.2000 Crore to a quantum jump of Rs. 39,000 Crores.

We have done a detailed documentation of developments in secondary education since independence earlier (Mukhopadhyay, 2007). There is yet another authentic documentation on development in secondary education in chapter 5 (by Dr. Biswal) in this book. For brevity, we'll flag, in this chapter, a few issues in secondary education, especially the issue of universalization of secondary education.

Evolution of Secondary Education through Policies and Plans

India got her first educational policy after 21 years (1947 to 1968) of independence; second policy was enacted after another 18 years (1968 to 1986). Though there is a sea change in India and the world scenarios during the last more than quarter of a century, Indian leadership is still to appreciate the need for a comprehensive third educational policy. Destiny of Indian education has largely been guided by Commissions and Committees, or of late by executive decisions of the Cabinet especially during the last decade.

Right at the dawn of independence, India rejected the Sargent Report (1944) largely out of new found enthusiasm and urgency of transforming the face of the nation. Government of India constituted a 10-member University Education Commission chaired by Dr. Sarvepalli Radhakrishnan, then Spalding Professor of Eastern Religions and Ethics at the University of Oxford (December, 1948–August 1949) to lay down the road map of development of university education. It was immediately followed by a Commission on Secondary Education under the chairmanship of Dr. A. Lakshmanaswami Mudaliar, a distinguished scientist and vice-chancellor of Madras University that recommended, among others 3 years of higher secondary education with multiple streams after 8 years of common schooling. The next important landmark was the constitution of the 16-member Education Commission under the chairmanship of Prof. D.S. Kothari, then Chairman of the University Grants Commission in 1964. One of the most distinguished thinker-educationist, Sri J.P. Naik, and then Head of the Department of Educational Planning, Administration and Finance, Gokhale Institute of Politics and Economics, Poona was the Member Secretary. The Commission submitted its report in 1966. The terms of reference, as well as the structure of the report of Kothari Commission, was substantially different; it looked into education as a whole and dealt with all the levels of education—primary to higher and professional education. As a result, it looked into the inter-structural linkages within education. The Commission recommended further structural changes in education. The current structure of 10+2+3—ten years of common schooling followed by two years of senior secondary education through diversified curriculum in several streams and three years of undergraduate education was recommended by the Commission. Thus, new structure demanded 15, instead of 14, years of education for graduation.

The 12-year school education has been divided into four stages -primary, upper primary, secondary and senior secondary comprising five, three, two and two years of education, respectively. Although India adopted a common pattern of 10+2 years of schooling, the internal structure of school education still varies. In many states, primary education comprises the first four years. In certain other states, primary and upper primary classes are not differentiated and comprise seven years of schooling followed by three years of secondary education. However, the common pattern is ten years of schooling leading to the first qualifying public examination followed by two years of senior secondary education as recommended by the Education Commission (1964-66).

Commission to Policy

The first National Policy on Education of 1968 was primarily based on the recommendations of Kothari Commission, and it supported the newly recommended structure and diversification. The National Policy on Education 1986 also extensively dealt with the secondary education, particularly the contents and processes of education. It found a place in the Programme of Action both in 1986 and in the revised version in 1992.

The National Policy of Education 1986 envisaged the building of a national system of education in which all students would have access to education of a comparable quality along with providing condition for success. It re-emphasized the need for developing a common school system. The Policy stated that access to secondary education would be widened with the emphasis on enrolment of girls, SCs and STs; particularly in Science, Commerce and Vocational streams. The Boards of the Secondary Education were recommended autonomy so that their ability to improve the quality of secondary education is enhanced. Vocational Education was to become a distinct stream intended to prepare student for identified occupation, spanning several areas of activity.

Following the NPE 1986, many new centrally sponsored schemes (CSS) were launched. Navodaya Vidyalayas (NVs) and National Open Schools (NOS) were also conceived and implemented during this period. The existing schemes of Integrated Education for Disabled Children (IEDC), Educational Technology and Computer Literacy (CLASS project) were strengthened. The Programme of Action 1992 specified programmes for providing adequate playground facilities, construction of additional classrooms and provision of laboratory facilities, improvement in curriculum, the textual material, teaching practices, examination/evaluation methods and for the improvement of pre-service and in-service training programmes. Many of these concerns continue to remain important, and need to be addressed with strategic interventions.

The Indian Parliament passed a Bill providing for free and compulsory education to all children aged 6-14 on 27th August 2009. The notification to enforce Article 21A in the Constitution and the corresponding legislation as 'Right of Children to Free and Compulsory Education Act 2009' has come into effect from 1st April 2010. Just as this bill came far too late for the country, it came truncated at both ends. It failed to recognize critical importance of pre-primary education for its contribution and impact on universalization of basic education. It also failed to recognize that without secondary and higher secondary education—a qualifying point, elementary education come cropper for young children. At 14, they are, at best literate, neither skilled nor qualified for any meaningful occupation. Gujarat's Children's University provides an interesting model of comprehensive prenatal to university education.

Policies to Plans

The five year plans are complimentary to the national policies. Plans provide the implementation mechanism. Furthermore, plans compliment the wide gaps between the policies enacted after decades.

During the first seven plans of 37 years including two years of plan holidays, emphasis was on expansion of educational facilities, often very poor. Huge proportion of dropout and grade repetition (stagnation) costing the institutional efficiency and effectiveness failed to attract the attention of the planners to the need for quality. The accumulated system deficiency and one-dimensional planning, namely access without quality, has taken its heavy toll on public exchequer as well as in the life of new generation learners. Even after, 67 years of independence, nationally not more than quarter of the children admitted in grade 1 complete 10th grade certification.

The 8th FYP (1992-97) followed the NPE 1986. This plan saw introduction of large number of centrally sponsored schemes like vocationalization of education, integrated education for disabled children (IDC), computer literacy, education technology, and science education, hostel facilities for girls, environmental education etc. The 8th FYP regarded vocational education as a priority area with reference to employment orientation and the need to establish meaningful linkages between the world of work and the world of learning. During the 9th FYP (1997-2002), the focus has been on reducing disparities, renewal of curricula with emphasis on vocationalization and employment oriented courses, diversification of the open learning system, reorganization of teacher training and the greater use of information and communication technology particularly computers, hostel facilities for girls, minorities' education, integrated education for the disabled, free education for girls, etc. have been some of the other issues in the secondary education that received attention.

An interesting feature of Indian policies and plans is its repeated emphasis on vocational education while turning a blind eye at its massive failure. The very positioning of vocational education as second rung education and a separate stream for students who are 'not good enough for academic courses' has defeated the very purpose. That it is wrong formulation from the angle of science of human learning has never been realized. According to science of human learning, 'application' is a higher order learning compared to knowledge and understanding that characterize academic courses. Vocational education is skill education, education in application of knowledge and understanding. Hence, it is possible to argue that vocational education demands higher order cognitive skills than academic education. It is the propensity and potentiality of the students that make them good enough for so called 'academic' or vocational courses. Vocational courses need to be put at the same pedestal, if not higher, with the academic courses. An illustrative case is that of the NOS. In 1994-95, National Open School allowed students to choose vocational subjects with academic subjects[1]; NOS also informed its potential students about the requirements of combinations and number of subjects by various universities. The net result was almost five times jump in choice of vocational courses by students of NOS. It also gave them an opportunity for skill development while pursuing their qualifying study. However, this innovation was discontinued later.

Although, secondary education was expanding with every five year plans, concept of universal secondary education had to wait till 2001 for the first articulation.

Universalize Secondary Education

The issue of USE was first raised in a Conference in 2001 hosted by NIEPA; it was followed by a paper in 2004 by the author creating alternative scenarios on demand for secondary education in 2010 due to success in SSA; this paper was circulated to the members of CABE Committee on USE. At the invitation of the CABE Committee, author chaired the CABE Subcommittee that drafted the report on USE in 2005.* Full report can be accessed at (http://www.teindia.nic.in/files/reports/ccr/cabe/use.pdf).

Plans in the Post CABE Report

In the 10th FYP, stress was laid on the expansion of secondary education. Greater access and reducing disparities were the bywords. The key theme of the plan was imparting of quality education. For this, a composite Centrally Sponsored Scheme (CSS) of 'Quality Improvement in Schools' was introduced by converging existing schemes (Improvement of Science Education in Schools, Promotion of Yoga, Environmental Orientation to School Education, National Population Education Project, and International Science Olympiads). During this period, NCERT unveiled the National Curriculum Framework in 2005 in an effort to give new directions to improve all aspects of school education.

The 11th FYP had proposed to raise the minimum level of education to class X and accordingly universalize access to secondary education (GER in secondary education was targeted to increase from 40 per cent in 2004-05 to 65% by 2011-12). It also aimed to ensure good quality secondary education with focus on Science, Mathematics, and English; and a reduction in disparities in gender, social, and regional gaps in enrolments, dropouts, and school retention.

Public spending on education saw an increase during the Eleventh Five-Year Plan Period (2007-2012) and expenditure on education as a percentage of gross domestic products (GDP) rose from 3.3 per cent (2004-05) to over 4 per cent (2011-12). Secondary education however received the least and

---

* For details, please see note at the end of the Chapter 1.

clocked 25 per cent while 43 per cent of the public expenditure on education was incurred for elementary education and 32 per cent for higher education.

Thus USE has been made an important goal so as to achieve universal access by 2017 and universal retention by 2020. To meet these, the Rashtriya Madhyamik Shiksha Abhiyan (RMSA), a centrally sponsored scheme was launched in 2009-10.

Rashtriya Madhyamik Siksha Abhiyan

Government of India has launched a comprehensive centrally sponsor scheme called 'Rashtriya Madhyamik Shiksha Abhiyan (RMSA)', in March 2009 with the objective to make good quality secondary education available, accessible and affordable to all young persons, irrespective of gender, socio-economic condition, disability, geographical and other barriers. The interventions supported under RMSA included (i) upgrading of upper primary schools to secondary schools; (ii) strengthening of existing secondary schools; (iii) providing additional classrooms, science laboratories, libraries, computer rooms, art, craft and culture rooms, toilet blocks and water facilities in schools; (iv) providing in-service training of teachers; and (v) providing for major repairs of school buildings and residential quarters for teachers.

In addition to the RMSA, five centrally sponsored schemes were launched during the Eleventh Plan: (i) setting up of model schools; (ii) setting up girls' hostels in secondary and senior secondary schools; (iii) National Scheme of Incentive to Girls for Secondary Education (NSIGSE); (iv) Inclusive Education for the Disabled at the Secondary Stage (IEDSS); and (v) National Merit-cum-Means Scholarship scheme (NMMS). In addition, the ongoing scheme of ICT in Schools was revised.

The present aim is to have a secondary school of acceptable norms and standards within 5 km of every habitation in the country, and similarly to have a higher secondary school within 8 km. RMSA has a funding pattern of 75:25 between Centre and States (90:10 for Special Category and NE States), was launched in 2009-10. It was proposed that all the ongoing Centrally Sponsored Schemes namely, ICT@ schools; Integrated Education for Disabled Children (IEDC); Strengthening of Boarding and Hostel facilities for Girl Students of Secondary and Higher Secondary Schools; and Quality improvement in schools would be subsumed in the new Scheme.

Despite all the efforts, combined GERs at the secondary and senior secondary (Classes IX-XII) levels were recorded at 49.3 per cent at the end of the 11th FYP. Further there is a significant dip in GERs from secondary (62.7%) to senior secondary level (35.9%) for all categories.

The 12th FYP claims that substantial progress has been made through this scheme as against a target of enrolling an additional 3.2 million students,

2.4 million additional students were enrolled in secondary schools during the XI Plan period.

The 12th FYP document proposes that the focus will remain on access, equity, quality and governance of education, but the greatest emphasis would be on improving learning outcomes at all levels.

The document acknowledges that we need to move towards universalization of opportunity to attend secondary schooling of adequate quality. The objectives for secondary education are laid down as:

- Achieve near-universal enrolment in secondary education, with the GER exceeding 90 per cent by 2017;
- Raise the GER at the higher secondary level to 65 per cent by 2017;
- Reduce Dropout rate to less than 25 per cent by 2017;
- Ensure quality secondary education with relevant skills including basic competency in mathematics, science, languages and communication;
- Implement common curricula and syllabi of nationally acceptable standards for Science, Mathematics and English in all schools in the country.
- Develop life skills including skills of critical and constructive thinking, use of ICT, organization and leadership, and community services.

Several initiatives have been taken to support moving towards universalization of secondary education. An initiative has been undertaken by NUEPA to create a comprehensive database on secondary education. This would aid the Government to manage educational expansion in a planned manner. School-based Annual Information System, SEMIS, has been collecting data on physical infrastructure and facilities of schools across the country, availability of teachers, enrolment and academic performance of students, professional development of teachers, etc. Extensive use of Information Communication Technology in management of secondary education has finally taken shape and will help in effective distribution of resources.

Evaluation Reforms

Assessment and evaluation pattern at secondary and senior secondary levels has been critiqued in many reports, policy documents (NPE 1986, Learning Without Burden,1992) and now the RTE Act also mandates child friendly systems of assessment. Still, reforms in the approach to assessment have been few and far between. Lately, class X and XII board examinations were being blamed for a spate of stress related problems among students. Consequently, the National Focus Group on Examination Reforms recommended bringing about structural and procedural change to reduce stress and anxiety among students (Position paper, National Focus Group on Examination Reforms,

2006). It suggested making the tenth grade board exam optional; presenting results through a wider range of performance parameters (absolute marks/ grades, percentile rank); and reforming 'paper-setting'. CBSE was quick to follow a few of these recommendations and has brought in landmark reforms by strengthening School Based Assessment and introducing Continuous and Comprehensive Evaluation at secondary level (Oct 2009) to cover both scholastic and co-scholastic aspects in assessment on an ongoing basis. In its policy to gradually fade out Board Examinations at class X, it has made them optional since 2011. Further, results are now being presented as Grades rather than marks (effective from 2009-10). CCE has been adopted by several other state boards of education. COBSE has taken serious interest in this innovative school based evaluation. These reforms have acted like a lever and focused the attention of teachers as well as students on coscholastic domain. The reforms in examination and evaluation have also impacted the entrance to institutes of higher education.

Changing Pattern of Entrance to Institutes of Higher Education

In an attempt to streamline the admission procedure to higher education, the Ministry of HRD proposed a common system for common admission into professional institutions in February 2010. A new format for admissions into Engineering Programmes has been forwarded after discussions among the councils of IITs, NITs and IIITs. Entrance to all engineering courses from the year 2013 onwards will be through Joint Entrance Examination (JEE). Care has been taken to give weightages to the performance of candidates in the class XII boards during this selection procedure. Similarly, for entry into Medical colleges, a common entrance test National Eligibility-cum-Entrance Test (NEET) from 2013 has been set forth thus eliminating the stress caused to students who had been appearing in multiple medical entrance examinations.

A common National Aptitude Test (NAT) has also been proposed for students seeking admissions to central Universities. NAT would test students' communication and analytical skills and its results along with class XII scores would decide the merit of students.

Renewed thrust on Vocational Education

Recognizing that only 5 per cent of the Indian population of 19–24 age group has acquired some sort of skills through vocational education, the 12th FYP has a renewed thrust on Vocational Education. The vision is to integrate and closely align vocational curriculum to the academic curriculum and contain modules on various generic and specific vocational skills for which industry should be involved. For this revamping the curricula of vocational courses to national occupation standard brought out by the Sector Skill Councils (SSCs) that determine the minimum levels of competencies for various vocations has been planned. National Vocational Education Qualifications Framework (currently being undertaken as a pilot project in Haryana) is to create clear educational pathways from school to higher education level and provide more options to students to choose vocational modules. Further, Vocational education at the secondary level would be aligned with skills training under the Ministry of Labour through Industrial Training Centres and modular training programmes as well as short-term training provided through National Skills Development Corporation (NSDC).

The 12th FYP conceives quality education by ensuring that all secondary and higher secondary schools conform to minimum standards in facilities and quality; overhauling of outdated curricula and syllabi; promoting examination reforms that would focus on problem-solving, critical thinking and reasoning skills and decrease the emphasis on rote memorization; promoting professional cadre development in education; and putting in place a *School Quality Assessment and Accreditation System* that would be established to cover all aspects of school functioning, including scholastic and co-scholastic domains, physical infrastructure, faculty management, school leadership, learning outcomes and satisfaction of pupils and their parents/guardians.

Some Concerns

Quality concerns in Education at Secondary Level

The experience of UEE has taught us valuable lessons. Instead of focusing just on providing access to schools to achieve USE, the vision of quality schooling should not be lost. Current policies reflect the same. But it is also important to take stock of the achievements of students currently moving out of the system.

Council of Boards of Secondary Education (COBSE, 2005) declared the total pass percentage of regular students of all Boards is 63.36 per cent. The pass percentage ranged from a high of [77.80%] by Boards of Tamil Nadu and Tripura to a low of [32.60%]. Madhya Pradesh. When this 63.36 per cent pass rate is superimposed on drop out till Xth grade, it provides indications of system effectiveness. With estimated 62 per cent drop out, number of students who take Xth board examination is 38; 63.36 per cent pass rate at the Xth indicates that only 24 out of children admitted in class 1 complete qualifying marks of Xth level schooling. Besides the concern on the numbers, the wide regional disparity in the system effectiveness is also a cause for worry. For example, the success rate in Kerala is 57 per cent (57 students out of 100 children admitted in class 1 complete and pass out of 10th Board examination) compared to less than 10 per cent in Bihar.

Furthermore, the reported percentage of success should be adjusted for mass copying in board examination as reported in the newspapers. (http://indiatoday.intoday.in/story/State+board+exams+marred+by+rampant+cheating/1/88997.html)

To give another example, when the Kalyan Singh government in Uttar Pradesh had introduced an anti-cheating rule in 1992 to prevent mass-cheating in Uttar Pradesh, the pass rate in High School exam fell from 57 per cent in 1991 to 14.7 per cent in 1992 (Kingdon, 2007).

The quality of education in Government run schools needs to be strengthened. Enrollment in private run schools in certain states has shown a steady increase over the years. It indicates lack of faith of parents in the quality of schooling provided in Government run schools. Today parents at all levels aspire to send their children to private schools or *English schools*. PROBE Report concludes that private run schools are becoming popular in states where the Government run schools are not performing well. As evidence, in *rural Himachal Pradesh, for instance, there is a good deal of purchasing power but the government schools function well, so that there are few private schools. In central Bihar, by contrast, poverty is endemic, yet private schools can be found in many villages due to the dysfunctional state of government schools (PROBE Team, 1999, p. 102).*

Inequalities in Secondary Education

Equality in education depends both upon both access and opportunity. Despite phenomenal expansion secondary education, this growth has not ensured that these institutions are within reach of the poorest and the weakest. Biswal, in the previous chapter substantiates this by reporting that, *'the availability of middle and secondary level schooling provisions in close proximity of households is relatively less for lower decile classes of the monthly per capita expenditure (MPCE). For example, in rural India, while 38.8 per cent of poor households (belonging to the lowest MPCE decile class) have access to a secondary school at a distance of less than 2 kilometres, 58.8 per cent of the rich households (belonging to the highest MPCE decile class) have access to secondary schools within the same distance (NSSO, 2010).* He adds, *'with 34.6 per cent of secondary institutions and 34.4 per cent of higher secondary institutions being private un-aided institutions (Government of India (SES), 2007/08), the poor may be economically as well as geographically excluded from secondary schooling facilities in the country.'*

It is difficult to measure in tangible terms the inequalities being created by denying equal opportunities to succeed.

Shadow Schooling

The perception that schools are not able to deliver has led to the rapid expansion of private run coaching business that may be termed as *shadow schooling/*

shadow education. An Asian Development Bank report (2012) claims that, in India, a whopping 60 per cent of primary school children and up to 83 per cent students in high schools receive private tutoring. The commercially run out-of-school-hours coaching/ tuitions are embraced for two main reasons: coaching to develop specific test-taking skills for entrance, aptitude and scholarship examinations (e.g. JEE coaching, Medical or Law coaching), and coaching to improve academic performance in particular subject areas (Board examinations and across different grades).

There are a number of implications of these private coaching. As the ability to access such classes depends solely on the ability to pay, it is increasing and perpetuating inequality by giving an edge in test taking skills to those who can afford. Attending coaching classes beyond school hours has become a norm in classes XI and XII and this is preventing students in engaging in sports, literary and other developmental activities. Also the existence of these coaching institutes questions the validity of class XII boards and schools itself.

There have been attempts to curb this growing menace by bringing in changes in school assessment and entrance to higher education. While the impact of these changes must be deliberated upon, it is also important to examine the reasons for popularity of tuition classes. What is it that our schools are not delivering? Why children across all grades and enrolled in all types of schools (Government as well as private) are lining up in front of tutors. Parents across all strata (even those who can ill afford these fees) aspire to send their children to private tutors.

Conclusion

School education has expanded significantly over the years. Along with the lateral expansion, there have been several innovative interventions to improve quality of secondary education. During this period, a national system of school education has steadily unfolded with increasing awareness for standardization and quality.

However, till the end of IX FYP, India was hesitant to fully respond to people's aspiration of secondary education for all. CABE committee report on Universalization of Secondary Education is a watershed. It's a massive task and may take several years to actually achieve universal secondary education. That the issue has been registered in the cognitive map of Indian education policy and planning process is a major step forward to universalization of secondary education.

Notes

1. The first author of this paper was then Chairman of NOS.

7

Revamping Student Assessment

A Paradigm Shift from Cognitive to Holistic Assessment

Haseen Taj

Assessment of student learning is the process of evaluating the extent to which participants in education have developed their knowledge, understanding and abilities. Most fundamentally, assessment seeks to *support and improve student learning.* It is the result of a movement toward accountability and involves a paradigm shift from the traditional view of what teachers provide (inputs) to a concern for what students actually learn, do, and achieve (outputs). Assessment is an ongoing process of setting high expectations for student learning, measuring progress toward established learning outcomes, and providing a basis for reflection, discussion and feedback to improve academic programmes. It is a systematic and cyclic process that makes expectations and standards explicit and public.

In education, 'assessment' describes any process that appraise an individual's knowledge, understanding, abilities or skills. There are many different forms of assessment, serving a variety of purposes. These include:

- promoting student learning by providing the student with feedback, normally to help improve his/her performance
- evaluating student knowledge, understanding, abilities or skills
- Providing a mark or grade that enables a student's performance to be established. The mark or grade may also be used to make progress decisions
- enabling the public (including employers), and higher education providers, to know that an individual has attained an appropriate level of achievement that reflects the academic standards set by the awarding institution and agreed UK norms, including the frameworks for higher education qualifications. This may include demonstrating fitness to practice or meeting other professional requirements.

Our present system of assessment is too narrow, passive and cognitive which only assesses the students' competence partially, what is required is active and holistic assessment approach which is capable of assessing the wholesome achievement and personality of the students.

Assessment need not take time away from learning. Assessment can be learning experiences in themselves. Active assessment strategies enhance students' understanding of contents and promote skills. The ability to see the big picture, developing effective oral and written reports (communication skills) and ability to work with peers are the skills promoted by active assessment. There are multiple forms of assessment that needs careful examination.

How to Use Assessment Strategies

Assessment need not take time away from learning; assessments can be learning experiences in themselves. Active assessment strategies enhance student content understanding and promote skills that will be beneficial to students throughout their lives. The ability to see the big picture, develop effective oral and written reports and the ability to work cooperatively with their peers are skills that are promoted by active assessment.

Strategies of Assessment

Some of the major strategies that can be used for holistic assessment of students are: Attitude survey, Concept Tests, concept mapping, project based learning, oral reporting, scoring rubrics, co-operative learning, peer review, jigsaws, role playing, portfolios, pre-testing, class participation, practice exams, and self assessment.

Portfolios

Portfolios are concrete and somewhat personal expressions of growth and development. Portfolios document student learning and improve student metacognition.

Showcase Portfolios

A showcase portfolio is a limited portfolio where a student is only allowed to present a few pieces of evidence to demonstrate mastery of learning objectives. Especially useful in a laboratory course, a showcase portfolio might ask a student to include items that represent: (i) their best work; (ii) their most interesting work; (iii) their most improved work; (iv) their most disappointing work; (v) and their favourite work. Items could be homework assignments, examinations, laboratory reports, news clippings, or other creative work. An introductory letter that describes why each particular item was included and what it demonstrates makes this type of portfolio especially insightful to the instructor.

Checklist Portfolios

A checklist portfolio is composed of a predetermined number of items. Often, a course syllabus will have a predetermined number of assignments for students to complete. A checklist portfolio takes advantage of such a format and gives the students the choice of a number of different assignment selections to complete in the course of learning science. For example, instead of assigning exactly 12 sets of problems from the end of each text chapter, students could have the option of replacing several assignments with relevant magazine article reviews or laboratory reports that clearly demonstrate mastery of a given learning objective. Additionally, class quizzes and tests can become part of the portfolio if that is what is on the checklist of items to be included. A sample checklist might require a portfolio to have 10 correctly worked problem sets, two magazine article summaries, two laboratory reports, and two examinations in addition to self-reflection paragraphs where the student decides which objectives most closely fit which assignments.

Open-Format Portfolios

An open-format for a portfolio generally provides the most insightful view of a student's level of achievement. In an open-format portfolio, students are allowed to submit anything they wish to be considered as evidence for mastery of a given list of learning objectives. In addition to the traditional items like exams and assignments, students can include reports on museum visits, analysis of amusement park rides, imaginative homework problems, and other sources from the "real world". Although these portfolios are more difficult for the student to create and for the instructor to score, many students report that they are very proud of the time spent on such a portfolio.

Use in Large Enrollment Courses

Portfolios can be used successfully in large courses provided there is an infrastructure for students and instructors to utilize. Most importantly, the format of each item in the portfolio needs to be in a similar format; the use of cover sheets, forms, and prescribed notebooks often helps. Second, students' creativity must be sacrificed to some degree for the sake of uniformity. This can be accomplished by assigning student tasks that have fewer multiple-correct solutions. Finally, if graduate teaching assistants are involved, each assistant should take responsibility for a particular series of learning goals, thus becoming an expert and seeing all student submissions. If announced to the students, this helps curtail academic dishonesty and variation in scoring.

Analysis

Because each portfolio is individualized, student assessment must be compiled by looking at the portfolio's contents relative to the course learning objectives.

Each piece of evidence should be graded according to a predetermined scheme. The items can be scored discretely as a 0, 1, 2, or 3 based on the grader's judgment about the student's presentation as related to the stated learning goals. (A larger scale can be used, but the reliability of different faculty giving the student the same score decreases.)

Assessing Project-based Learning

"Student projects are culminating experiences, activities designed to bring together a number of strands in a unit. As culminating activities, projects often consist of higher-order objectives, which are integrative in nature."

Project-based learning provides students with the opportunity to tackle real world situations that by their nature have no easy solution, or have no solution at the present time. Project-based learning helps students to understand that sometimes one needs to be satisfied with asking the right questions rather than focusing on the "right" answers. Students learn to manage their time, interpret data sets, resolve value conflicts between group members and prepare and communicate the results of their investigation. In other words, they will use their experiences to learn to manage real life situations. Problem-based learning module engages students in defining a situation, gathering information on what is known and not known about the situation, developing an Earth Systems analysis and reporting on their recommendations. Because the tasks involved in Project-based learning are so varied there are several methods that may be used together to assess student learning.

Assessing Oral Reports

We all have a sense of what constitutes a good presentation and what constitutes one that is less than satisfactory. Assessing an oral presentation can be a very subjective endeavor, but with a bit of forethought, instructors can ease student anxiety surrounding oral reports and make the process of preparing for an oral report a valuable learning experience for the student. Organizing what elements need to be in the oral report also makes the task of assessing and substantiating student work easier.

Organization: Although oral reports will vary in length and depth of detail they generally follow a set structure. The advice regarding oral reports that I once recieved from a seasoned faculty member was, "Tell them what you are going to tell them; tell them; then tell them what you told them". Very good advice, but let's see if we can make it a little more specific. Good oral reports usually begin with the equivalent of a topic paragraph, a statement that will draw the listener into the substance of the talk. Then data is presented to support the assertions made in the opening stage of the report. Finally the report draws to a conclusion with a summary and closing statement.

Content: Oral reports usually have accompanying overhead transparencies or PowerPoint presentation that provides the audience with visuals of data, supporting evidence and conclusions. The ability of students to make appropriate choices in what data they show varies with their experience in developing oral reports. This process involves several higher-order process skills. They must evaluate the data or information they have collected, make choices about what findings are and are not essential to the presentation and then organize their thoughts.

Presentation: Are students presenting oral reports that are highly organized and well researched? Are their presentations "stream of consciousness" reports that move from point to point without structure, or are they reading from a written page or from the power point slides.

Attitude Surveys

While attitudinal surveys may take many forms and address a range of issues, they typically consist of a series of statements that students are asked to express their agreement or disagreement (using a scale.)

This type of survey provides valuable information on student perceptions of their classroom experience. This includes general attitudes toward the course, the discipline, and their own learning. The results from this survey can also help you identify elements in your course which best support student learning. An attitudinal survey (also known as an affective survey) can provide information on student perceptions (emotions, feeling, and attitudes) of their classroom experience. For example it can reveal perceptions on:

- the content of a course
- specific components of a course
- course components which aid or are detrimental to learning
- the effects of course innovations

Attitudinal surveys may also focus on students' needs in taking a course, how well those needs are met, student interest in or appreciation for the subject matter or field, student confidence in their ability to perform in a course, or their beliefs about the nature of the discipline itself, e.g.

- the nature of a discipline (chemistry, physics, mathematics, engineering)
- the nature of learning within a discipline
- their ability to learn within a course
- useful strategies for learning within a course or discipline
- their own learning style or preferences for learning

Suggestions

Attitudinal surveys can be used at the beginning of a course to identify the ways students perceive they learn best or to determine their attitudes toward the course or discipline. This information can be used to adapt instructional strategies. Another use is a comparison between attitudes at the beginning of the semester (pretest) and again at the end of the semester (posttest). This allows the instructor to discover the impact of their course on student perceptions on the variety of topics mentioned above. They also can be used at any point during the semester to make corrections to existing curricula or methods in a course.

The surveys can be taken in any location and require little time. A very long survey with eighty or so items usually requires no more than 20 minutes. Gender, ethnicity, major, year in school, and previous coursework can all be included in a survey.

Another feature that makes data collection and analysis easier is to use an optical scanning form and scanner (e.g. Scantron). This allows these data to be directly imported into a spreadsheet or statistical application for analysis.

Concept Maps

A concept map is a diagram of nodes, each containing concept labels, which are linked together with directional lines, also labeled. The concept nodes are arranged in hierarchical levels that move from general to specific concepts. Concept Maps assist students in "seeing the big picture".

Concept maps assess how well students see the "big picture". They have been used for over 25 years to provide a useful and visually appealing way of illustrating students' conceptual knowledge.

Description

A concept map is a two-dimensional, hierarchical node-link diagram that depicts the structure of knowledge within a scientific discipline as viewed by a student, an instructor or an expert in a field or sub-field. The map is composed of concept labels, each enclosed in a box or oval; a series of labeled linking lines, and an inclusive, general-to-specific organization. By reading the map from top to bottom, an instructor can:

1. gain insight into the way students view a scientific topic;
2. examine the valid understandings and misconceptions students hold; and
3. assess the structural complexity of the relationships students depict.

In addition to these applications in assessment, faculty have also used concept maps to organize their ideas in preparation for instruction, as a graphic organizer during class, and as a way to encourage students to reflect on their own knowledge and to work together and share their understandings in collaborative group settings.

Limitations

Concept maps provide a useful and visually appealing way of depicting the structure of conceptual knowledge that people have stored in long-term memory. As a result, they offer a readily accessible way of assessing how well students see "the big picture." They are not designed to tap into the kind of process knowledge that students also need to solve novel problems or for the routine application of algorithmic solutions. Because they probe an individual's or a group's cognitive organization, they are very idiosyncratic and difficult to compare, either among individuals or groups, or across time for the same individuals or groups.

Scoring Rubrics

"Learning increases when learners have a sense of what they are setting out to learn, a statement of explicit standards they must meet and a way of seeing what they have learned." (Loaker, Cromwell and O'Brien 1986). Scoring Rubrics help students focus on content, and Instructional Rubrics guide them in developing presentations, written and oral reports. One of the usual student psychology is that students will focus on learning material that will impact their grade. Rubrics are a way to make explicit our expectations of what students will need to know and be able to do in order to receive a given grade. Rubrics help instructors to develop clear and attainable learning objectives for their students and if provided to students prior to the activity, serve to guide their efforts.

Scoring Rubrics Focus and Promote Learning

Assessment sometimes carries a sense of the mysterious for students. They may be told to take notes in class, read the chapter and answer the questions at the end, but they may get few specifics regarding what material will be assessed, and at what depth. In contrast, rubrics given to students before the learning activity starts help them get a clear sense of what knowledge and skills they need in order to achieve a given grade. In their book Learner-Centered Assessment on College Campuses, Hubba and Freed (2000) point out those Scoring rubrics usually contain the following elements:

- Clear statements of the level of knowledge you expect the student to achieve for them to receive a given grade.
- The dimensions of the quality of work you expect the student to achieve.
- Commentaries describing your expectations of knowledge and quality that distinguishes each grade band (e.g. ABCDF).

Keep a few questions in mind while developing an instructional rubric.

- What are the essential elements of high quality work?
- How many levels of achievement are to be described?
- Are the criteria for each level clearly described?

Cooperative Learning

Cooperative learning involves a number of students working together on a lab or field project. It requires teachers to *structure* cooperative interdependence among the students. These structures involve five key elements which can be implemented in a variety of ways. There are also different types of cooperative groups appropriate for different situations. It is more than just working in groups.

Cooperative learning exercises can be as simple as a five minute in class exercise or as complex as a project which crosses class periods. These can be described more generally in terms of low, medium, and high faculty/student time investment.

- Low (simple, informal, less than 15 minutes, in-class)
- Medium (one to two meeting sessions, more formal, in or out of class)
- High (complex, formal, across multiple class periods, in and out of class)

Cooperative learning can be used across a wide range of classroom settings ranging from small to large lecture, as well as in online classes.

- Recitation and laboratory sections
- Small enrollment classes
- Large enrollment classes (by using personal response devices, Smith *et al.*, 2009)
- Online classes (Roberts, 2004)

Five key elements differentiate cooperative learning from simply putting students into groups to learn (Johnson *et al.*, 2006).

1. *Positive Interdependence*: You'll know when you've succeeded in structuring positive interdependence when students perceive that they "sink or swim together." This can be achieved through mutual goals, division of labour, dividing materials, roles, and by making part of each student's grade dependent on the performance of the rest of the group. Group members must believe that each person's efforts benefit not only him-or herself, but all group members as well.
2. *Individual Accountability*: The essence of individual accountability in cooperative learning is "students learn together, but perform alone." This ensures that no one can "hitch-hike" on the work of others. A

lesson's goals must be clear enough that students are able to measure whether (a) the group is successful in achieving them, and (b) individual members are successful in achieving them as well.

3. *Face-to-Face (Promotive) Interaction*: Important cognitive activities and interpersonal dynamics only occur when students promote each other's learning. This includes oral explanations of how to solve problems, discussing the nature of the concepts being learned, and connecting present learning with past knowledge. It is through face-to-face, promotive interaction that members become personally committed to each other as well as to their mutual goals.
4. *Interpersonal and Small Group Social Skills*: In cooperative learning groups, students learn academic subject matter (task work) and also interpersonal and small group skills (teamwork). Thus, a group must know how to provide effective leadership, decision-making, trust-building, communication, and conflict management. Given the complexity of these skills, teachers can encourage much higher performance by *teaching cooperative skill components* within cooperative lessons. As students develop these skills, later group projects will probably run more smoothly and efficiently than early ones.
5. *Group Processing*: After completing their task, students must be given time and procedures for analyzing how well their learning groups are functioning and how well social skills are being employed. Group processing involves both task work and teamwork, with an eye to improving it on the next project.

There are three commonly recognized types of cooperative learning groups. Each type of group has its own purpose and application.

Informal Cooperative Learning Groups

These *ad-hoc* groups may be organized "on-the-fly" as an aid in direct teaching. Informal groups are particularly useful in breaking up a lecture into shorter segments interspersed with group activity. While this method leads to less time for lecture, it will increase the amount of material retained by students as well as their comfort working with each other. (Johnson, *et al.*, 2006, p. 3:10)

Formal Cooperative Learning Groups

This type of group forms the basis for most routine uses of cooperative learning. Groups are assembled for at least one class period and may stay together for several weeks working on extended projects. These groups are where students learn and become comfortable applying the different techniques of working together cooperatively. (Johnson, *et al.*, 2006)

Cooperative Base Groups

Cooperative base groups are long-term, stable groups that last for at least a year made up of individuals with different aptitudes and perspectives. They provide a context in which students can support each other in academics as well as in other aspects of their lives. The group members make sure everyone is completing their work and hold each other accountable for their contributions. Implementing cooperative base groups in such a way that students meet regularly for the duration of a course completing cooperative learning tasks can provide the permanent support and caring that students need "to make academic progress and develop cognitively and socially in healthy ways." (Johnson *et al.*, 1998)

Why Use Cooperative Learning?

Will cooperative learning help students learn? Research has shown that students who work in cooperative groups do better on tests, especially with regard to reasoning and critical thinking skills than those that do not (Johnson and Johnson, 1989).

- "In extensive meta-analyses across hundreds of studies, cooperative arrangements were found superior to either competitive or individualistic structures on a variety of outcome measures, generally showing higher achievement, higher-level reasoning, more frequent generation of new ideas and solutions, and greater transfer of what is learned from one situation to another." (Barkley, *et al.*, 2005)
- In Slavin, 1991's review of 67 studies, 61 per cent of the cooperative-learning classes achieved significantly higher test scores than the traditional classes. He notes that the difference between the more and less effective cooperative-learning classes was that the effective ones stressed group goals and individual accountability.
- Slavin (1996) further argues that "cooperative learning has its greatest effects on student learning when groups are recognized or rewarded based on the individual learning of their group members".

Cooperative learning has also been observed to enhance achievement of female and African American students (Herreid, 1998), members of groups that are underrepresented in various disciplines.

- Students in mixed groups (different races, genders, learning styles) tend to have a deeper understanding of the material and remember more than those in homogeneous groups (Wenzel, 2000).
- "In a study of 2051 students at 23 institutions, Cabreara (1998) found that minority students expressed a greater preference for learning in groups than did majority students." (Barkley *et al.,* 2005, p. 21)

Jigsaws

In a jigsaw, the class is divided into several teams, with each team preparing separate but related assignments. When all team members are prepared, the class is re-divided into mixed groups, with one member from each team in each group. Each person in the group teaches the rest of the group what he/she knows, and the group then tackles an assignment together that pulls all of the pieces together to form the full picture, hence the name jigsaw.

The jigsaw is an effective way of engaging students both with course material and with each other. The peer teaching aspect requires that each student understands the material well enough to teach it to others (individual accountability), and each student is required to contribute meaningfully to a group problem-solving component (group goals). Research on this and other cooperative learning techniques shows significant benefits for students not only in terms of level of learning but also in terms of positive social and attitudinal gains.

Designing an effective jigsaw requires different, but overlapping, team assignments and a meaningful group task, plus attention both to how students will prepare effectively for peer teaching and how the instructor will evaluate what individual students have learned.

Class Participation

Class participation can be an alternative method of assessing the student. A good way to encourage class participation is to make it part of the overall course grade. Class participation may include answering reflective questions in a course module, taking part in weekly class discussions, providing peer review critiques of fellow students' assignments, or locating and contributing online resources to a class-created knowledge-base.

The quality and quantity of submissions can be used to determine the grade.

Peer Review

"For generations, the academic community has relied on peer review as a way of enhancing the knowledge base and encouraging serious scholarship. Peer review can offer many of the same benefit to students. [and] computers [can] mediate the interaction among peers." — *Gehringer* (2000)

Introductory-level courses can integrate the process of having students review and comment on materials written by their peers. Traditional peer-review exercises can also be modified with the addition of technological tools to facilitate the process. Students can write and review the writings of their peers.

Peer review is useful for instructors of large introductory-level courses that want to challenge their students to think critically, synthesize information, and communicate science in nontechnical language. Through use of technological tools, electronic peer review provides the option of not restricting the peer-review process to a particular location and/or time, while the grading load is lessened on an instructor.

Peer review assignments can be developed for individual communication exchanges or collaborative team projects. Electronic tools can facilitate the peer review process.

Pre-testing

It is helpful to find out whether our students meet the basic knowledge and skill levels required to learn your materials. Use a pre-test to find out. Pre-tests are often paired with remedial materials.

Some instructors offer self-assessment pre-tests prior to the beginning day of class and offer students ways to catch up before the first day. Others provide time during the first week for students to do such things.

Practice Exams

Practice exams and problem set homework are popular with students in courses which use exams for grading. Students who complete a practice exam usually encounter fewer problems on the official exam. Technical problems have been worked out, and the student knows what to expect in terms of types of questions.

It's important to let the student know that practice exam questions will be similar to what they will find on their exams. However, the specifics will differ based on course content. For example, a nursing case study will be presented and students will need to identify specifics relating to the case. In exam, they will view case studies, but the details will differ. Students are very likely to complete a practice exam which parallels the real exam even though it does not count toward their grade.

Role-Play

> "Walk a mile in my shoes" is good advice. Our children will learn to respect others if they are used to imagining themselves in another's place. — Neil Kurshan (*Raising Your Child to Be a Mensch*, 1987)

In most role-playing exercises, each student takes the role of a person affected by an issue and studies the impacts of the issues on human life and/or the effects of human activities on the world around us from the perspective of that person. More rarely, students take on the roles of some phenomena, such as part of an ecosystem, to demonstrate the lesson in an interesting and immediate manner.

Role-playing is simultaneously interesting and useful to students because it emphasizes the "real-world" side of science. It challenges them to deal with complex problems with no single "right" answer and to use a variety of skills beyond those employed in a typical research project. In particular, role-playing presents the student a valuable opportunity to learn not just the course content, but other perspectives on it.

- Reasons to Use Role-Playing: explains how role-playing exercises motivate students, augment traditional curricula, and teach real-world skill.

How to Teach Using Role-Play

The instructor needs to decide the context for the exercise and the role(s) that the students will play. If the students are taking human roles, the context is generally a specific problem such as global warming or dealing with an active volcano. Lessons need to be carefully explained and supervised in order to involve the students and to enable them to learn as much as possible from the experience. However, a well-done scenario never runs the same way twice, teaches people things they might not ordinarily have learned, and tends to be fun for all involved.

Self-assessment

Self assessment types of assignments are provided for quick student feedback. Self assessments:

- help the learner check if they have mastered a topic
- provide opportunity to measure learning progress
- are usually voluntary and may allow multiple attempts
- inform the learner, but not the teacher
- can occur whenever a performance activity is linked with feedback about that performance.

Self assessment examples:

- practice quizzes
- games, simulations, and other interactive exercises
- practice written assignments
- peer reviews
- true-false questions

Conclusion

By deliberately using different strategies of Assessments at specific times during the learning process students will have a clearer vision of what is expected of them and generally will be more positive about their course experiences. They will also learn to use skills that will help them understand how scientists analyze and present findings. In addition, a programme of sustained student assessment is the foundation for evaluation of courses.

8

Higher Education

Story of the Past and Reconstituting the New

Sudhanshu Bhushan

The first wave of institution building relates to the post independence phase of higher education when the challenge was to free it from the colonial policy of developing an elite oriented education. The challenge was not only to establish few high quality institutions but also to expand the base of higher education to cater to the needs of mass education. The vision of higher education was to prepare the youth of India in higher education institutions for meaningful participation in the industrial revolution launched since second plan. The second wave of institution building consists in preparing the youth to meet the challenges of knowledge economy which is different from that of industrial economy. The growth of services sector and skill requirement in the services sector at the high end as well as at the low end of knowledge requires restructuring higher education reconstituting the past.

An immediate challenge is to present a vision for the future. If second wave is interpreted to mean paradigm shift, as it is sometimes argued, how does the past legacy support or inhibit the progress on the second wave? What needs to be given up? What elements of the past need to be remodeled? What needs to be introduced afresh? Reflections on these questions will provide insights to the issue of institution building, new sets of policies, role of state and planning, new initiatives and programmes. Needless to say, components of second wave require us to learn from past, in fact, evaluate the past development, assess the present strengths and weaknesses and given this understanding plan for the future on the basis of realistic assumptions.

The objective of the paper is to analyse the post independent phase of institution building and provide some inputs to the second wave of institution building in higher education. To achieve the objective the Part I, rather briefly, notes the directions of past developments. Part II evaluates the past developments in higher education, based primarily on three parameters-access, equity and quality. Part III develops new directions and the key elements of paradigm shift and Part IV notes the scenario for future directions.

Directions of Development

Higher Education in India has two phases. Pre-independence colonial phase set the beginning of modern higher education in 1854 with Wood's dispatch and creation of Universities at Calcutta, Madras and Bombay in 1857. Higher education remained elite institution with a view to fulfill colonial agenda—social, political and economical. The post independence phase marks the transition from elite to mass higher education. The first commission on higher education in the post independence phase, popularly known as Radhakrishnan Commission that completed its task in short span of time from December 1948 to August 1949 is a truly remarkable piece of literature on higher education with its recommendations covering all aspects of higher education right from aims of university education in independent India to the standard of teaching, courses of study, post graduate training and research, professional education, rural education, women's education, examination and finance. It provided a definite direction amidst uncertainties as even the Constitution of India was not adopted by the time the report was published. Significantly, the recommendation of the first commission for the University Grants Commission to regulate the standards of higher education was later fulfilled with UGC Act 1956, granting UGC, established in 1953, a statutory status. Since then the history of higher education at the policy and planning level was in a way the history of initiatives and programmes of UGC based on numerous committees, Kothari Commission recommendations and the government policy on education. The period between 1956, the statutory status to the UGC and the establishment of Education Commission in 1964 under the Chairmanship of D.S. Kothari was the period of supporting the expansion of colleges and universities established under central and state legislation[1].

Another important event in the history of education and higher education, in particular, was the establishment of Kothari Commission (1964-66) that made its recommendations on all aspects of higher education—both academic and administrative, as well as on the roles of the UGC. What directions were set by the commission? The detailed discussion on higher education is covered from Chapter XI to Chapter XVI. The major issue in the wake of expansion was the issue of 'governance of universities' that could facilitate quality in teaching, research, extension as well as the development of science, vocational and technical education that could successfully support the industrial development of the country. The issue of the autonomy of university, the role and appointment of Vice-Chancellor and expansion of affiliated colleges to fulfill the demand and the coordination and maintenance of standards were issues of critical importance. In particular, Kothari Commission recommended closing up any fragmentation that occurred within higher education and suggested professional councils in agriculture, engineering, medicine to coordinate the developments within a particular sector and coordination between different councils and UGC. Kothari Commission felt that "In view of the magnitude and importance of the problem facing the commission. considerably larger funds will have to be made available to enable it to deal effectively with them" (p. 345). It suggested that 6 per cent of national income be devoted to education—a point that was endorsed by the National Policy on Education, 1968-but a dream that is yet to be realized. NPE, 1968 also endorsed the 10+2+3 pattern of education. It noted very briefly yet emphatically the provision of essential facilities for maintaining high standards of universities, promotion of postgraduate courses, Centres of advanced study and increased support to research in universities.

Various committees setup by the governments and the UGC also determined the directions in which the higher education moved. Sen Committee submitted its report in 1974 on the issue of minimum qualifications for lecturers and their pay scales. V.S. Jha Committee (1974-77) reviewed the functioning of UGC with regard to coordination and determination of standards of higher education. There were also a number of conferences of Vice chancellors convened by the UGC and the government to decide number of issues such as admission and facilities for weaker sections, role and responsibility of teachers, autonomous colleges, on women's participation etc.... Committees that deserve mention in the area of management of universities were D.S. Kothari on Model Act for Universities (1964), P.B. Gajendragadkar Committee on Governance of Universities and Colleges (1971), A. Gnanam Committee on Towards New Educational Management (1990), Soneri Committee on Review of Gnanam Committee Recommendations (1995) and P.C. Alexander Committee on The Role of the Governor as Chancellor of the Universities (1997) (Approved 2003)

Consultation with the state governments was ensured through the Central Advisory Board of Education, an apex body, that constituted various committees from time to time to consider their recommendations. The latest two such committees were on the financing of universities and on the issue of autonomy in higher education.

In the financing of higher education two committees—one on central universities, under the chairmanship of Justice K. Punnayya [UGC 1993], and another on technical education institutions under the chairmanship of D. Swaminadhan [AICTE 1994], to outline methods of mobilisation of resources for higher education-deserve special mention. Both committees stressed the importance of state financing of higher education and suggested ways for nongovernmental sources of finance. Other recommendations that attracted the attention of the government include (i) raising fee levels, (ii) raising of resources by the institutions through consultancy, and sale of other services, (iii) introduction of self-financing courses, and (iv) introduction/ revitalisation of student loans. The trend towards privatization reflected in the approach to financing was rather supported by Birla Ambani Report that vehemently supported out and out privatization of higher education.

An important milestone and the last word is the prevailing National Policy on Education, 1986. Concept of autonomy was given a big push through developing autonomous colleges and post graduate department's autonomy. Greater flexibility to the courses were permitted. Teaching methods, teachers' orientation, assessment of teachers were to receive priority. Delinking of degree from job and the rural university were to be setup.

It is no secret that official policy treats higher education as non-commercial social activity, yet the current trends defy it. The conflict came to the surface when attempts were made to contain commercialization. Supreme Court had to interfere time and again to allow privatization without commercializing education. Recent Supreme Court Judgement delivered on 12 August 2005 created another controversy on the issue of reservation in private unaided institutions. There seems to be tension and official policy on higher education demands a fresh round of discussion in the wake of events overtaking higher education in recent years on grounds of commercialization, internationalization of higher education, potentials of knowledge economy and also to realize the potentials of ICT revolution.

Assessing the Past

Access: Educational structure in India consists of a large network of 33023 colleges, 659 universities/Deemed universities/Institutions of National Importance and 12748 Diploma level institutions, thanks to the unprecedented expansion during 11th plan as a result of second wave of institutional expansion. The growth of private institutions is an interesting development during this period (*see* Table 8.1).

Table 8.1: Post Secondary Higher Education Institutions in 2011-12

	Centrally funded	*State funded*	*Private*	*Total*
Universities/Degree awarding institutions	152	316	191	659
Colleges	69	13024	19930	33023
Diploma		3207	9541	12748
Total	221	16547	29662	46430

Source: 12th Plan, Planning Commission of India.

Enrolment of students in higher education institutions was 25.9 million of which 21.7 million was in face to face teaching mode and 4.2 million was in open and distance education mode. It amounted to the GER of 18.1 per cent during 2011-12. Enrolment in Government institutions and the private institutions accounted for 41 and 59 per cent respectively (*see* Table 8.2). It is important to note that enrolment in Engineering alone was 25 per cent of total enrolment. Undergraduate, postgraduate and diploma enrolment accounted for 74, 11 and 15 per cent respectively.

Table 8.2: Distribution of Enrolment

	In Millions	*Per cent*
Government	89.63	41.1
Central	5.63	2.6
State	84.00	38.6
Private	128.23	58.9
Total	217.86	100.0

Source: 12th Plan, Planning Commission of India.

With over 8 lakhs teachers and a pupil teacher ratio of over 25, the higher education institutions in India continue to grow, although shortage of teachers is growing. As per All India Survey on Higher Education. 19249 foreign students are estimated to be studying higher education in India in 2010-11. There are, in addition, 66 Academic Staff Colleges for academic training to the teachers. The above scenario of growth over base year 1950-51 is a tremendous feat of success on account of access and expansion.

Target for the Twelfth Plan is to increase enrolment capacity by another 10 million. Of this, 1 million will come from ODL, 3.3 million through large scale expansion of skill-granting diploma programmes and remaining 5.7 million will come from further expansion of degree programmes with accelerated expansion of postgraduate and doctoral programmes. Therefore, additional enrolment capacity of 10 million students would enable roughly 3 million more students in each age cohort to enter higher education and raise the gross enrolment ratio broadly in line with the current global average from 18.2 per cent now to 25.2 per cent by 2017. It means further capacity of institutions has to go up by 2012. Higher education in India, therefore, may be said to approach the 'critical' level of enrolment-something like 30 per cent of GER by 2020.

Going little deeper into the statistics per cent enrolment in technical and professional courses at 25 per cent, amounts to high absolute number placing India as having 3rd largest scientific manpower. Enrolment in science is at present 14 per cent. Science enrolment has come down in recent years causing great concern. University system has a large responsibility to manage graduate students. Affiliated colleges where graduate students are enrolled, therefore, places heavy burden on the university system (See Table 8.3).

Table 8.3: Faculty wise Distribution of Enrolment

	in lakhs	*Per cent*
Arts	65.78	30
Science	30.57	14
Commerce/Management	34.34	16
Education	13.00	6
Engineering/Technology	54.68	25
Medicine	12.02	6
Agriculture, veterinary science	1.21	1
Law	3.48	2
Others	2.78	1
Total	217.86	100

Source: 12th Plan, Planning Commission of India.

There has been continued fall in percentage expenditure on higher education although share of public expenditure on higher education in GDP shows a continuous improvement in 1990's. This, it is argued, is the product of a wrong mind set of the government to treat higher education as non merit good[2] (Tilak, 2004).

Equity

Inclusive development is another important objective of planned development in higher education. This is tougher to achieve in higher education as this system receives a limited pool from the school education system and most socio-economic disparities often force students out of schools after primary and secondary levels. The GER statistics across categories and genders point to the huge disparities that already exist amongst various categories and amongst genders. Rajasthan, Odisha, Chattisgarh, Jharkhand, Assam and Bihar are amongst the lowest in terms of gender parity in higher education, with alarmingly low levels amongst the ST and SC populations.

Table 8.4: Social Group Composition in Enrolment of Students and Staff

	SC			*ST*			*OBC*		
	M	*F*	*T*	*M*	*F*	*T*	*M*	*F*	*T*
Student	10.3	10.1	10.2	4.3	4.6	4.4	27.3	26.8	27.1
Teaching Staff	7.7	6.7	7.4	2.7	3.1	2.9	23.8	22.5	23.3
Non Teaching Staff	11.8	13.8	12.2	3.8	4.6	4.6	22.3	24.7	22.9

Source: All India Survey in Higher Education, Government of India 2012.

Higher education is no longer an elite constituency. An argument contrary to this notes that subsidies that went to finance higher education was cornered by the elites and the policy of affirmative action such as reservation benefited largely the creamy layer of the society. Thus social and political forces at work shaping the policy of the state ultimately benefited the rich. Notwithstanding the merit of this point of view the role of state in promoting equity is well recognized. State policies in higher education must, therefore, provide space for increasing gender and social parity, as first wave of state supported higher education opened the doors of job opportunity for both sexes and socially deprived sections.

Regional Bias: There has developed a strong regional bias in the distribution of professional institutions. Here the divide exists between the north and the south. Southern states such as Andhra Pradesh, Maharashtra, Tamilnadu, Karnataka and to some extent Kerala account for the bulk of the professional institutions in India, mostly in the private sector. Similar north-south divide exists in other branches of professional education in India. This has an important implication for the northern states. Since most of the students from the poor northern states take admissions in the private professional institutions, higher the fees structure higher is the drain of money from the north to the south. This fact has very important implication in terms of policy and planning design of professional institution. The institutional density and enrolment pattern given in Figure 8.1 suggests that states with high enrolment but low institutional density should attract attention of planning.

Quality: There is no published index of quality either in terms of input, process or output indicators in higher education that could to a certain extent assess quality objectively. There are, however, views that have been expressed. Balance of opinion gives the verdict that except for islands of excellence overall quality is far from satisfactory[4]. System of higher education that allowed upward mobility of heitherto unaccessed could manage to get job but at the system level quality deteriorated. Much remains to be done if India has to meet the challenge of knowledge economy as latter considers issue of quality of supreme concern for meaningful participation in knowledge economy. In the triangle with its vertices as access, equity and quality, it is sometimes argued that quality in higher education has suffered due to the trade off with quantity. The posing of the problem in this manner implies that as the resource is simply said to be exhausted in expansion and diversification with little left for quality intervention, the casualty is the loss in quality. It, however, misses the inner dynamics of development—the structural, institutional, political or the issue of governance. In reconstructing the past, the understanding of the inner dynamics assumes importance. Hence the reflection on development process assumes importance.

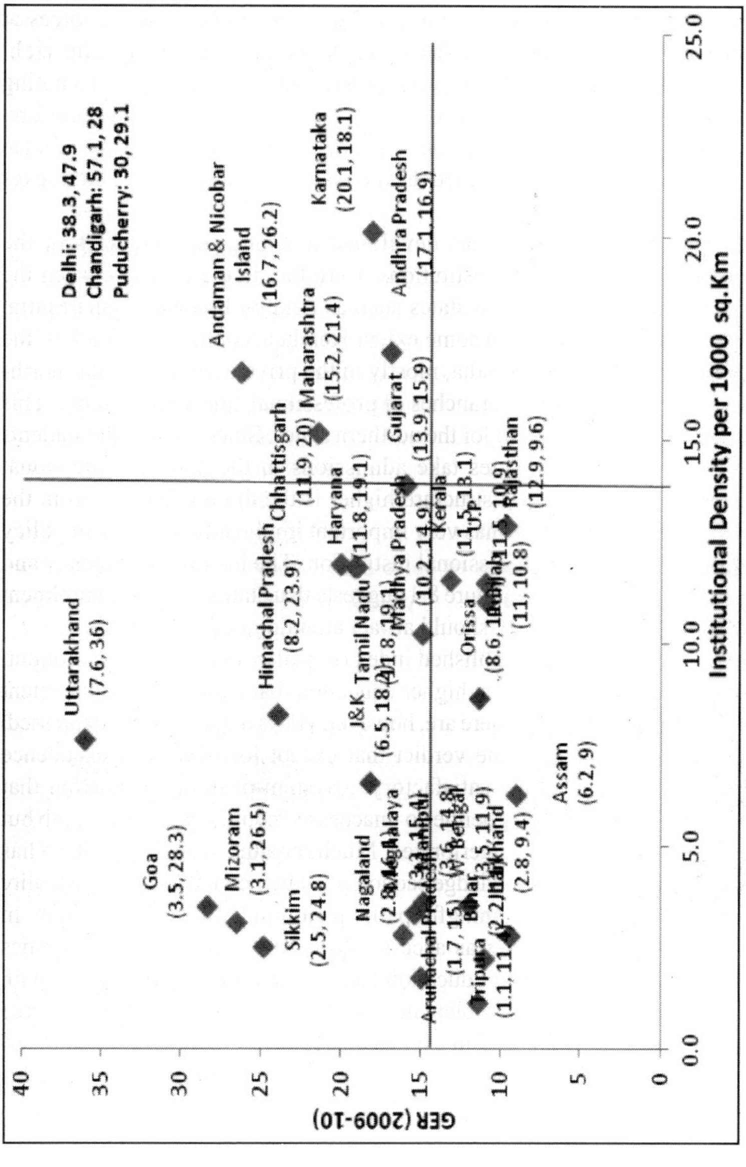

Fig. 8.1: GER and Institutional Density by State/UT (2009-10)[3]

Roots of Decline in the First Wave of Institution Building

Mediocrity of Research: A.M. Shah (2005) concludes that "A cumulative effect of various developments both within and outside the field of education is the declining enrolment of talented students, and therefore the declining availability of trained researchers and teachers in the basic physical sciences, the social sciences and the humanities for appointment in colleges, universities and research institutes. This development is contributing to further decline of teaching standards." He analyses the following factors for the decline of quality that arose either due to poor implementation or wrong strategies of various programmes launched by UGC: (a) Personal promotion scheme became movement for mass promotions to higher ranks shorn of academic merit, (b) Failure to induct a researcher into a long term commitment through M.Phil, (c) Failure of Academic Staff College to develop quality among teachers, (d) Downgrading eligibility test for researchers and for recruitment of the teachers, (e) Substandard syllabi, (f) Emphasis on teaching rather than research re-asserted itself in universities and growing isolation of research institutes in the style of functioning, (g) UGC's encouragement to research through Centre of Advanced Study, Departmental Assistance, award of research and teacher fellowship failed to develop quality with poor funding support to the libraries, (h) Flight of talented students to professional courses, private and foreign universities and the competitive populism within universities. Why these problems arose? Author feels that the structure of university system was unable to take the load of managing too big a system in its entire dimension. As a result, quality of teaching and research at the postgraduate level suffered. The author thus suggests a structural reform to reduce the burden of universities to manage affiliating undergraduate colleges and concentrate on post graduate teaching and research. He would then support developing a culture of meritocracy devoid of political interference.

Institutional structure created in the phase of expansion failed to develop meritocracy as a general phenomenon. As a result legacy presents us with mediocrity. Future vision calls for excellence in research. *Restructuring of universities narrowing the focus to manage research in a manner that develops in-built mechanism for scholastic achievement should be the cornerstone of policy*. The form of such restructuring should not detain us here but the principles may clearly be laid down in terms of strict recruitment policy of teachers, reward and incentives to teachers for excellence in teaching and research, student evaluation of teachers, training to the teachers, freedom and resources to participate in academic programmes and infrastructural and academic support to teachers.

Failure in Co-ordination and maintenance of Standards: University Grants Commission and various professional bodies of higher education were established by the Union Government under Article 246 of the Constitution of India to co-ordinate and maintain standards in higher education[5]. At the system's level, Amrik Singh (2004) notes that ' The real major lapse has been in not having set up the National Council of Higher Education as recommended by the 1986 Policy of Education' (*ibid.,* p. 14). As a result the task of co-ordination was left with the Ministry of Human Resource Development. Various professional bodies including Distance Education Council could not sit together to benchmark standards and study the developments relating to the growth of private professional colleges, issue of fake universities, upsurge of unrecognized private institutions partnering with foreign universities to confer foreign degrees illegally, the growth of correspondence and distance education and the hidden commercialization. The co-ordination was also required to be achieved to supervise the growth process itself—issues of required expansion in general and technical/professional courses in accordance with the demand, regional balanced development and issue of gender and social participation across different courses and various other matters that cut across different disciplines.

Not only that the benchmarking of standards ignored, Singh (2004) also notes that the UGC at present is toothless body as it has no right to give the final approval to the establishment of university nor can it derecognize the degree granted by the university, in case the violation in maintaining the minimum standards is noticed by it. Various other professional councils may have some difficulties or the other in terms of needed statutory support to maintain standards. The whole issue, therefore, is to empower statutorily and financially the professional councils and asking them to co-ordinate. The accountability of professional councils needs to be ensured at least in maintaining the minimum standards for postgraduate department, research, professional and technical courses, recruitment of quality teachers, if not all the undergraduate colleges. The role of NAAC and NBA as accrediting agencies will then be to promote quality above the benchmarked standards in preferential areas and institutions and to encourage all UG colleges to progressively improve the quality. Accrediting agencies role should be to create awareness and motivation among teachers to improve the quality and inform the students about the standards of particular institutions. For a large size country like India, accrediting agencies need to evolve appropriate mechanisms for accreditation.

Thus if we take stock of the first phase/wave of institution building, the strength of higher education is large and diversified structure of institutions with few institutions of excellence. The weakness of the system is that quality is not only poor, there seems to be systematic erosion of quality particularly research and teaching. Hence the biggest threat is dominance of private and foreign institutions offering programmes which have high market demand in view of decline of public institutions, adversely affecting equity. Hence the strategy from past experience should be to introduce reforms at the level of universities by narrowing the focus of management to improve research and teaching and evolve suitable structure to regulate admission, fees, examination etc. that at present overburden the university system. The second set of strategy should be restructuring and empowering the professional councils, evolving a system of co-ordination through the National Council of Higher Education that will constantly monitor the developments in higher education and issue guidelines for professional councils.

The point about willingness of political elite to do so is important and has been pointed out by many authors. Kapur and Mehta (2004) notes that Indian higher education system has suffered both from the state as well as market failures and has paid the price for it in terms of sub-optimal level of higher education reflected in mediocrity. Nonetheless the state is the mechanism through which the reform process in higher education has to take place by understanding the new directions which defines the contours of the paradigm shift and believing in the promises made by the Prime minister for state induced second wave of institution building, state needs to assume a new role of further strengthening institutions to improve quality and strategically invest in institutions and programmes and at the same time promote and regulate the market.

New Directions

1990's may be said to be the beginning of new phase chiefly characterized by the privatization, internationalization of higher education, emergence of knowledge economy and the technological breakthrough due to ICT. Remnants of the past presents us with a strong institutional base with few quality institutions but large number belonging to average and less than average category of institutions.

State vs. Market: Notwithstanding the role of state in the first wave of institutional expansion, the role of market gradually became predominant. Empirical evidence suggests that the private sector, which accounted for just 15 per cent of the seats in engineering in 1960, now accounts for 86.4 per cent of seats (and 84% of all engineering colleges). In the case of medical colleges the proportion of private seats has risen from 6.8 per cent in 1960 to 40.9 per cent in 2003 (See also Natrajan, 2004 and Table 8.7 in the appendix). Similarly majority of the business schools are in private sector. The trend of privatization in professional courses also points to a trend towards commercialization.

Central government's decision to amend the UGC Act, 1956 to allow Deemed University status in 1986 to private/public institutions may be said to promote private co-operation, yet in practice it permitted the trend towards privatization and commercialization to flourish. State even permitted the expansion of self financing courses in colleges and universities. The whole episode of private universities, beginning from private university's bill introduced in Parliament to the Supreme Court Judgement (2005) abolishing the private universities established under Chhattisgarh legislation is a telling example of state's failure to even regulate the market in a meaningful way to increase access and quality in higher education through private participation. The growth of private institutions has been chaotic to the extent that many of them exist outside the purview of university system. They offer courses that have market induced demand such as fashion design, computer applications, tourism and all such courses that can fetch money. Many courses may have employment potentials but are not offered by public university system. Diversified providers operate to take advantage of such situation and no mechanism exists to certify the quality of programmes.

Privatisation is now a force to reckon with. The existential reality whether at home or abroad created material conditions to its development. Sadly enough, the privatization has brought the new direction in the form of commercialization and is substantially different from the older philanthropist tradition[6]. This trend in Indian context is also different from American system where government increased federal support for basic scientific research 25 fold in real dollar between 1948 to 1968 to reach almost $ 3 billion per year and considered new ways of linking university research to the needs of business[7]. Government's pro active role of strengthening infrastructure, investing in research and facilitating academia through enabling laws will create productive synergy between universities and corporate world.

Internationalisation of Higher Education: It refers to the international, intercultural and interdisciplinary aspects of curriculum and the teaching/ learning process and is reflected in increasing mobility of students, programmes, teachers, researchers, scientists and institutions. Movement of students[8] and the movement of teachers, researchers and scientists[9] are the embodied form of Cross Border Higher Education (CBHE) and the movement of programmes, institutions[10] and the mode of delivery through the distance electronic way[11] may be said to be the disembodied form of CBHE. An interesting phenomenon is the universities moving beyond the national frontiers in a global knowledge economy. Internationalisation of higher education provides a new dimension to the growth of higher education. At the more practical level foreign universities have begun to collaborate with the private institutions in India to impart education and confer degree to the students[12]. Bhushan S. (2005 b) notes that "At present this phenomenon is symbolic and market driven, and as yet there is no policy guideline on foreign universities. Given the strong demand for foreign degrees by Indian students, market-driven trends may dominate in the future." It may be noted that India is also the destination of international students, notably from developing countries[13] and in recent years there has been strong tendency to export education abroad. However, for Indian students, USA is the most preferred destination followed by UK, Australia, Canada and France.

Besides India is a signatory to the WTO. General Agreement on Trade in Services (GATS) promotes the philosophy of trade in education. The developments relating to trade related internationalization have raised new dimensions to the policy issues. New dimensions are added, as hitherto protected system of public higher education is exposed to competition from the newly emerging structure of education providers-private as well as foreign.

The new trend of internationalization of higher education is in a sense inevitable. Government regulation to assure quality and check profiteering should be put in place. The university system in India should collaborate in the area of basic sciences with leading research universities to upgrade faculty, programmes and generate new knowledge. If internationalization has to be admitted as a fact of life, the system of mutual recognition of qualifications should be promoted through bilateral and regional agreements.

Knowledge Economy: A knowledge economy is ability to create and disseminate knowledge and use it for economic growth and improved standard of living. In knowledge economy human resource endowed with education and skill is considered important as knowledge can only be produced by human resources who can then transform knowledge into tangible products-technology and goods and services—for the market. Carl Dahlman and Anjula Utz (2005, p. 9) in 'India and the Knowledge Economy: Leveraging Strengths and Opportunities' note a number of strengths of India for transforming itself into a knowledge based economy—skilled human capital in sciences, democratic institution, widespread use of English, macro economic stability, dynamic private sector, free market economy, large local market, well developed financial sector abroad and diversified S&T infrastructure and booming IT sector[14]. India is also a sought after venue for services in global production chains—away from call centres, financial accounting and database production to international firms that are using India in banking, insurance, technology and telecom, engineering and business services and further more striving to move high up in the value chain towards high knowledge end. The potentials of India as knowledge economy can be realized if higher education adapts to demand for changes in a knowledge economy. Hence the second wave of institution building in higher education must cater to the needs of knowledge economy.

India's Score Cards in Knowledge Economy: To improve India's score cards in knowledge economy tertiary enrolment needs to be raised. Higher education has also the responsibility to improve the quality of science and math. Education and develop expertise to train the employees. Policies must stop the emigration and attract talents in Indian universities.

Information and Communication Technology: ICT has tremendous potential to increase access and quality in higher education institutions at affordable cost. There is need for an enabling environment for the widespread availability and application of ICT in varied fields in higher education institutions. Critical factors for such an enabling environment are widespread availability of access devices such as telephones and PC's, connectivity to the internet through internet service providers, ICT literacy among students, teachers and educational administrators and the availability of knowledge

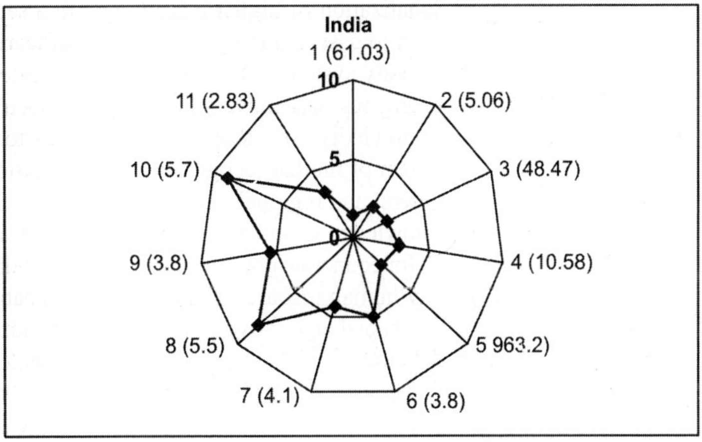

1-Adult Literacy Rate (% age 15 and above), 2-Average Years of Schooling, 3-Secondary Enrollment, 4-Tertiary Enrollment, 5-Life Expectancy at Birth, years, 6-Internet Access in Schools, 7-Public Spending on Education as per cent of GDP, 8-Quality of Science and Math Education, 9-Extent of Staff Training, 10-Availability of Management Education, 11-Well Educated People Do Not Emigrate Abroad.

Note: Each of the 80 variables in the KAM is normalized on a scale of 0 to 10 for 128 countries. The fuller the scorecard, the better poised a country is to embrace the knowledge economy. But an economy should not necessarily aim for a perfect score of 10 on all variables. This is because the scorecards may be shaped by the particular structural characteristics of an economy or by trade-offs that characterizes different development strategies. Values in parentheses denote actual values for the most recent period for which data are available.

Source: World Bank, "Knowledge Assessment Methodology," http://www.worldbank.org/kam

Fig. 8.2: India's Score Card on Knowledge Economy

professional in the higher education institutions. It is also important to understand different specific areas in which efficiency can be increased through greater transparency and substantial cost reduction and quality of education can be increased through availability of reading materials, innovative delivery practices and offering web based courses. There are following areas in which ICT coverage can be extended. (a) Admission processes can be computerised and further application and testing services can be offered online. (b) Results of college and university examinations can be computerised. (c) Payrolls, leave systems, accounting etc. soft wares can be adopted as part of the e-governance. (d) Use of multimedia in the classrooms can be promoted (e) College libraries can be accessed from different points i.e. from students' computer centers and faculty's desktops. Further through a dedicated server and a downlink facility, networking of libraries can be assured. (f) Internet, intranet and extranet facility can be promoted among students and teachers. (g) Digital campus through campus pipeline web platform and appropriate soft wares and services in select institutions can be planned. At present ICT integration in higher education is not satisfactory and exploiting ICT for improving quality must be an important strategy of development in higher education

Recent reforms in higher education policies and higher education institutions: The policy of the Government is to bring about improvement in information infrastructure and develop quality education through Information Communication Technology (ICT) integration in the higher education institutions in the country. The UGC has launched an ambitious programme to bring about a qualitative change in the academic infrastructure for higher education. Under this initiative UGC is modernizing university campuses with state-of-the art campus wide networks and setting up of its own nationwide communication network named UGC-Infonet. Under E-Subscription initiative the universities across the country will also be provided with access to 9000 journals with full text through gate way portal access. Various schemes for library automation, Software for University Libraries (SOUL), creation of Indian bibliographic databases and various training programmes are being launched. Consortium of Educational Communication established by UGC provides education to students across the country via electronic media. Among recent initiatives is the promotion of multi media techniques, video streaming of educational programmes on Internet. UGC has been increasingly supporting colleges and universities for establishing computer facilities. The government has already launched EDUSAT-a dedicated educational satellite with the capacity to telecast 72 channels only for educational purposes.

The 10th plan notes that the basic issue of quality improvement would be addressed through the modernisation of syllabi, increased research, networking of universities and departments and increased allocation of funds. Networking through Local area Network (LAN), Wide Area Network (WAN), Information and Library Network (INFLIBNET) would also lead to increased academic activities and research. The university system would be expected to utilize the autonomy it enjoys for innovations in teaching and for pursuing high quality research. The emphasis would be on conferring autonomous status on more colleges, improving the infrastructure and more rationalised funding of research. Through the provision of the means to interact across geographical boundaries of institutions, integration will be increased during the Tenth Plan. Steps will be taken for increased access to Scheduled Caste/Scheduled Tribes (SCs/STs) students and minorities. Besides, the activities of distance/open universities will be supported to increase access for the northeastern and backward areas. In this regard UGC has taken initiatives in the first two years of planning.

Key Elements of Paradigm Shift in Higher Education: Can we therefore say that against past trends the new directions define the trajectory of development that calls for paradigm shifts in higher education? Is government through the proposed measures of reforms prepared to face the paradigm shift? How should the newer elements for change be reconstituted in higher education based on past experiences? To answer those questions the issues relating to paradigm shift need to be discussed.

Teaching Learning Process: An important aspect of paradigm shift in higher education is the fundamental change in the way learning takes place and the relationship between learner and teacher. Learner should be able to develop technical, interpersonal, and methodological skills. Technical skills include literacy, foreign language, math, science, problem solving, and analytical skills. Interpersonal skills include teamwork, leadership, and communication skills. Methodological skills include the ability to learn on one's own, to pursue lifelong learning, and to cope with risk and change. (World Bank 2003)

Traditional classroom setting is the one in which the teacher is the sole source of knowledge. Teamwork, problem solving, motivation for lifelong learning—cannot be acquired in a learning setting in which teachers dictate facts to learners who seek to learn them only in order to be able to repeat them. This therefore demands that instructionist paradigm that defines classroom situation in India needs to be changed. Teacher should work as facilitator, as guide to source of knowledge. Learners learn in teams. They learn in the process of doing. The new paradigm is multi-channel learning system (MCLS) supported by constructivist learning paradigm (*see* Mukhopadhyay 2004). This paradigm shift is necessary to be introduced in Indian classroom. Teachers should equip themselves for such a change.

Nature of Universities: The traditional view of university is based on linear model of innovation, presuming only long term contributions of academic knowledge to the economy. Universities in the global knowledge economy must develop strategic alliances with industrial sector where both co-evolve. This may not require some sort of paradigm shift. However, there are various other compulsions that may require universities to consider some sort of paradigm shift, as without that it may not be possible to deal with the challenges. George Andrew Gekas (2004) notes four major challenges facing Universities. It has been difficult to obtain adequate government funding to develop first-rate Universities. University system is over-regulated. Centralized decision-making may take 3-5 years to introduce a new programme. University programmes are driven by the faculty interests not the client (student) needs. Universities may be unresponsive or late to respond to emerging market needs. Can university system solve the problems and challenges facing it within its traditional structure? If not, the structure needs to be strengthened. It has to be less bureaucratic and more professional. The pace of decision making may have to be fast to respond to changing realities and needs. A little more autonomy may go hand in hand with more of accountability. In considering the future of Universities, we also notice a new trend of world-class Universities in the era of globalisation. This also requires a new way of thinking in university management, as standard rules and procedures may not work to attract talents.

Competition: A paradigm shift is taking place in the approach to protection inherent in public system of higher education. Although subsidy is considered desirable from social point of view, it has provided too much protection to the public provider of services and these institutions in turn have tended to be inefficient and less quality conscious. It will amount to a paradigm shift if competition in higher education is accepted as a philosophy to guide it. Competition will amount to either of the following in an excess demand situation: (i) At a given price raise the supply by increasing the efficiency and (ii) to increase the supply price to raise the supply[15]. Former may be easily pursued, although implementation difficulties exist. However, latter strategies would mean privatization and free trade approach to higher education. It is the second approach that will mean paradigm shift for which situation may not exist, yet policy makers will have sometimes to strike a balance and resolve the conflict.

Future Perspectives in Higher Education

Where should we go from here? Consistently we have been referring to a weak spot in higher education system. Mediocrity has taken a toll of higher education system. Mediocrity needs to be repaired and indeed eliminated. Excellence in teaching and research has restricted to select few institutions. Excellence must be all pervasive. Besides there has been a whole paradigm shift in teaching learning process and teachers hardly seem to be aware, let alone be practicing. Hence legacy presents a mixed picture-some excellent teachers and institutions as well as majority teachers and institutions of most ordinary quality. Excellent institutions need to be taken a step further. Many issues of paradigm shift will be easily accepted. Most of the ordinary institutions need a dose of institutional reform before some elements of paradigm shift can be introduced gradually. For example before introducing changes in classroom practices to improve quality there must be institutional preparedness to put in place requisite infrastructure and training facility to the teachers. Hence a two pronged approach to enhance the quality should be taken up—promotion of excellence in select institutions and institutional reform measures to prepare the ground for promoting excellence in average institutions. Future directions in higher education call for investment in quality on the basis of institutional assessment and planning. State commitment to provide financial resources for the same should be total.

As pointed out above, a tradeoff between quantity and quality may exist given the scarcity of resources. To reduce this trade off private investment in higher education needs to be encouraged. Diversified providers may introduce programmes and supply education services. There are two concerns here, namely, equity and the quality. Within the framework of Supreme Court Judgement it is possible to form committees at the central and state level that can regulate admission and fees. Similarly appropriate body can be established to certify quality before institutions begin to operate. All these private providers can be effective educators and trainers in non-degree courses, as they enjoy the requisite flexibility to work according to the signals received from the market quickly.

So far as future directions are concerned, government should declare its policy in no unambiguous terms the commitment of state for improving quality through institutional reform and promoting excellence in public institutions and establish mechanisms for regulating admission and fees and the quality before unscrupulous providers begin to market education.

It has also to be noted that the university as an institution has changed. Past legacy in terms of bureaucratic, heavily burdened and professionally and technologically weak structure cannot deal with the challenges that 21st century higher education faces. At least few of the universities can be developed as world class research universities where international scholars may keep visiting and where both way flow of ideas could take place. Universities also need to take up the load in meaningful manner. The burden of graduate colleges upon universities can be reduced in two ways: (1) by declaring large number of colleges as autonomous colleges and giving them required autonomy with close supervision of quality, (2) creating separate structures in a university to manage undergraduate colleges, allowing university to concentrate on Postgraduate and research.

Future directions of higher education should also revolve around the integration of technology. Teachers should be enabled to use technology to access large repository of knowledge existing in digital form. Modern technology should also be used in class rooms. The networking among institutions should be effective. ICT technology has enabled to connect various colleges and universities. An institutional dimension to this connectivity can be put in terms of a virtual university through a consortium approach working together in practical way to programme, develop the contents and ensures the delivery of the programmes.

The future directions must also look at the issue of funding Higher Education. Fully subsidized higher education, that has been the feature of higher education expansion till 1990 can not continue on account of constraints and contradictions facing state. On the other hand there are enough potentials for private initiatives in higher education.

Notes

1. See Sharma Kavita A. (2003) for a detailed analysis of developments of UGC that set the directions of development in higher education.
2. "Decline in per student expenditure means decline in real resources available per student on average, seriously affecting the quality in higher education. After all, there were steep cuts in budget allocations for libraries, laboratories, scholarships, faculty improvement programmes, etc. Serious effects on the quality of higher education were also widely felt." (Tilak, 2004,) See the pattern of decline in 1990's in Table 8.5 in the appendix.
3. Chapter on Higher Education, XII Five Year Plan, Planning Commission of India, New Delhi, 2012
4. See observation on quality in Mehta V.R. (2003). He notes that "We have failed to sustain a sound teaching learning process, or to provide a right kind of fodder to the job market...we have failed to provide authentic process of certification....people are so much uncertain about the qualities of our product that they no longer take university certification seriously" (p. 5) Another observation can be found in Jayram N. (2004). He notes " The undue emphasis on certification rather than on the teaching and learning process-a proverbial case of the tail wagging the dog-has distorted the orientation of university education" (*ibid.* p.93)
5. Entry 66 of list I in the VII Schedule of the Constitution of India vests Central Government with the power to legislate for "Co-ordination and determination of standards, in institutions, for higher education or research and scientific and technical institutions". The Constitutional provision clearly lays down that entry 25, list III by which the state government has the power to establish university is subject to the power of Parliament to legislate under entry 66 to maintain the required standards of higher education. It is thus the constitutional obligation upon the Central government to regulate maintenance of the standards of higher

education. The UGC Act, 1956 says "the Constitution of India vests Parliament with exclusive authority in regard to "co-ordination and determination of standards in institutions for higher education or research and scientific and technical institutions". UGC Act, clause (f) and (g) of Section 26 guides UGC regarding minimum standards and its maintenance in universities.

6. See Kapur and Mehta (2004). In section VI on Philanthrophy or Privatisation, he notes that there is a good deal of confusion between the two terms in financing higher education.
7. See Bok Derek (2003). He refers to Bayh-Dole Act, passed by the Congress in 1980 which made it much easier for universities to own and license patents on discoveries made through research paid for with public funds. These initiatives paid dividends. By the year 2000, universities had increased the volume of their patenting more than 10 fold and were earning more than $1 billion per year in royalties and license fees.
8. Movement of students to another country for study abroad is popularly called mode 2 under GATS.
9. Movement of natural persons such as teachers, scientists, and researchers to another country for a short period is covered under mode 4 of GATS articles.
10. Movement of programmes and institutions such as under franchisee, twinning, programmatic collaboration or branch campuses leading to single or joint foreign degree in foreign country is covered under commercial presence abroad which is mode 3 supply of education under GATS.
11. Distance education particularly in electronic version is covered under mode 1 supply of education under GATS.
12. See Bhushan S. (2005 a) for a fuller analysis of foreign institutions partnering with private institutions in India under different modes such as twinning, franchising, programmatic collaboration in different programmes.
13. See Bhalla Veena (2005).
14. India's strength in IT and IT related services sector is not something in terms of high end IT tasks. It is geared towards low skill, low wage competition. See D'Costa (2003).
15. See Bhushan S. (2005c) for a detailed analysis of competitiveness in higher education.

9

Global Trends in Reforms in Higher Education

N.V. Varghese

The expansion of higher education in the first decade of the twenty first century has been phenomenal. Enrolment in higher education was 158.7 million in 2008 (UIS, 2010), denoting an annual average increase of 7.2 million students, which is the highest level attained for any decade. This rapid expansion in enrolment is also associated with non-state funding. It can be argued that reforms that facilitated an active role of non-state actors in the provision of higher education have contributed to the surge in enrolment in higher education in this millennium.

The market-friendly reforms in the economic sectors helped extend similar reforms to education. Reforms initiated in many countries reduced state control over higher education and opened the sector up to market operations. The international agreements/commitments and changes in the national economic policy have, no doubt, influenced the direction of reforms in higher education. The General Agreement on Trade in Services (GATS), the Bologna process, external quality assurance mechanisms, and cross-border provisions are factors affecting reforms in national systems of education, and they link national systems with regional and international networks and global markets.

The privatization of public institutions of higher education and the emergence of private institutions as an alternative are examples of policies moving closer to markets and market principles of operation in education. Based on a review of reforms in higher education in several countries, this paper argues that the reform efforts in general indicate an effort to reposition higher education in the changed external environment, to reassert its relevance, and a tendency to replace the state as the dominant player in the decision-making process by the market.

This chapter will deal with rationale for recent reforms, approaches to introduce reforms in higher education, some of the reforms in higher education in different countries, some general trends in the reforms of different countries, and some conclusions from the preceding discussions.

Reforms Attempt to Re-assert the Relevance of Higher Education

Reforms, in general, refer to planned changes of a basic nature that affect the whole education system, or at least a sub-sector such as higher education. Since reforms are *generic in nature and holistic in their effects*, it is usually the state that has the authority to initiate education reforms.

Some reforms are influenced more by the external environment than others. For example, reforms designed to respond to the market requirements are efforts by the education system to support production and, in a sense, are derived reforms to align the sub-sector with other sectors. Many reforms that are aimed at effecting changes in the mode of knowledge generation may be playing a lead role in shaping changes in the decision–making process, both in the education and production sectors.

With the increasing importance of knowledge in production and economic growth, there is a heightened interest in higher education and reforming higher education to suit the requirements of production. Recent studies (UIS/OECD, 2003) indicate that investment in human capital has been the driving force of economic performance, and that human capital has been 'the single-most important engine of growth in OECD countries in the past three decades' (OECD, 2000: p. 17). The key to economic success lies in a country's 'capacity to mobilize knowledge and use it to the full' (World Bank, 2008: 3). Mobilization of knowledge implies the capacity to innovate to produce knowledge and absorb knowledge produced elsewhere. Both are positively associated with the availability of those who are higher educated. Thus expanded higher education became a necessary condition for faster economic growth.

Globalization has underlined the need for an expanded higher education system because the demand for higher educated people has increased, primarily due to the 'capital-skill complementarities' and 'technology-skill interaction' (Griliches, 2000) in production. The skill premium in the labour market is on the increase, and the returns from investing in higher skills are also high. This is reflected in the increased labour market returns to the higher educated, especially in the knowledge-based professions (Feenstra and Hanson, 1999). The rate of return studies, which in the 1960s and 1970s showed higher returns to primary education (Psacharopolous, 1994) started showing higher returns to higher education from the late 1980s (World Bank, 2002a). The higher returns to higher education graduates act as an incentive for households to invest in higher education and promote non-state actors in the provision of services in the sub-sector.

Expansion of the higher education sector is considered a necessary condition for growth and to overcome the human capital constraints in economic growth. However, public institutions alone may not have the capacity to meet the growing demand for higher educated graduates. Therefore, alternatives to public provision are sought in the sector. In other words, the weak fiscal capacity of the state to finance an expanding system of higher education, the inability of public universities to offer courses relevant in the market, and the willingness of households to invest in market-friendly courses have led to the initiation of reforms to open the sub-sector to non-state actors, especially to private providers, in order to expand the pool of higher educated workers. Therefore, one can see that most of the reforms have resulted in an expansion of the sector, even when public investment in higher education has not increased sufficiently to accommodate the social demand for higher education.

Approach to Introducing Changes in Higher Education

Any radical change in higher education that encompasses the whole system is always difficult to implement. Therefore, changes are very often introduced on a small scale and incrementally. As well as being incremental in nature, these changes are also sometimes introduced individually rather than in a coordinated fashion. Hence such an approach to introduce changes are called 'disjointed incrementalism' (Braybrooke and Lindblom, 1963).

The other approach to introduce changes is called the 'staged theory of organizational change' (Fullan, 1991). It considers that changes can be introduced incrementally and in stages, such as an initiation stage, an implementation stage, an institutionalization stage, etc. Many incremental changes introduced in stages together and cumulatively may lead to a transformational change (Fullan, 1991). It is argued that a gradual and incremental approach to introduce reforms encounters less political resistance than comprehensive reforms, since such a piecemeal approach reduces the national spotlight and the resultant public debate (Haddad, 1994) on the negative implications of any reform measure.

The punctuated equilibrium theory of change (Tushman and Romanelli, 1985) takes into account long-term changes. Organizations experience 'long periods of relatively stable equilibrium punctuated by short periods of intense, deep change' (Parson and Fidler, 2005). The nature of the changes will depend on whether or not they transform the deep structure of an organization consisting of—(a) core values and beliefs; (b) a strategy and organizational priorities; (c) distribution of power; (d) an organizational structure and control systems (Tushman and Romanelli, 1985). The incremental changes may lead to improved operational efficiency of the organization, but they do not necessarily change the deep structure and do not fundamentally change the organization.

In periods of equilibrium there will be a resistance to change, especially to introduce major changes. The transformational changes take place when there is a crisis type situation or when there is a change in the leadership. Punctuations are for short periods, when an organization undergoes profound changes that result in the transformation of the deep structure of the organization. The brief periods of punctuation may cause distress to members and disorientation to the organization. The period following the punctuation ushers in an era of stimulated thinking, new organizational rules, and long periods of equilibrium and incremental change (Gold, 1999).

Irrespective of the approaches adopted to introduce reforms, it takes a long time for the system to overcome the resistance to change, to accept the changes, and to assimilate them. Further, all reforms, in order to be successful in their implementation and institutionalization, require legitimization. The three constituents of legitimization of higher education reforms are the state, the market, and academia (Slantcheva and Levy, 2007). Legitimization takes place when the reform measures are translated into legislative provisions by the state, when providers and the market adhere to these regulations, and when the professoriate and other stakeholders socially accept the reform measures. Continued public support is needed at all stages in the process of legitimization. It is interesting to note that in past experiences, even when reforms implied a move away from state control and demanded more institutional autonomy, public support was sought to implement and legitimize them.

An Overview of Reforms in Higher Education

Many reforms taking place in the world reflect a focus on the importance of knowledge production, the role of the market in knowledge production, and the importance given to higher education in knowledge production and knowledge use. This is more so with regard to reforms in higher education in the developed world (Varghese, 2011 for a detailed discussion). An analysis of reforms in Europe indicates that most of the recent reform measures have been efforts to reposition European higher education in order to improve international and global competitiveness (CHEPS, 2009) following an understanding that economic growth and global competitiveness are increasingly driven by knowledge. The effort to develop world class universities is a good example of this. Some of the basic features of world class universities are: highly qualified faculty; excellence in research; quality teaching; high levels of funding; international and highly talented students; academic freedom; autonomous governance structures; and well-equipped facilities for teaching, research and administration. Salmi (2009) summarizes these attributes under three categories: (a) concentration of talents (faculty and students); (b) abundance of resources; and (c) favourable government. The university rankings added another impetus to align universities with market-led growth, global competitiveness, and the need to develop world-class universities.

Higher education reforms in many countries of South East and East Asia, too, aimed at enhancing their capacity to produce knowledge to improve economic and market competitiveness. The Chinese reforms of Project 1985 or Project 2011, the Centres of Excellence (COE 21) in Japan, Brain Korea 21 (BK 21), and the Accelerated Programme for Excellence (APEX) in Malaysia are good examples of this trend. US higher education reforms were also an attempt to closely align the system with the market in order to improve economic competitiveness by relying 'far more on marketplace forces, local authority, and professional autonomy in controlling and coordinating tertiary education' (Mclendon and Hearn, 2009) than on the state. Most countries would like their universities to be among the highest-ranked universities in the world.

The recent reform measures in India attempt to look closely at the higher education system to improve the relevance of its study programmes and the quality of graduates from the system. The Yashpal Committee report and several bills introduced in parliament in recent years indicate an earnest effort to change the system. The establishment of a new constitutional body—the National Commission for Higher Education and Research (NCHER), the setting up of a national accreditation agency, and permitting entry of foreign educational institutions are measures that are subjected to discussion and debate in the country (Sunder, 2010; Tilak, 2010).

In Europe, the Bologna Process was central to higher education reforms in the period 2000-2010. Most of the 46 countries constituting the European Higher Education Area have adopted new higher education legislations, a credit system (180+120 credits equivalent to 3+2 years of full-time study), effected curricular changes, and embraced quality assurance processes. The development of the European Standards and Guidelines for Quality Assurance in Higher Education (ESG), and the creation of ENQA, the association of quality assessment agencies, were all efforts to improve the quality of higher education (Martin and Antony, 2007).

The reforms in higher education in the Commonwealth of Independent States (CIS) were intended to reposition and facilitate transition from a centrally planned to a market economy. Higher education in the Soviet Union and in East European countries was a state-funded and controlled activity. Political changes in the region in the 1990s marked an end to centralized planning, a marked reduction in public funding, rapidly declining academic standards, and high levels of unemployment among university graduates. One of the major areas of reforms in this region was curricula. Curricular reforms were intended to reflect market-orientation in the curricula by introducing market-friendly courses in the study programmes and courses on economics, accounting, financial analysis, marketing, business administration, law, information systems, international relationships, psychology, etc. The number of courses offered by the CIS countries, mostly market-friendly, increased greatly. For example, the number of courses in Belarus University increased from 19 in 1991 to 56 in 2005, and the number of specializations rose from 105 to 230 during the same period, most of which were in new, market-friendly areas (Varghese, 2009b).

Other reforms in higher education in the CIS region include the introduction of the credit system, and changes in course structure and student evaluation methods. These were efforts meant to align universities in CIS countries with international standards and their education systems with those of the west. There was also regional pressure to develop a comparable structure for the purpose of credit transfer systems between universities located within the CIS countries. They developed a new structure of higher education, which allowed the different levels to be clearly distinguished—undergraduate, graduate, post-graduate, and doctoral studies. Having a comparable structure of higher education promotes regional mobility and facilitates credit transfer, as is the case in the EU countries today.

The CIS countries also introduced cost-recovery and cost-sharing measures to finance universities in order to retain teachers in public universities. During the transition period the salaries of professors in some of the most prestigious universities in Moscow and St. Petersburg did not exceed US$ 2 a day (Shattock, 2004), leading to a mass exodus of professors from public universities. The universities started generating their own income to provide higher salaries to the professoriate. Levying fees from the students was the easiest way to generate sustainable income without substantial initial investment. This led to changes in the admission policies and procedures—fee paying and non-fee-paying students. The non-fee-paying students, supported by the state budget, were called 'budget students' (Kitaev, 2004, Varghese, 2009b). The share of non-budget students increased over a period of time.

An analysis of reforms in Latin America indicate that the reforms in this region were, perhaps, more related to privatization, promoting the private sector, and diversification of institutions, programmes and clientele. For example, in Chile, there are 25 traditional universities belonging to the Council of Rectors of Chilean Universities (CRUCH), which receives direct public funding (Araneda, 2010). The universities created after 1981 by the private sector are self-funded institutions, and other tertiary institutions are also self-financed private institutions offering courses directly relevant to the market.

An analysis of reforms in higher education in Africa indicates several measures to enhance the financial position of universities. The university enterprise scheme (UNES) and parallel programmes of the university of Nairobi, the dual track admission policy—with sponsored and private students in Makarere University, the institutional transformation programmes, cost-sharing, and revenue diversification strategies of the University of Dar-es-Salaam, dual track systems in Zambia etc. are examples of efforts of universities to respond to the decline in public funding support. Apart from the move towards privatization, most of the countries in Africa encouraged the establishment of private higher education institutions, and this segment of higher education is expanding very rapidly. These reform measures have helped expand higher education in Africa. The growth rates of enrolment in higher education are high in most countries in Africa (Mohammedbhai, 2008). More importantly, the private segment of the public institutions (fee-paying students) and private institutions witnessed a faster growth than the public-funded sector.

It can be seen that the motivation behind reforms in most cases in several regions was to reposition higher education vis-à-vis the external environment. In most cases this move implied aligning institutions of higher education more closely with the market—local, national, or global. It seems that the system is internalizing a realization that the external environment of operation of institutions of higher education has changed from serving the public sector to serving the private sector and the market.

Some General Trends in Reforms in Higher Education

The state traditionally enjoyed a monopoly in funding and managing institutions of higher education. While this status of the state in decision making remained unquestionable until the 1980s, most reforms in the past quarter of a century questioned the dominant role of the state in decision making. The central question in many reforms concerns the role of the state. Most reforms have tried to reduce the role of the state and enhance the role of the market. This transition took different forms in different countries.

The fiscal capacity of the state weakened in the 1980s, and this is reflected in its investment in the social sectors, including education. Further, the state was considered to be investing in non-productive sectors and was inefficient in operation. The structural adjustment programmes further enforced conditionalities to a reduced role of the state in general and in social sectors in particular. Within education, the structural adjustment regime demanded a re-prioritization, which meant a diversion of resources from higher to basic education (World Bank, 1986). The fiscal crisis and the reduced capacity of the state to finance an expanding higher education system further questioned the state's legitimacy to be the sole provider and paved the way for the emergence of an evaluative state model (Neave, 1988; Neave and van Vught, 1991). This move, in a sense, was a movement away from direct control to a 'steering from a distance' model of governance. This change implied less direct control by the state and more autonomy for institutions.

The next stage saw a more direct entry of the market in the operations of institutions of higher education. Many countries embraced the new market-oriented management framework—New Public Management (Dent, 2007). Public universities adopted corporate models and became entrepreneurial (Clark, 1998), leading to changes in university activities, organizational structures, and management practices. Further, private higher education institutions emerged and expanded their share of total enrolment (Levy, 2006; Varghese, 2006). The prevailing ideology seems to be that 'even if a service is to be provided at public cost, it need not actually be provided by public agencies if the private sector is able to provide the same service in a more cost-effective manner' (Patel, 1993: 45). This stage saw an enlarged role of the market.

A move towards the market implied either privatization of public institutions, or the operation of private higher education institutions. Privatization implied applying market principles in the operation of public higher education institutions. The move towards a market-oriented system focused on notions of efficiency in operation, performance evaluation, and accountability measures, and implied several changes at the institutional level. It is this market approach to the provision of public services from a 'managerialism' perspective that lies at the core of the changes introduced in many universities.

The emergence of the market as an important partner in decision-making helped respond more effectively to the demands emerging from the production sectors, whose operations, in any case, are moderated by the market. The emergence of a knowledge-based production and globalization process put pressure on the higher education sector to respond not only to domestic market demands, but also to global markets. International agencies and institutions became a part of decision-making in higher education. The emergence of GATS, accreditation agencies, and harmonization efforts such as the Bologna process reinforced the influence of international inputs in national decision-making (Leuze *et al.*, 2007). In other words, the role of the market has become all pervasive and its influence omnipotent.

With the entry of market operations, universities have become both managerial and entrepreneurial in their approach as well as in their operation. An entrepreneurial response provides a formula for institutional development that places autonomy on a self-defined basis: diversifying sources of income, reducing governmental dependency, developing new departments and modes of training, rationalizing structural changes that provide a stronger response capability, creating a central steering capacity, focusing on institutions, etc. These changes, individually and collectively, have led to a major re-organization of university activities. Such re-organization, especially in public institutions, may be called 'institutional restructuring' (Varghese, 2009a), which is, in fact, the major change one notices in the higher education sector.

The restructuring process has changed the orientation and operation of institutions of higher education. Institutions of higher education are expected to fill the role of intellectual enquiry and academic preparation, high level professional preparation, and skill impartation. The intellectual tradition, in many instances, is on the decline and the professional orientation is on the increase. However, with the entry of market operations, the state still encourages the academic orientation and research tradition, while the market influences more of professional orientation.

The introduction of some of the reforms was very painful and faced severe resistance. In some countries the process was incremental and in line with the changes introduced in the economic sectors. The reforms in most of the developed countries were introduced individually and incrementally. The higher education institutions in these countries continued to enjoy state support and a long-term equilibrium. The system accepted and absorbed the changes with little resistance. However, the reforms in the CIS countries and in the African context experienced severe challenges and they punctuated the long-term equilibrium enjoyed by the system. When the deep structure was affected, some universities in Africa experienced direct confrontation between the authorities, students, and staff. The reforms in the CIS countries affected the core structure but did not face direct confrontations, not because the constituents accepted the changes but because there was no alternative other than to close down the universities. In South East Asia, protests were limited but resistance was felt. Although the introduction of reforms faced resistance in the 1990s, it has become more acceptable now.

One of the common factors in all the reforms is the expanding role of the market in higher education decision making. It can be argued that this is the core of most reforms. The exception to this trend may be in the Nordic countries, where the higher education institutions continue to receive state funding, private institutions are not common, and most reforms focus on quality and equality in higher education (Fagerlind and Stromqvist, 2004).

At the close of the decade, the economic crisis has led to a questioning of the role of excessive market operations in all sectors, including education. The need for state action and regulation is more felt now than before the crisis period. The implication of the crisis at the institutional level was a need to do more with less. Many universities were forced to re-prioritize activities at the institutional level and re-organize the functioning of the institutions.

Concluding Observations

A review of reform measures across countries indicates a move of the locus of decision-making away from the government to institutions and markets. The move towards the market is either executed through privatization or through private institutions. In many cases, these reforms did not imply a total reliance of public institutions on market forces for their income. They continued to receive a large share of their operational costs from the public authorities. The income generated by public institutions through market operations is an addition to the public funding support they receive. However, income generation has become a major concern for institutions of higher education, which at times overshadows the core academic concerns.

How are different stakeholders affected by the reforms? All reform implementation has been the result of a process of negotiation between the government, the professoriate, the students, and the households. The professoriate argued against government control but preferred a public institutional image to a private sector image of the institutions in which they were working. It seems that the professoriate was more against bureaucratic control than government policy interventions and public funding. They were more in favour of maintaining academic freedom and institutional autonomy than of opening the sector to the market.

The student community reacted to the reforms based on the given political situation in the country. They were at the forefront of agitations when reforms were introduced. However, given the transitory nature of their stay in the universities, the cohort of students that followed those who opposed the reforms accepted them as part of the rules of the game.

The reforms also implied a shift in the financial burden away from government to the households. The final incidence of the financial burden as a result of the move towards the market was borne by households. This was true irrespective of the influencing factors or drivers of reforms. Reform measures pertaining to privatization of public institutions faced severe resistance, even when cost recovery in private institutions was tolerated. The private institutions became a convenient arrangement to facilitate the shift in the cost burden from the general public to households with less resistance.

It is important to note the most recent change, especially during the period of economic crisis. The crisis questioned the role of the market in replacing the functions carried out by the public institutions. The need for regulations is underlined in all instances, which implies that the state is back in a different role—more as a regulator and facilitator than a role related to funding and controlling the sector (Varghese, 2010). State intervention has also reprioritized investments in higher education. The state is increasingly targeting its investments towards science and technology programmes, which help retain and improve the market competitiveness of the economy, and in the education of certain groups and subject areas to improve equity. Both sets of strategies followed by the state have helped to expand the role of the market. In other words, what is being noticed is a clear case of public intervention as a means to strengthen market processes. The state, through its regulatory role, keeps expanding the sphere of market operations in education.

Linking higher education reforms too closely with economic production and market processes belittles the important role played by higher education in several areas of educational and social life. Further, the implications of market-oriented reforms for long-term equity in access to education and income distribution needs to be analyzed before reform measures are implemented. In other words, the social desirability and acceptability of reforms should be considered when reforming the higher education sector. This aspect of the reforms is very often overshadowed by market considerations of improved efficiency and returns to investment.

10

Open and Distance Education*

Madhu Parhar

Open and distance education, like all other sectors of education, experienced massive expansion since independence, especially since 1962 when Delhi University for the first time introduced correspondence education in India. This was a step forward in extending academic help to thousands of students who were appearing as 'private candidates' in many universities in India. Correspondence education provided tailor made learning material with some provision of tutorial support. Some of the interesting initiatives came from unconventional sources. Institution of Engineers introduced AMIE course in Engineering, and Chartered Accountants Association of India introduced on Chartered Accountancy, respectively. Counting 1962 as the founding date of open and distance education with Delhi University setting up the Directorate of Correspondence Education, Indian open and distance education has 52 years of history.

During this period of expansion and qualitative changes in open and distance education, it came to occupy a place of prominence compared to its earlier location in the periphery of the system. It found places in the national policy statements, and planning paradigms. In this chapter, we will deal with the evolution of the system and flag a few issues that deserve our attention.

Emergence of the System

The first three open learning institutions were set-up in Australia, Canada and New Zealand in 1916, 1919 and 1922, respectively (Mukhopadhyay and Philips, 1994). Incidentally, all three initiatives were in the domain of school education with the sole agenda of reaching out with education where formal

---

* This chapter draws from author's chapter on ODE published in *Education in India: Dynamics of Development* (2007).

mechanisms were not viable or feasible. Higher education adopted open and distance education almost after 35 years. Pioneer was, probably, Chinese correspondence education initiated by People's University of China in 1952 (Jhang 1997). First Open University was set up in 1969 in UK with another 15 years of time lag.

Indian initiative in distance education was cradled by conventional universities. They offered same courses through formal face-to-face as well as distance education modes. They are now called 'dual mode universities'. There are about 250 dual mode universities, now. First Open University was set-up in 1982 in Andhra Pradesh, 20 years after the beginning of correspondence education in Delhi University and 13 years after the first Open University in the world, e.g. UKOU. Probably, the popularity and success of distance education programmes in the dual mode institutions had created enough ground for setting up dedicated open universities in India. Further, while market forces were the driving force for correspondence education in the dual mode universities, open universities owe their emergence to policy thrusts of the state and union governments on India.

Policy Thrusts

Expansion of higher education since independence was uneven in terms of establishment of institutes, academic programmes and enrollment. The Planning Commission proposed, in 1960, setting up of evening colleges; starting correspondence courses and awarding external degrees. Later, Education Commission (1964-66) recommended introduction of correspondence education. This was reflected in the first National Policy on Education of 1968. It is interesting to note that University of Delhi introduced correspondence courses in 1962 as a pilot project much before the recommendations of the Education Commission and the National Policy on Education 1968.

The national seminar on Open University system organized by Government of India in 1970 recommended establishment of a National Open University to offer quality education to "much larger body of population which remains outside the university system". Based on the recommendations, a draft bill was prepared by the Union Government for the establishment of a National Open University. Despite the bill was for setting up a 'national' Open University, Andhra Pradesh wrested the initiative and pioneered Open University in India by setting up Andhra Pradesh Open University in 1982. Indira Gandhi National Open University was established in 1985, three years later, by an Act of Parliament.

The second National Policy on Education (1986) also recommended open and distance education, to "augment(s) opportunities for education, provide access, to ensure cost effectiveness and for promoting relevant, flexible and innovative system of education".

ODE through Five Year Plans

Study of five year plan documents provides an interesting insight into the growth and development of open and distance education in India. The first five year plan (1951) referred to the need for increasing the opportunities for higher education outside the formal system without articulating the nature of the programme outside the formal system. Since then almost all the five year plan documents emphasized on open and distance education system, in some form or other, to provide educational opportunities to large number of people.

In 2009, Ministry of Human Resource Development drafted a New Policy on Distance Learning in Higher Education. The document was uploaded on the website of MHRD for information of the public and the stakeholders. The draft policy stated that "ODL can provide opportunity of learning to those who do not have direct access to face to face teaching. Through ODE, India can achieve the GER target of 20 per cent by the end of 12th five year plan. It also pointed out that institutions offering distance education must use ICT in delivery of programmes, management of students and university affairs through Web Portal. Institution must make optimal use of e-learning contents for delivery of programmes through distance mode". This document, however, could not be formalized as a policy.

The 10th and 11th Five Year Plan documents provided distinct coverage to distance education system. The highlight was to expand the activities of Gyan Darshan and Gyanvani". The 12th Plan (2012-2017) was much more exacting on open and distance education. To quote the 12th Plan document, "Support will be given to open and distance learning institutions to expand access. Programmes will be regularly evaluated for learning outcomes to maintain the quality of ODL programmes. Traditional institutions can offer part of the curriculum online. This will promote blended learning and help universities reach out to more students and nontraditional learners".

Open and Distance education finds a place of prominence in the documents and recommendations of the Ministry of HRD (MHRD) and Planning Commission. However, RUSA (National Mission on Higher Education) that forms the backbone of higher education reforms especially in state colleges and universities is silent on open and distance education that actually provides education to more than 20 per cent students in higher education.

[http://mhrd.gov.in/sites/upload_files/mhrd/files/upload_document/RUSAguidelines30102013.pdf]

The National Knowledge Commission (NKC) which was created in 2005, recommended paradigm shifts in teaching learning, evaluation, infrastructure, organization and management and quality assessment in open and distance education system. It emphasized on establishing autonomous credit bank, a national repository of Open Education Resources and use of advanced information and communication in access, pedagogy and governance. It recommended an independent External Quality Assurance Cell to evaluate ODE institutions at regular intervals.

Another important policy shift in the distance education system was the creation of a regulatory mechanism, namely, Distance Education Bureau (DEB) replacing Distance Education Council (DEC). DEC was set up in 1991 as a statutory mechanism under IGNOU Act. Role of DEC was for promotion, coordination and maintenance of standards of open and distance education system in the country. It developed guidelines for regulating the establishment and operation of ODL institutes in the country. MHRD in 2010 constituted a committee to revisit the regulation of standards of education imparted through distance mode. The committee recommended the creation of a new regulatory body of ODL system to be named as Distance Education Council of India (DECI). It also decided that DEC be shifted from IGNOU to UGC. Thus in 2012, MHRD transferred DEC from IGNOU to UGC by an order. IGNOU notified the repeal and deletion of Statute 28 of IGNOU act and dissolution of DEC in 2013. Since then DEC has been renamed as Distance Education Bureau (DEB) under UGC. This is an interim arrangement till DECI is created by the Parliament of India.

Market Forces

So far as dual mode universities are concerned, there were two major reasons for initiating the correspondence courses. One compelling reason was to create a balance between the demand and number of places available in the universities. For example, Delhi as a city produced more school graduates than the university and its affiliated colleges could accommodate. To accommodate the demand, Delhi University created Directorate of Correspondence Courses and another center for non-collegiate women students. Though started as a second option to cope with social demand, students all over the country saw the advantage in flexi time education leading to degree. Hence the demand grew.

Some perceptive vice-chancellors did not miss to see the economic, rather commercial, prospect of the new phenomenon. Backed by the recommendations of major committees and commissions, some universities started correspondence education to bridge the gap and build financial health of the universities. They focused on courses that offer richer dividends. The economic studies of correspondence courses in several universities indicate that correspondence courses generate substantive revenue for the university. The 'commercial' dimension is also indicated by the transfer of funds from correspondence education departments to the central kitty of the university to support the formal departments, which depended all along on state subsidy. This transfer of funds from correspondence education to support conventional departments often cost of quality of distance education.

The open universities emerged out of social demand, economic viability and non-commercial motives backed by government policies and also academic adventure.

The dual mode institutions had already established the acceptability of distance education mode among Indian students. They had also proved that students in correspondence education are prepared to pay; hence, open learning can be viable through social financing. However, the dual mode universities remained conventional so far as courses and course delivery are concerned, may be guided by the requirements of the examination since student of both formal and correspondence education take the same examination. Structural innovations over the conventional institutions -innovative courses, open course choice, open age, open entry qualification, open or flexi-time, credit accumulation, multi-channel course delivery, etc. were the academic adventures of open education.

Thus, social demand, commercial potential and academic adventure are the three important driving force for the emergence of open and distance education in India.

Expansion

Beginning with the directorate of correspondence education in Delhi University in 1962, presently there are more than 242 dual mode universities offering distance education programmes. During the last few years, some conventional as well as the private universities have established new departments of distance education. The growth of DE institutions (both dual mode and single mode) is given in Table 10.1 below:

Table 10.1: Growth of ODL Institutions

Year	*Dual Mode Institutions*	*Single Mode Open Universities*	*Total*
1962	1	—	1
1975	22	—	22
1982	34	1	35
1985	38	2	40
1990	46	5	51
2000	70	9	79
2005	106	13	119
2010	242	14	256

Source: http://www.ugc.ac.in/deb/pdf/growthDEB.pdf.

There are two interesting features of the expansion.

- Maximum growth of distance education institutions happened during 2000-2005.

- Many prestigious institutes of national importance, like IISc (Bangalore), IIT (Chennai, Bombay and Kharagpur) also offer DE programme.
- National Law School of India, International Institute for Population Sciences, and Indian Institute of Taxation are also offering distance education programmes.

There has been equally impressive growth in enrolment (Table 10.2).

Table 10.2: Growth of Student Enrolment

Year	*Conventional Universities*	*CCI/DEI/Open Universities*	*Percentage share of Distance Education*	*Total*
1962-1963	7,52,,095	1,112	0.147	7,53,207
1975-1976	24,26,109	64,210	2.578	24,90,319
1980-1981	27,52,437	1,66,428	5.701	29,18,865
1985-1986	36,06,029	3,55,091	8.964	39,61,120
1990-1991	49,24,868	5,92,814	10.744	55,17,682
1994-1995	61,13,929	8,03,176	11.611	69,17,105
1995-1996	65,74,005	10,03,000	3.237	75,77,005
2000-2001	83,99,443	13,78,000	14.094	97,77,443
2005-2006	110,28,020	18,33,524	14.256	1,28,61,544
2009-2010	124,68,560	37,36,744	23.35	160,00,000 (approx)

Source: http://www.ugc.ac.in/deb/pdf/growthDEB.pdf.

Enrollment in distance education in higher education increased from 1,112 students in 1962 to around 38 lakhs in 2009-2010. Thus the share of distance education in the GER is about 23.35 per cent. IGNOU, with more than 3 million students (cumulative) on rolls, is one of the mega universities of the world.

In higher education, till 1999-2000, Open and distance education accounted for 17 per cent of total enrolment in higher education (Kaul, 2005); As per the 12th plan document, during 2011-12 there were 42 lakh students in ODL which is targeted at 52 lakhs during 2016-17 (Planning Commission estimate).

Along with the expansion of the institutions and enrollment, there have been important developments and diversification in course offerings. General programmes like B.A., B.Com. etc. were offered during the beginning of DE system in India. Later programmes like B.Ed. and technical programmes were introduced by the distance learning institutes. Open Universities moved from traditional programmes to professional and vocational programmes like plumbing, sericulture, bee keeping, textile and apparel designing etc. During 2009-2010, 1138 academic programmes were offered at 14 open universities (Srivastava, 2012). Universities also moved from certificate, diploma, and graduate programmes to M.Phil. and Ph. D. programmes.

Relevance

The issue of relevance of open and distance education can be seen from more than one angle.

- Who does it serve—rural or urban, male or female, youth or age, disadvantaged or privileged people?
- What kinds of courses are offered -conventional or unconventional, degree or continuing education based on system need, or economic viability, or commercial profitability?
- Is it self-renewing-changing with the changes in employment market demand, pedagogy/andragogy, and technology communication?

There are several research contributions on socio-economic background of open learners. Unfortunately, equity is not the hallmark of the system. In the dual mode universities, about 90 per cent students are urban. Similarly, only about 40 per cent are female students (Srivastava and Ramegowda, 2006). The proportion of students from disadvantaged sections is also low. Reasons are not far to seek. Since distance education is fee charging, it discourages the rural disadvantaged and the women students. Further, the student support services are available largely in the urban areas. The composition in open universities is a shade better, marginally more equitous than the dual mode universities.

So far as the courses are concerned, conventional universities restrict themselves to conventional courses like B.A., B.Sc. and B.Com. They offer the same graduate and postgraduate programmes through correspondence education and formal conventional methods. Of late, the trend has changed. Some of the dual mode institutions also offer courses like B.Tech., M.Tech., Paramedical, Journalism, Astrology and Yoga studies. Many universities offer shorter duration certificate, diploma and postgraduate diploma programmes through distance education.

Dual mode universities offer courses not on the basis of any specific need assessment—at least such studies have not been referred to in professional literature on distance education. They use their 'gut feeling' and/or 'learnt-from-the-neighbor'; if a particular programme generated good response, similar course was offered elsewhere. Conventional undergraduate programmes in liberal arts and commerce (B.A./B.Com.) are in this category. Another kind of courses was launched on the basis of understanding of the market conditions; B.Ed., Courses on Computers and MBA courses fall in this category. These courses are the single largest source of revenue to the dual mode universities. This need assessment is also not a common feature in the open learning institutions, though IGNOU has done need assessment studies on couple of occasions.

The Open Universities, IGNOU in particular, broke new grounds. During 2014-2015 IGNOU offered 266 programmes with lot of built in flexibilities. There are many unconventional stand-alone courses and modular courses that can be opted as standalone module. such modules can, however, also be learnt to accumulate credit leading to diploma or degree. Each School of IGNOU is steadily building up its repertoire of unconventional courses, primarily for continuing education, ranging from construction workers to creative writers to college and university teachers or corporate managers. Courses like Appreciation Course on Environment, Course on Intellectual Property Rights and awareness package in the area of Environment, Poultry etc. are some such examples.

The YC Maharashtra Open University also gave a lead in designing and offering unconventional courses deliberately creating an affront to the conventional elitist concept of a 'university'. For example, it designed courses for farmers, grape growers, who may or may not be even literate. (The architect of this new form of university, Prof. Ram G Takwale, then Vice-Chancellor of YCMOU, called it Mass-varsity). On the other end of the continuum, the same university offers distance education programmes to doctoral students.

Whether the open and distance education system is learning from its own experience and self-renewing itself is an important question that does not seem to have a straight answer. In dual mode universities, courses have continued to be conventional, learning material has continued to be textual. Some of the new-entrants, particularly in B.Ed., brought down the quality of material to save on cost compared to their counterparts in Madras, Annamalai, etc. Thus, in many of the conventional dual mode universities, economic and commercial considerations outweighed the issue of relevance and quality (Mukhopadhyay, 1997).

The distance education in the dual mode universities has remained largely entangled with the bureaucratic structures of the universities. The concerned discipline, Faculties and Boards of Studies, determine the courses for the university; the same courses are prescribed for the distance education programme. Universities also differ in their structures so far as the status of the correspondence education unit is concerned. Internal structures are also not uniform. For example, while Bombay University manages its correspondence education unit with few academic staff and a tiny secretariat staff, Delhi University has more than 90 academic staff in the School of Open Learning.

Quality of Distance Education

Quality is the major issue in distance education. Popularly, the formal system is used as the benchmark for quality. This may not be the right reference point since the quality of formal education itself is questionable, besides the wide variation in quality from one university to another. By all pedagogical analysis and assessment, distance education is far more scientific so far as the instructional design and delivery is concerned (Parhar, 1998). The assessment of quality of distance education, hence, will have to be with reference to a different framework.

As the open and distance education has grown all over the world, as well as in India, it is classified by various authors into different levels of generations (Mukhopadhyay, 1996, Taylor 2000, Anderson and Dron 2011) depending upon the nature and combination of delivery modes and pedagogy used by the distance education system.

Mukhopadhyay and Taylor provide a theoretical framework for adopting latest technologies in distance and open education system. Both authors have described that distance education has moved increasingly from single print material mode (first generation) to a multi-channel mode (fifth generation). Not only that the later generation distance education has incorporated many more alternatives learning paths, including electronic, satellite and internet based communication, but also has incorporated major change in the structure and pattern of print and contact modes also. While the earlier generation distance education used conventional textual material, the later generation converted them into self-learning material (Self-learning material of later generation distance education is different from the conventional textbook-mode lessons used in the correspondence education) which, by all research evidence, facilitates learning better. Similarly, the personal contact programmes are increasingly being upgraded from one way lectures to interactive ones. One way television and radio communication is being complemented and supplemented by two way interactive video and radio. At present many institutions have adopted online learning with virtual classrooms and mobile learning.

Anderson and Dron (2011) classified open and distance education differently into three generations of pedagogy in distance education. These are cognitive-behaviourist, social constructivist and connectivist pedagogy.

Against this parameter, it is interesting to note that the Indian distance education system vary widely among themselves in their choice of instructional media. The conventional dual mode universities still hold on to the textual print material, and personal contact programmes dominated by lectures. Open Universities uses

- Self-instructional print material,
- Short and Extended personal contact programmes in both lecture and tutorial modes,
- Assignments,

- Interactive Radio and Television,
- Computer Communication (Online Education), and
- Web Conferencing.

Exceptions apart, most dual mode universities have satisfied themselves with the conventional delivery modes of distance education. This remains compatible to their economic and other considerations for the programmes. Certain conventional universities, however, supplement print material with audio and video programmes. It is, however, necessary to mention that they have all the relevant skills and expertise to upgrade their own systems. This is indicated by the composition of the course teams in IGNOU. IGNOU programme and material design is largely the contribution of the academia from the conventional universities.

An important feature of DE pedagogy is that the onus of learning is on the learners as compared to that in the formal system. Distance education builds its pedagogy around self regulated learners. It stands on a sound foundation of instructional design. The pedagogy is based on constructivist approach of learning as compared to the instructivist learning approaches practiced in formal system. In realistic assessment, it is possible to infer that the conventional dual mode universities have retained their original tradition despite their knowledge and expertise about the emerging pedagogy of distance education. Whereas the open universities have been able to adopt and utilize the new modes, though there is quality variance between the national and state open universities as well.

Technology Initiatives

With the revolution in information and communication technologies (ICT), open and distance education institutions made massive advances in the use of technology in the delivery of programmes. In late 1990s and early 2000, open universities introduced interactive radio/TV counseling, FM radio stations. EDUSAT which was launched in 2004 changed the distance education learning environment especially at IGNOU. With further innovations in ICT, ODL received major impetus.

To improve learning, National Mission on Education through Technologies (NMEICT) was started during the 11th plan. Under this mission universities and colleges were provided broadband connections. Virtual labs were developed and creation of e-content was made the priority. 12th plan carried forward the legacies of the 11th plan. There was a major shift in the use of technologies in the five year plans as well as the way learners were using technology.

A major new thrust was the promotion of Open Education Resources (OER) and Online Courses. Open Education Resources originated from the developments within the open and distance education. OERs are free openly licensed educational material that can be used for teaching, learning, research and other purposes. The various types of resources are the course material, content modules, learning objects etc. Students have improved access to different programmes and courses, with higher quality and low cost (Rory, 2013 and Parhar, 2013). Large number of initiatives are being taken by open universities as well as few conventional universities. Some examples are; IIT Bombay, National Programme on Technology Enhance Learning (NPTEL), NIOS, Sakshat, NCERT etc. NPTEL is an important project funded by MHRD is an indication of government policy thrust on ICT enabled distance education. It provides E-learning through online Web and Video courses in Engineering, Science and Humanities streams. The mission of NPTEL is to enhance the quality of engineering education in the country by providing free online courseware.

The latest buzz in education is about MOOCs (Massive Open Online Courses). There are many MOOC websites like Coursera, edX, Futurelearn, Udemy, ITunes, Carnegie Mellon Free Courses, Khan Academy etc. which are offering free education. Through MOOCs learners learn on their own, watch videos, involve in online discussions, online laboratories and also involve themselves in other learning tools. In India, IIT Bombay started the MOOCs movement partnering with edX for training large number of engineering teachers. IIT Bombay is now working on blended MOOCs model where students study available digital material on their own, including viewing of pre-recorded lectures. They then attend classroom tutorials and discussion sessions, and practise solving problems in groups, under the supervision of a teacher. Through this 'flipped class-room' model of teaching, teachers can conduct group discussions and problem solving sessions rather than mere lecturing.

Few private organizations have taken Initiatives in providing education by using latest technologies. Xerox Research Centre for Innovation has created innovative online programmes for students anywhere, anytime in the world, offered through TutorSpace. The TutorSpace comprises seven components, namely, Information, Lectures, Deadlines, Quizzes, Discussion, Students, and Attendance. 'Information' provides the basic outline of the course and/or the theme. Contents are delivered through video-lectures, usually short and crisp without the noise and clustering of electronic aids. Most speakers use electronic pen to elaborate on the electronic boards. The video presentations are complimented with discussion where students can post their questions and comments and thereby generate a discussion. The learning outcome is assessed by quizzes which are actually a series of multiple choice questions. Then there are normal data on student identity, attendance and deadlines. TutorSpace is one step further to NPTEL video programmes. With carefully produced video complimented by discussion and quizzes, it provides a mechanism of quality assurance.

Amrita University created a powerful platform, A-VIEW for extending online education to various types of learners. To quote from the website www.a-view.in, “A-VIEW is another advanced multi-modal, multi-platform, collaborative e-learning solution which allows an instructor to teach or interact with a large number of learners transcending geographies on a real-time basis through live audio video streaming and synchronized content sharing. A-VIEW allows the instructor to perform live evaluation of the learners and to get real-time feedback from attendees on the go. A-VIEW can also act as an online meeting tool that can support online social collaboration and interactions with multiple users from various locations simultaneously.” Collaborating with IIT, Bombay, A-VIEW has trained literally thousands of teachers. A-VIEW is now used by various types of institutions.

Research in Distance Education

Distance Education is an innovative and steadily growing system of education in the world. Research in Distance Education is a distinct area of academic interest. With the beginning of the British Open University in 1969, a more serious and systematic attempt to study the components of Distance Education started which helped to improve the distance teaching learning process. The focus of research in distance education differs from one country to another.

Number of authors reviewed researches in distance education (Sherman and Nedza 1990, Scriven 1991, Panda 1992, Rekkedal 1993, Jegede 1994, Calvert 1995, Mishra 1997, Koble and Bunker 1997 and Holmberg 2000) (Berge and Mrozowski (2001), Rourke and Szabo (2002), Parhar (2003), Lee *et al.* (2004), Zawachi-Richter (2009) from various angles.

Panda (1992) found that most of the studies are descriptive, surveys or experimental studies with poor methodological footing. Mishra (1997) critically analyzed 361 papers published in four leading international journals on distance education. Later in another review Mishra (2002) categorized techniques into eight areas. Naidu (2004) suggested five, namely, case studies, co-relational studies, experimental, phenomenological studies and research synthesis, research methods for pursuing research in distance education.

Parhar (2013) analyzed the studies in the various areas as evident from the review earlier done by various authors. She found two major areas of concentrations of research in distance education, namely, characteristics of distance learners and economics of distance education. There are certain areas where the status of research is still in the form of touch and go, especially, in andragogy and pedagogy of distance education. Distance education has, all over the world, adopted a multi-channel learning format. There is no study on the effect of multi-channel learning on distance education. There are separate studies on various components of the instructional process. Within the instructional process there are very few studies on electronic media. TV and radio as media of distance education have remained almost unexplored. Similarly, researches in other components of instructional processes are few and scanty to derive any meaningful conclusions about the pedagogy and andragogy in distance education.

Studies are totally missing on what constitute quality and what determines quality in distance education. The number of studies on organization and management of distance education are small. Another relatively unexplored area is the staff development through distance education at a time when the nature of jobs is changing rapidly. The need for on-the-job training, in industries, business organizations as well as in service sectors is much more important now than ever before. Research is needed on worker reeducation—programme and course design, instructional design and delivery, costing and cost effectiveness and impact on productivity.

Although number of universities—both open and dual mode universities are offering on-line education, research is still too scanty in this area. More and more agencies at all levels will resort to use Internet for educational programme delivery. There is, however, little evidence of research base on the basics of pedagogy of on-line education. Future research will have to address the nitty-gritty of web-based instruction as a mode of distance education.

Conclusion

There are few clear trends. Open and Distance education is no more on the sideline; it has arrived at the mainstream policies in higher education. The lateral expansion of open and distance education will continue unabated. Its current contribution of about 22 per cent to the GER of 20 per cent in higher education is likely to stay as India moves to 30 per cent GER in higher education by 2020. The space is shared by dual mode universities and open universities. Irrespective of the crying concern of quality and relevance of distance education, it is the conventional dual mode universities that serve the educational needs of maximum number of students in the country.

The Open and distance education will continue to be invaded by innovations especially through technology enabled delivery. As technology enabled delivery occupies more and more space, new and unconventional institutions will continue to enter the fray. For, it is these kinds of institutions that exploit the fruits of technology.

A natural corollary of innovative institutions with innovative methods is the change in the type and structures of courses as indicated by OER and MOOCs. Parallel to conventional long term graduate programmes, there are short focused courses on life enrichment, vocational and technical skill Upgradation. By implication, job enrichment will emerge as a parallel focus in open and distance education in not to remote future in India.

11

Reforms in Teacher Education

Sherwin M. Sungoh

A sound programme of professional education of teachers is essential for the qualitative improvement of education. Investment in teacher education can yield very rich dividends because the financial resources required are small when measured against the resulting improvements in the education of millions. In the absence of other influences, a teacher tries to teach in the way in which he himself was taught by his favourite teachers and thus tends to perpetuate the traditional methods of teaching. In a situation like the present when new and dynamic methods of instruction are needed, such an attitude becomes an obstacle to progress. It can be modified only by effective professional education which will initiate the teachers to the needed revolution in teaching and lay the foundations for their future professional growth. First-rate teacher-training institutions can thus play a crucial role in the development of education.

The destiny of India lies in its classroom. This has been pointed out by the Education Commission Report, 1964-66. Teachers as organizers and controllers of the classrooms are mostly responsible for the future of India. Teachers are supposed to build future citizens of the country. Teachers have a lot of responsibilities to discharge their duties effectively. So teachers should be equipped with necessary knowledge, skills and abilities to deal with children. It is in this context that the education of teachers becomes most important in the country.

Teacher education has been struggling with the challenge of preparing and retaining sufficient numbers of high-quality teachers who can work effectively with students from diverse cultural backgrounds. A good teacher education programme, first of all, is coherent. That is, it has an idea about what good teaching is and then it organizes all of its course work, all of the practical experiences, around that vision. So it's not just a random assortment of courses and experiences for people. The courses are very much connected to practice as well as to theory. Good teacher education programmes should have student teachers in the classroom working constantly with expert master teachers/teacher educators while they're also teaching them for a variety of ideas about how students learn, about how to assess their learning, about effective teaching strategies that will allow them to build a repertoire. The most important issue in teacher preparation is getting prospective teachers into real-life classroom settings early with mentor teachers.

It is really important for an opportunity for prospective teachers early on to have experiences that put them in the classroom, that give them, in a sense, the practical experience. The other really critical element about preparation is this idea of being able to have mentors, people who are already very experienced and knowledgeable. We're talking about a knowledge base that grows over time and can be shared between the novice and the expert.

Moving it from theory to practice is what a really good programme can do. And again, the notion that we're not just thinking about it and we're not just talking about teachers and teaching, rather that they're actually participating in seeing how it has made a difference in the lives of children.

A good teacher preparation programme that prepares student-teachers to understand what they're going to be meeting, that understands what it takes for them to be successful, is really important in the retention of teachers. In very poor programmes, on the other hand, teachers are challenged by walking into the classroom for the first time when they're the actual teachers in school records. And they are literally scared of the children, they're scared of the parents, and of the community. Why would anybody want to stay in a job like that? No one with any kind of common sense would stick around.

Weaknesses in Teacher Education

Unfortunately, the professional education of teachers has been comparatively neglected. Several seminars were held and study groups were appointed to discuss improvements in elementary and secondary teacher education. But their recommendations have not yet been implemented in any large measure. By and large, training institutions for primary and secondary teachers have remained isolated from the mainstream of the academic life of the university, as well as from the daily problems of the schools. The quality of training institutions remains, with a few exceptions, either mediocre or poor. Competent staffs are not attracted; vitality and realism are lacking in the curriculum and programme of work which continue to be largely traditional; and set patterns and rigid techniques are followed in practice-teaching, with a disregard for present-day needs and objectives.

Forms of Isolation

Isolation takes place in three forms:

Isolation from University Life. The professional education of primary teachers is not looked upon as a concern of the universities. The professional education of secondary teachers is with the universities, no doubt, but it has become separated from other intellectual disciplines in the university and is treated almost as a Cinderella in university life. No significant improvement in teacher education is possible unless this isolation is broken. Education should be brought into the mainstream of the academic life of the universities. In India, the general trend has been to equate education with pedagogy. It has been taught mostly in training institutions and is studied only by those who decide to enter the teaching profession, after such a decision has been made. In the educationally advanced countries, however, education has developed considerably as a social science and a separate academic discipline. The realization that education is an instrument of change -social, political and economic -is having far-reaching implications, not only for education as an intellectual discipline of great scientific and philosophic import, but for other disciplines as well. It is also worth noting that philosophers and social scientists have begun to give special attention to education as an important part of their fields of study. In view of its increasing scope and importance, 'education' should be recognized as a social science or an independent discipline. 'Education' as an elective subject should be introduced at the undergraduate and postgraduate stages on the lines indicated below:

(i) The courses in undergraduate education should give an orientation in three broad areas-sociological, philosophical and psychological foundations of education. The contributions of great educators, comparative education and a study of some of the current educational problems could be included in the course. Moreover, the interrelationship of education with national development in all its aspects needs to be stressed in these courses. A wide choice should be offered so that it would be possible for a student to choose education in combination with any other subject, e.g., one or more of the natural sciences, mathematics, behavioural sciences, most subjects in the humanities, and even professional courses like engineering or social work.

(ii) At the postgraduate stage, an M.A. degree in Education/M.Ed, to be taken two years after the first degree in any subject should be introduced. In addition, it should be possible at this stage to combine education with one other subject selected from a wide range in the humanities and the sciences. To begin with, this may even be left as an additional option and scholarships may be given to students who offer it and who agree to be teachers after the completion of the course.

(iii) In all these courses—undergraduate or postgraduate—a minimum teaching practice should be obligatory just as laboratory work is a compulsory part of the study of sciences. It should be possible for a student who has taken these courses, to become a teacher, after a period of internship and, if necessary, after some in-service education provided through summer institutes.

Isolation from Schools: Teacher education, both at the primary and secondary levels, has become isolated from schools and current developments in school education. To break down the isolation from schools, every training institution should be required to guide neighbourhood schools and their staff in planning their work and in using improved methods of teaching. Such extension work is needed as much for the improvement of schools as for the improvement of the training programme itself. An extension department should be established in each training institution—pre-primary, primary or secondary—and should be regarded as an essential part of the programme and the responsibility of the training institution as a whole. All members of the staff should participate in it, and it should not be left to the coordinator only.

One other way in which training institutions can keep in active touch with schools would be through their old students. Institutions for teacher education should have effective alumni associations which would periodically bring together old students from far and near to discuss problems of common interest with the college staff. Such discussions which would cover achievements of individual teachers and difficulties experienced in implementing the programmes envisaged while under training, would benefit the institution as well as the past students now working as teachers, and provide opportunities for a follow-up of the schemes of work planned in outline during the training period. If there was anything that was unrealistic or impractical in them, the staff would see their way to modifying their approach. If the failure to implement was due to lack of enthusiasm or want of support from the school and the staff, attempts would be made to overcome the obstacles. The very idea that old students and the college staff would meet periodically to discuss reports of work and frame future programmes would keep up the enthusiasm of the students and lead them to try out their own ideas and projects instead of following routine methods. Such a close link between old students and the staff has immense potentialities for making teacher education dynamic and progressive.

Yet another method of breaking this isolation is to make student-teaching a comprehensive internship in which trainees are able to observe the entire work of the school and to participate actively in all the important professional activities of a teacher, both in and out of the classroom. Such comprehensive and fruitful internship will be possible only when there is a systematic collaboration and cooperation between the schools and the training institutions and when student-teaching is regarded as the joint responsibility of the producers (i.e., the training institutions) and the users (i.e., the schools and State Departments). Departments of Education should develop such collaboration by giving special recognition and status to schools selected for the programme as 'cooperating schools' and by providing them with adequate grants for equipment and maintenance (i.e., to meet the entire cost of allowances to the supervising teachers).

Collaboration between schools and training institutions could advantageously be extended beyond the internship programme. Selected teachers from cooperating schools could join the training college staff, on deputation, from time to time and participate, not only in the general programmes of the college, but also in evolving new plans of work and methods of teaching or in preparing teaching aids. They may teach in the experimental or demonstration school of the training institution and in exceptional cases, even work as members of its staff. The training college staff itself, which will find a fruitful field of research in educational methods and practices opened up to them through their collaboration with schools, will benefit considerably if they can do some continuous teaching in the cooperating schools. For this purpose, they may be deputed annually to teach at least for a month or so in a school or to complete at least one unit of the school syllabus. A combination of training college staff trying out their principles of teaching, and school teachers drawing generalization from their practical experience, would be of great benefit to student-teachers and would assist in a continuous improvement in teaching techniques. Schools should gradually become responsible partners in teacher education, not only by the facilities they offer for student teaching, but by their active participation in professional studies and educational research.

Isolation from One Another: The different types of teacher-training institutions are isolated from one another and do not form an integrated community. Teachers for the different stages of school education or for special subjects are now trained in separate courses and in separate institutions. The training institutions for pre-primary and primary teachers have the status of lower secondary schools only, in terms of qualifications and remuneration of staff or the scale of contingent expenditure. There is also a total separation between training institutions for secondary school teachers and those for primary or pre-primary teachers. An important reform, therefore, would be to raise the status of training institutions for pre-primary or primary teachers to a collegiate standard and to end the fragmentation of teacher education which results in weakness at each level and greatly reduces the effectiveness of the programme as a whole.

Improvements in Teacher Education

A comprehensive programme of improvement is urgently needed in teacher education which can be done by:

1. Removing the isolation of training institutions by bringing them into the mainstream of the academic life of the universities and by building up closer relations with the schools and between the training institutions preparing teachers for different levels;
2. Improving the quality of training programmes and training institutions;
3. Expanding training facilities:
4. Making adequate provision for the continuing professional education of all teachers; and
5. Creating appropriate agencies, both at the Centre and in the States, for the maintenance of standards in teacher education.

Training Programmes and Training Institutions

Programmes for Teacher Education should be sponsored by the UGC in a few selected universities and developed speedily on a large scale. In each selected university, a Department or Institute should be established to develop research and training programmes in collaboration with other disciplines. Its main functions would be:

1. to conduct undergraduate and postgraduate courses in education;
2. to conduct courses in professional education for different categories of teachers—pre-primary, primary and secondary;
3. to provide extension services to a few institutions of teacher education at all levels and to assist them to grow;
4. to organize summer institutes and in-service programmes in subject content as well as in professional education;
5. to work in close collaboration with a few schools of all types with a view to developing research and evolving better curricula and techniques of teaching; and
6. to promote research in education, especially with an interdisciplinary approach.

A practice should also be adopted of appointing eminent professors in different disciplines as part-time professors in the colleges of teacher education or training institutions to explain new developments in their fields and the manner in which they will affect education at the school stage. Apart from the intrinsic value of such contacts for improving professional education itself, this measure will incidentally help in raising the status of professional education and in interesting leading intellectuals in school education.

This programme will have two incidental advantages. As education can be studied without any commitment to being a teacher and in combination with other subjects, many talented students will study it and if their interest is aroused sufficiently, some of them may join the profession. The study of education itself will also begin to receive the enriching inter-disciplinary attention that is now lacking.

Role of Teacher Education

Teacher Education plays an important role in shaping and moulding the habits, manners and above all the characters of student teachers to become effective teachers. The institutional climate of teacher-training institutions is dependent not only on teacher educators, but also on the principal, administration, infrastructure, quality and the background of student teachers. The teacher is the key factor and the most important element in the educative process. Education is an effective means for social reconstruction and to a great extent it offers solution to the problems a society is faced with. Since the teachers play a major role in education of students, their own education becomes a matter of vital concern. Teacher Education should enable the student teachers to meet the challenges of the explosion of knowledge. Teacher Education programmes should help teachers to overcome the commonest disease teachers suffer from i.e. arteriosclerosis (long set habits that become a second nature forcing them to act always in the old well established way, independently of the transformed world around them). Breaking outdated habits, attitudes and practices that hamper marching ahead towards wholesome innovative teachings, also deserves attention. The role of teacher is changing so fast and teacher education programmes should help them cope with the changes in the society. The teacher needs to be conceived as a "change agent" and not as a mere transmitter of knowledge.

Objectives of Teacher Education

By implementing a mentoring programme for all beginning teachers we should aim to impact teacher retention, teacher practice, student achievement, and school culture. The main objectives of teacher education are:

1. to improve teaching performance;
2. to increase the retention of promising beginning teachers;
3. to promote the personal and professional well-being of beginning teachers;
4. to satisfy mandated state or district requirements; and
5. to transmit the culture of the educational system to beginning teachers.

Issues in Teacher Education Programmes

1. *Teacher-pupil Ratio:* In India the teacher-pupil ratio is about 1:50 while it is 1:30 in England and 1:28 in the United States. Moreover in India, the proportion of trained teachers to the total number of teachers in service is about 60 per cent, i.e. 40 out of 100 or 1 out of every 5 teachers is always a serious drain on the financial and human resources of education. Such a large number can be a menace to any education system.

2. *Number of Training Colleges:* At present the number of teacher training colleges is increasing irrespective of the place and importance of the area. Though NCTE has temporarily recognized these institutions, they do not fully satisfy the required conditions. These institutions do not appoint qualified and talented teachers and do not pay them enough salary. But they charge high capitation fees from the students at the time of admission. Therefore to restrict these processes of commercialization of teacher education, strong measures are needed to be taken by the State and the Central Level.

3. *Opening of New Training Colleges:* New teacher education institutes should be permitted on the basis of need assessment study. For this purpose, regular surveys have to be undertaken by the State Planning Department to ascertain the manpower requirement of teachers in various subjects at different levels. The inspection teams should comprise of eminent educationists.

4. *Practical Training/Practice Teaching:* Today, greater emphasis is being placed on the theoretical side of training. In the present scheme of studies practical training is the most neglected link in the whole system. Quality of teacher education depends on the quality of teaching practice because it is only through practice that teaching skills can be developed. Teaching practice is being neglected because there is more emphasis on theory. The duration of teaching practice is too short to provide sufficient experience and opportunity to the trainees to understand all the aspects of the school programmes. It is felt that the duration of the practice teaching in schools should be increased because it is the core of the teacher education programme. The remedy lies in increasing the number of working days and working hours. Another solution is to increase the practical and functional aspects of the programme and reduce non-productive activity. Teacher Education institutions should utilize the time available and how to bring the trainees nearer to actual working of the school. They must plan their activities and programmes in such a manner that the impact on the trainees is deep and permanent. Even in most of the training colleges teaching practice is not taken seriously. The number of teaching practice days should be increased. One month block practice should be conducted. Three months internship may be made compulsory in schools after theory examination. Trainees may be assigned at the rate of ten per school and they should work under the guidance of the School staff, and the

headmaster should be made responsible for the progress of the trainees assigned to the school. During their stay the trainees should not only participate in actual teaching but should also be involved in all the co-curricular and other assignments that are part of every school programme.

5. *Classroom lecture:* Lecture is the most common method of teaching used in the classrooms. This method should be supplemented with occasional seminars, discussion, tutorial and self-study, inquiry-based learning, Cooperative learning, information processing strategies etc.

Content of Teacher Education Programmes

Teacher Education programmes should be broad-based so as to allow versatility of knowledge. In this context the following contents may be taken into consideration.

1. Elective Courses should be introduced inorder for student teachers to opt for them.
2. Educational Foundation Courses (psychology, sociology, philosophy and school management) are required to give the student teachers a sound background.
3. Value Education should also be introduced in teacher education programmes.
4. Education on Human Rights to enable the student teachers to become aware of them and forming correct values and attitudes among students.
5. Environmental Education to create environmental values, attitude, capacity and environmental ethics among student teachers.

Strategies for Teacher Education Programmes

Teachers and methods of teaching are to change with the new information technology which keeps on changing from time to time. An attempt should be made to develop the teacher trainee's maturity through experience, self study and discussion.

1. Activity-based learning should be emphasized.
2. Teaching methodologies will need to emphasize inquiry dialogue and student participation in developing knowledge in addition to focusing on how to learn.

Professional Development and Career Paths

1. *Teacher License*: Teachers should be professionally equipped before they teach. Teacher education programmes should prepare teachers for a role which is both complex, demanding and challenging. Accomplished teaching

simultaneously involves command of subject matter and how to teach it. Teacher License is an important element to assure quality of teaching workforce. Licensure is used to identify students with required knowledge and skills that certify that candidates have earned the right of passage to teaching profession. License should be issued by the State Government after conducting licensure test.

2. *Preparing Teacher to meet the demands of Inclusive Education*: Teacher development has to be the heart of initiatives for developing inclusive practices in schools. This necessitates building competencies of all regular teachers to deal with diverse population of students and to learn pedagogical strategies that facilitate the learning of all students in their classroom. Teachers need to be prepared to teach in inclusive setting, meeting the needs of all students. The inclusive education system requires a more knowledgeable, highly skilled teaching force. It is now widely accepted that the most effective way to improve the quality and effectiveness of education programme in inclusive setting is to reach teachers and teacher educators. There is need for strengthening knowledge, skills and attitudes of teachers for creating inclusive ethos and learning environment in schools. The triangulated effect of knowledge, skills and attitude building develop the awareness among teachers and comprehensive perspectives of inclusive education as part of their role and responsibilities. Sensitizing teachers to the requirements of children with special needs will be ensured by regular in-service training of teachers in inclusive education at the elementary and secondary level.

3. *Competency-Based Teacher Education:* Teacher Education Colleges or Institutions have two functions to perform. The first is the training function and a gate-keeping function. The training function requires that they make students competent practitioners of the teaching profession. Secondly the gate-keeping function requires that they graduate only those students who actually become competent practitioners. In the past, by far the greater share of the resources and effort of training programme faculties have been devoted to fulfilling the training function while the gate-keeping function has been largely neglected, which has inspired the crisis of confidence that we face. Teacher Education Programmes should identify competencies that are specific to their programmes. According to Dave (1998) there are ten competency areas: (i) contextual competencies, (ii) conceptual competencies, (iii) curricular and content competencies, (iv) transactional competencies, (v) competencies in other educational activities, (vi) competency related to teaching and learning material, (vii) Evaluation competencies, (viii) management competencies, (ix) competencies related to parent contact and cooperation, and (x) competencies related to community contact and cooperation. These competencies lead to five areas of commitment by teachers. (1) learners, (2) society, (3) profession, (4) excellence, and (5) basic human values. Thus

the quality of teacher education is a product of the (a) knowledge, (b) skills and (c) competencies working in perfect harmony to produce good students.

4. *Performance Areas:* According to Dave (1998) there are five performance areas for teachers: (i) performance in the classroom, (ii) school level performance, (iii) performance in out-of—school activities, (iv) performance related to parental contact, and (v) performance related to community contact and cooperation.

5. *In-service Teacher Education:* Various in-service programmes need to be organized by Teacher Education Colleges/Institutions to enable the teachers to update themselves. One time training does not ensure effective teaching. There is a need for follow-up trainings which can be organized through periodic programmes. For example: (1) Peer coaching is recognized as a way in which teachers are provided with opportunities to work in a collegial setting. Peer coaching model requires that teachers be provided with (a) theory, (b) practice in observation, (c) practice with note taking as a source of data collection and practice in observing video-taped teaching episodes. According to Miller (1991) peer coaching is a model that allows teachers the opportunity to observe and learn from each other. (2) Orientation programmes conducted by various academic staff colleges will help in mentoring new teachers. (3) Refresher courses for teachers and teacher educators are compulsory every five years to keep themselves abreast with the changing curriculum.

6. *Teachers' performance evaluation:* Appraisal of Teachers' performance based on peer evaluation or students' evaluation if conducted objectively might help the teachers to improve professionally.

Conclusion

The highest function of education is to bring about an integrated individual who is capable of dealing with life as a whole. (J. Krishnamurti) The need of today is teachers who can ensure quality education with professional perfection. This can be attained through Teacher Education Programmes. The basic concern of teacher education programmes is to enable teachers to make sense of life and develop their own potential.

12

Implementing the National Curricular Framework for Teacher Education 2010

A Strategic Approach

Sweta Singh

As India is achieving its goal of Universal Enrollment, issues of quality are becoming critical. It has been felt that in our quest to provide universal education we have somewhere compromised on the quality of education. When we explore the factors that promote quality we emerge with some broad category of factors, namely, teachers, schools, and communities as 'the engines of quality', with teacher quality identified as a major driver. A number of studies undertaken around the world substantiate that the quality of teaching makes a difference for students. It follows that the system for teacher education and preparation must place priority on preparing teachers who can deliver high quality pedagogy and provide all students with quality learning experiences.

The UNESCO 2005 Education For All report captures this view in the following quote:

> "What goes on in the classroom, and the impact of the teacher and teaching, has been identified in numerous studies as *the* crucial variable for improving learning outcomes. The way teachers teach is of critical concern in any reform designed to improve quality" (UNESCO 2004, p. 152)

Moreover, parents, teachers, and administrators repeatedly emphasize the fundamental role that teachers play in the determination of school quality. There is a common perception that novice teachers lack adequate knowledge and skills, but a number of researches have demonstrated that there is no statistically significant relationship between years of experience and quality of teaching (Bressoux, 1996; Pass, Riccomini, & Switzer, 2005; Gore,

Williams, & Ladwig, 2006). This bears an important implication: if quality does not necessarily improve with experience then the preservice education of teachers is far more critical for the education system. However at the moment, preservice education of teachers is also a subject of apprehension.

National Council for Teacher Education in its document NCFTE 2010 has expressed similar concerns.

> "The training of teachers is a major area of concern at present as both pre-service and in-service training of school teachers are extremely inadequate and poorly managed in most states. Pre-service training needs to be improved and differently regulated both in public and private institutions."

Exploring the Meaning of Quality of Education

Before an attempt is made to explore the framework to assure quality in teacher education, we must understand the term itself. Buchberger, *et al.* (2000:14) indicates that the concepts quality, quality assurance and total quality management evolved in the industrial and business setup, where quality is defined by a product. Harvey and Green claim that the quality movement seems to have evolved over the years and diffused to other areas beyond the manufacturing sector and presently includes education (1993:27).

To pinpoint and define 'quality' it seems, is as elusive as achieving it. UNESCO in the document '*2005 EFA Monitoring Report: The Quality Imperative*' reiterates this. It points out that different notions of quality are associated with different educational traditions and approaches:

- *The humanist approach*: Quality within this tradition is interpreted as the extent to which learners translate learning into social action.
- *The behaviourist approach*: Quality in this context is measured in precise, incremental learning terms.
- *Critical approaches*: Quality education within this tradition is seen as prompting social change, encouraging critical analysis of social power relations, and ensuring that learners participate actively in the design of their learning experience.
- Indigenous approaches to quality reject mainstream education imported from the centers of power, assure relevance to local content, and include the knowledge of the whole community (UNESCO 2004, pp. 32–35).

Harvey (1995) provides a useful framework for thinking about quality by outlining five goals for education that define the vision of quality within individual systems:

- Education quality as *exceptionality*: excellence is the vision that drives education, quality education is education that is exemplary, schools should maximize the pursuit of the highest potential in individual students.

- Education quality as *consistency*: equality is the vision that drives education, quality requires equitable experiences, schools and classrooms should provide students with consistent experiences across the system.
- Education quality as *fitness-for-purpose*: refinement and perfection in specific subject areas is the vision that shapes the system, quality is seen as preparing students for specific roles, instructional specialization is emphasized.
- Education quality as *value for money*: education reflects reasonable correspondence to individual and societal investments; quality is interpreted as the extent to which the system delivers value for money.
- Education quality as *transformative potential*: social or personal change is the vision that drives education, quality education is a catalyst for positive changes in individuals and society, education promotes social change (Kubow and Fossum 2003, pp. 125-126).

Vision for Teacher Education

While envisioning the new Teacher Education Programme, National Curriculum Framework for Teacher Education elaborates on the following five key points and thus provides the broad guiding lines which should shape the teacher education system.

- Our thinking on teacher education is integrative and eclectic, free from the hold of 'schools' of philosophy and psychology, non prescriptive, open and flexible. aim(ing) to empower the teacher to relate himself/herself to them.
- To make teacher education liberal, humanistic and responsive to the demands of inclusive education. The emphasis in teaching is not on didactic communication but on non-didactic and dialogical explorations.
- Modern pedagogy derives its inspiration more from sociological and anthropological insights on education. There is increasing recognition of the worth and potential of social context as a source for rejuvenating teaching and learning. Multi-cultural education and teaching for diversity are the needs of contemporary times.
- We acknowledge the existence of a diversity of learning spaces and curriculum sites, the diversity of learning styles that children exhibit and learning contexts in which teachers have to function—oversized classrooms, language, ethnic and social diversities, children suffering disadvantages of different kinds.

- The tentative and fluid nature of the so-called knowledge-base of teacher education. This makes reflective practice the central aim of teacher education. Teacher education needs to build capacities in the teacher to construct knowledge, to deal with different contexts and to develop the abilities to discern and judge in moments of uncertainty and fluidity, characteristic of teaching-learning environments.

(*National Curriculum Framework for Teacher Education, Towards Preparing Professional and Humane Teacher, 2009, pp. 19, 20*)

This vision of Teacher Education views the newly qualified teacher as one who, having successfully completed a programme in initial Teacher Education, can function as an effective facilitator of pupils' learning in a diverse context, and has developed a capacity to engage in reflective practice.

NCFTE 2009, however, does not lay down clear guidelines to implement this ambitious vision. If the teacher education programmes are to prepare teachers capable of motivating a new generation of learners, then the implementation of this curriculum in its true spirit is vital. Without proper strategy in place for implementation, the NCFTE will remain yet another policy document, which will be often quoted and referred by people but would not have the desired impact.

Strive for Quality Improvement through Strategic Planning

While planning is an intelligent preparation for action, the term strategy finds its origin in military parlance. Strategic planning provides major directions in the quest of quality for any institution, be it a small department, school, college or a university. It ensures efficient and optimum use of resources to meet defined goals and provide maximum benefit to stakeholders. In teacher education, these stakeholders are—

- external: students, employers i.e. schools, funding agencies, and society,
- internal stakeholders: faculty and staff.

Organizations committed to quality education must have some type of strategic planning in place. All strategic planning deals with at least one of three key questions (Bradford and Duncan, 2000):

1. What we do?
2. For whom do we do it?
3. How do we excel?

Unlike long term planning, strategic planning is more sensitive to the external environment, involves the stakeholders and is less oriented to the maintenance of status quo. There is great emphasis on strategic planning in the area of business and industry. But today it is widely used by educational organizations too. It is difficult to directly apply various strategy-planning models to sectors such as education because of the following reasons

- The basis of strategy planning in business communities is differentiation. Educational institutions do not have the complete freedom to determine their directions unlike the private business setups. They work under the broad umbrella of national policy frameworks and similar goals and much differentiation is not possible.
- Strategy-planning models work under the assumption that the operating environment is predominantly competitive and a profit motive is the driving force. Educational institutions usually strive to maximize output within a given budget rather than fight for survival in a stiff competitive environment or be driven only by profit motive.

Despite the above, it is possible to adapt various strategic models to suit the needs of an educational institute especially when more and more private institutes are entering this arena and the environment is becoming competetive. Bryson (1995) also emphasizes this, strategic planning, can help public and nonprofit organizations anticipate and respond effectively to their dramatically changing environments.

Mukhopadhyay (2005) proposed a 'workable strategic plan' to ensure quality. Its steps are:

- Belief, vision, mission, goals;
- Learners' needs assessment and client education;
- Institutional assessment and SWOT analysis;
- Quality policy and intervention plan;
- Cost of quality;
- Planning for implementation; and
- Evaluation and feedback

Phases of Strategic Plans

A different way of looking at strategic planning from vision to outcomes is by breaking down the whole process into four sub-steps or phases, namely environmental scanning (analysis), strategy formulation (planning), strategy implementation and evaluation and control (*see* Fig. 12.1).

(A) Environmental scanning: It involves the monitoring, evaluation and distribution of information from the external and internal environment of an institute in order to undertake the planning process with a sound researched background (*see* Fig. 12.2).

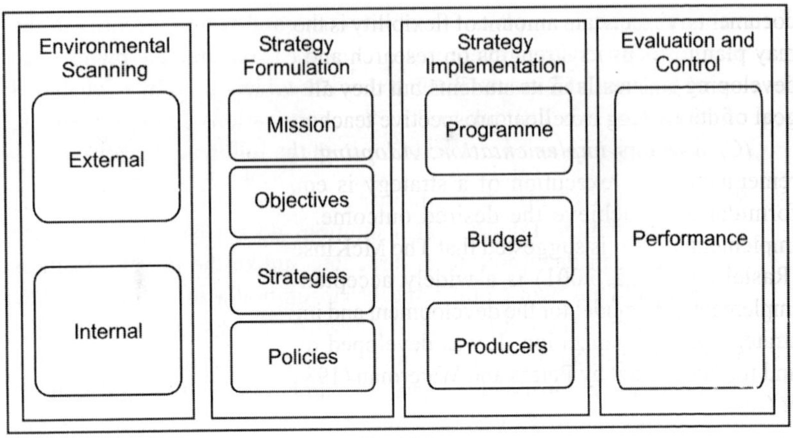

Fig. 12.1

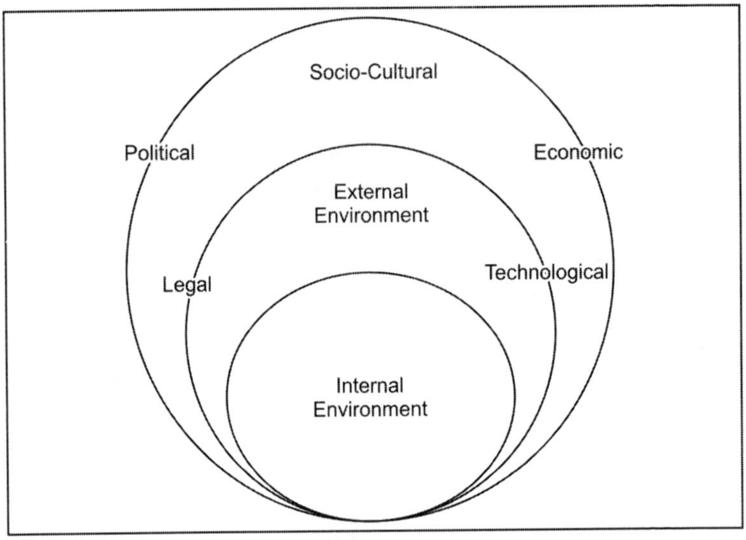

Fig. 12.2

(B) Strategy formulation: It is the development of plans for effective management of the organization. At this stage the institute's vision crystallizes, mission is refined and documented, achievable objectives are specified and strategies and policies defined.

An institution's mission describes the purpose of its existence. It announces what the organization is providing for the society. In educational institutes the missions emerge from and within the broad parameters of the broad visions of education. For ex., the mission of a specific teacher education institute can not differ too widely from the programme envisioned in policy documents. Yes, certain amount of flexibility is there. For instance one institute may plan to focus its strengths on research and extension while another on developing ICT skills in its students but they all would do this with the main goal of developing excellent prospective teachers.

(C) Strategy implementation: Adopting the 7-S-Model: It must be remembered that execution of a strategy is equally important as strategy formulation to achieve the desired outcome. To resolve the problem of implementation, it is suggested that The McKinsey 7 "S" be adopted. The 7S (Rasiel and Friga, 2001) is a widely accepted and robust analytical and implementation model for the development and implementation of the selected strategy of an organization. It was developed by Pascale and Athos (1981) and further refined by Peters and Waterman (1982), consultants at McKinsey & Co.

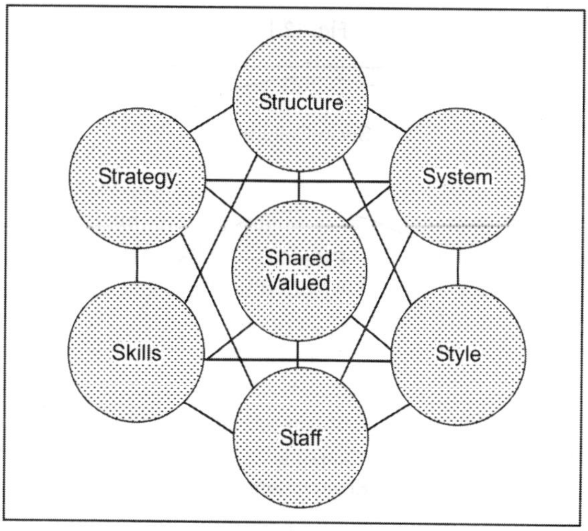

Fig. 12.3

The model starts on the assumption that an organization consists of seven elements, distinguished in so called hard S's and soft S's. The hard elements (green circles) are easy to identify. They can be found in strategy statements, corporate plans, organizational charts and other documentations. The four soft S's however, are difficult to describe since capabilities, values and elements of corporate culture are continuously developing and changing. The coherence between all elements is important. All the 7 "Ss" in the system should be balanced and consistent. By using this tool any academic institute can identify those areas that need to be focused upon and changed. In order to implement the vision of quality education alignment of all the 7 elements towards the same goal is important.

(1) Structure: Chandler (1962) described the structure as the design of an organization through which the enterprise is administered. This design has two aspects:

(a) The line of authority and communication amongst the different administrative offices and officers; and
(b) The information and data that flow through these lines of communication and authority.

The structure is understood by analyzing the reporting relationships (who is reporting and to whom), division of labour (job descriptions), and integrating mechanisms (special committees, etc.) within an institute. The structure should facilitate the translation of the institute's vision. A flexible, decentralized structure in an academic institute would empower the faculty. Too rigid and hierarchical structure is not conducive for the growth of the staff in any institute. Shawyun also supports this by saying "a networked and inter-disciplinary structure could bring about the streamlining of innovative curricula and synergy in the pool of academic and administrative resources and expertise".

(2) Systems: The systems in any organization are evident in the processes and procedures in place through which things get done on a day-to-day basis. These patterned responses to tasks support the strategy and structure by facilitating work. Systems are both formal and informal. Formal systems usually include resource allocation systems, performance management systems, and management information systems. Informal systems may include procedures to resolve conflict, organize meetings etc.

When we view the teacher education programme, a number of systems or routinized processes and procedures are followed within each institution. To name a few, there are systems in place for selection of student teachers, implementation of the theoretical component of the programme, organization and implementation of the practicum component especially the school experience programme, assessment and evaluation of student teachers, feedback and monitoring system, placements, performance appraisal of the faculty and staff etc.

The efficiency and effectiveness of each system determines the capacities of the final products. A number of systemic concerns are mentioned in section 1.6 of NCFTE. Some of these are language proficiency, reflective thinking, SEP, linkages between theory and practice etc. It is important for institutes to examine and modify the systems in place, which address these areas. Research based evidence should be used to develop healthy procedures. For example, the study exploring the reasons behind Finland's excellent programme of teacher education Tryggvason (2009) reports that Finnish teacher educators transmit theoretical and pedagogical aspects by using them in their own teaching thus, the student teachers not only hear and read about them, but they also experience them. The teacher educators' method repertoire has a wide range and thus they offer a variety of approaches instead of pure lecturing. Therefore the systems in place to develop pedagogical knowledge should not focus simply on transmitting its meaning but help the students to evolve and apply these in different contexts.

(3) Strategy: This is the plan or course of action decided upon to achieve the stated mission of the organization. These constitute handful of carefully considered decisions that shape most of an institute's subsequent actions. They have an immense impact on whether the organization's strategic objectives are met or not. While developing an effective strategy decisions regarding the allocation of resources to achieve identified goals over time are taken.

It is a rare teacher education institute that has a strategy in place. Usually people continue to work on a day-to-day basis in a mechanical manner. It is important to develop a strategy, which has been deeply thought and discussed with all the stakeholders.

(4) Staff: This element implies the people employed. It is important to review how they are appointed, developed, deployed and motivated. In academic institutes staff should be viewed both as potential weaknesses and as strengths. The knowledge, competencies and values of the academic and administrative staff have an immediate impact on the quality of teachers being produced.

This is an area, which demands tremendous attention. NCFTE also laments about this. Ample opportunities to develop and enhance their skills must be provided; their morale, attitude and motivation should be boosted with appropriate schemes.

(5) Skills: Skills are differentiating characteristics of the company's products and services. From the point of view of an academic institute, these are key functions and dispositions, which an institute promotes in its products (here novice teachers). What skills are most important/ valued in the institute? Where and when and how these skills are learnt and honed?

One skill, which NCFTE mentions a number of times is skill of critical and reflective thinking. This is one essential tool that helps the prospective teachers develop the capacity of directing their own professional development in future and thus empowers them as autonomous learners and teachers. In fact this skill is so important that it should feature in mission statements, strategies should be developed to fulfill these and the teacher educators (staff) should work systematically towards achieving this.

(6) Style: It implies the way in which the members of an organization interact with each other. It includes the way problems are approached, manner in which day to day activities are undertaken and the areas that form the focus of attention. An academic institute demands a democratic and participative style of functioning. Empowered environments where all members take

responsibility towards achieving laid missions and collaborate for professional development is the need of the hour.

(7) Shared values: Values are the feelings of worth we attach to something and they guide our behaviour. Shared values of an organization are principles adopted by the members to guide their style and behaviour. The shared values become evident in the culture of the organization. These are few consistent themes, which drive an organization, and traditions with which it identifies. We can see the importance of this component from its placement right in the centre of the construct of the 7S model. It is imperative for an institution to proactively define shared values, communicate them with stakeholders and align all actions with them. These values should percolate to all stakeholders, be it the faculty and staff, students, collaborating schools and NGOs, or parents so that each person's actions are directed to achieve excellence. It is these shared values that form the guiding lifeline of any organization. A common set of values binds all members together and directs their actions towards the same goal. It also ensures continuity and focus on the broad vision even when heads and leaders change, which is a fairly common phenomenon in educational management. Whether the institute values educational excellence or community service or reflective teachers, it is important to identify them and state them with courage in implicit terms and reinforce them repeatedly. This is especially more important in the Indian and Asian sub context where we slip to a '*chalta hai*' attitude.

(D) Evaluation and Control

The final and last phase of strategic management is Evaluation and control. Questions regarding whether objectives established have been achieved or not, whether we are moving towards our mission are answered here. Careful thought has to be given before deciding on the manner in which the programme is evaluated.

Some ways are:

- judging the output i. e. the teachers prepared by the institute. This can be done by following their placements, taking feedback from stakeholders (students, parents and employing schools)
- using prepared tools like those developed by accrediting bodies. For example the assessment tool developed by National Assessment and Accreditation Council (NAAC), India in collaboration with the Commonwealth of Learning (COL), Canada to judge "continuous quality improvement and to energize and sustain the institutions' quality enhancement efforts" (NAAC). This comprises 75 Quality Indicators spread under the six key areas of functioning of a TEI.
  - Curriculum Design and Planning

- Curriculum Transaction and Evaluation
- Research, Development and Extension
- Infrastructure and Learning Resources
- Student Support and Progression
- Organisation and Management

Conclusion

If the management, administration and the faculty gets together and plans the management of institutions in a systematic manner the implementation of the vision for teacher education would not be difficult.

13

Adult Education in India after Independence

Between Recent Past and Imagined Future

H.S. Bhola

To make sense of the development of adult education in India since Independence in 1947, the historical discourse on the subject needs to be located within a larger framework defined by two intertwined historical processes: Decolonization —some would say Neo-colonization (Sartre 2001); and Globalization that has reduced the world to a "global village" effecting structures and processes of politics, economics, culture, technology—and *education* —of all nations around the Globe (O'Meara, Mehlinger and Krain 2000; Burbules and Torres 2000).

The Global Discourse of Adult Education

Globalization can be seen to have begun in earnestness with European colonization of the non-Western nations, but in our times, it is being systematically mediated through the United Nations Organization (UN), which was officially established on October 24, 1945. The United Nations Educational, Scientific and Cultural Organization (UNESCO), a United Nations affiliate, came into existence on November 16, 1945. Over the years, an extended family of organizations, affiliated with the UN has come into existence, among them: Food and Agriculture Organization (FAO), World Health Organization (WHO) and International Labour Organization (ILO), to name a few from many equally important organizations today on the world stage. It should also be stated that alongside of these official intergovernmental structures, hundreds of Non-Governmental and Civil Society institutions have come into being, also dedicated to the cause of peace and prosperity of nations around the globe.

UNESCO and Adult Education: A Special Relationship

UNESCO was to be dedicated to three great global causes—Education, Science and Culture; and within the sector of Education, it came to deal with all aspects and levels of Education, from Primary through Secondary to University. It is noteworthy that UNESCO since its very birth has had a special interest in Adult Education. The Preamble to the UNESCO Constitution had declared "that since wars begin in the minds of men, it is in the minds of men that defenses of peace must be constructed." The "Men" that the Preamble had in mind were adult men and women, bypassed by school, already engaged in the political economy of their communities.

This special interest of UNESCO in Adult Education has been realized in UNESCO's project of "United Nations Conferences on Adult Education," held every twelve years. The first such Conference was held at Elsinore, Denmark in 1949, and the sixth, most recently at Belem, Brazil in 2009. At every conference some grand theme for the education of adults has been proposed for consideration of the power elite, policy makers, and educators invited from around the world, encouraging them to look before and after, and in togetherness develop new ways of policy borrowing and policy sharing in the service of their peoples and nations through adult education (Bhola, 1998).

Emergent World Perspective and Directions: In Ideology, Theory and Policy of Adult Education

UNESCO's influence on Adult Education around the World has been extensive. In *Ideology*, adult education is now meant to be people-centered, always serving the people's interest of all nations. UNESCO has also contributed significantly to the processes of development of *Theory of adult education*. It is now widely accepted that *adult literacy* is the fundamental instrument of *adult education* at the front end of adult education process. On the other end, adult education has come to be seen as continuous with the never-ending processes of *lifelong education and learning*—in interface with basic education through both formal and non-formal structures. Regarding *Policy Development*, adult educators are now advised to attend to the total cycle of policy processes of adult education promotion, from Policy Analysis, through Policy Formulation to Policy Implementation to policy Evaluation (Bhola, 2003).

While, UNESCO has played a major role in this regard, other Global institutions have also made important contributions, particularly the World Bank, and UNICEF. In 1974, a study sponsored by the World Bank had introduced a new taxonomy of education that included Formal Education (FE), Non-formal Education (NFE), and Informal Education (IFE) (Coombs and Ahmed 1974). In 1990, an Interagency Commission of several international agencies organized the World Conference on *Education for All* (EFA). In the implementation of EFA Goals, Adult Education was first equated with NFE which was then construed as education provided to out-of-school children, using non-formal settings and methods (WCEFA 1990; UNESCO 2000, 2002). Later in the 1990s, fast-developing free market economies re-packaged adult education as Adult Basic Education (ABE), as a second chance for schooling for adults. Adult Basic Education and Training (ABET) was then invented to serve the objectives of professional formation of labour for the benefit of the workplace.

The most recent calls for adult literacy and adult education are included in The United Nations Literacy Decade (United Nations 2001 June, 2002 July); and The United Nations Summit on Sustainable Development held at Johannesburg (United Nations 2002).

Parallel with these developments and differentiations of adult education, the concept of Lifelong Education was coined and promoted, asserting hat adult education was not a one-shot affair, but needed to be a lifelong process. In the 1990s, the Europeans started talking of knowledge-based societies, and "adult *learning*" to emphasize self-direction on the part of adults in their own learning —to access education which they needed, on their own, using a variety of sources, governmental, non-governmental and private. With adult learning came the phrase Lifelong Learning (OECD 2003). It should be noted that in the Third World, adult *learning* will have to follow adult *education* for quite some time. Self-directed adults, accessing education they need, on their own, from the education market, is still a long way off in developing societies.

Convergence and Confluence: Adult Education and Adult Literacy

In Oral Cultures of earlier times, most knowledge was, of course, transmitted by oral communication, both within and across generations. In our times of slowly but surely unfolding processes of modernization, all the knowledge that we need to receive or to diffuse among our families and communities is no more amenable to merely oral means for mutual sharing. More and more of this knowledge needs to be in *print*, first to be understood and then to be recalled. There are indeed limits to human memory. Knowledge of new technologies of agriculture and of new productive skills used on the factory floor, challenge the limits of human memory. Ability to read and write becomes a necessity. In other words, more often than not, Adult Literacy becomes the foundational skill for Adult Education (Bhola, 2009).

There is another significant detail in the relationship between Adult Literacy and Adult Education. Literacy being the "skill" to read and write is *observable* and also *measurable* by testing. By using particular numbers of words, to be first taught and then tested—word lists of 850 words to 2,500 to cover Equivalence range of grades within Basic Education—literacy tests could be differentiated by levels of literacy competence, responding to various grades. Again, *Equivalent* word lists resonating to different interest areas—e.g., agriculture and health, work-place skills, Sustainable development, Environment protection, etc.—could be developed that yet have equal conceptual loads while using different words. Adult Education by itself is too generic to be similarly treated for testing by levels. Consequently, and unsurprisingly, literacy data have come to be used as surrogates for measurement of Adult Education, by all educational institutions from the local to the global. Lastly, Adult Education need not stop there and could combine numbers with narrations. In-depth evaluations of successes of Adult Education with objectives of poverty eradication, democratization, social inclusion, green energy, and now Mitigation and Adaptation to Global Warming could all be undertaken using Quantitative with the Qualitative data, collected from specific groups in particular contexts (Bhola 2008).

Before moving on to the task of showing how history (and particular history of education) at the global level has cast its shadows on the history of adult education in India, we must make a quick reference to the new world's technologies, hard and soft. The Media have become agents of history-making on the world stage and have had nothing less than a transformational impact on histories of "education for development" around the world, during the last two decades.

Imagining a Future Made Possible by Soft Media Technology

Technology in today's world is more than merely *instrumental,* but has the potential to change the very *objectives and processes* of projects wherein modern technology is applied. This has been dramatically true in the case of "*communications technology*" with its two intertwining threads of *Hard* Technologies (focused on computers) and *Soft Technologies* (involving curriculum design and programmed instruction). The miracles that can be wrought by Soft Media—Facebook, Twitter, YouTube and such—has been exemplified in the dawn of the "Arab Spring" of 2011 that has shaken the foundations of Middle Eastern countries and challenged their ideologies, political economies and most significantly their traditional definitions of the role and status of women.

These Hard and Soft communication technologies have an equally significant possible role in the more mundane sectors of development and delivery of education around the world. These technologies are waiting to be put to work for motivation, mobilization and implementation of projects for the eradication of poverty, for universalizing literacy and healthcare, for promotion of sustainable development, for adaptation of daily lives to mitigating an adaptation to Global Warning, and for inclusion of the excluded for reasons of class, caste and gender. *Instructional Systems Technology (IST)* —born in the 1960s in USA on Indiana University campus in Bloomington, Indiana —is today a highly advanced area of study and research at Western Universities; and has already well demonstrated what a systematic integration of *computer technologies* and *instructional technology* can do to overcome time and space, in the delivery of instruction to all who need it—in otherwise unreachable learning groups in villages, townships, fields and factories, spread all over the globe, (Access: Google for further information)

The Indian Scene

The Language of Discourse and Ideology of Adult Education in India

In India, the phrase "Adult Education" has held its sway for most of the history of adult education, except for a brief flirtation with other descriptors, such as, "social education", "fundamental education" and "polyvalent education" (Sohan Singh 1957; Dutta 1986, Shah 1999). At the Seventh International Conference of Adult Education held in UNESCO Institute of Education (UIE), Hamburg (UNESCO 1997), the phrase "Lifelong Learning" was suggested to inform the vision for adult education. Indeed, UNESCO Institute of Education (UIE) has since re-named itself as UNESCO Institute for *Lifelong Learning* (UIL). In India, the new descriptor—Adult and Lifelong Education " has been preferred over "Lifelong Learning"—the assumption, perhaps, being that "Education," more often than not, may have to help in Learning, both in groups and more so for independent learning.

The Ideological Roots of Adult Education

India won its Independence in 1947 after a long struggle. There had been repression by the colonial powers during the struggle for freedom but the masses responded with *Satyagraha* (meaning Truth-Force) involving civil disobedience with passive resistance and without violence, as taught by Mahatma Gandhi, now the revered Father of the Nation. It worked with the British colonizers but not in avoiding the occurrence of most cruel and extensive communal riots between Muslims and Hindus during the partition of India which created two states of India and of Pakistan. Pakistan's Eastern province later became a separate country, namely Bangladesh.

Adult Education as "Culture" and "Structure"

A useful distinction can be made between "adult education as culture" and "adult education as "structure". Adult Education as "Culture," has come in process for ever, and whenever adults engaged in learning from each other across their own generation, or sought transmission or diffusion of knowledge to future generations.

Mahatma Gandhi was an activist in "adult education as *culture*." His project of adult education as culture came to cover every nook and corner of the country, and his learners constituted the whole nation. His curricular objective for the nation was to create a new national consciousness, and a new culture of free people, moral in thought and action, steeped in non-religious secular spirituality. His unwritten class primer kept the millions of men and women spellbound by the metaphors embedded in the texts forming the collective memories of the people. He talked of a return to *Ram Rajya* (the Kingdom of God Lord Rama); and he bestowed on half the nation, comprising of untouchables and outcasts, the dignity and equality due to them, by re-naming them as *Harijans* (Peoples of God). Mahatma Gandhi can indeed be credited for capturing of the minds and souls of the people of India transforming the personal identities of millions.

Adult Education as Structure Invented by State and Civil Society

Mahatma Gandhi did also make contribution to "*Adult education as structure,*" as well by way of offering and implementing *Bunyadi* Talim, meaning Foundational Education for children of school age which was essentially rural in character, and obsessively focused on a pedagogy based in teaching traditional crafts for generating both instruction and income—using the spinning wheel as an icon as also in learning activities (Steele and Taylor 2000).

What we have called "Adult education as structure" also come to India as part of the Independence movement with the ideology of freedom. To learn, to read and to teach others was called a sacred duty. The struggle for freedom from alien rule was aligned with the fight for freedom from hunger, ignorance and disease. Mahatma Gandhi had defined education as one of his constructive programmes, and supported *mass literacy* campaigns in some districts of India. During the ten years from 1937 to 1947, some wonderful initiatives, were undertaken, among them The Maharajah of Baroda's supplementation of literacy efforts with public libraries; and the coming into existence of Karnataka Adult Education Council, of Gujarat Social Education Committee; and Bombay City Social Education Committee, to name a few. Most significantly, the Indian Adult Education Association (IAEA) was set up in 1939 and registered as a non-governmental voluntary association in 1947. Early in the 1950s, Mrs. Welthy Fisher's, the wife of a Bishop that became a Gandhian, had established the Literacy House in Allahabad—which later moved to Lucknow, Uttar Pradesh in 1953 on a larger campus on the outskirts of the city (Sohan Singh, 1957; Shah, 1999).

Constitutional Commitments and Policy Initiatives

Constitutions first and foremost are instruments for codification of political, economic, cultural and educational ideologies of nations. The Indian Constitution as codified and adopted in 1950 was a mixture of the American and English constitutional patterns and principles. The Preamble of the Indian Constitution affirmed a determination to secure liberty of thought, expression, belief, faith and worship and equality of status and opportunity and to promote amongst the people a feeling of fraternity, ensuring the dignity of the individual and the unity of the nation (Constitutional Review Commission 2001). Some later day critiques of the Constitution, have suggested that in application it has ended up creating a bourgeois nationalist order (Myrdal 1968), side-lining the poor.

Directive Principles of the Constitution did require arrangements for providing free formal education for all up to the age of 14 years for all, within 10 years of the commencement of the Constitution (that is, by 1960). However, there was no clear and direct reference to the provision of adult literacy or adult education to those bypassed or not served by regular schools. Consequently, the ideology and policies of adult education and adult literacy in post-Independence India are derived by "implications and amplifications" of the Constitution. In official rhetoric, adult literacy (and adult education) has come to be called the cornerstone for making the provision of equality of opportunity a reality. (See: Constitutional Review Commission, 2001).

Adult Education in India's Five-Year Plans: Twists and Turns of Commitment and Allocations by he State

Eradication of illiteracy through adult education was part of the political rhetoric as politicians talked of their future agendas for an Independent India. In the real world, however, emphasis during early years of Independence was on *Economic Growth* through *Industrial Growth*. In the various Five Year Plans developed by India's Planning Commission—the lead agency for the implementation of the national vision and purpose, in all aspects of policy, foreign and domestic—allocations for Adult Literacy and Adult Education got a short shrift.

The First Five Year Plan of 1951-56 allocated 3.5 per cent of the planning budget to "social education" (another name for adult education) that would include literacy, and was to be integrated with the Community Development programme of India. Even commitments at this level were not held up in the subsequent Five Year Plans that made much lower budgetary allocations. The Second Five-Year Plan for 1956-61, for instance, had allocated 1.6 per cent; the Third Five-Year Plan of 1961-66 had 0.3 per cent; the Fourth Plan of 1969-74 had 0.1 per cent; and Fifth Plan of 1974-79 had 0.3 per cent (Bhola 1987; Bhola 2000). In subsequent Five Year Plans, there were several twists and turns in Budgetary Allocations: the allocations to Literacy in the 11th

Five Year Plan (2007-2012) were 2.9 per cent of the total education budget. At the same time, percentage of Literate adults in India in the year 2011 had risen to an impressive 74.07 <http://planningcommission.nic >An explanation for this contradictory set of statistics will be offered later.

A Related Policy Initiative: The Education Commission of 1964-66

Looking back to beginning, The Report of the Education Commission of 1964-66 (Ministry of Education, 1966) could easily be seen as a benchmark in the development of the ideology and policy of adult education and adult literacy. To prick the conscience of the nation, the Commission had pointed out that some 20 years after Independence the literacy percentage had still hovered around 28.6 per cent. The Commission, therefore, had emphasized the need for an accelerated programme for literacy promotion, using a combination of the *selective* and *mass* approaches that could mobilize all men and women in the country including students and teachers.

They had also pointed out that for literacy to be worthwhile it would have to be *functional.* As a specific recommendation, they had asked for a provision of part-time general and vocational education to the young adults in the age group 15-30. They also showed sensitivity towards the need for use of media as a tool for building a literacy environment. Finally, the Commission had suggested the establishment of a National Board of Adult Education to provide a national focus and direction, both to the state and the civil society institutions.

The National Policy Resolution of 1968 accepted the recommendations of the Commission of 1964-66 and asked that adult education be harnessed to the movement of total national development and to enable peoples' participation not only in improving economic productivity but also in building democratic institutions promoting national integration and for realizing the socialistic patterns of a future society (Bhola 1987; Bhola 2000; Constitutional Review Commission 2001).

The National Policy on Education 1986

More than two decades after the Education Commission Report, came the National Policy on Education of 1986 reiterating the objectives of universalizing elementary education as also of adult literacy. Specifically, they asked for not only for universal elementary education but also universal retention of children up to 14 years of age; a systematic programme of *non-formal* education—meaning out-of-school education for those bypassed by schools—to supplement formal primary education in the educational backward states.

Prior and Parallel Developments in The Struggle for Universal Literacy

For a comparative perspective on the roles of the State and Civil Society institutions, both prior and parallel plans and projects of adult education and adult literacy, undertaken by non-State agents and institutions, are included below.

Important changes were taking place during the 1990s, with the Marxist states having crumbed, and capitalist-democratic forces becoming strident, in disseminating and imposing neo-liberal ideologies in politics, economics and education, around the world. India, too, opened up to the West. At the same time, the World Conference of Education for all came to be held (WCEFA 1990) in Jomtien, Thailand. The Conference did talk of adult education but did nothing much about it. Neo-liberalism and modernization, with their emphasis on the formal economies and formal education was inimical to adult education, except for small-scale projects for the professional formation of labour in workplaces and production facilities.

With the shift to neo-liberal political economy in India, came another shock to adult education as a secular humanist project for the nation. The BJP (Bhartiya Janata Party) came to power during March 1998 and stayed until May 2004, with Prime Minister Atal Bihari Vajpayee at the helm. BJP was a party that propagated the ideology of Hindutva (the Hindu realm): seeking to give India, a predominantly Hindu country, back to Hindus (Appaiah 2003). The BJP-led government was accused of attacking secularism by systematically Saffronizing (referring to the saffron coloured clothing of BJP political workers) the curricula for History in schools. They were also accused of "communal fundamentalism" and were condemned for their fascination for the "corporate glitz". While in power, the BJP did not initiate any educational policies or projects that could qualify as adult education, though they had had a history of having undertaken some highly successful" agitational mass mobilization" of youth and adults in the form of a Rathayatra (chariot-journey), and organization of a million protesters that were to demolish the Babri Masjid—a Mosque built by the Muslim Emperor Babar in the 16th century at a place which Hindus of the BJP Party claimed was the site of a Hindu temple repossessed by Babar). (wordIQ.com/definition/Babri_Mosque)

Civil Society Contributions and Contestations of Policy Directions: Institution Building for Organization of Partnerships

Policy-making and institution building go together so that quite often the process of policy development includes the process of designing and establishing new institutions, or re-structuring already existing institutions to achieve intended policy objectives. And on the other end, policy analysis and institutional analysis are often undertaken at the same time. India during Independence was able to establish a strong network of institutional structures that span the whole range from the center to localities. There is a separate

Division in the Ministry to develop adult education policy and with an attached Directorate of Adult Education to organize training and delivery of adult literacy and adult education. There are Departments (or similar organizational units) for adult education at the state levels, complemented by well staffed "State Resource Centers" that provide professional services to adult educators and adult education institutions in their jurisdictions.

Indian Adult Education Association

India, of course, is a country where Non-Governmental Organizations (NGOs) and Community-Based Organizations (CBOs), numbering in thousands, are spread all over the land. In this civil society sector, the Indian Adult Education Association (IAEA) remains the crown jewel of the adult education family.

The Indian Adult Education Association (IAEA) established in 1939, and duly registered as a voluntary association with the Government in 1947, has been the most prestigious institution of adult education in the country. The office bearers of the IAEA have included cabinet ministers, legislators, ambassadors, high level government officials, Maharajahs, princesses, and professors. One of the presidents of the Association, Dr. Zakir Husain, was to become the third President of the Indian Republic from 1967 till his untimely death in 1969.

Thc IAEA had had a strong influence on the ideology, policy and general professional development of adult education in India. Through its annual conferences and, later on, through Annual Zakir Husain Lectures, the IAEA was able to contribute to the agenda setting in adult education in the country. At home in India, the IAEA has served as the bridge between the legislature and the government, and between the Union Ministry and the Planning commission. Internationally, IAEA has been the conduit for ICAE and UNESCO to bring discussion and dialogue on adult education around the world, and to the community of professional adult educators at home. Its official journal, the *Indian Journal of Adult Education*, has had an uninterrupted career of more than 70 years and has continued to be the repository of the history of adult education in India. In 2002, the IAEA had made another big leap forward by establishing an International Institute for Adult and Lifelong Education, as an extension of the IAEA; and by publishing a new scholarly journal (International Journal of Adult and Lifelong Education) to promote the professional formation of the of adult education.

University Departments of Adult Education

Establishment of Faculties of Adult Education, accompanied with Centers for Research and Development in the area, has been a historic development and already has a long history. The first Masters' degree programme in adult education was offered at the University of Rajasthan, Jaipur in the early

1960s. Half a Century later there are as scores of them, training thousands of professionals every year, who in turn go to train field level workers within the contexts of local, district and regional projects and programmes and campaigns.

Adult Literacy and Adult Education in the Lives of Peoples and Their Communities

For several years after Independence nothing much had happened by way of state-sponsored adult literacy and adult education. Some excellent work had, however been done by Non-governmental Organizations (NGOs) and other structures of the Civil Society—among them the oft-quoted "Gram Shikshan Mohim" in Satara District, Maharashtra in 1959. The volunteers associated with the Mohim spent 3-6 months in each village until they had taught everyone in the village to read. A Farmers' Training and Functional Literacy Project during 1968-69 attracted great attention because of the partnership among three national ministries: viz. Education, Agriculture and Information and Broadcasting. The University Grants Commission during the early 1970s planned a programme to "Send the University to the Masses" which did not go much beyond its declaration. The ivory tower remained unshaken. Visits to India by the American missionary, Frank Laubach, who had invented and used the method "Each One Teach One", did create some stirring but it did not last for very long. In our times, the work of Bharat Gyan Vigyan Samiti that came on the scene some 20 years ago and now has presence in 22 states and 316 districts of India, has won well-deserved appreciation (Saldan 2010).

Adult Education in Sharp Focus

Adult Education, and with it Adult Literacy, came into sharp focus on October 2, 1978, with the launch of the National Adult Education Programme (NAEP) under the leadership of Prime Minister Morarji Desai, a committed Gandhian. The declared intent of the NAEP was to organize adult education programmes, *with literacy as an indispensable component*, for approximately 100 million illiterate persons in the age-group 15-35, with a view of providing them with skills for self-directed learning leading to self reliant and active role in their own development, and in the development of their environment. In a historical perspective, it can surely be seen as a marker, the First Milestone on the road onto a fully literate India.

The National Literacy Mission (NLM), the Second Historic Marker in Literacy Promotion on India came about a decade later in 1989, under the leadership of Prime Minster Rajiv Gandhi. The NAEP was revisited and was vitally reconstructed as the National Literacy Mission (NLM)—with the hope of adding a *missionary* zeal to literacy promotion in India.

The Unfolding of the National Literacy Mission

The NLM launched in 1989, was a significant organizational innovation using the strategy of a nationally funded planned programme with the time-bound and participative Total Literacy Campaigns (TLCs) at the district levels. Once again, while it seemed to be doing better than NAEP, it needed a shot in the arm by way of "Operation Restoration" in 1994. Nonetheless, at its peak, the National Literacy Mission (NLM) of India had covered 574 out of the total of 598 districts of India, using the Total Literacy Campaign (TLC) approach. Three hundred and two districts had already entered in the post-literacy phase; and 112 districts had received sanctions for initiating Continuing Education Programmes. Weaker sections of the Indian society, such as women and scheduled castes and tribes, had received special attention (Constitution Review Committee 2001; Bhola 2002).

More than a decade later "An Evaluative Account of individual and social effects of the NLM based on 97 evaluation studies showed that the impact attributable primarily to the NLM had indeed been substantial. Adult education groups and literacy workers were a welcome presence in the lives of people; and literacy did acquire the status of a social need. Literacy did also find its uses by individuals whenever it was possible within their contexts and loci of control. Literacy helped many to emerge out of their silence and speak up with a new sense of self-worth. Individuals did begin to be more effective in transactions with their political, social and economic environments. Even more would have been possible, if there had been concomitant structural changes (Bhola 2002)."

But even when all this was happening, ill winds had started blowing. The Government had practically withdrawn most of the resources allocated to adult education. In 1999-2000, adult education budget was 113.4 crores as compared to 3,037 crores for elementary education (a ratio of 1: 0.037). There was no special item for Rural Functional Literacy Projects, even as the overall allocations for adult education had increased to 40 per cent. The state is now playing with the idea of using ICT to carry the burden with donor assistance. The bureaucrats are discussing new ways of fiscal management of education; another ruse used by the states to withdraw from it responsibilities for adult education and leaving it all to NGOs and private entrepreneurs.

A Renewal of NLM!

The NLM was most recently soldered with a new programme named "Saakshar Bharat" (that is, Literate India)—essentially a programme of Adult Literacy that would go on to flower into an ambitious set of projects of Adult Education, of both non-formal and formal categories.

The Saakshar Bharat Mission was launched on September 8, 2009 by the then Prime Minister of India, with the objective of creating a literate society through a variety of teaching learning programmes for non-literate and neo-literate persons of 15 years and above. Seventy million illiterate adults—60 million of them women—will be made functionally literate by 2012, reducing the gender gap from 21 per cent to 10 per cent. The final goal is to take the national literacy levels from 64 per cent currently to 80 per cent by 2017.

To achieve the goal set by the President, the Government's other initiative, Bharat Nirman, will be linked with "Saakshar Bharat" (Literate India) with its prime focus on women —and at the same time transforming rural realities. Investments will be made in the infrastructures for irrigation, all-weather roads, rural housing, rural water supply, and rural electrification. Rural telecommunication connectivity will also be enabled, beginning with telephones, all of which will be the source for the general development objectives and general educational content embedded in plans of Saakshar Bharat—all in partnership between the Government of India, state governments, and Panchayati Raj Institutions (2009).

At the same time, the Constitutional mandate of affirmative action in behalf of Scheduled Castes and Scheduled Tribes is to be maintained also in the provision of Adult Literacy leading onto Adult Education Programmes. Auxiliary target of the Mission is stated to be to offer 1.5 million adults Basic Education (who now already have Basic Literacy) and to another 1.5 million impart vocational skills (i.e., teaching them development related skills) programmes (Bhola, 2011a).

Another Feather in the Cap

The assertive connection of Adult Literacy (and Adult Education) with Women's Inclusion in the structures of political economy was reaffirmed in the *International Conference on Women's Literacy for Inclusion and Sustainability*, hosted by the Government of India, sponsored by the of UN for the E-9 member States during September 8-10, 2011, New Delhi, India (Bhola 2011b).

Spread of Literacy in Indian Population: India's Census Bureau Records

Statistical data inevitably assume a common definition of an entity of interest to continue with the process of its conceptual analysis until quantifiable indicators for characteristics of the entity become available. Indicators can then be used in tests to be administered to individuals or groups as appropriate, to generate quantifiable data to be entered in data sets for use of interested professionals at various levels of a programme system. This has been impossible to do in the case of "Adult Education" because of the amorphous character and content of adult education. However, adult literacy being a skill is much more amenable to testing and grading for quantification. For this reason, over a long historical period, in all programmes and countries around the globe, Adult Literacy has come to be a surrogate for Adult Education. Data Sets on Adult Literacy are available at all levels from Local to District, to Province, to sub-Region, to national and Global.

In India since Independence Adult Literacy Date have been collected by the National Census Bureau which conducts a national Census every 10 years, providing a most useful perspective on Adult Literacy—and thereby on Adult Education:.

Table 13.1: Literacy Ratios -1951-2011

Year	*Percentages of Literacy*		
	Total	*Male*	*Female*
1951	18.34	27.16	8.86
1961	28.31	40.40	15.34
1971	34.45	45.95	21.97
1981	43.56	56.37	29.75
1991	52.11	63.86	39.42
1997	62.00	73.00	50.0υ
2001	64.83	75.26	53.67
2011	74.04	82.14	65.46

As we can see from the Table 13.1 above, India crossed the mark of 50 per cent literacy for the first time in 1991; and the 2011 estimates for literacy now were 74.04 per cent. At first glance, these achievements look impressive. Yet, when we look at number of Literates and Illiterates in absolute numbers, the task ahead appears to be daunting indeed, as the following related statistics will show:

	Population in Absolute Numbers (2011)	*Decadal Growth*
Total	1,210,193,422 (in b./m.)	17.64%
Males	623,724,248 (in m.)	17.19%
Females	586,469,147 (in m.)	18.12%
	Literates in Absolute Numbers (2011)	*In Percentages*
Total	778,454,120 (in m.)	74.04%
Males	444,203,762 (in m.)	82.14%
Females	334,250,358 (in m.)	65.46%

Literacy in Rural-Urban Perspective

At the outset, it can be stated that in terms of Rural versus Urban data, out of the Total of 778.5 Literates in 2011, 493.0 million were Rural, and 285.4

were Urban In the following, a Rural-Urban perspective is added to the Male-Female differences in literacy in India as tabulated in Table 13.2 (a) and Table 13.2(b) which should be read together.

Table 13.2(a): Distribution of Literacy by Rural/Urban Location

	Total		*Total (Male)*		*Total (Female)*	
	1991	*1997*	*1991*	*1997*	*1991*	*1997*
All Areas	52.20	62.00	64.10	73.00	39.30	50.00
Rural Areas	44.70	56.00	57.90	68.00	30.60	43.00
Urban Areas	73.10	80.00	81.10	88.00	64.10	72.00

Table 13.2(b): Literacy of Population by Gender and Rural/Urban Residence—From a Decadal Perspective, 2001-2011

Year	*Percentages of Literacy*		
	Total	*Male*	*Female*
1951	18.34	27.16	8.86
1961	28.31	40.40	15.34
1971	34.45	45.95	21.97
1981	43.56	56.37	29.75
1991	52.11	63.86	39.42
1997	62.00	73.00	50.00
2001	64.83	75.26	53.67
2011	74.04	82.14	65.46

Affirmative Action in Literacy

In India, affirmative action on behalf of the weaker sections of the society—Scheduled Classes, Scheduled Tribes and Other Minorities —is constitutionally protected and had led to gains made by the weaker sections of the nation.

Celebration, Yes! Complacency, No!

The National Census Board of India, at the end of the 2001 census, was so impressed with the improvement of literacy statistics during the past decade of 1991 to 2001, that it decided to designate the years 1991-2001 as "India's Literacy Decade". UNESCO gave their seal of approval to the achievements of the NLM by awarding it the international "Noma Prize" for literacy. The 2011 Census data is likely to evidence the same trend.

Celebrations seem to be in order, but complacency is not, neither on the part of policy makers nor practitioners (Bhola 2003). Looking behind and beyond the statistics, we need to add several qualifications to the data and take note of several unpleasant realities. Percentages in Table 13.1 hide the stark realities inherent in absolute numbers. India's population in 1991 was

846.30 million. Estimates for 2001 are 1031.63 million. That means a huge backlog of illiterate adults that may take decades to teach, to read and write and to participate in the politics and the economy of the country.

It is of great significance to note that all individuals, who were reported to be literate during the 2001 Census, had not learned to read through the work of any adult literacy programme, but instead had acquired their literacy through schooling. The estimates of those who became literate through primary education programmes in schools during 1991-2001, are estimated to be 162 to 196 million (that is as many as 75 per cent of the total literates added to the pool of literates during the decade; and it is thus deduced that the NLM may not have contributed more than 50 million (25% of the total) to the aggregate of total literates during the decade of 1991-2001 (Mehta, 2002).

It does matter whether literacy is acquired in elementary schools or by joining adult literacy groups. First, a smaller contribution of literate adults to the total deducts from the perceived success of the NLM. Second, there is the question of the quality of literacy obtained in schools. It has now become clear to the development policy makers that school literacy does precious little to contribute to the social and economic development of the country in the short and in the middle run; because primary schools, as run at the present time, do not impart much of the development-related knowledge enabling participation in the economic, social, political and cultural institutions of the society, and the children coming out of the elementary schools are too young in any case to imbibe such knowledge. Literacy workers conducting literacy projects and programmes are discovering that quite often as many as half of the adults in literacy classes may have gone through school as children. They have come back to literacy classes only to refresh their literacy and numeracy skills, to pick up useful developmental knowledge to be used in life and at work and be able to connect with the ongoing development activities of the government. To sum up, the adult educators' task remains undiminished. Schooling does not preempt the tasks of the adult educator. Indeed new needs and challenges emerge: the need to work with the school-leavers, new and old, to impart to them the developmental knowledge and values they will need regarding agriculture, health, environment, local self-government through Panchayats (Singh 2003), gender sensitivities (Patel and Dighe 2003), and the HIV/AIDS pandemics.

Ups and Downs on The Road

Ups and downs on the road to a fully literate India have continued, even as some important strides ahead are attempted. As the Working Paper for the 50th All India Adult Education Conference, held in Shegaon, December 19-22, 2001, observed (p. 19): "In recent times some of the statutory bodies that carried out the NLM-such as the NLM Authority and the Executive Committee supervising the NLM Authority-had become inactive. The links established between the center and the states on the one hand, and between the state and civil society on the other hand had also broken down. The allocation of funds for the NLM of Rs. 970.47 Crores during the Eighth Five Year Development Plan (1992-1997) had gone down to Rs. 650.97 crores in the Ninth Five Year Development Plan (1997-2002)—a 33 per cent decrease. Regrettably, even this lower allocation had not been fully spent. As should have been expected there has also been a lowering of aspirations for achievements in education. In the approach paper to the Tenth Five Year Plan—prepared by the BJP-led government—the revised target year to achieve universal access to primary education had been pushed to 2007. Targets for national literacy achievements had then been fixed at 72 per cent by 2007 and 80 per cent by 2012."

Concomitantly, the downward slide of literacy achievements had already begun. The bad news about adult literacy could have been expected, yet it has proved startling because the bad news came also from Kerala which had become famous beyond India for its illustrious work in literacy during the 1990s (Basheer 2003). Within a few years, after the change of Government, literacy rate in Kerala has fallen from 95 per cent down to 80 per cent.

Social Media: A Great Hope in The Near Future

To smooth all ups and downs and fill all potholes in the road to a fully literate India, Great Hope today lies in the Soft Media that could give a real shot in the arm to adult literacy and adult education in the immediate future.

What the brand new Social Media, with the crowd-source Internet and cell phone technology; and the not so new Mass Media, such as Radio and Television all together, are doing in India and elsewhere around the Globe, is nothing less than amazing. The Soft-Media are helping young people re-invent new personal-identities and group solidarities; new aspirations for social mobility and brooking of insatiable consumer wants and desires; offering people "Virtual" socialization and new fast streams of knowledge, both competing and cooperating with the old plans for education for all, and of all kinds, is quite another matter (The Economist 2011). Cyber-schools with cyber-curricula are sprouting like mushrooms, around the globe.

India has not been closed or immune to such developments in the Hard and Soft Technologies of Education under Globalization. It should be stated that while India started later than the United States and Western Europe, its history of Development of Instructional Technologies has been impressive. It should also be noted that in India as in various other emerging countries, advances in Hard Technologies and their use in instruction has been comparatively much more impressive than in the area of Soft Instructional Technologies.

The Report of Dr. S.P. Gupta Committee, "India: Vision 2020" which brought together some 30 experts from different fields and spent two years deliberating on inventing the Vision 2020, had examined many important policy issues "but the one's that stand out most powerfully are employment and education."... "Greater coverage and better quality education at all levels from basic literacy to hi-tech science and technology [were emphasized]." ... "The report calls for concerted efforts to abolish illiteracy, achieve 100 per cent enrolment at primary and secondary levels and broader access to higher education and vocational training through both traditional and non-traditional delivery systems (page iii)."

Responses to Vision 2020: From Planning Bodies to Structures of Governance

The Structures of Governance of the Government of India have all responded to the Vision 2020. Among the various Ministries of the Union Government, the Ministry of Communications and Information Technology, through its two departments—The Department of Information Technology and the Department of Education may have done yeoman's work.

The Department of Technology has focused attention on more technological initiatives, such as: Promotion of Information Technology education and Information Technology-based education; Matters relating to Cyber Laws, administration of the Information Technology Act of 2000, and other IT Laws; and establishment of two important structures—Center for the Development of Advanced Computers; and National Information Center. *The Department of Education* has also created an important structure: National Institute of Electronics and Information Technology. It has designed a Special Project, "All Government Services to be at Your Mouse-tip" whereby "citizens across 28 states of Indian Union will be able to avail of all government services including payment of utility bills and applying for a driving license, through common internet portals being developed.

India is by no means a new comer to the movements. India was already a well-connected all across its length and breadth, by telegraph, telephone, radio and television. It can now boast of one diversified communication network that links all part of the country by Internet and which is based on some of the most sophisticated technologies in the world, enabling further developments in the future, for a national, indeed global communication network.

The existent System is heavily in use by India's mobile phone users, over 881 million as of October 2011. India is also the world's third-largest internet user numbering over 121 million Internet users as of December 2011. Future developments are most promising. India is regarded today as the world's most competitive and one of the fastest growing telecom market.

Conclusion: Future of Technology in Adult Education in India

Speculating about directions of movement in the future is a hazardous intellection talk. But straws in the wind are making intriguing and promising patterns. India is already producing the world's best computer engineers, and already has some 881 million mobile phones, ringing in the nation's ears, day and night. The real challenge before us is to use these new technologies to expand the coverage of literacy for achieving universal literacy; and to ensure effective delivery of education to adults for them to use in life and work—to change economies, to sustain democratic politics, to remake communities and cultures that are inclusive of women and the weaker sections of the society.

It is by no means impossible.

14

Education of Persons with Disabilities

Sudesh Mukhopadhyay

Important changes are being witnessed in the education scenario in general since the turn of this century. India has made some specific statements to address the issues of disadvantaged and marginalized in its development planning and policy to the extent that Eleventh Plan (2007-12) is referred to as the "Inclusive Plan". This trend is going to dominate the scenario also in the Twelfth Plan (2012-2017). Interestingly the term Inclusion was coined and used mainly by such social scientists who were concerned with the process of marginalization especially for the Persons with Disabilities. Today, in tune with the international trends, the Term is being used even in India to cover the concerns for all marginalized including Persons with Disabilities.[1] Inclusion in education is an approach to educating students with special educational[2] needs. Under the inclusion model, students with special needs spend most or all of their time with non-disabled students. Implementation of these practices varies. Schools most frequently use them for selected students with mild to severe special needs.

Inclusive education differs from previously held notions of 'integration' and 'mainstreaming', which tended to be concerned primarily with disability and 'special educational needs' and implied learners changing or becoming 'ready for' or deserving of accommodation by the mainstream. By contrast, inclusion is about the child's right to participate and the school's duty to accept the child. Inclusion rejects the use of special schools or classrooms to separate students with disabilities from students without disabilities. Rights based approach places emphasis on full participation by students with disabilities and upon respect for their social, civil, and educational rights. The Right of Children to Free and Compulsory Education (RTE) Act, 2009 (Government of India) as implemented on First April 2010 reflects this spirit and provides for imbibing it in practice. Going by the spirit of RTE, 2009 fully inclusive schools are not to distinguish between the so far used terms like "general education and special education programmes"; instead, the school process are so structured so that all students learn together.

Existing Practices

Inclusion as practiced in India and also word over has many practices imbibed in the philosophy of full inclusion to partial inclusion as against the early practice of total segregation in special schools. Though overtime a relationship between the special schools and general schools have emerged in terms of supporting the education needs of the child.

As can be seen from the figure below (Mukhopadhyay, Sudesh, 2004), inclusion is in all aspects of the schools/educational institutions. Starting from the policy and practice of admission, through all the processes of curriculum related decisions and transaction to the way the general environment of the school is structured. "Inclusive practice" is not always inclusive but is a form of integration. For example, students with special needs are educated in regular classes for nearly all of the day, or at least for more than half of the day[3].

As was provided for in the Scheme of Integrated Education of the Disabled (GOI, 1986, 1992) the students receive additional help or special instruction in the general classroom and are treated like a full member of the class. However, most specialized services are provided outside a regular classroom, particularly if these services require special equipment or may not gel with the ongoing activities of the rest of the class. These may include activities such as speech therapy, learning Braille etc. The student may be pulled out of the regular classroom for these services. Resource Room is established in the schools wherever feasible in terms of number of students and resources available; else service may also be provided by the Itinerant resource teacher who may be shared by few schools.

In the "full inclusion" setting, the students with special needs are always educated along-side students without special needs, as the first and desired option while maintaining appropriate supports and services. Some educators say this might be more effective for the students with special needs[4]. SSA Framework as revised for RTE 2010 promotes this vision and provides for such practices. As in other countries thought is to consider special education as a service, not a place and those services are to be integrated into the daily routines and classroom structure, environment, curriculum and strategies and brought to the student, instead of removing the student to meet his or her individual needs. Students with mild or moderate disabilities, as well as disabilities that do not affect academic achievement, such as using wheel chair or special spectacles are most likely to be fully included. However, experience of including students with all types of disabilities from the different disability categories have been reported in general education classes, working and

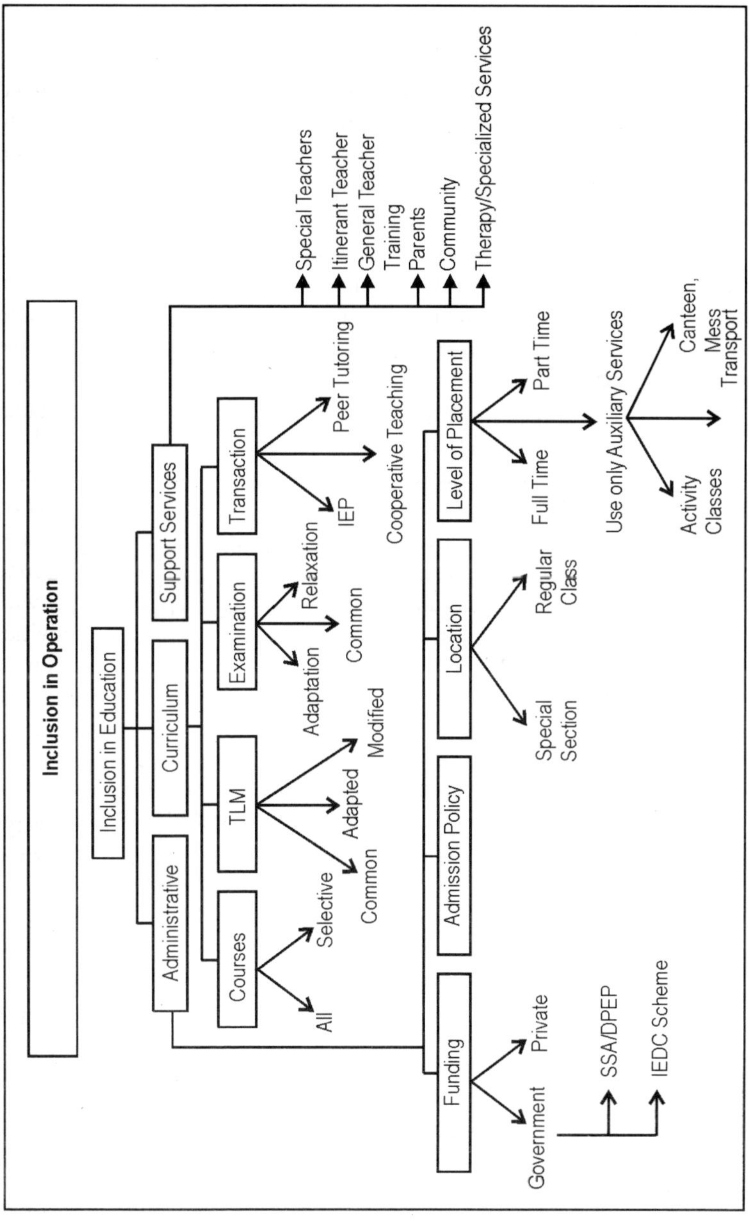

Fig. 14.1: Inclusion in Operation, © **Sudesh Mukhopadhyay**

achieving their individual educational goals in regular school environments and activities (Mukhopadhyay, Sudesh, 2000)[5]. SSA has also supported home—based education for very severe cases[6].

Today, being a signatory to Convention on Child's Right and the anti-discriminatory climate as being advocated in the country and internationally; Inclusion has been accepted as the larger framework as a policy. This framework also is reflected now in the Draft Disability Bill (2011)[7] under consideration. It is very important that inclusion should not lead to lip-service and counting numbers and meeting physical targets. Important is to ensure the academic education of students with disabilities which would imply:

- Adequate supports and services for the student,
- Well-designed individualized education programmes,
- Professional development for all teachers involved, general as well as special educators,
- Time for teachers to plan, meet, create, and evaluate the students together,
- Reduced class size based on the severity of the student needs,
- Professional skill development in the areas of cooperative learning, peer tutoring, adopting curriculum including learning materials and evaluation procedures as well as life-skill components,
- Collaboration between parents, teachers, administrators and other service providers with onus being on the system and not on the student and/or parents, and
- Sufficient funding so that schools will be able to develop programmes for students based on student need instead of the availability of funding.

In the Indian context, the current programmes for school education such as SSA, RMSA, RTE Act 2009, IEDSS, 2009, the proposed Disability Bill provide this spectrum. Need of the hour is to academically prepare the system to respond so that inclusion is not perceived as a governance issue only.

Inclusion is also about Social and Cultural Inclusion

As used by UNESCO, inclusion refers to far more than students with special educational needs. It is centered on the inclusion of marginalized groups, such as religious, racial, ethnic, and linguistic minorities, immigrants, girls, the poor, and students with disabilities, HIV/AIDS patients, remote populations, and more. In some places, these people are not actively included in education and learning processes[8]. Although inclusion is generally associated with elementary and secondary education, it is also applicable in postsecondary education.

According to UNESCO, inclusion "is increasingly understood more broadly as a reform that supports and welcomes diversity amongst all learners." Under this broader definition of inclusion, steps should also be taken to eliminate discrimination and provide accommodations for all students who are at a disadvantage because of some reason other than disability. This is in a way the reason for promoting 25 per cent admissions for children from the disadvantaged groups under RTE 2009.

Evolving Pedagogy of Inclusion

The emerging scenario of the schools during Twelfth Plan period (2007-2012) which would also be the completion of period earmarked by RTE to prepare the schools for implementation on many accounts; may be as under:

- Students in an inclusive classroom are generally placed with their chronological age-mates, regardless of whether the students are working above or below the typical academic level for their age (Age Appropriate Placement as per RTE Act).
- Schools to encourage a sense of belonging, emphasis being placed on the value of accepting diversity and social inclusion.
- Practices evolved to nurture a relationship between a student with special needs and a same-age student without a special educational need.
- Visible practice of assigning *buddy* to accompany a student with special needs at all times (for example in the laboratory, academic grouping, canteen, on the playground, on the bus and so on). Thus removing barriers to friendship and encourage cooperation.

Classroom interactions and teacher behaviour reflecting a climate of openly dealing with individual differences by mutual sharing and understanding There are many positive effects of inclusions where both the students with special needs along with the other students in the classroom both benefit. Research has shown positive effects for children with disabilities in areas such as reading individualized education programme (IEP) goal, improving communication and social skills, increasing positive peer interactions, many educational outcomes, and post school adjustments. Positive effects on children without disabilities include the development of positive attitudes and perceptions of persons with disabilities and the enhancement of social status with nondisabled peers[9]. These findings have also been reported in Indian studies as early as 1984.[10]

A fundamental feature of inclusive education is that of teacher expectations and styles. Teaching diverse groups and being concerned about the learning experiences of all pupils and students is of crucial importance[11].

Talking of students and teacher expectations, it is important to understand the students that are likely to pose relatively more challenges. Who are these disadvantaged and/or Children from Economically Weaker Sections? What are past experiences and capacity of the system? Is there a common trend across the perceived diversity that these may bring to the classrooms? As can be seen from the Table 14.1, inspite of the perceived diversity, all these learners share a common requirement from the system. This is because they all tend to be cases of lost opportunity due to a number of factors in their circumstances and may be some are the push-out of the system itself.

Children with disability would need may be some extra inputs (also known as Plus Curriculum) depending on the nature of the disability and the impact caused either due to delay in identification and interventions or at times the progressive nature of the condition. Important is to note that we are not staring at point Zero; there are experiences, expertise and systemic interventions in place, we need to realize this potential and take the first step! Today we do have access to information on Universal Design not only for addressing the physical barriers but also for creating learning strategies.

Universal Design for Learning (UDL)

Universal design as an architectural construct refers to creating structures that are accessible to all-a ramp with railings, for example, works for those who can walk, those who use wheelchairs, those pushing strollers, and those who need extra time or support. And a ramp can be beautiful. It does not have to be a signifier that something is wrong or that some people are different (i.e., regular people can enter here, and those with disabilities use this entrance). The ramp can be the way that *everyone* enters the building. —In Instruction, universal design means that the curriculum and teaching can be broadly designed so that all students can access it and be part of it.—We design the lesson from the *beginning* so that a wide range of learners can access it.— And the materials that students access to learn can also vary widely and include print materials, audia books, interactive software, personal interviews and more.—Using the priciples of universal design communicates that all students belong in the classroom and that the curriculum is designed for all of them. By providing broad, diverse options from the beginning, as part of the original design, teachers are much less apt to be surprised or distressed by the variations in the classrooms.[12]

Universal Design for Learning is an educational framework based on research in the learning sciences, including cognitive neuroscience that guides the development of flexible learning environments that can accommodate individual learning differences.[13] Recognizing that the way individuals learn can be unique, the UDL framework, first defined by the *Center for Applied*

Table 14.1: Age-appropriate Service Model
(Developed by Sudesh Mukhopadhyay, Aug. 2011)

Age Appropriate Placement for	*Special training areas*	*Earlier Expertise*	*Who?*	*Possible Location near to school*	*Challenges as per RTE*	*Requirements*
Sch. drop outs	Catching up with lost competencies	EGS, Alternative Schooling	Para Teachers NGOs KGBV, NPGEL	Cluster Level in case of rural areas, different models for urban pockets including NGO run initiatives	Age appropriate Academic & Life skills Special Training Arrangements Maintaining interest Record keeping Monitoring Progress Convincing parents, trs etc. Time table design Space Resources	• Respecting them as "Child/ student/ learner" • Competence assessment mechanism for identifying strengths • Enrichment materials • Pool of support persons
Never Enrolled	Catching up with lost competencies	EGS, Alternative Schooling	Para Teachers NGOs KGBV, NPGEL	Cluster Level in case of rural areas, different model for urban pockets	-do-	-do-
Migrants	Catching up with lost competencies	Para Teachers NGOs KGBV, NPGEL	Cluster Level in case of rural areas, different model for urban pockets	Cluster Level in case of rural areas, different model for urban pockets	-do-	-do-
Working Children	Catching up with lost competencies	Para Teachers NGOs KGBV, NPGEL	Cluster Level in case of rural areas, different model for urban pockets	Cluster Level in case of rural areas, different model for urban pockets	-Do-	-do-
CWDs	• Identification of Edu Needs • Readiness • Plus Curriculum • Catching up with competencies	IE Programmes Resource Teachers	Schools Support Groups Special schs	Itinerant Teachers NGOs Special Schs	-do-	-do-

Special Technology (CAST) in the 1990s[14], calls for creating curriculum from the outset that provides:

- *Multiple means of representation* to give learners various ways of acquiring information and knowledge,
- *Multiple means of expression* to provide learners alternatives for demonstrating what they know, and
- *Multiple means of engagement* to tap into learners' interests, challenge them appropriately, and motivate them to learn.

Curriculum, as defined in the UDL literature, has four parts: instructional goals, methods, materials, and assessments (Rose & Meyer, 2002). UDL is intended to increase access to learning by reducing physical, cognitive, intellectual, and organizational barriers to learning, as well as other obstacles. ***UDL principles also lend themselves to implementing inclusionary practices in the classroom.***

Individuals bring a huge variety of skills, needs, and interests to learning. Neuroscience reveals that these differences are as varied and unique as our DNA or fingerprints. Three primary brain networks come into play:

Recognition Networks	*Strategic Networks*	*Affective Networks*
The "why" of learning	The "how" of learning	The "what" of learning
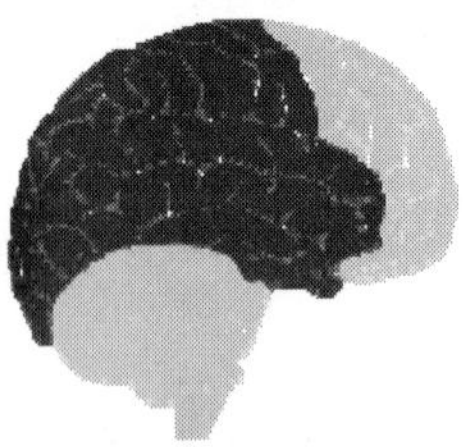	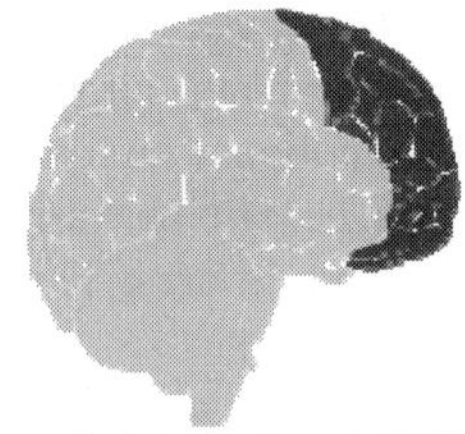	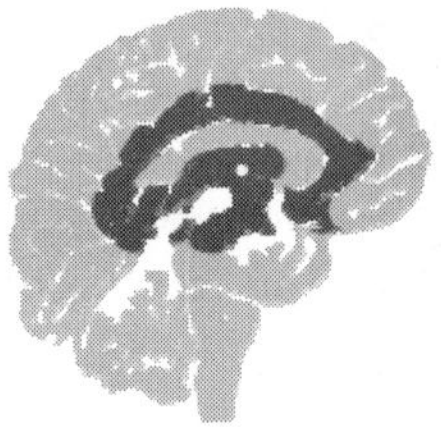
How we gather facts and categorize what we see, hear, and read. Identifying letters, words, or an author's style are recognition tasks.	Planning and performing tasks. How we organize and express our ideas. Writing an essay or solving a math problem are strategic tasks.	How learners get engaged and stay motivated. How they are challenged, excited, or interested. These are affective dimensions.

Fig. 14.2: Universal Design for Learning

Hence Pedagogy of Inclusion[15] implies:

- *Imbibing Courage* to leave behind something we know well and embrace (even tentatively) something unknown or frightening and decide to do things differently. Courage is recognizing that things familiar are not necessarily things that are right or inevitable.

- *Being Inclusive* so that all children are accepted and no one has to fight for a chance to be part of a classroom or school community. Although children require different levels of support and resources, the concept of inclusion means all children-not just those who are clean or who have agreeable parents or who come to school ready to learn. *It is like living inclusion rather than being told.*
- *Value* self and value all and act on the belief that every one counts. Schools need to practice strategies and tactics that focus on what children can do rather than on what they cannot do or their weaknesses or areas of need. This keeps us from seeing the whole child and narrows our lens of appreciation. Value the strengths and capabilities that each individual have.
- *Practice Integrity.* Integrity means wholeness. Litmus test is look at our response to diversity—differences to be avoided, ignored, worked around, minimized or accepted as characteristics to be understood, valued, appreciated, supported and celebrated?
- *Promote and Practice Cooperation* to realize "None of us is as smart as all of us". Peers are seen as allies and not as enemies or opponents. Structuring schools and classrooms cooperatively would imply looking closely at not just how we teach but also what we teach as well as enacting that belief in all aspects of curriculum, pedagogy and school management.
- *Ensure Safety-physical and emotional.* We all may have some notion of physical safety such as banning corporal punishment, safety against accidents, abuse etc. Emotional safety is about being 'oneself' and to be vulnerable to seek help, to be warmly supported and not being afraid of taking risks and failures. This is a must for growth and development.

Universal Design also implies that teaching and learning are both planned but flexible phenomenon. Preparation has always been an important part of teaching (Lesson Planning, Unit planning etc.). It is particularly important when interacting with students with disabilities (age and maturation also plays an important role in this case as is for all children!) because their needs are often different (sometimes real and at times so perceived) to those of other students. We should remember as the representatives of system that it has consequences for the student with special needs, for teachers and administrator as well as for all other students if we fail to respond adequately, appropriately and timely. Preparation covers three main areas:

- Developing an appropriate and inclusive teaching strategy.
- Making appropriate reasonable adjustments.
- Providing an accessible and safe teaching environment.

India also has taken tentative steps to actualize these and be in tune with developments at home and abroad. Noticeable are the latest changes to the Copyright Act[16] which draws inspiration from these concepts and also the interventions being planned under Barrier Free access to education.

Box 14.1: The Copyright (Amendment) Act, 2012

The text of the amendment as applicable to Persons with disability is given below:

Section 52 (1) The following act shall not be an infringement of copyright, namely: (zb) the adaptation, reproduction, issue of copies or communication to the public of any work in any accessible format, by:

(i) any person to facilitate persons with disability to access to works including sharing with any person with disability of such accessible format for private or personal use, educational purpose or research; or

(ii) any organisation working for the benefit of the persons with disabilities in case the normal format prevents the enjoyment of such works by such persons:

Provided that the copies of the works in such accessible format are made available to the persons with disabilities on a nonprofit basis but to recover only the cost of production:

Provided further that the organisation shall ensure that the copies of works in such accessible format are used by persons with disabilities and takes reasonable steps to prevent its entry into ordinary channels of business.

Explanation. For the purposes of the sub-clause, "any organisation" includes an organization registered under section 12A of the Income Tax Act, 1961 and working for the benefit of persons with disability or recognized under Chapter X of the Persons with Disabilities (Equal Opportunities Protection of Rights and Full Participation) Act, 1995 or receiving grants from the Government for facilitating access to persons with disabilities or an educational institution or library or archives recognized by the Government.

Developing Road Map for Inclusion

All these examples and analysis of Policy to Practice indicate that irrespective of countries and the enabling conditions being created, there is a need to address effectively the fundamental rights of children and increase the responsive practices to prevent exclusion of children. *A system-wide change is necessary*. Inclusive Education does not happen on a child by child basis rather inclusive education is a system-wide approach (Miles 1991 b)[17] dedicating to making school accessible and amiable. This would imply that:

- All students come to school with diverse needs and abilities, hence students are different, and they are individuals with their own contexts, personality and aspirations.

- It is the responsibility of the general education system to be responsive to all students; RTE Act offers an opportunity.

According to Fullan (2001)[18] Educational Policy goes through three phases: initiation, implementation and institutionalization. As also corroborated by UNESCO Report (Lynch, 2001)[19] the worldwide approach towards Inclusive Education is still patchy and uncoordinated, which is attributed to lack of system-wide change. It would mean that the Educational Policy has not even crossed the second stage (implementation).

May be one can begin by a SWOT on the current situation in the selected geographical unit both for education in general and education of children and youth with disabilities. Needless to say this would be a participatory exercise. This is one area of capacity building and intervention for planners, NGOs, government agencies and even serious researchers committed to policy research.

Next step would be developing an action plan-which should be more like institutional planning process. The crux of institutional planning is that you have a vision/a goal and plan to achieve building on the available strengths (Will to do; Committed NGOs, Existing mandate, etc.). Purpose is not of developing a charter of demands at this stage but initiating the process of first exhausting all the options available—doing all that is within ones' own control, within reach before looking outward. Problem with developing roadmaps is that most people first try to list what they do not have—thus creating an atmosphere of despair! As a researcher, trainer and development worker many of us had the opportunity to witness and learn about work with potentials and possibilities in various types of locations and situations; enough strengths are always available to begin with positives; it is matter of discovering and inculcating that mindset.

Another need of the hour is to see Higher Education as a continuum for education of Persons with disabilities. Higher Education is perceived as one of the important institutions created by the society for its own betterment and to generate knowledge as well as workforce for the society; and is seen as synonymous with better quality of life. Hence, with this logic, reason and necessity flowing from the word 'Higher Education' the disabled people have the same rights as anyone of us has. According to Leslie Wagner, "University is an elastic term used by some to include and some to exclude" (as quoted by Reisz Mathew, 2008[20]). While there is a lot of debate on what is a university and what is its purpose and scope; for this particular paper, it is restricted to the viewpoint that modern university and institutions of higher education tend to emphasize on one hand the pursuit of knowledge and research for its own sake as well as to generate workforce to meet the challenges of industrialization and other requirements of the society. All our countries today are debating on a vision of a world where all are able to benefit from "transformational education experience and a mission to create a vibrant, multi-cultural learning community enabling people to transform their lives by participating in excellence, innovative education, scholarship and research. Does this mean that persons with disability across our region are also able to acquire these opportunities for learning?

Higher Education is not about learning alone but it is the place for generating dreams and manpower. Persons with disability reach higher education after a lot of hard work, commitment and more than anything with dreams like others to be, to do and to make a change in the world. Hence, we need to find out mechanisms to address the requirements of this group of people. Normally, increased enrolment is seen as a measure of addressing diversity. Most of the institutions of higher education work through a process of diversification leading to creating multi-cultural societies, compensation and correction for the present and past discrimination with admission policy and practice as one of the significant intervention. *This would imply that the admission policy to institutions of higher learning needs to be critically analyzed and interpreted for the persons with disabilities.*

While over a period of time the number of persons entering the higher education streams has increased in absolute terms but in relative terms the trend is not very different. With about 3 per cent persons being enumerated as disabled, the representation in higher education is less than 0.1 per cent. To quote from this source, "*Though the percentage of disabled students in the respondent colleges was as low as 0.52 per cent very few of the respondent colleges expressed their concerns openly. Only about 15 of the respondent colleges reported lack of infrastructure and trained staff as their apprehensions*" (NCPEDP, 2005).[21] This phenomenon indicates two more points: first is the school sector really preparing persons with disability for entrance into higher education and secondly, is higher education really open for persons with disabilities? I think both these issues need to be debated and understood consciously and conscientiously. Needless to say that depending on the definition of disabilities there is further discrimination and denial of opportunity among the disabled. For example, visual impaired persons may have relatively a better chance of participation and empowerment as compared to a person with mental retardation or hearing impairment.

Added to this are other reasons of discrimination such as gender, geographical disparities, caste, race, ethnic origin etc. etc. This whole process further gets complicated by two more factors i.e. what happens in the families in terms of the poverty status, the family expectations and also what do the service providers or an elite society perceive about the access of persons with disabilities to higher education (such as class assumptions and expectations from these people).

All these impact policy statements and practices in higher education in general and some specialized courses and institutions in particular. It is an established fact that courses in higher education should be available to all those who are qualified by attainment to pursue them and who wish to do so. In case of persons with disability, as mentioned earlier this general trend cannot be followed until and unless the system becomes sensitive to create means to overcome class differential, these people are also equally affected by the socio-economic status of their families. The spirit of this statement has remained same unfortunately since 1981 when this debate and dialogue started; two quotes from the yesteryears are applicable even today:

> "There is a basic and unacceptable inequity in preservation of an expensive, privileged, conveying education and social experience for socially unrepresented elite". (Fulton, 1981 p. 11)
>
> "*When more is taken for education in one generation more tends to be available in the next*". (HMSO, 1963 as quoted by Gordon in Fulton, 1981 p. 126)[22]

Some of the more observable and multiple sources of discrimination are rooted in the concepts of the relative prestige status of institutions where these people may get admissions, divide created by the public and private institutions, paying capacity of these people, the location and facilities available to access these institutions and above all the choice of courses, which may be available to these people as well as the employability. At times relatively excessive personal funds are spent to overcome the difficulties imposed by the disability by the families of the persons with disabilities, as many of our countries do not have social security policies in place like other advanced countries in the North.

Hence, the first step would be to facilitate them to overcome this sense of exclusion, which is created not only by behaviour but also by routes taken by these people like so many other marginalized groups for higher education. For example, many of the disabled persons, who complete school, leaving certificate may have come through open learning system, home-based education provisions, special schools and may be at times through softer courses. While in many resource-starved countries the cost of school education may have created these conditions; issue is should they continue to be marginalized even in the higher education systems, which is comparatively rich in resources? Vocational education should not be the only choice for these people. Part time and distance learning courses also require flexibility. Hence, some of the recommendations, which have been put forward in higher education by the previous conferences, should now be revisited and interpreted for persons with disabilities.

Concrete answers are not readily available because of the fact that even the voluntary organizations and some of the international agencies like DFID, UNICEF, UNESCO, World Bank, ADB, etc. though actively engaged in the issues of basic education, poverty, etc.; education of the youth and the manpower implications of disability and their adult years have not still caught the attention of many people. However, literature generated by these agencies does indicate that disable people are over-represented among the poor and they are more vulnerable to poverty. According to the Work Bank estimates 20 per cent of the world over people are disabled (Elwan, A., 1999)[23]. Coming to the specific point of what can institutions of higher education can do; relatively concrete answers would be to:

- Create role models by recruiting persons with disabilities at all levels
- Create disability support centers, initiate and promote disability studies, carry out research and share information.
- The countries can also launch vouchers and additional resources as incentives.
- Wherever reservation policy is in place, it should be implemented sincerely along with relaxation in marks in admissions and recruitment.
- Within the competence of individual institutions and government policies one can also think of generous financial policies which anyway will be required as many countries are signatories to the United Nations Convention on the Right of Disabled Persons, 2008.
- In terms of higher education it will also mean flexible and modular courses. The issue of credit system has already addressed by many forums to deal with the issues of interruption and transfer of study as well as mature learners as the clientele of higher education.

In the end, I will also draw the attention to the policy statement by the International Association of Universities as adopted by the International Association of Universities in its 13th General Conference at Utrecht in July 2008: *Access to higher learning should be made possible to all regardless of race, ethnicity, gender, economic or social class, age, language, religion, location or [dis]abilities. The goal of access policies should be successful participation in higher education, as access without a reasonable chance of success is an empty promise.*

This also gels well with one of the cautions sounded by Philip O'Keefe (2007)[24].

The number of people with disabilities in India is substantial and likely to grow-disability does not "go away" as countries get richer. Social attitudes and stigma play an important role in limiting the opportunities of disabled people for full participation in social and economic life, often even within their own families. One also needs to be sensitive to the fact that higher education brings stress because of increased academic demands, challenges of living independently for the first time, changes in social and sexual identities, peer pressure and unrealistic expectations from parents. Need is for dedicated staff and professionals to support the first timers. Number of students opting for higher education has increased world over, and what used to be an elite pursuit once has now become more mass-based by the growth in enrolment in colleges and universities. Equal Opportunity Office in each University to begin with may be a good beginning for large countries to be followed by provisions in constituent colleges as well. Beginning has been made in the XI Five year Plan, but more is expected to be in terms of actualizing these commitments, may be next plan will witness more concrete results!

Notes

1. Earlier chapter has already covered the developments in the historical context, hence this writing takes the dialogue further.
2. Inclusion (education) http://en.wikipedia.org/wiki/Inclusive_education
3 http://en.wikipedia.org/wiki/Inclusive_education cite note Bowe, Frank. (2005). *Making Inclusion Work.* Merrill Education/Prentice Hall.
4. http://en.wikipedia.org/wiki/Inclusive_education cite note Understanding Psychology Eighth Edition", Feldman, Robert S. (2008), page 309. Retrieved 2010-06-10.
5. Mukhopadhyay, Sudesh, *Case Studies on Inclusive Education and Quality Improvement*, Shared in the Regional Workshop on Building National Capacity for Quality Improvement of Primary Schools, UNESCO sponsored, Hiroshima, Japan, February 26-4 March 2001.
6. Government of India, *Sarva Shiksha Abhiyan* (2000). Ministry of Human Resource Development . Accessed from:http://www.educationforallinindia.com/page119.html
7. The Rights of Persons with Disabilities Bill, 2011 (As submitted to MSJE Presented by Committee appointed by Ministry of Social Justice and Empowerment Government of India, 30 June 2011.
8. http://en.wikipedia.org/wiki/Inclusive_education cite note UNESCO (2009) Policy Guidelines on Inclusion in Education. UNESCO: Paris. http://unesdoc.unesco.org/images/0017/001778/177849e.pdf
9. http://en.wikipedia.org/wiki/Inclusive_education cite note Bennett, T., Deluca, D., & Bruns, D. (1997). Putting inclusion into practice: perspectives of teachers and parents. *Exceptional Children,* 64.
10. Mukhopadhyay Sudesh and Renu Singh, (2008). *Access to Education for the Disabled: A Case Study of India*, NUEPA, New Delhi (Mimeo).
11. www.ioe.ac.uk/study/MMAINC)
12. Sapon-Shevin Mara (2010). *Because we can change the world: A Practical Guide to Building Cooperative*, Inclusive Classroom Communities. California: Corwin, p. 163.

13. http://en.wikipedia.org/wiki/Universal_Design_for_Learning cite note Rose, DH, & Meyer, A (2002) *Teaching Every Student in the Digital Age: Universal Design for Learning* Alexandria, VA: ASCD
14. http://en.wikipedia.org/wiki/Universal_Design_for_Learning cite note Orkwis, R., and McLane, K. (1998). A curriculum every student can use: Design principles for student access. ERIC/OSEP Topical Brief No. ED423654. Reston, VA: ERIC/OSEP Special Project.
15. Adapted from the conceptualization of Civics Curriculum—Courage, Inclusion, Value, Integrity, Cooperation Safety by Sapon-Shevin Mara (2010) *Because we can change the world: A Practical Guide to Building Cooperative, Inclusive Classroom Communities*. California: Corwin, pp. 7-19.
16. The Copyright (Amendment) Act, 2012, no. 27 of 2012 , An Act funther to Amend the Copyright Act, 1957, and June 2012
17. Peters, S. et al. (2005). A Disability Rights in Education Model for Evaluating Inclusive Education. In *International Journal of Inclusive Education*, Volume 9, No. 2, p. 142.
18. *Op cit.*
19 Lynch, J. (1994). *Provision for Children with Special Educational Needs in the Asia Region*. World Bank Technical Paper Number 261. Washington: The World Bank.
20 Reisz Mathew (2008) *Diversity Challenge*, Times Higher Education www.timeshighereducation.co.uk accessed on 2/13/2009.
21. National Centre for Promotion of Employment for Disabled People (NCPEDP), (2005) Journey Towards Promotion of Inclusive Education (Mimeo).
22. Fulton Oliver (ed.) (1981) *Access to Higher Education*, Surrey: The Society for Research into Higher Education at the University of Guilford.
23. Ellan A. (1999) *Poverty and Disability: A Survey of the Literature*, Washington: The World Bank.
24. Philip O'Keefe (2007), *People with Disabilities in India: From Commitments to Outcomes,* The World Bank, 2007.

15

Women's Education in Post-Independent India

Manju Narula and *Gauri Srivastava*

Promotion of women education has been one of the prime concerns of India since independence. There was a realization that for the overall growth of the country education of women was a pre-requisite. Article 45 of the Constitution enjoined that the state shall endeavour to provide within a period of 10 years from the commencement of the constitution, compulsory education for all children until they complete the age of 14 years. For fulfilling the Constitutional commitments and achieving the agenda of girls' education the Government of India appointed several Committees and Commissions from time to time; some exclusively for women's education and their development. In this chapter, an attempt has been made to examine the growth and development of women's education in post independent India especially reviewing the provisions in the Constitution, Five Year Plans, Policies and Programmes of the government.

Constitution of India

There are several articles in the Constitution that have direct or indirect bearing on women's education and development. Article 15 prohibits discrimination against any citizen on grounds of religion, race, caste and gender. The Article 15(1) emphasizes on right to equality, provides the basic policy framework that enshrines the vision of girls' education and the spirit in which their education is to be provided. Article 15(3) made a special provision enabling the state to make affirmative discriminations in favour of women. Articles 16, 29, 30, 39A, 39C also have implications for girls and women's development. Article 42 directs the state to make provision for ensuring just and humane conditions of work and maternity relief. Article 51A(e) imposes a fundamental duty on every citizen to renounce practices derogatory to the dignity of women. To make this de-jure equality into de-facto one, many policies and programmes were put into action from time to time, besides enacting/enforcing special legislations, in favour of women.

Until 1976, education was a state subject. Since its transfer to the Concurrent List by the 42nd Constitutional Amendment in 1976, the Central Government has played a more proactive role in the sector through several centrally sponsored schemes that had a distinct bearing on promoting education for girls. In 2002, the 86th Constitutional amendment made education as a 'Fundamental Right' for the children in the age group of 6 to 14 years committing 'the state shall provide free and compulsory education to all children of the age of six to fourteen years in such manner as the State may, by law, determine' (Article 21A). However, Right to Education (RTE) Act was passed in 2009. It makes reference to gender and girls education in different sections. To bring all the children, especially girls from disadvantaged communities it stated the duties of appropriate government authorities at various levels. In addition the Act stresses on age appropriate classes (which will largely apply to girls), inclusion of women in school monitoring committees.

Commissions, Committees and Policies

The University Education Commission (1948-49) devoted a full chapter to women's education. The Commission's observation indicates role stereotyping for women—the wife-mother's role. The Commission mentioned, however, that a woman's world should not be limited to only one relationship. It was forced to take note that women were entering the world of work.

Women's education figured prominently in the report of the Secondary Education Commission (1952-53). This Commission too viewed girls' education to be more closely connected with the home and the community. Accordingly, Commission recommended teaching of Home Science in Girls' School (and wherever possible, for girls attending boys' schools) to be radically improved o fulfill her two-fold duty of family and society.

'The National Committee on Women's Education' (1958-59) chaired by Durgabai Deshmukh shifted its focus from higher education to school education. The major purpose of this Committee was to look into the factors that hindered the progress of girls' education and make recommendations for bringing girls' education on par with that of the boys. It made recommendations of far reaching consequences; if implemented, it would have changed the picture of women's education totally. The Committee recommended constitution of a National Council for the Education of Girls and Women; urged UGC to set apart special funds for the promotion of women's education; highest priority should be given to schemes prepared to close the existing gap between the education of men and women in as short a time as possible.

Government of India generally accepted the recommendations made by the National Committee and decided to accord a high priority to women's education, especially in the Third Five Year Plan.

This was followed by Committee on Women's Education, better known as Hansa Mehta Committee (1962-64) appointed by the NCWE. This Committee suggested adoption of co-education as the general pattern at the elementary stage; separate primary and middle schools as a transitional measure where necessary; and at the secondary level, to be left to the choice of the management and parents. Committee recommended induction of women teachers in boys' schools to encourage girls to join these institutions; and, common curricula for boys and girls at the elementary stage.

The NCWE appointed another Committee (M. Bhaktavatsalam Committee in 1963) to investigate into the cause for lack of public support for education of girls, particularly in the rural areas and to suggest suitable measures to secure public cooperation. In 1970, NCWE reviewed the development of women's education after Independence and recommended priority for women's education; curbing discrimination between boys and girls; government to encourage states to launch various programmes for girls education; providing proper facilities and protection for women teachers serving in rural areas; and giving scholarships to local girls to complete their education to overcome women teacher shortage.

The Education Commission (1964-66) stressed that where co-education was not acceptable, separate schools for girls should be provided. In addition, hostels for girls should be encouraged wherever possible; subsidized transport should be arranged; and girls should be given special preference in scholarship programmes. The Commission emphasized the need to give adequate attention to the training and employment of women teachers. Part time and vocational education should be developed for girls. The Commission found the state of female literacy particularly distressing and observed that the effort being made in the direction of making women literate left much to be desired.

The Commission's recommendations came into force with the National Policy on Education, 1968. The most far reaching recommendation of the NPE, 1968, is that of ten years of common curriculum for all children, which resulted in girls also studying science and mathematics up to 10th class.

A further important development in post-Independent India was the constitution of 'The Committee on the Status of Women in India (CSWI)' in 1974. Its report "Towards Equality" was placed before the Parliament in 1975. The Committee examined the Constitutional, legal and administrative provisions which had bearings on the status of women. Low female literacy, declining sex ratio, declining work participation rates, low paid jobs for women and deprivation of basic needs of health, nutrition, and education of women were the expressed concerns. The CSWI report coincided with the International

Women's Year and the beginning of the Women's Decade. The Committee recommended co-education as a long term policy in view of the economic constraints and equality of opportunity. Separate institutions for girls were, however, recommended in areas where there was continued sex segregation.

A new thrust was provided to girls' education in the National Policy on Education (NPE) 1986, and its Programme of Action (POA). The policy went beyond the equal opportunity and social justice approach and exhorted education to become an instrument of women's equality and empowerment. The policy states that education would promote the value of gender equality by removing gender bias and stereotyping in the contents and processes of education. It would also involve training and orientation of teachers, decision-makers and administrators on gender issues. The policy proposed a dual track approach designed to promote simultaneously adult literacy and primary education with a focus on girls and other disadvantaged groups.

For promoting self reliance among girls, the policy especially stresses on encouraging participation of women in vocational and technical professions. In the context of vocational education the policy specially emphasizes on non-discrimination to eliminate sex stereotyping and encouraging participation of women in unconventional occupations and in new and emerging technological fields.

The subsequent revised version of NPE in 1992 recognized that it is impossible to achieve Universal Elementary Education (UEE) unless concerted efforts are made to reach out to the girl child. It recommended specially designed NFE programmes for out of school and adolescent girl dropouts with a view to getting them back into the formal stream; use of distance education to reach out to girls in rural/remote areas and urban slums; special efforts to recruit women teachers and to augment teacher training facilities for women; guidance and counseling for girls as a necessary pre-condition to encourage participation.

The NPE 1986 came soon after the UN Development Decade for Women (1985-95) and reflected adequately the national aspirations for removal of all disparities, caste, sex, region, and to carry basic education to all sections of society living in every nook and corner of the country. This was also a period when experience showed that for raising the status of women, the interventions have to be made very early and the entire South Asian Region committed itself to working for the survival, protection and development of the girl child. As part of the SAARC Decade of the Girl Child, all national governments including India prepared a Plan of Action to operationalize various aspects of the development of the girl child to include health and education.

The Government of India enacted a National Policy for the Empowerment of Women in 2001. The goal of this policy is to bring about the advancement, development and empowerment of women. Specifically, the objective of this

Policy was to create an environment through positive economic and social policies for full development of women to enable them to realize their full potential.

In 2004, the Government of India had re-constituted the Central Advisory Board of Education (CABE), to examine existing schemes, incentives and special measures to reduce gender disparity and increasing the participation and retention of girls, in all sectors of education. The report submitted in 2005 emphasized on the constitutional commitment to provide education of a comparable quality to all, hence, there is no alternative acceptable to regular schooling of good quality to all the girls. The Committee mentioned that incentives offered for promotion of girls' education to be revisited and the measures taken need to be of such nature, force and magnitude that they are able to overcome the obstacles posed by factors such as poverty, domestic/ sibling responsibilities, girl child labour, low preference to girls' education, preference to marriage over education of the girl child, etc.

Five-Year Plans: Expansion of Girls' Education

Five Year Plans provide the framework for implementing the policy decisions. The recommendations of the Committees and Commissions and national policies on education were only as effective as their implementation through the five year plans. There has been significant development in girls' education from 1st to the 11th FYP (Table 15.1)

Table 15.1: Women's Education through FYPs

Plan Period	*Thrust*	*Increase in Girls' Enrolment*
1st (1951-55)	Different targets were set for boys and girls. The target for the girls' enrolment was set to 40 per cent	Primary from 5.4 m to 7.5 m, Middle: from 0.5 m to 1m High/Higher Secondary: from 0.2 m to 0.4 m
2nd (1956-60)	To study the situation in each area separately, and to explore methods for overcoming the difficulties in the acceptance of co-education and alternative to separate schools for girls in some areas.	Primary: from 7.5 m to 11.4 m Middle: from 1 m to 1.6 m High/HS: from 0.4 m to 0.7 m GER Primary: 41.4% Middle: 11.3%
3rd 1961-65		Primary: from 11.4 m to 18.3 m. Middle: from 1.6 to 2.8 m
4th 1969-73		Primary: 24.5 m girls among 64.10 m children enrolled. Middle: 4.6 m girls among 15.30 m Girls' GER 61% in Classes I-V and 22% in Classes VI-VIII.
5th 1974-79		GER for girls: Primary: 66% (100.2% boys). Middle: 28% (52% boys).

Contd.

Plan Period	*Thrust*	*Increase in Girls' Enrolment*
6th 1980-84	from 'welfare' to 'development' of women	Primary: 35 m out of 84 m girls; GER for girls was 76.7%. Middle: (9.72 m out of 27 m were girls; GER for girls was 36%.
7th 1985-90	Girls' education will be free up to the higher secondary stage. The focus of effort was on promotion of girls' education through appointment of women teachers, attachment of pre-school centres to primary schools, provision of free uniforms and other incentives.	Primary: 40 m girls among 97m children. Middle: 12 m girls out of 31m children.
8th 1992-97	Stressed on the need to ensure a definite flow of funds from the general developmental sectors to women. It stressed on expansion of secondary schools particularly to cater to the needs of deprived sections like girls and SCs/STs and in rural areas	Primary: increased from 40 m to 47 m Middle: from 12 m to 15 m. GER: 80% (primary); 48% (middle).
9th 1998-02	Women as empowered partners in the political and decision-making process; Additional hostel facilities for girls, particularly in tribal and remote areas. The National Agenda for Governance stated that plans will be instituted for providing free education for girls up to college level i.e., under-graduate level including professional courses. Launched SSA in partnership with states	Primary: increased from 48 m 50.3m Middle: increased from 15.9m to 18.7m
10th 2002-07	'Empowering Women' as agents of social change and development continued as thrust through social and economic empowerment and gender justice. RTE was formulated. Vocationalization of secondary education and vocational training for women was another priority area. Rs. 13,780 Crores were earmarked in the central budget of the Department of Women and Child Development. Women-specific programmes such as the existing Mahila Samakhya, Kasturba Gandhi Swatantra Vidyalaya and the National Programme for the Education of Girls at the Elementary Level.	
11th 2007–2012	Focused on bridging regional, social and gender gaps; New range of initiatives, e.g. setting up 410 additional Kasturba Gandhi Balika Vidyalayas. To increase the participation of girls up to elementary level the National Programme for Girls at Elementary Level (NPEGEL) Scheme was started. CABE Committee on girls' education.	

Note: From 1966 to 68 was declared as Plan holiday. During the Plan holiday period there were 20.57 million girls among 55.49 million children enrolled in primary classes. At the upper primary level, there were 3.51 million girls among total of 12.27 million children. The enrolment ratio of girls at the primary stage reached 58.5 per cent but was only 18.8 per cent at the middle stage.

As would be evident, there have been some major efforts to improve equity and access for girls' education during all the five year plans. In addition to elementary education, the Government of India introduced a range of schemes and programmes at the secondary and senior secondary levels viz. National Scheme of Incentive to Girls for Secondary Education, Nutrition Programme for Adolescent Girls, Computer Literacy and Studies in Schools project (CLASS), strengthening boarding and hostel facilities for girls students, Meena Manch, Kishori Shakti Yolanda, etc. In view of improving access and participation of education the Government of India under the welfare scheme provide free uniform, free text books, free noon-meals, free bus passes, free bicycles to all SC/ST girls students, remedial and special coaching to SC/ST student in classes IX to XII. During the XI five year plan secondary education has been accorded relatively high priority in the development agenda. In 2004, Central Advisory Board of Education (CABE) formed seven committees. Among them one was on Universalization of Secondary Education and other was on the issues of girl's education. As mentioned earlier, for Universalization of Secondary Education RMSA was launched.

Development of Girl's Education

Access to education has improved dramatically after independence and there have been a number of encouraging trends in girls' and women's education. One of the major achievement was the reduction if gender gap in literacy. The gap of 21.59 percentage points in 2001 Census has reduced to 16.68 percentage points in 2011.

Enrolment by Gender and Marginal Groups

Because of the affirmative actions by the government, female enrolment, and among them participation of women of socially backward communities, increased, though inequalities were prominent among these groups. Total female enrolment in 2000 at the elementary level was 67.3 million; this increased to 85 million by 2005. Same trend was observed for SC and ST women. SC women enrolment increased from 11.8 million to 15.1 million and ST enrolment increased from 11.8 million to 8.6 million (Table 15.2). Furthermore, though female enrolment is increasing over the years, their participation at the elementary level is still less than 50 per cent.

Secondary Level

Enrolment of girls of socially backward groups at secondary level of education has grown at a faster rate than those of the boys, thereby reducing the gender in-equalities over the period. The increase in enrolment has been higher for the girls belonging to Scheduled Castes (9.8 times) in comparison to Scheduled Tribes.

Table 15.2: Percentage of Female Enrolment in Elementary School

(In Millions)

Year	Female Enrolment			Total Enrolment			% Female Enrolment		
	Total	SC	ST	Total	SC	ST	Total	SC	ST
2000	67.3	11.8	5.9	156.6	27.9	14.1	43.0	42.3	41.8
2001	69.0	12.2	6.3	158.7	29.0	15.1	43.5	42.1	41.7
2002	77.9	12.8	6.7	169.3	29.2	15.1	46	43.8	44.4
2003	81.4	13.7	7.3	177.0	31.2	16.2	45.99	43.9	45.1
2004	83.8	14.6	8.1	182.0	33.5	17.9	46.1	43.6	45.2
2005	85.0	15.1	8.6	184.2	34.4	18.5	46.1	43.9	46.5

Source: Selected Educational Statistics: 2005-06 Ministry of Human Resource Development, GOI, 2008. (Provisional).

The decadal growth rate of enrolment at the secondary level suggests that from 1980-81 to 2005-06, the increase in the growth of enrolment at the secondary level was more for SC and ST population than general population. The growth in enrolment of SC and ST girls is growing by more than 9 per cent per annum compared to a little over 6 per cent in case of total girls enrolment. Similarly, total enrolment of SCs and STs is growing at a higher rate of over 6 per cent per annum compared to a little higher than 5 per cent in case of general population (see Table 15.3).

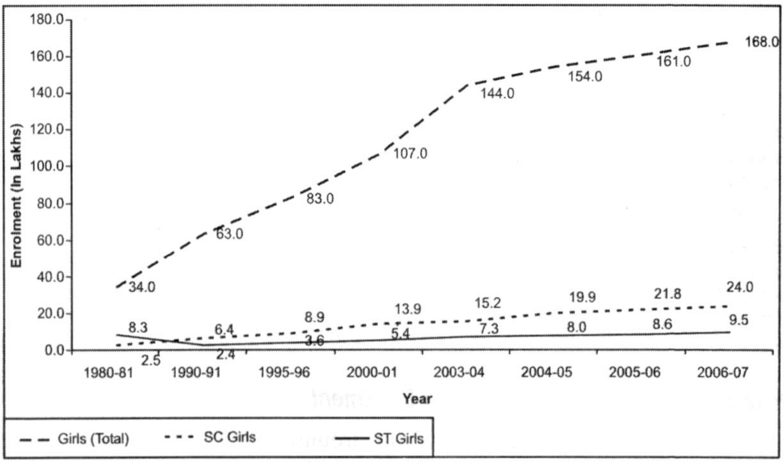

Fig. 15.1: Growth of Girls Enrolment at Secondary and Higher Secondary

Enrolment by Location and Gender

Though around 70 per cent of population in India lives in rural areas but they remain educationally backward in comparison to the urban areas. Table 15.4

Table 15.3: Average Annual Growth Rate of Enrolment at the Secondary Level

Years	Girls	Total	SC Girls	SC Total	ST Girls	ST Total
	Average Annual Growth Rate					
1980-81 to 1990-91	8.52	7.36	15.81	10.30	7.13	14.47
1990-91 to 1995-96	6.35	3.38	7.94	3.44	10.16	7.87
1995-96 to 2000-01	5.78	4.10	11.43	7.81	9.80	6.56
2000-01 to 2005-06	10.09	7.80	11.31	9.38	12.22	9.69
A.A.G.R. 1980-81 to 2005-06	6.4	5.1	9.1	6.5	9.8	7.9

Source: *Ibid.*

Note: A.A.G.R.—Average Annual Growth Rate is calculated on the basis of formula= ((LY/BY)^(1/NY)-1)*100)

depicts the inequitable distribution of enrolment in rural areas at the secondary and senior secondary levels. Girls' enrolment is quite dismal at both secondary and senior secondary levels, with 19 per cent and 22 per cent respectively in rural and urban areas at secondary and 16 per cent and 25 per cent at the senior secondary levels.

Table 15.4: Percentage of Enrolment in Grades 9-12 by Location and Gender, 1993 and 2002

Source (Year)	Urban			Rural			Total
	Total	Boys	irls	Total	Boys	Girls	
Sixth All-India Educational Survey (1993)							
Grades 9-10	62	37	25	38	27	11	100
Grades 11-12	49	29	20	51	35	16	100
Grades 9-12	45	26	19	55	37	18	100
Seventh All-India Educational Survey (2002)							
Grades 9-10	54	31	22	46	27	19	100
Grades 11-12	58	32	25	42	26	16	100
Grades 9-12	49	27	21	51	31	20	100

Source: All India Education Survey, 1992 and 2002, NCERT, New Delhi

Share of Differently Abled Children in Enrolment

Table 15.5 indicates that during 2005-06, around 1.24 million in I-V grade and about 0.38 million were in upper primary grades across the country. Gender wise bifurcation shows that out of the total disabled children, 0.51 million girls were in I to V grades, and 0.15 million girls were in VI to VII/VIII grades across the country. The Gender Parity Index is 0.71 at I to V grades and 0.67 at I to VII/VIII grades. This indicates that much greater attention is needed to bring differently abled girls of this category into the fold of regular primary schools.

Table 15.5: Enrolment and Gender Parity Index of Children with Disability: 2002-03 to 2005-06

Grades	*All Areas*		
	Girls	*Total*	*GPI*
2002-03			
I-V	3,11,024	7,81,314	0.66
VI-VII/VIII	75,554	1,99,850	0.61
I-VII/VIII	3,86,578	9,81,164	0.65
2003-04			
I-V	5,58,481	13,46,186	0.71
VI-VII/VIII	1,61,655	4,12,297	0.64
I-VII/VIII	7,20,136	17,58,483	0.69
2004-05			
I-V	4,10,860	10,17,392	0.68
VI-VII/VIII	1,58,600	3,81,951	0.71
I-VII/VIII	5,69,460	13,99,343	0.69
2005-06			
I-V	5,12,993	12,36,891	0.71
VI-VII/VIII	1,52,684	3,79,965	0.67
I-VII/VIII	6,65,677	16,16,856	0.70

Source: Elementary Education in India. Analytical Report. 2006-07. NUEPA.

(ii) Gender parity Index

Gender participation has been examined using indicators of share of girls to total enrolment with gender parity index. From 1950-51, girls' enrolment is continuously increasing. It has taken over more than five and half decades to increase the proportion of girls' enrolment. The efforts have brought Gender Parity Index at the primary level to over 98 per cent. Gender Parity Index increased from 0.22 to 0.91 per cent for upper primary level, 0.38 per cent to 0.96 per cent at elementary level (grade I to VIII) and 0.27 to 0.82 per cent at secondary level (Table 15.6).

The Gross Enrolment Ratios (GER)

The growth in enrolment appears to be quite impressive but looses effectiveness when compared with the size and growth of corresponding age population. Gross Enrolment Ratio (GER) is one of the crude indicators that give idea about the participation of corresponding age population in education. The GER moved in respect of primary level from one fourth per cent in 1950-51 to more than 100 per cent (114.4) in 2007-08, as underage and overage children

Table 15.6: Gender Parity Index at the School Level

Years	*Gender Parity Index*	*Gender Parity Index*	*Gender Parity Index*	*Gender Parity Index*
	Primary	*Upper Primary*	*Elementary*	*Secondary*
1950-51	0.41	0.22	0.38	
1960-61	0.50	0.34	0.47	0.27
1970-71	0.63	0.45	0.59	0.40
1980-81	0.67	0.53	0.63	0.47
1990-91	0.75	0.61	0.71	0.59
1995-96	0.82	0.73	0.80	—
2000-01	0.82	0.75	0.80	0.73
2003-04	0.95	0.86	0.93	0.80
2004-05	0.95	0.88	0.93	0.79
2005-06	0.95	0.88	0.92	0.80
2006-07	0.95	0.90	0.93	0.81
2007-08	0.98	0.91	0.96	0.82

Source: *Ibid.*

were included at this level. With respect of middle level also GRE increased massively i.e. from 12.7 per cent to 78.2 per cent (see Figure 15.2).

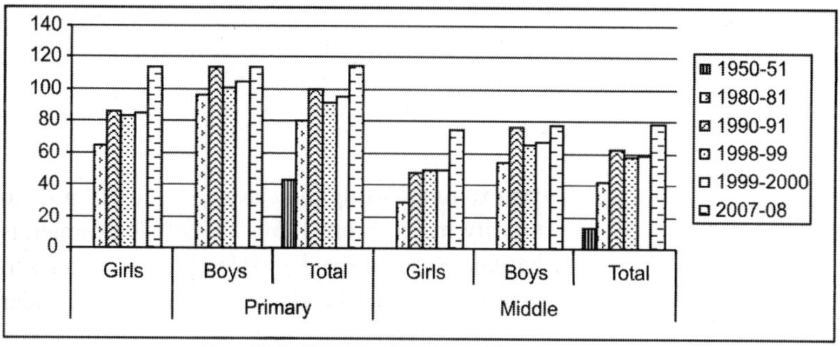

Fig. 15.2: Gender wise Gross Enrolment Ratio

The Figure 15.2 also indicates that girls GER increased from 28.6 per cent during 1980-81 to 74.4 per cent during 2007-08. However, the boys GER at middle level reduced from 76.6 to 65.3 per cent during 1990-91 to 1998-99, while GER of girls during the same period showed an increasing trend (47.8 to 49.1%).

Dropout Rate

The Figure 15.3 sum up that during 2007-08 near about 25 per cent children of classes I-V and more than 40 per cent children of the classes I-VIII and 57 per cent students from classes I-X dropout of the system. The Figure 15.3

also reveals that at classes I-V more boys dropout in comparison to the girls; at classes I-VIII and classes I-X more girls dropout of the system.

The Figure 15.4 and 15.5 reveals that rate of drop out among SC and ST students are higher in comparison to general students. It was also observed that less SC and ST girls' dropout from the classes I-V and classes I-VIII in comparison to the boys studying at the classes I-X. It shows that out of 100 SC students enrolled in grade I, only about 45 per cent reach grade X, 23 per cent ST children reach to grade X.

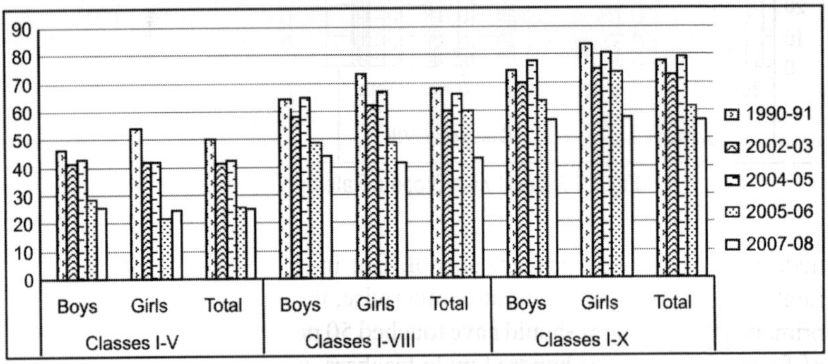

Fig. 15.3: Level-wise Dropout Rate

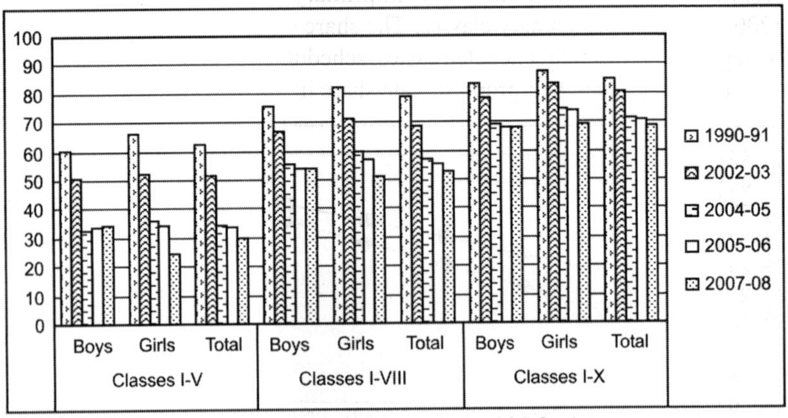

Fig. 15.4: Level-wise Dropout Rate of SC Students

Growth of Female Teachers

Primary and Upper Primary Level

In absolute terms, substantial increase in the number of female teachers has been registered since 1950-51 in all types of schools (Figure 15.6). As per the Operation Blackboard Scheme (OBS), there has to be one female and one

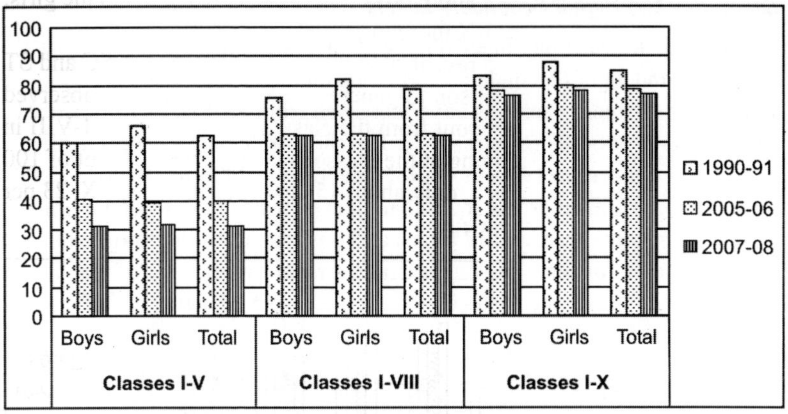

Fig. 15.5: Level wise Dropout Rate of ST Students

male teacher in every primary school. But in rural and difficult areas this might not have happened, because otherwise, the share of female teachers in primary schools/stages should have touched 50 per cent. If we see, the number of female teachers per hundred male teachers, we find that it has increased from 20 (1950-51) to 66 (2003-04) in primary classes, 18 (1950-51) to 69 (2003-04) in upper primary classes. The share of female teachers belonging to deprived groups like scheduled castes, scheduled tribes and other backward classes are less than their proportionate share in population. However, over a

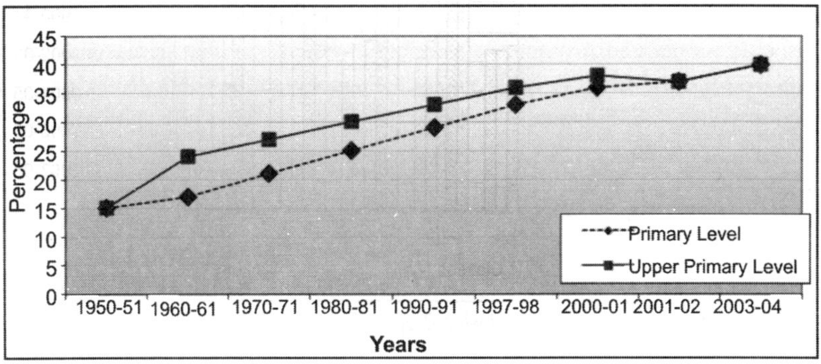

Fig. 15.6: Share of Female Teachers at primary and Upper Primary Level

period of time, the number of teachers belonging to these groups has increased partly due to intervention strategies (job reservation policies). In many states, qualification for recruitment of teachers belonging to deprived groups like scheduled tribes are relaxed and reduced at the time of recruitment.

Secondary and Higher Secondary Levels

Substantial increase has been observed in the number of teachers at the secondary and higher secondary level. Total numbers of teachers in secondary and higher secondary schools have increased from 1.27 lakhs in 1950-51 to 22.22 lakhs in 2006-07 (Figure 15.7). The share of female teachers increased from 15.74 per cent in 1950-51 to 38.36 per cent in 2006-07. Between 1950-51 and 2006-07, the increase in total number of teachers in secondary/higher secondary schools is around 18 times, and it is around 13 times for males and about 43 times for females. The average annual growth rate of teachers at secondary/higher secondary level of education is 5.5 per cent (4.7% for males and 6.9% for females).

Women in Higher, Technical and Professional Education

The level of participation in higher education is invariably indicative of the collective aspiration of the people for national development and for improving the quality of life at the individual level. India has one of the largest systems of higher education. Up to 2009-10 there were 504 universities and university-level institutions and 25,951 colleges including 2565 woman colleges. The enrolment of woman students was 65.49 lakhs constituting 41.40 per cent of the total enrolment.

There are over 10 exclusive women's universities. There are also exclusive Engineering colleges and a Medical college for women. Thus women have access to both women as well as co-educational institutions.

However, participation of women in higher education is quite low. The Table 15.7 shows the enrolment in higher education in recent years. In 1995-96 only 36 per cent women were in higher education that increased to 40.5 per cent in 2005-06. The Table also reveals that over the years gender gap has reduced from 28.00 per cent to 19.00.

Table 15.7: Women's Enrolment in Higher Education

Year	*Total Enrolment*	*Women Enrolment (in lakhs)*	*% of Women*	*MF Gap*
1995-96	67.54	23.64	36.00	28.00
1999-2000	8051.00	31.12	39.00	22.00
2005-06	110.28	44.66	40.50	19.00
2009-10	136.42	65.49	41.40	—

Stream-wise Women Enrollment in Higher Education

Women's participation in higher education is found more in traditional subjects like Arts, Science and Commerce, and not in technical and professional subjects. The Table 15.8 reveals subject wise choices made by women in higher education.

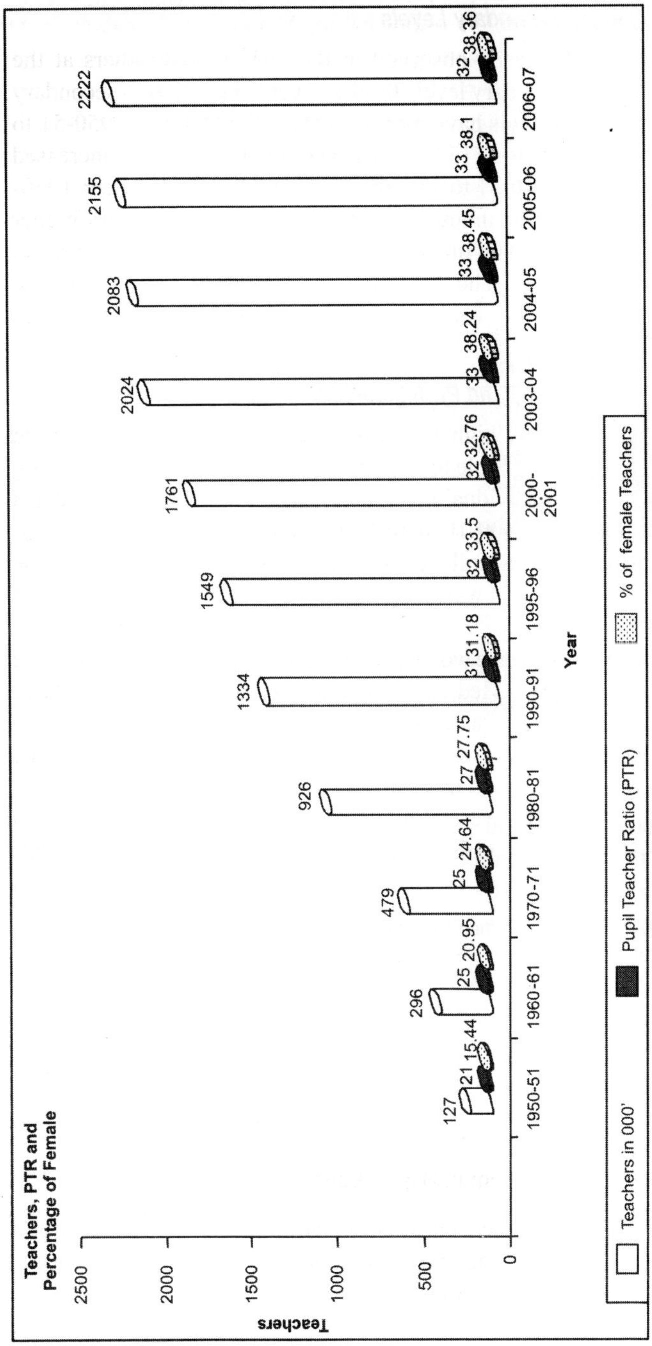

Fig. 15.7: Growth of Teachers, Pupil-Teacher Ratio and Percentage of Female Teachers at Secondary and Senior Secondary Levels,1950-51 to 2006-07

It was observed that most preferred choice is for Arts stream. Near about 50 per cent of the women opts Arts stream. The Science and Commerce stream occupy the second position with around 19 to 20 per cent. The share of women in technical and professional courses like Engineering, Technology and medicine continuous to be low with less than 5 per cent of women enrolled in these streams. However, the enrolment has slightly increased from 2.1 per cent in 1997-98 to about 5 per cent in 2007-08 in Engineering and Technology. Same situation is observed for Medicine, Law, and Agriculture.

Table 15.8: Distribution of Stream-wise Women Enrolment

Year	*Arts*	*Science*	*Comm./ Mangt*	*Edu.*	*Engg/ Tech.*	*Med.*	*Agril*	*Vet. Sc.*	*Law*	*Other#*
1995-96	54.4	20.1	14.1	3.9	1.2	—	—	—	1.8	4.5
2000-01	51.1	19	16.7	2.4	3.6	3.9	0.4	0.1	1.8	1.00
2005-06	51.01	20.18	16.46	1.85	4.16	3.64	0.24	0.08	1.64	0.74
2008-09	49.08	19.99	16.21	3.02	4.90	3.59	0.27	0.08	1.58	1.10

Note: # 'Other' in 1995-96 includes Agriculture, Medicine, Veterinary Science, etc.

Source: UGC Annual Reports Various Years (1995-96 to 2008-09), New Delhi.

Gender Budget

The Eighth Five-Year Plan, for the first time, highlighted the need to ensure a definite flow of funds from general developmental sectors to the education of women. But it could not make much dent in ensuring adequate flow of funds and benefits to women. The Ninth Five-Year Plan, while reaffirming the earlier commitment adopted women component Plan as one of the major strategies and directed both Central and State Governments to ensure that 'not less than 30 per cent of the funds' should be earmarked for all the women related sectors. It also directed that a special vigil be kept on the flow of earmarked funds/ benefits through an effective mechanism to ensure that the proposed strategies bring forth a holistic approach towards empowering women.

The Tenth Five Year Plan (2002-07) marked another significant step forward as it envisaged "immediate action in tying up these two effective concepts of Women's Component Plan (WCP) and Gender Budgeting to play a complementary role to each other, and thus ensure both preventive and post facto action in enabling women to receive their rightful share from all the women-related general development sectors". The need for taking up Gender Budgeting was also recognized in the *National Policy for the Empowerment of Women, 2001*, which observed "Availability of adequate financial, human and market resources to implement the Policy will be managed by concerned Departments." and that this process will include, among other initiatives, "Assessment of benefits flowing to women and resource allocation to the programmes relating to them through an exercise of gender budgeting."

During XI Five Year Plan to increase the access in higher education. In addition to increase women participation in higher education institutions, 343 polytechnics have been provided a first instalment of Rs. 20.00 lakh each during 2009-10 for the construction of women's hostel.

Barriers to Girls' Education and Areas of Intervention

There are several factors for the low levels of participation among girls. They are as follows:

- Lack of qualified female teachers.
- Lack of transport facilities.
- Lack of hostel facilities for girls.
- Fear of sexual harassment.
- Fixed schooling hours.

The enrolment rates of girls and their retention can be improved if educational facilities are made available to girls during periods suitable to them when they are free from domestic chores. Flexible school timings have been tried in Rajasthan through the Shiksha Karmi Project and Lok Jumbish, and the results are encouraging.

Conclusion

Despite significant policy initiatives, there exists gender disparities in education at all levels. More than half a century after independence, universal elementary education still remains elusive. Near about 65 per cent of the girls and women have the opportunity to acquire education; even if they do enroll, chances are that the poorest and the most disadvantaged among them will drop out. The question is how pressure can be mounted on the Government and non-governmental organizations to put resources (financial and human) to realize the goal of universal educational for girls and women.

It is necessary for promotion of women and girls education through special affirmative measures viz. providing free education, appointing more women teachers, creating a gender-sensitive educational system, increasing enrolment and retention rates of girls through provision of hostels, mid-day meals and improving the quality of education to facilitate life-long learning as well as development of vocational/technical skills and thus eliminate discrimination against women and girls in respect of education. In addition to achieve the distant dream of UEE community awareness and support is also very essential.

16

Empowerment of Junior Youth Programmes in India

A Study by Baha'i Educators

A.K. Merchant

My background in the study of English Literature, teaching of English Language and literature at school and college levels, as well as work in the non-formal education sector has led to understand that "education" is both an art and a science. As a science it is necessarily concerned with models and theories. However, it also becomes apparent that many educators, in their great zeal to be scientific, have elevated collections of assumptions, observations, and prescriptions to the level of models and theories and in doing so have made the field of education a rather confusing one. This paper, therefore, focuses on educational materials for children in secondary school education, that is, the junior youth, aged 12 and 15 years, and how events and happenings in an age of globalization shape their thinking and outlook to life.

Literature, as most people will agree, has brought to fore issues that humanity is trying to come to terms with such as gender equality, economic deprivation, violence and exclusion inter alia because at the core of these challenges is the vast untapped potential of millions of youth in this subcontinent and elsewhere. How to prepare oneself effectively for the future; to make appropriate choices in life; to see the different aspects of one's life as coherent without being torn by endless dichotomies and how to be able to translate one's ideals into purposeful action are just some of the collective anxieties that countless young people have to go through in their social spaces. An underlying philosophy behind the Junior Youth Empowerment Programme is that the ages between12 and 15 years is that period of life when habits and attitudes are still being formed and which become the guiding principles for the rest of one's life. The Programme is premised on the posture of humble learning in trying to address the "collective anxieties".

The Junior Youth Empowerment Programme: The underlying Principles

The work of this Programme has therefore been on two levels: firstly through the space of a junior youth group accompanying junior youth for three years. The second aspect is to train older youth to become animators/mentors so that they can in turn form their own junior youth groups.

A Vision for the Junior Youth

The vision in place for the junior youth groups is that they become the nucleus of their community in a village or neighbourhood. Animators are helping them build a foundation for the community. For instance, the groups are assisted to explore fundamental social, scientific and spiritual concepts through the study of certain texts, complementary activities and small of acts of service within their communities.

They are assisted to develop the skills of asking questions, reflecting on various social processes, scientific and cultural ideologies and learning to analyze what is happening in the world around them. Such an environment aims at raising the capacity of these youth to develop a language and power of expression that can empower them to participate in the decision-making processes within that nucleus. They are accompanied to navigate a crucial stage of their lives towards an ongoing positive social change. For instance, with so much discourse on conflict-resolution, it is apparent that prejudices and differences are major forces of disintegration in the world today. It is reassuring to see these young people realize the futility of these differences and the power that lies in unity and cohesion. The words of a young girl from Banthra, a village in the state of Uttar Pradesh, who had been participating in a junior youth group after her school hours still rings in my ear: that the members of her group, in spite of belonging to different castes, and discouraged by their families to mix with each other, have learned not to discriminate and accept the fact that ultimately they are all the same. They are happy to be with each other and play together.

There are a number of such examples that can be cited given the fact there are at present some 100 junior youth groups receiving the benefit of the curricula of materials developed for their advancement. It is hoped that with the proliferation of such groups, thousands of junior youth would be sensitized, their capacities raised and a cadre of animators and coordinators would emerge to reach out to the masses of youth in the country. So far the programme has been launched in 18 states covering 52 cities, districts and numerous villages and towns within India as well as some of the neighbouring countries such as Nepal, Bangladesh and Malaysia.

Being in Charge of One's Own Education and Spiritual Growth

One of the first things the curriculum does is to prompt the participants to understand what it means for us to be in charge of our own education and spiritual growth? What is it that really motivates us to grow? This is a question which I feel has deep implications for elaborating the conceptual framework of the course materials. Serving humanity while bringing with it tremendous joy and enthusiasm, also at times brings with it disappointments and getting worked up in the process. However, having an understanding that the dialectical forces of integration and disintegration at work in the world today is part of the collective evolution of humanity helps the individual not to get overwhelmed by the terrible amount of turmoil that the world is going through. Rather, the conditions of humankind should motivate the person to work harder in doing one's bit to free humanity from the "yoke of oppression". (The Universal House of Justice in a message dated Ridván [21 April—May] 2009).

Moreover, if the person understands that he or she has the capacity to strive for excellence, despite the limitations and imperfections that are inherent in every human being, one will never feel disillusioned, since there is hope that the more effort one puts in, the more assured and confident one be to overcome challenges and obstacles. There is no competition and comparison with others in this process and hence when an individual doesn't understand something, it doesn't make the person disheartened.

Another very important insight for our conceptual framework that the text gives with regard to the identity of the individual and society is the fact that human beings are born noble and have the potential to manifest perfections such as unity, love, justice and forgiveness. Furthermore, there is no dichotomy between one's physical/material self and one's spiritual self. In order to develop a holistic individual and create a harmonious society, both elements need to be coherently integrated. This implies that by civilization we don't only mean intellectual and material advancement, but having at its foundations a value or ethical system that enables individuals and communities to contribute meaningfully for the forward march of civilization as we know it.

An understanding such as this would naturally influence the way the society governs and educates itself; the way the people see the relationship between the individual and society; the promotion of art, culture and aesthetics; the functioning of civil society; the process of nation-building, etc. Everything that we do would be with a consciousness of enhancing this nobility and building greater and greater coherence between the material and spiritual aspects of life.

The question that we might then ask ourselves is what is it that contributes to raising this consciousness? Antonio Gramsci emphasized the role of education in raising mass consciousness. He also stated that everyone is an intellectual, in other words each member of the human race is a protagonist in working towards social change. This would imply universal participation, where everyone has a responsibility towards establishing world peace. He also linked theory with practice, that change cannot be brought about living in a cloister segregated from society but one needs to act upon beliefs. There is therefore an intimate relationship between individual and collective change.

True Education must Address the Human, Material and Spiritual Aspects of Life

The curricula of materials take this theme further and suggest that true education is human, material and spiritual. Thus education should be able to contribute to awakening one's latent capacities towards being able to become a means of advancement for the human race. The text also speaks of how education is not something we limit to academic degrees and for procuring good careers. Rather, it is a life-long process and spiritual and intellectual empowerment.

The junior youth empowerment programme might be seen as one such educational programme whose aims are to raise the consciousness of adolescent youth towards devoting their energies to the advancement of material and spiritual civilization. Because this is a time when one's habits and character is still being formed and are not yet fixed. Their environment, upbringing, relationships and culture is what influences the youth to think and act in a certain way. If they receive the right environment, education and space to grow, in the word of one educationist, they possess that "magic of transformation".

In this process of education which is for three years from 12 to 15 years, these youth learn to develop certain capabilities that will empower them to resist pressures from the old social order.

Here the junior youth learn to acquire qualities, attitudes and concepts that will develop their moral capability. This is also about elaborating their conceptual framework. They also engage in social action and take part in the life of their communities. They learn to study, consult, act and reflect on their actions by doing service projects in their groups systematically and simply participating in random events. The group first consults together; then they make a plan, for instance what materials do they need or who would be responsible for the different tasks among each other and after carrying out the project they come back and evaluate their actions. There are instances where junior youth have on their own initiative embarked on acts of service even without having been told or brought together to consult on it by their animator; they carry out service activities such as conducting devotional gatherings, children classes, planting trees, helping neighbours in the fields etc. (This is also I think related to capacity building). I know for sure that in my days as a junior youth nobody bothered to assist us to develop such capacities and neither was there any encouragement to enhance our level of confidence.

Since we spoke about interpretation, understanding and action, in other words, learning how to translate what is written into reality, one another aim of the programme in this context is to enhance the power of expression of junior youth. They try to understand the moral implications of speech and action in their daily lives. We can imagine how disempowered one would feel if one is unable to share and express their thoughts. Junior youth start thinking about their society and community around them; they start reflecting on various social processes, scientific and cultural ideologies and learn to analyze what is happening in the world around them. For instance, one activity that several groups undertake is to analyze the influences of advertising. This is also about developing justice—seeing with their own eyes and independently investigating the truth rather than getting brainwashed by propaganda.

One of the things animators become conscious of while working with the junior youth, is that they also learn to apply in their daily lives the concepts they are studying. Otherwise, this would mean acquiring knowledge but not understanding. Thus, one more capability that we are striving to enhance in the youth is spiritual perception. For instance, in one group while discussing about service to humanity, the junior youth gave the analogy of the mountain and how it inspired them to be steadfast and firm even through storm and rain. The programme is as such trying to help junior youth elevate their thoughts to engage in profound moral discussions. It helps them to change their goals in life. I remember some of the remarks made by a group of junior youth I interacted with sometime ago. While sharing what they had learnt in their group some of them said that they now know the purpose of their lives. They said their goal used to be to study, get jobs and earn money. But now they know that that is not enough. They were very clear that central to whatever they do in life is their service to humanity. Some of them also said that they wish to take classes for children like the one being held in their neighourhood. Here they were very clear what implications the concept of service has in their lives. Again, I feel their consciousness towards the purpose of their lives is being raised through helping them to enhance their power of language and thought, which is helping them to gain a better insight into social reality. From my study of the texts of the junior youth programme, one thing I feel is relevant to this idea of individuality and romanticizing the individual is how having an understanding of the concept of trust in the Divine, (which is the main theme in the first book for junior youth) is conducive to humility than trying to develop more and more confidence in one's own capabilities. The concept of individuality and individualism in the West does not have this concept of reliance on God and Divine Assistance.

Social Action for Empowerment of Adolescents and Youth

The text also highlighted that social action is about having a correct reading of society and this will affect our choice of methodology and approach. When I reflect on the approaches taken by some of the other organizations and the manner of working for the empowerment of adolescents and youth, and the materials developed by them, one thing I have observed is that most of the times, the way they try to tell junior youth to make the correct choices etc. is through entertaining them, thinking that they can understand serious issues merely through the garb of fun, and even the standards are relativistic. For instance, I remember seeing a documentary, in which an organization working for the empowerment of some tribal children, junior youth and youth, while showing them movies based on different themes about making them socially aware of the workings of society, (I don't remember what exactly those themes were, but something like about emancipation for instance,) were also showing them negative elements of violence and promiscuity as well.

In many institutions, I have noticed that junior youth are told, "let's study first, then we'll go out to play and have fun". This notion that they need 'fun' and that the study of the text is a burden, and all the time thinking of different ways that the group can be entertained and engaged in fun is detrimental. One might feel that this is the only thing that can motivate them to come to their group. But having fun or just having extra curricular activities is not the purpose of the group. Too much emphasis on these other activities can actually distract the group from their overall purpose. Therefore, the Baha'i approach to transacting the texts for the junior youth ensures that the animator is well prepared and understands those concepts in the texts and the junior youth are also made aware of their purpose and goal of coming to the group—I have noticed that they truly enjoy taking part in the discussion and serious consultation of the texts and the concepts. And then again the approach in this curriculum towards extra curricular activities is not according to deplorable norms of present-day society, but an understanding that these activities' are to help us achieve the goals of spiritual and material excellence and becoming agents of change for the society. Having a good understanding of one's purpose definitely helps one to advance better towards those goals.

Certain Unique Features of the Junior Youth Empowerment Curricula

What is important for the animator is not for him or her to decide what the group will do, but to consult with them on what they think they can do together. With regard to the dynamics of the group, each group has its own identity and may do different things they like to do. We don't have to give them a list of things to do like some sort of recipe. This would only hamper their creativity and space to think. My experience is that the programme tries to avoid rigidity. Rather, it endeavours to create a dialogical communication between the junior youth and animator as well.

Another issue of which those who are using this curriculum must be mindful of is that sometimes organizations and institutions unconsciously transmit meaningless rituals and practices in name of preserving one's culture or protecting one's religious identity. I have seen such textual materials and with diffidence would like to recommend that our aim should to assist the youth in understanding the necessity of a healthy convergence between science and religion or technology and spirituality and not perpetuate dogma and shibboleths of a by-gone era.

Although at this point I have only insights into what I think might work best with junior youth, the fact that one's belief in the nobility of every human being as a central idea is at the heart of the educational process. That one's primary source for the illumination of human thoughts and morals-the Word of God-makes us have at least a different approach and methodology that strives to combat relativistic tendencies in society, where our goal is not simply to help these youth adjust themselves to a materialistic society. At the same time, we are also not inculcating in them any sort of bigotry or fundamentalism in their understanding of society, religion and their aims in life.

In the above sense the texts may appear relativistic and allow room for ambiguity—a certain level of uncertainty and at the same time, giving room to everyone to share their perspectives; but not to the extent of excessive individualism and nihilism. In trying to assist with the systematic expansion of the junior youth programme for instance, there is always room for ambiguity in terms of the methods and approaches that one may adopt as well as the strategies that we implement. We cannot say that the approach we are using now is the only way. Many times we don't know what the outcome of a particular approach or strategy will be and have to just try and see what works. So for instance if when consulting with the coordinators about what strategy they have for increasing the number of groups, I can give my suggestions and overall learning that we have from experience, but at the same time, I make it clear that they need to see what they think is best and who knows they might come up with something different and more useful. At the same time, there cannot be an extreme that when they ask for suggestions to just leave them entirely on their own. Neither is there this endless debate and argument over how to go about things. We ourselves have to be careful not to fall in the trap of either-or, but learn how to consult with each other and enter in a dialogue. I remember that sometimes talking to coordinators or accompanying other friends or just talking about our goals would make me nervous—in a sense that I have always wanted to know what the exact thing to do is. But this idea of a dialogue, of searching and seeking and not being concerned in a rigid way with one way of doing things has helped a great deal in truly showing the way for fruitful consultations and actions—this is hard to explain but many times admitting "I don't know" has led to new doors being opened and new things to learn each time. I have to remind myself to first listen to the other point of view, understand what is being said and I realize that in a consultation there is no wrong opinion or suggestion ever being given. If everything is done in a spirit of oneness and for the sake of seeking the truth, the whole outcome of the consultation leads to the development of a new insight that one could have never imagined. I think it is also about trusting each member of that dialogical community and believing in their capacities.

The dialogue and conversation that is taking place is also not just between the animator and the junior youth, but is at several levels:

- between the junior youth and junior youth
- between the animator and the junior youth
- the animator and the parents of junior youth
- the animator and the animator (in animator reflection gatherings)
- the coordinator and the animator
- the coordinator and other institutions such as the institute board and resource persons

What the Junior Youth Empowerment Programme helps to Achieve

At every level of the programme, there are certain things we are trying to achieve.

Good level of coordination: Humility and attitude of learning at every level of coordination—in animator towards junior youth; in coordinator towards animators; in those accompanying the coordinators. The responsibility of the coordinators is likened to that of a gardener tending to his garden. At the same time, coordinators need to be vigilant of imbibing disempowering attitudes such as paternalism, self righteousness and authoritarianism. With regard to always have a learning attitude, one of the things most animators find challenging to overcome is how not to prolong the childhood of junior youth. Those animators who are teachers at school find it particularly challenging to overcome habits of paternalism and authoritarian control. There is always this challenge of how to balance between love and discipline, especially towards those youth who display a tendency to be aggressive and disobedient. One such animator who is also a teacher, however, commented that he has been trying to let his role as an animator influence his way of teaching middle and high school students at school and which he has found very effective. The quality of the junior youth groups depend greatly on the willingness to change and the amount of effort one is ready to put into it. Hence for the animator to remember that there is much learning from the junior youth; for the coordinator to remember that it is not just about instructing the animator what needs to be done, but learning from his experiences as well. It seems that this is also something that one needs to learn—how to learn from each other, how to listen and understand what the others are saying.

Accompaniment: There is so much to this term and these are just a few points I have gathered from my interactions. In the context of the principles of oneness and justice, qualities such as patience and an attitude of self restraint have deep implications in the process of accompaniment. For instance, being ready to give the one we are accompanying the space to act and even to make mistakes. There is unity, since we need to remember that we are working as a team and not pointing instructions at each other. Being patient in conveying ideas to others, in listening to them and trying to understand them. I know of people and even that we have a certain way of doing things, but we fall in the danger of becoming rigid that we find it difficult to adapt to the way others work. So our own capabilities and capacities don't help to empower others to release their potential. If someone is slow or someone is fast, either ways one needs to exercise patience, to learn from others and to also pass on certain information or knowledge to others. Team work involves sharing learning/ experience, planning, consulting and finally reflecting together. I even need to be patient with myself when I don't understand something, instead of feeling restless. Also when friends find it difficult to put their plan in action then we have to accompany them and help them see the possibilities and potential of what can be done—this is something that takes time. All these are implications of this principle of oneness, as well as fighting against notions of the "cult of the individual" and balancing between individual initiative and collective endeavours. For me it is hard sometimes to understand things from the perspective of others—this is essential for practicing justice—for instance when having to explain things more than twice to people we are accompanying or they see something in a different way than I do. Taking this a step further I want to add what I heard at a consultative session, that humanity has never seen such a relationship between individuals, community and institutions, since here, it is not that institutions dominate individuals or for that matter we are doing away with notions of power struggle/conflict that have since time immemorial existed between groups and individuals who wished to bring about change (one fundamental belief in Marxist ideology). In the context of animators accompanying junior youth, and exercising justice and equality, I had felt that for the animator to be just he/she has to devote equal amount of time to each junior youth. But then I learnt from others in similar service, that this is not necessary. The animator can still be just even if he/she does not give equal amount of time, but devotes time as per the need of the junior youth and at least does not favour some over the others. This is because there is also the challenge of fostering cooperation as against competition in the groups. The relationship between the junior youth also tends to be influenced by forces of competition. Experience has shown that the greater the unity between the junior youth, the better the group is able to sustain itself. For the animator it is a challenge of how to create a strong sense of belonging among the members of a junior youth.

Reflection and analysis: Sometimes, while in the path of service, we become so preoccupied that we might just end up doing our tasks mechanically. We might forget the spiritual nature of the enterprise that we are engaged in. For instance, I might just be going to my junior youth group every week and feel that it is becoming a burden, something I have to do as an obligation.

This might happen if I don't reflect on the purpose of taking a junior youth group. Hence we need to reflect and question ourselves: for instance, does being an animator bring me joy? The coordinator who is accompanying the animator both reflect together on the relationship between the junior youth: Are they able to build those bonds of unity, trust and friendship between each other? What is the relationship of the animator with the parents? Are they becoming more conscious of their role in the spiritual empowerment of their children? For the animator and coordinator to think that through the service that they are rendering are they in the process developing their own spiritual qualities and perception?

Raising consciousness: This again is enhanced through the process of reflection and analysis. For instance, the junior youth and animators becoming more conscious of the purpose of what they are doing, like why they are coming to a junior youth group, the role of service in our lives, choosing forgiveness over revenge etc.

Capacity building: Accompaniment eventually leads to capacity building as well. Are our animators now confident to take their groups on their own or meet the parents and talk to them without assistance from the coordinator? So at each stage that the coordinators work with the animators they are trying to build capacity in them to carry out different tasks without having to each time become dependent on the coordinator.

Role of generation, application and acquisition of knowledge in social transformation: This takes place at all levels starting with the junior youth themselves. So generating learning from the grassroots and how it needs to be disseminated from the animator to coordinator and then, for instance, to other agencies who then come up with a body of worldwide learning which then needs to be disseminated back to the grassroots. This knowledge that is being disseminated definitely does not have at its core a materialistic vision alone. We are learning what it means to sustain junior youth groups for 3 years and empower them spiritually and intellectually which is what is going to contribute in constructing a civilization. This is perhaps what the text is trying to say with regard to presenting knowledge as an alternative model so that it does contribute to true development. So here we are trying to transcend the rigid and strict approach to knowledge where it is not merely a collection of facts and information but that teaches us towards fulfilling the purpose of our life. For otherwise as we see today, the knowledge that we gain is mostly theoretical and we don't learn how what we are learning can be applied fruitfully and practically in our daily lives. Furthermore, the junior youth empowerment programme is an educational programme with a universal curriculum that transcends all barriers of nation, caste, class and race, and in this way also demonstrating the oneness of humanity. This is as against those beliefs that a different curriculum must be catered to people coming from different cultures or economic backgrounds.

Another major element of my conceptual framework is about leading life in an integrated way, which I feel is quite challenging: how to be conscious at all times of the interconnectedness of things (for me it is mostly in terms of family life, service, education and work.) Is there a reciprocal relationship between this and raising my understanding of social reality? From my understanding, it seems that this is related to the relationship between language and reality. The more I enhance my language and thought, the more my consciousness also expands: learning to apply the concepts in the realm of science and religion/spirituality to the world around me in order to generate a deeper understanding of reality. For instance when I learn that I can experience true happiness only when I serve others I will not be busy looking for happiness in something that is just about me—one finds in various magazines and newspapers suggestions for bringing happiness to yourself by doing something you like, pampering yourself (idea of self/individual being romanticized) or even indulging yourself (idea of privacy). What makes me happy is not looking at my accomplishments, but those whom I am accompanying in the path of service. For instance, as an animator what makes me happy is seeing my junior youth group engage in service to their communities. Another example that comes to my mind related to the aims of the junior youth programme is comprehending the term 'empowerment'. When I understand that it is not about possessing wealth, fame, position and the ability to manipulate others, it helps me to change the goals in my life. We instead strive to direct our efforts from the prison of self to selfless service to humanity.

Developing a Language of Coherence

Also, as the text explained, we need to constantly develop a language that can explain reality in a coherent way. Even David Bohm wrote about the intimate connection between language and thought and reality. According to 'Abdu'l-Bahá, the mass of the people are uninformed as to those vital agencies that will be the remedy for the social ills around us. They lack the language and vocabulary to even explain what they want. The word/concepts I realize have to be inspired and illumined with the spiritual principles in the Sacred Scriptures if they are to convey meaning closest to reality. For instance, my understanding of the purpose of life remains limited if it is not inspired with what is written in the Scriptures. How far I am able to understand that and translate into action is the issue.

As we go long I realized the need to enhance my language towards being able to convey to in the wider society what is meant by social action in the Bahá'í community, its perspective of history, how doing a junior youth group is part of the civilization-building process etc. Sometimes, friends and contacts ask me what I am doing—how to say it in a way that does not give the impression that this is not simply a service by a religious community but it is all about contributing to social change. Over the years the Bahá'í community has been developing a common vocabulary to understand the society building processes inspired by the teachings of Bahá'u'lláh. For example, use of words such as "core activities", "growth-related activities", "study circle", "devotional meetings, "home visits", etc. What does it mean to launch an intensive programme of growth? What does it mean to take a study circle? What does a study circle do, etc.?

Ironing Out Some of the Contradictions

In terms of ironing out contradictions in my conceptual framework, for sure I haven't been able to iron out many of them, but at least I see myself recognizing those contradictions more consciously and reflecting on them. For instance, why do I think this way, or why did I act that way or say this thing to someone. But then of course there are times when I find myself slipping back into the same cycle of making the same mistakes over and over; but as the guidelines point out this is something that can be overcome through spiritual discipline.

One contradiction that comes to my mind is the kind of attitude the followers of a particular religion living in urban cities have towards their fellow co-religionists in rural communities, even though they profess the same set of beliefs. This is also true of the members of the Bahá'í community who strongly believe in the oneness of humanity. I remember in this gathering for junior youth coordinators last year, we had participants from both rural and urban clusters. But the ones who dominated the gathering were the youth from the urban clusters. They were more loud and hence the atmosphere seemed to imply that they were the ones with most of the experience and better understanding of what we were consulting and reading. The ones from the rural cluster were mostly quiet, but because they were not as loud, not much emphasis seemed to be given to them. Also, it seemed like there were two different groups of people and initially they did not mix and it took a lot of time for them to interact. One question which then comes to my mind, is how many of us youth from the city have really good friends living in the rural communities? This perhaps highlights in many ways what it means to manifest this oneness and unity in our efforts to build a better world.

Walking Together in the Path of Service

In the path of service for instance, to really serve humanity I need to believe in people's potential, be free of these prejudices concerning the rural and the poor, or any other culture, tribe, race and people.

Interactions within my social spaces like my community need to be founded on the principle of oneness which is indeed the bedrock to working towards change. This can happen with the unity of the hearts. For me this means not even having a thought of dislike. Even at the level of thought this feeling of oneness needs to be created. One point that the book Revelation and Social Reality suggests is that the whole world is truly our common homeland, then how to treat diversity in a way that does not lead to conflict?

This relationship would also imply that individual freedom cannot be valued at the cost of the freedom of others. It comes with being aware of one's responsibilities towards that collective whole that one is part of. Any suggestion I make or any act on my part, I first need to think, if it is contributing to unity. Is the criticism constructive? I also want to relate how a learning attitude helps one in maintaining unity and putting collective interests before individual priorities in this life long educational process. I remember when we received guidance from our institutions that it was now time for our community to decentralize its monthly community gatherings called "19-Day Feasts" into certain neighbourhoods, since the community had grown quite large and having one Feast was not ensuring maximum participation, comments could be heard on various fronts from long standing members that this was disturbing the unity of the community and it used to be so nice to have everyone together in one place, etc. There was unfortunately a lot of criticism and this really became a test of obedience for some members. Hence it seems that being involved in a learning process would necessarily entail that we should be ready to do away with our notions and mindsets that we previously considered to be true. The individual's role in building a divine civilization is that whatever potential he or she is endowed with is to be used towards this collective interest and goal, since the individual is a part of the whole.

Conclusion

The challenges confronting those involved in developing an integrated curricula for a certain purpose and the junior youth age group were, of course, very complex. However, trusting in divine assistance and committed to the wellbeing of society and working for a long period of time an acceptable level of curricula materials were generated. In the words of Dr. Farzam Arbab, "Integration of capabilities does not imply that the way to go about designing curricular elements is to first analyze thoroughly a capability; then think of all the concepts, bits of information, skills, abilities, attitudes, and spiritual qualities that contribute to it; and finally come up with an educational activity. The development of curriculum is a creative process, and I do not think creativity can easily be made to follow a linear progression.... Action, reflection, consultation... help to sharpen the objectives, content and methods and, through a series of approximations, the curricular element gradually approaches a final and well-defined form."

17

ICT Policy and Missions in Education

Shakila Shamsu

India stands at the threshold of a revolution triggered by the advances in information technology and the digitization of knowledge, skills, processes and services. The prime mover of this mammoth change is the multi-pronged and all pervasive interventions of Information and Communication Technology (ICT) in all aspects of life and in almost every sector of the economy.

India has achieved impressive progress in the field of science and technology and is emerging as one of the strongest economics in the developing world. Information and communication technologies have brought significant changes in development of the Indian society through information dissemination. No other technology is as profound as information and communication technology in human history. The term Information and Communication Technology refers to the diverse set of technological tools and resources used to create, store and communicate information. ICT in education refers to the usage of the technologies for the dissemination of knowledge. It utilizes tools such as computers, internet, broadcasting technologies (radio, television), telephony, satellite etc.

ICT has had a great influence on the economy and lives of people across the world. The concept of India Vision 2020 floated by Dr. A.P.J. Abdul Kalam identified ICT as one of the core competencies and a wealth generator. He proposed ICT for education along with its applications in medicine, e-governance etc.

In India, the benefits of ICT are being seen in a pronounced manner and the impact of these benefits are creating great change. It is also true that the use of digital technologies in the world has not only improved people's day–to–day life but it has also divided the world into information rich and information poor, *i.e.* the information haves and have–nots. The unequal access to information and communication technologies has led to a massive divide digitally and has posed challenges to the government to take appropriate steps to bridge the gap. Although India has been one of the emerging super powers in ICT, the benefits have been remarkably slow, particularly in rural and remote areas. Besides socio-economic factors, geographic, educational and attitudinal factors have been some of the challenges for the government when introducing ICT-oriented programmes.

Information and communication technology (ICT) has given rise to many benefits in our society. ICTs allow people, anywhere in the world, to access information and knowledge almost instantaneously. Individuals, organizations and communities should benefit from access to knowledge and information. Technological change is the major contributor to the growth and development of the information society; e-learning, e-libraries, e-health, e-governance, etc. have become pillars of the information society. A World Summit was organised by the United Nations in 2003 in Geneva to develop a common vision and understanding of the information society and to draw up a strategic plan of action for concerted development towards realising this vision.

The Information and Communication Technology is considered the driving force behind the long unprecedented economic growth period of the last decade. It provided the infrastructure for economic development, helped create the knowledge society, contributed to innovation and created value for the economy. More importantly, it brought the world closer together by improving the dissemination of knowledge, accelerating research, stimulating innovation and facilitating collaboration.

As we have all witnessed, the advent of the internet, broadband communication, open source collaboration, and the rapidly improving computing capacity has changed the world economy drastically. The knowledge economy and the globally integrated enterprise have become a reality. The economies of industrialized countries are moving into services. Business models and processes are globalized. ICT is changing quickly, shortening its life cycle and speeding up its obsoleteness.

The effective participation of the government and all stakeholders is vital in developing the Information Society requiring cooperation and partnerships among all of them. To maximize the benefits of initiatives undertaken, these should include the concept of sustainability. The private sector should also be engaged in projects to develop the Information Society at local, regional and national levels.

India has made substantial progress in the creation of an Information society which signifies a digital revolution on several fronts and domains. Today, the Government provides adequate access through various communication resources, particularly, the internet, to public official information. Governments, in collaboration with other stakeholders are establishing sustainable multi-purpose community public access points, providing affordable or free-of-charge access for the citizens to the various communication resources such as the internet. These access points have sufficient capacity to provide assistance to users, such as in rural community centres with basic information related to health, agriculture, land records, access to library resources, educational institutions, public administration, post offices or other public places, with special emphasis on rural and underserved areas, and encouraging the use of information and sharing of knowledge. It is important to facilitate accessibility of ICTs for all, including disadvantaged, marginalized and vulnerable groups.

It is worth mentioning that the National Knowledge Commission has *inter alia*, recommended setting up of a knowledge network, portals and e-governance. The knowledge network will interconnect all knowledge institutions throughout the country, through an electronic digital broadband network with adequate capabilities to encourage sharing of resources and collaborative research. Creation of national web based portals for basic needs on certain key sectors such as Water, Energy, Environment, Education, Food, Health, Agriculture, Employment, citizen Rights to provide access to government data. E-governance includes mainly re-engineering government processes to change basic governance pattern for simplicity, transparency, productivity and efficiency, develop common standards and deploy common platform/infrastructure for e-governance, selection of important services that make a critical difference, simplify them and offer them as web-based services and ensure speedy delivery, productivity and efficiency of services making them citizen centric and ensuring that the right people get the benefits. The XI Plan envisages the creation of core infrastructure such as SWAN (State Wide Area Network), Common Service Centres (CSCs) and State Data Centres (SDCs) for creation of a common service delivery platform. These initiatives are well underway and coverage is substantial. Most of the State governments have followed the Central Government and created their own portals and introduced basic e-services which have brought immense benefit to the common people. Also, e-governance projects are being implemented in various departments mainly to bring in transparency and efficiency of services both in terms of time and costs.

India's ICT applications support sustainable development, in the fields of public administration, business, education and training, health, environment, agriculture and applications of science and technology in defence and other strategic sectors. Some of these sectors are:

- *E-governance*: Implementing e-governance strategies focusing on applications aimed at innovating and promoting transparency in public administrations and democratic processes, improving efficiency and strengthening relations with citizens. Developing national e-governance initiatives and services, at all levels, adapted to the needs of citizens and business, to achieve a more efficient allocation of resources and public goods.

- *E-business/commerce*: Government policies favour assistance to, and growth of Small Micro and Medium Enterprises, in the ICT industry, as well as their entry into e-business, to stimulate economic growth and job creation as an element of a strategy for poverty reduction through wealth creation. Through the adoption of an enabling environment, and based on widely available Internet access, governments should seek to stimulate private sector investment, foster new applications, content development and public/private partnerships.
- *E-health*: Promoting collaborative efforts of governments, planners, health professionals, and other agencies along with the participation of international organizations for creating a reliable, timely, high quality and affordable health care and health information systems and for promoting continuous medical training, education, and research through the use of ICTs, while respecting and protecting citizens' right to privacy. Facilitating access to the world's medical knowledge and locally-relevant content resources for strengthening public health research and prevention programmes. Encouraging the adoption of ICTs to improve and extend health care and health information systems to remote and underserved areas and vulnerable populations, recognising women's roles as health providers in their families and communities.
- *E-environment and energy conservation*: Government, in cooperation with other stakeholders is encouraging the use and promotion of ICTs as an instrument for environmental protection and the sustainable use of natural resources. Today, Government, civil society and the private sector are initiating actions and implementing projects and programmes for sustainable production and recycling as well the environmentally safe disposal of wastes. Establishing monitoring systems, using ICTs, to forecast and monitor the impact of natural and man-made disasters. ICT can also play a vital role in energy conservation.
- *E-agriculture*: Ensure the systematic dissemination of information using ICTs on agriculture, animal husbandry, fisheries, forestry and food, in order to provide ready access to comprehensive, up-to-date and detailed knowledge and information, particularly in rural areas. Public-private partnerships should seek to maximize the use of ICTs as an instrument to improve the quantity and quality of agricultural and other allied sector production.

- *Transportation and urban planning* is another sector which is benefitting greatly from ICT based processes and applications.
- *E-Learning* is discussed at length under ICT in education.

Information and Communication Technology in Education—The Indian Context

Innovation has become the main focus for many countries looking for job creation and better living conditions. Research is needed to use existing knowledge and to create new knowledge. Knowledge management is the solution for sustaining a competitive edge in a knowledge economy. Higher education plays a major role in all these processes by preparing and providing the required human capacity through education, creating and disseminating knowledge to society, and directly contributing to economic development.

For India to emerge as a knowledge super power of the world in the shortest possible time, it is imperative to convert our demographic advantage into knowledge powerhouse by nurturing and honing our working population into knowledge or knowledge enabled working population. Capacity building and ICT literacy are essential so as to empower all with the necessary skills to benefit fully from the Information Society. ICTs can contribute to achieving universal education worldwide, through delivery of education and training of teachers, and offering improved conditions for lifelong learning, encompassing people that are outside the formal education process, and improving professional skills. ICTs must be fully integrated in education and training at all levels, including in curriculum development, teacher training, institutional administration and management, and in support of the concept of lifelong learning. There is a need to develop and promote programmes to eradicate illiteracy using ICTs. There is a need to develop projects which demonstrate the impact of ICT-based alternative educational delivery systems mainly for achieving Education for All targets, including basic literacy targets. These capacity building programmes should aim at creating a critical mass of qualified and skilled ICT professionals and experts. We should design new forms of ICT-based networking, linking education, training and research institutions between and among developed and developing countries.

ICT can empower teachers and learners, making significant contributions to learning and achievement. ICT changes education from institution-centric to learner-centric, from classroom-based to being pervasively connected through e-learning, and wireless. ICT allows us to have the flexibility in space, time, and content. The most important impact of ICT is that the majority of the education institutions have adapted a blended model of learning which combines both distance learning with on-site learning. In addition, many universities have decided to share their intellectual capital by putting their course materials on line for free access.

Roles of ICT: In course delivery through open and distance learning modes with delivery of course content through internet, satellite and other mediums, ICT provide a technological platform linking universities and other agencies for collaborative research and e-content development in all disciplines. It can be harnessed to develop appropriate teaching aids in classrooms, and make available free educational content for all students on online repositories. In educational administration, it can facilitate better educational management by developing IT systems for educational institutes including complete student management and recordkeeping. In collaborative learning, ICT provide technology platform linking universities and other agencies for collaborative research and content development.

ICT can foster:

- *Greater equity*: By providing a better access to students from various socio-economic groups, leading to greater inclusion. Good quality institutions are then not restricted to a few pockets but are made accessible to students located all over the country. Global content from all over the world can benefit students irrespective of time or place.
- *Better Access*: Lower costs of education, increased flexibility, providing anytime anywhere access to students, reduction in capacity constraints can make large enrolments possible in courses run by reputed institutes.
- *Improved Quality*: Can be ensured by using supplementary teaching aids, better and more efficient processes and management systems, access to up-to-date content, increased knowledge sharing, leveraging technology to access courses in new and emerging fields to greater number of students, scientists and by creation of comprehensive centralized digital repositories for reference material.

The ICT Schemes in Indian Education

In the Education domain, the Central Government through the Ministry of Human Resources Development, has launched ICT based Schemes both at the school and higher education levels. These two major initiatives in the XI Plan by the MHRD are aimed at transforming both school and higher education. The Information and Communication Technology (ICT) in Schools Scheme is revised to cover all Government and Government-aided secondary and higher secondary schools, in-service teachers' training, computer teachers, computer literacy, providing broad band connectivity and development of e-content. The National Mission on Education through Information and Communication Technology (ICT) has been launched to leverage the potential of ICT in the teaching learning process with an aim to enhance the GER in

Higher Education by five percentage points by the end of the XI Plan. The National Mission on Education through ICT has been launched and will provide internet connectivity with 10 MBPS bandwidth to over 20,000 colleges and 10,000 departments in the universities. The mission has two major components viz., (a) course content generation and related issues for all subjects and all types of learners, and (b) connectivity and access issues for institutions and learners. While implementing the ICT Mission, it is being ensured that all knowledge domains have e-content and that the tertiary general education is given equal importance with science and engineering areas. It is envisaged that colleges and universities will become digital campuses with online teaching and virtual classrooms.

The ICT in Schools is not a new scheme, but an expansion and modification of one component of the existing scheme of ICT@School, introduced in December 2004. The revised Scheme of Information and Communication Technology (ICT) in Schools will increase the outreach of the scheme to cover all Government and Government aided secondary and higher secondary schools in the country with emphasis on Educationally Backward Blocks and areas with concentration of SC, ST, minority and weaker section, development and dissemination of appropriate e-content in regional languages, making available internet connectivity and most importantly training the teachers in the use of ICT based teaching learning processes, and to set up smart schools in the district to serve as demonstration models for neighboring schools. The scheme also envisages an exclusive, suitably qualified ICT teacher for each school. The main objectives of the scheme are to establish an enabling environment to promote the uses of ICT in all higher secondary and secondary govt. and govt. aided schools and to provide an effective learning environment for all children, including those with special needs, through ICT tools. It is proposed to cover 1,08,983 schools during the XI Plan period and setting up of 150 more Smart Schools by States/UTs by conversion of one of the existing State Govt. Schools, to serve as role model and also to share the infrastructure and resources available with the neighborhood schools.

The objectives of the revised ICT in Schools are:

1. To establish an enabling environment to promote the usage of ICT in the teaching-learning process in Government and Government-aided secondary and higher secondary schools.
2. To ensure the availability of quality content on-line and through access devices.
3. Enrichment of existing curriculum and pedagogy by employing ICT tools for teaching and learning.
4. To enable students to acquire skills needed for the digital world for higher studies and gainful employment.

5. To provide an effective learning environment for children with special needs through ICT tools.
6. Promote critical thinking and analytical skills by developing self-learning. This shall transform the classroom environment from teacher-centric learning to student-centric learning.
7. To promote the use of ICT tools in distance education including the employment of audio-visual medium and satellite-based devices.

The National Mission on Education through Information and Communication Technology (NMEICT) has been envisaged as a Centrally Sponsored Scheme to leverage the potential of ICT, in teaching and learning process for the benefit of all the learners in Higher Education Institutions in any time any where mode.

The objectives of the National Mission on Education through ICT shall include:

1. building connectivity and knowledge network among and within institutions of higher learning in the country with a view of achieving critical mass of researchers in any given field;
2. spreading digital literacy for teacher empowerment:
   - development of knowledge modules having the right content to take care of the aspirations of academic community and to address to the personalized needs of the learners;
   - standardization and quality assurance of e-contents to make them world class;
   - research in the field of pedagogy
3. learning modules for disparate groups of learners:
   - making available e-knowledge contents, free of cost to Indians;
   - experimentation and field trial in the area of performance optimization of low cost access devices for use of ICT in education;
   - providing support for the creation of Virtual Technological University;
4. identification and nurturing of talent:
   - certification of competencies of the human resources acquired either through formal or non-formal means and the evolution of a legal framework for it; and
   - developing and maintaining the database with the profiles of our human resources. The Mission has two major components:
     - providing connectivity, along with provision for access devices, to institutions and learners;
     - content generation.

   The Mission aims to extend computer infrastructure and connectivity to over 20,000 colleges in the country including each of the departments of nearly 418 (now 504) universities/deemed universities and institutions of national importance as a part of its motto to provide last mile connectivity. Therefore, the Mission, in addition to utilize the connectivity network of BSNL/MTNL and other providers, shall explore the possibility to provide connectivity utilizing Very Small Apperture Terminal (VSAT), Very Personal Network (VPN) and EduSat channels.

It seeks to bridge the digital divide, i.e., the gap in the skills to use computing devices for the purpose of teaching and learning among urban and rural teachers/learners in Higher Education domain and empower those, who have hitherto remained untouched by the digital revolution and have not been able to join the mainstream of the knowledge economy so that they can make best use of ICT for teaching and learning.

The Mission would create high quality e-content for the target groups. The peer group assisted content development would utilise the Wikipedia type of collaborative platform under the supervision of a content advisory committee responsible for vetting the content. Interactivity and problem solving approach would be addressed through "Talk to a Teacher" component, where the availability of teachers to take the questions of learners shall be ensured appropriately.

The Mission also envisages, promoting on line research with the objective to develop new and innovative ICT tools for further facilitation of teaching and learning process. It plans to focus on appropriate pedagogy for e-learning, providing facility of performing experiments through virtual laboratories, on-line testing and certification, utilization of available Education Satellite (EDUSAT) and Direct to Home (DTH) platforms, training and empowerment of teachers to effectively use the new method of teaching learning etc. Central Government would bear 75 per cent of the connectivity charges for 5 years even for institutions not belonging to it. Renowned institutions would anchor various activities in their areas of excellence. The Mission would seek to enhance the standards of education, in Government as well as in private colleges. Enlistment of support and cooperation of States/Union Territories, Institutions and individual experts would be an integral part of the Mission.

One of the mandates of the Mission is to generate a data base of the human resources in different fields/disciplines and also to predict the availability and demand of the human resources in different disciplines. It shall also develop certain testing modules to test and certify the skills of the human resources acquired through various formal and non-formal means.

The Mission also seeks to give further impetus to NPTEL (being implemented by IITs and IISc. It would also promote open source culture and provide platform for sharing of ideas, techniques and pooling of knowledge resources. While about 100 premier institutions are being provided 1 Gbps connectivity under National Knowledge Network initially and the number is slated to go up in future, under this Mission, without any duplication, 20000 other institutions of higher learning and nearly 10000 University Departments will be provided connectivity as per their requirement, beginning with a minimum of 5 Mbps for each one of them, through satellites and terrestrial means. Vocational education would be strengthened through ICT and class room teaching would be supplemented under the Mission. Under the Mission, quality enhancement of teaching through digital empowerment of teachers would bridge the digital divide and there would be on-line availability of experts and teachers to remove doubts of students.

Challenges of Implementation

India is a multicultural, multi–language and multi–religion country with complex socio–economic conditions. A fundamental requirement for reducing the digital divide in countries is to give priority to the development of their communication infrastructure and provide universal and affordable access to information to individuals in all geographical areas of the country. There are a number of barriers to bridging the digital divide. Although underserved communities in India are gaining access to computers and the Internet, their benefits are limited because of the factors such as infrastructural barriers. Faster networks, higher level machines, more complex software and more capable professionals are required, but in many nations including India the funding is not available to support these developments. In a country like India where roughly 50 per cent of people do not have reading and writing skills for functioning in everyday life, IT literacy is out of question. Generally, online content and information have been designed for an audience that reads at an average or advanced literacy level and those who can afford it. Education in information literacy will play an important role in keeping the society from fragmenting into a population of information haves and have–nots. The lack of skill in using computer and communication technology also prevents people from accessing digital information. Poor access to computer and communication technology also causes a digital divide. Preference for local languages in small towns and rural areas underscores the need to develop content in multiple languages. There is equally critical need to develop content in all domains of learning particularly social sciences, humanities, arts, commerce and management.

We need to examine some of the issues and likely impediments in the effective roll-out and implementation of the ICT schemes. As regards, ICT in schools, the challenge of providing uninterrupted power supply, for successful implementation of the scheme, calls for convergence with the Ministries of Power, IT and New and Renewable Energy. Most of the States have been successfully implementing state policies on ICT education. In order to provide guidelines with minimum common standards and capture best practices, an ICT policy in schools is on the anvil. This would certainly encourage more States to adopt an ICT based education in schools and thereby enhance learning outcomes and empower students to become technology savvy. The obsoleteness of the technology needs to be addressed with clear guidelines for changing both the hardware and software. This is both from the point of view of sustainability as well of ensuring cost effective model. Ensuring capacity of all teachers is crucial to success of this scheme failing which students would merely become computer literate without acquiring in depth knowledge on how to use computers for effective curriculum transactions in all subjects. The over emphasis on the use of computers in limited subjects such as Maths, Science and Languages is not desirable as all subjects and courses can equally gain by ICT based pedagogic interventions. A well thought strategy for development of e-content in all courses is equally critical. This is applicable to the Mission in higher education where there is surfeit of digitized material and interactive e-learning modules in engineering, technology, management and other application based disciplines but there is dearth of such content in pure and basic sciences, social sciences and humanities. Unless a concerted effort is made to ensure generation of e-content in all knowledge domains, we would be guilty of creating a new divide in the knowledge domain. In the long run, this would result in the fading out of certain core subjects in these areas leading to a new kind of educational imbalance and inequality.

Conclusion: Path Ahead

Merely implementing a massive nation-wide Mission need not make us proud as India is relatively in its infancy as compared to several developing and developed countries in ICT enabled education. We need to clearly identify our strengths and weaknesses and ensure collaborative efforts in a multi-pronged manner to reap the benefits of both the schemes. The Vision of catapulting India as a knowledge super-power is undoubtedly captured in the Schemes which will empower our youth and make them more productive and creative. But merely having the will cannot transform this goal and vision into a sweet reality unless all stake holders are focused on effectively contributing to the successful implementation of these schemes. A pro-active attitude of planners, policy makers, civil society, the academia, students, parents and the corporate private sector in this venture constitutes the core of such a transformation which will change and revolutionize the education domain in particular and largely the society and economy. It would serve our students to meet the global competition and ensure that India becomes an intellectual giant in the near future.

18

Educational Reforms in Gujarat

A Versatile Venture

Rajendrasinh Jadeja and *Nishant Joshi*

"Now that Gujarat is completing 50 years of its formation, the state is celebrating its Golden Jubilee. The celebrations are not only for achievements of past i.e. the glorious journey that Gujarat has been through over the years and for landmark achievements across sectors but also for *a vision*—A vision of even better Gujarat, A vision of a prosperous Gujarat, A vision where every Gujarati person is educated, A vision where every Gujarati person is healthy, A vision of a clean Gujarat, A vision of Green Gujarat, A vision of modern Gujarat."[1]

This is the vision statement of the Government of Gujarat as it appears on its special website for 'Swarnim Gujarat Celebration 2009-10'. One significant aspect of this celebration is the attitude of the government and the people. The purpose is not only to launch a grand celebration but also to create an opportunity to sum up the journey of Gujarat and its pros and cons and to look forward to create a new Gujarat for the 21st century in all the fields like education, business, administration, public services, arts, literature, living standards and health of the people etc. To realize this vision the government has undertaken various programmes in the fields mentioned above, but the most important among them is education as it has been perceived as a means to achieve all other aims and goals, and also as an agent of change, reformation and creation. As Gujarat is becoming the business hub of India, the government of Gujarat has decided to do the same in the field of education simultaneously. The initiatives and programmes undertaken in the last five years have introduced many reforms in the system of education at all levels and the process is still continuing. These initiatives and programmes in the field of education have four major dimensions, namely physical resources, education system, curriculum and faculty development and teaching-learning process. These four dimensions have been taken care of at three main levels of education: (i) Primary Eduaction, (ii) Secondary Education, and (iii) Higher Education. The government has harmoniously endeavored to strengthen all three by planning and implementing various programmes and initiatives.

Primary Education

The vision statement of Gujarat says that every Gujarati should be educated and healthy. To achieve these goals Primary Education is the best tool. In the last five to ten years, the government of Gujarat has aimed at 100 per cent enrollment and 0 per cent drop-out rates. Not only that, the government has developed innumerable schemes and spent crores of rupees to expand the horizons of Primary Education—both qualitatively and quantitatively -in all four dimensions that will be discussed here in detail.

Physical Resources

Construction of Classrooms and School Complexes: The government has built 64,390 classrooms in the last ten years for the Primary Schools. During the year 2010-11 Rs 7492.12 Lac have been allotted to build another 1711 classrooms including 441 in tribal area, 1029 in non-tribal area and 241 in special areas. In the 11th year planning, 13,000 schools will be covered under the scheme of Safety School Complex where the schools will get the grants for building a compound wall, creating playground and planting trees and thus making the environment natural as it has been suggested by Rabindranath Tagore in his educational philosophy. These facility of creating a healthy and natural environment will definitely influence the learners and increase their interest. The State government has also set up 50 supplementary schools for the tenure of six to eight months in the desert and coastal salt pan areas since 2006-07. Under the SSA scheme the government has planned to build 50 seasonal hostels for the students coming from migrating families. Simultaneously the repairing of the classrooms through state efforts is also going on. The government has built around 500 quarters for the teachers working in the interior areas to attract good teachers.

Creating All Basic Facilities-Clean Gujarat: Till today most of the primary schools have been equipped with all sorts of basic facilities like electricity, lights, fans, water facility, toilet facility especially for girls. The school time sanitation units were specially built for the girls of the standard 5 to 7. Following the vision of clean Gujarat the government began the mission from primary schools and doubled the grants for the cleanliness and maintenance in all primary schools. The yearly grant now for it is about Rs. 5000. As far as furniture is concerned, the government has distributed 3,78,237 benches in all the districts of Gujarat in the primary schools in the last five years.

Preparing Primary Schools for Modern Gujarat: If Gujarat is to become modern Gujarat, its primary education should also become modern education. To develop interest in science and to clarify the concepts of science right from childhood, the government has devised a scheme from the year 2002-03 under which each and every primary school will have a well-developed science laboratory with equipments necessary for primary education. Under the SSA (Sarva Shiksha Abhiyan) scheme the government implemented Child Mapping System—monitoring the educational progress through creating computerized database. Under the scheme of computerization, computer education will start from standard VI; the government has provided computers, printers and internet connection to each school. Around 5,500 computer labs and 8000 BISAG receiving centers have been developed for the purpose.

Free Learning Material: The government of Gujarat provides free of cost textbooks to all the students of all the primary schools. In addition, under the SSA mission, children registered in III to VII standard are given self-learning books free of cost. Experiment book and map book are provided free of cost to VI and VII standard students. The upper primary schools are provided educational magazines from the government like 'Safari', 'Vignan Darshan', 'Vignan Jagruti', 'Yojana' and 'Bal Bharti'.

Education System

Compulsory Education Related Reform: In Gujarat 1st to 7th standard is called Primary Education. The Right to Act of 2009 made education compulsory for the children coming in the age group of 6-14 years. So the first reform was to include 8th standard in the primary school rather than in secondary. This reform is going on in large scale. The government has divided the primary education in two levels namely, lower primary-standard 1 to 5 and higher primary-standard 6 to 8. In order to improve the quality of education, the government is recruiting trained teachers (with B.Ed. degree) for subjects like Mathematics, Science and English. For this reform total 5000 additional classrooms will be built and 10000 trained teachers will be recruited.

Moving towards 100 per cent Enrollment, 100 per cent Retention and Girls' Education: In order to achieve 100 per cent enrollment and 100 per cent retention, the government implemented special programmes keeping in mind girls' education. One of these is Pravesh Mahotsav and Rathyatra. It has been allotted special grants for celebration where the teachers, Sarpanch and other dignitaries present, celebrate a day and motivate the villagers for the enrolment of their children especially girls in first standard. The specialty of both these programmes is that for the first time in the history of Gujarat Chief Minister, Ministers, MLAs and the government officers all participate in these programmes in villages. Under the scheme of Vidya Lakshmi Bond (started in the year 2002-03), each girl of below poverty line is given a bond of Rs. 1000/- at the time of enrollment in 1st standard and the amount is returned, with interest when she passes 7th standard. Vidya Deep Insurance, another scheme under which all the primary students of the state are covered and compensation of Rs 50,000/- is awarded to the parents of diseased child.

To encourage girls' education, the government has set up one separate fund named Kanya Kelavni Nidhi. For this donations from the donors and institutions are accepted. This fund is used to support the girls at every step of their education in various ways by the chief minister under various schemes. With these successful efforts, the government has achieved its targets of decreasing drop outs in girls and in general and increasing the rate of retention which becomes evident in the following chart.

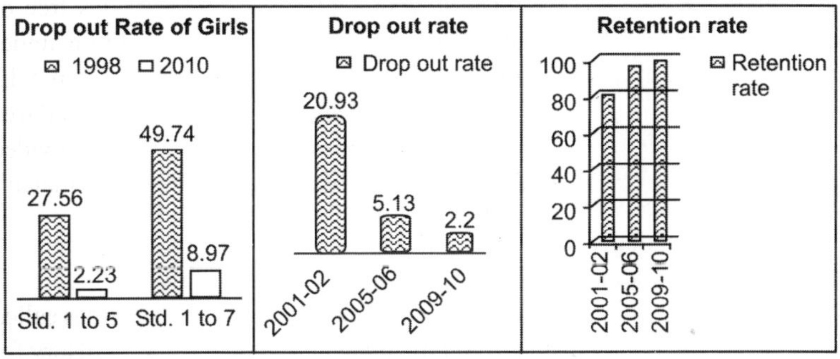

Fig. 18.1

Gunotsav—A Quality Enhancement Programme: After achieving targets in enrollment and retention, recruiting teachers, providing every kind of necessary facility and training the teachers to improve their proficiency, in 2009-10, the government felt the need for quality check and enhancement in Primary Education in the State. Therefore to check the educational proficiency of the students and teachers and to decide the educational level of the school, the government started a unique and innovative quality enhancement programme, viz., Gunotsav. The programme was implemented from September 2009 to November 2009 in two phases for the first time. In the first phase, self-assessment was carried out in all 32331 schools and in the second phase the government officials assessed 7939 (25%) schools. The assessment team consisted of total 3000 officials including IAS officers, IPS officers, IFS officers, class-I and class-II officers of govt., Ministers and MPs etc. They all worked on the specific guidelines and worked for the whole day in the school and uploaded the evaluation form on the prescribed website. The assessment included evaluation of reading, writing, languages and computing skills of the students. The average of overall assessment was 60.0 per cent. Majority of the schools were found below average in the analysis. Therefore the government has planned out the follow-up work in which the remedial teaching classes have been started and the teachers have also been trained for that. Recruitment of 20000 thousand teachers has been planned out. The other recommendations are under consideration so far.

School Gradation Project (SGP): This project was implemented by the GCERT (Gujarat Council of Educational Research and Training) for the first time in the year 2008 and it continued in 2009. It accredited all the government primary schools and the grade was awarded on the basis of the educational achievement of the student of std. 4th and std. 7th. The result analysis showed that in 4th std. only 38 per cent schools got A/A+/A++ grades and in the 7th standard only 29 per cent schools have reached to A/A+/A++ grades which suggested a great need for improvement in primary education in Gujarat in terms of quality. The gradation functioned well in raising awareness about quality education in teachers and concerned government officials and provided a realistic picture of "where do we stand?" and what should be our future plans.

Other Reforms: From the year 2006-07, the government has also started the project of modern school where the schools covered under this scheme get Rs 2.5 lac specially to increase the educational facilities in the schools and to make it a modern school. Another centrally sponsored project, Kasturba Gandhi Balika Vidyalaya (KGVB), Kasturba Gandhi Balika Vidyalaya (KGVB), was undertaken by Gujarat Primary Education Council called. These are residential schools for girls from SC/ST category, minority community and below poverty level families. 63 schools in 19 districts have been started till date.

Curriculum

Gujarat State Board of School Textbook: This separate board of textbook helps the government to implement new curriculum reforms. Since 2006, for standard 1st and 2nd the new textbooks in double Demi size have been introduced. From June 2008, new textbooks have been introduced in 7th standard according to new syllabus in Gujarati, English, Hindi and other mediums of instruction. From June 2008, Self-learning books for 3rd and 4th standards have been given to children learning in District Panchayat and Municipal schools. A revised edition of bilingual (English-Gujarati) dictionary based on text books of English (as a second language) for 5th to 7th standard students has been published in the year 2010. From June 2009 onwards, Self-learning books for 5th to 7th standards have been prepared for all mediums for English (as a second language), Social Science, Science and Technology and Maths. From the year 1999, a children Magazine, "Balsrushti", published by the board, has been performing a pivotal role in improving reading habits of students and in disseminating new knowledge and information. It also motivated the students and the teachers to involve themselves has publishing their stories, poems and other forms of creative writing.

Strengthening of Curriculum through Various Activities: The Science-Maths unit of the GCERT is doing various activities that can be referred to as curriculum reforms. The unit is developing and managing Science-Maths Mandal in each of the primary schools. It organizes the Science-Maths Exhibition in the schools. Curriculum here also includes environment education and in primary education Eco-club has been formed as an association of the students and teachers of the schools who are interested in nature and environment. They undertake various projects and activities in primary schools and all DIETs (District Institute of Educational Training) to develop an awareness among students and teachers about environment and how to save nature. The activities include preparing clean soil, Botanical gardens and gardens of flowers and vegetables, working for plantation in schools and public places, celebration of Van Mahotsav, World Environment Day, cleanliness of public places etc. Another initiative is organizing yearly sports festivals by GCERT from Cluster Resource Centre (CRC) level to state level to encourage the primary students, PTC student-teachers and teachers.

NSS and Scout-Guide Programme: In all the DIETs, for the PTC trainees, NSS units have been recently formed and under this scheme various activities for the benefit of the local society, for the development of the youth and educational institutions contributing to nation building and national development are undertaken. Like NSS, Scout-Guide Programme is also being considered a part of the curriculum by the National Syllabus Committee. Following this recommendation, under the guidance of the Education Department, Scout-Guide Programme has been started since 2007-08 in the upper primary schools to develop love for the nation, discipline, adventure and human values in children. A Troop Development Committee has been formed at district level and the teachers and people involved in this activity were trained by the experts from Bharat Scout Guide Federation.

SRG (State Resource group): The government has established a State Resource Group in order to create a group of expert primary school teachers to review and reform curriculum, syllabus, textbooks, evaluation system etc. It works in two groups. One group works on standard 1st to 5th and another group works on 6th to 8th standard. Recently a new State Resource Group of 144 members has been re-established by GCERT for 1st to 5th standard for reforms in curriculum.

Faculty Development and Teaching-learning Process

Training Branch of GCERT: For the development of professional efficiency of the primary teachers, the GCERT has a separate branch and its district centers work on research based, need based and area based training programmes. In the year 2009-10, 1281 Key Resource Persons and Resource Persons were given a 20-day training. The branch has prepared 26,780 experts in the form of CRG (Cluster Resource Group) for the CRC (Cluster Resource Center) level teacher training. A workshop was organized in 2010-11 to write modules on subjects like effective class interaction, positive attitude and language teaching for further training which trained 1467 Key Recourse Persons and Recourse Persons and 23359 CRG experts. All primary teachers were given an innovative training through teleconference mode by BISAG Studio organized by SSAM and GCERT jointly which was a new beginning in the field of faculty development. The Readers, education faculties, principals, and lecturers participated in the Value Education Workshop organized by Senior Citizenship Development, New Delhi at Gandhinagar. Under the guidance of Dr. Swaroop Sampat Life Skills through Drama training was held at DIET Vadodara in four phases. About 150 resource persons were trained during December 2009 to March 2010. Poems in subjects like Gujarati, Hindi and English of VII standard were recorded in the voice of primary teachers with the help of UNICEF.

ADEPTS Progamme: Advancement of Educational Performance through Teachers' Support is a programme implemented since 2007 as a support to the Learning Enhancement Programme with an objective to improve the classroom performance of the primary teachers. In phase-I, 456 schools and 28,000 teachers and in phase-II, 6,676 schools and 48,000 teachers were included under this programme. The programme has been strengthened by workshops, teleconferences and review meetings. A list of various activities and a booklet have been prepared specially to provide a framework to the programme. In the year 2010-11, 15,000 more schools will join this programme to improve the professional ability of their teachers in terms of classroom work.

Distance Education Programme and Teaching-Learning-Training Through BISAG: BISAG (Bhaskaracharya Institute for Space Applications and Geo-informatics) studio in Gandhinagar has radically widened the horizons of education in Gujarat. It is a State level nodal agency to facilitate the use of spatial and geo-spatial technologies for the planning and developmental activities pertaining to Agriculture, Land and Water Resource Management, Wasteland/Watershed Development, Forestry, Disaster Management, Infrastructure and Education. It records, prepares and telecasts educational programmes as well as establishes a live source of communication among the people involved in the process of education using EDUSAT satellite and thousands of receiving centers established all over

Gujarat. In primary education there are several teaching-learning programmes implemented through BISAG. One of them is Distance Education programme in which GCERT organizes lessons for students of V to VII standards in subjects like Maths, Science and English. The students from Educationally Backward Block's (EBB) come from the interior areas of Gujarat to Gandhinagar, stay there for a few days, participate in the activity based lessons, visit the important places and institutions in Gandhinagar and Ahmedabad and other teachers and students of Gujarat participate from their respective receiving centers. Through BISAG, Gujarat Primary Education Council trained 1,94,000 primary teachers of the state where the experts interacted with all the teachers through broadcasting and teleconference.

Secondary Education

To help secondary education realise the vision of Gujarat, two state level government bodies are working. One is the Gujarat Secondary and Higher Secondary Education Board (GSHSEB), Gandhinagar and another is the Secondary Teacher Training Institution (STTI), Gandhinagar. In addition, to these state level bodies the Commissioner of School also plays a vital role in implementing and coordinating various educational programmes and schemes of the government.

Physical Resources

Under Rastriya Madhyamik Shiksha Abhiyan (RMSA), it has been decided to setup a secondary school in the vicinity of 5 kms and higher secondary school in the periphery of 1 to 10 kms to achieve the goal of universal availability of secondary education in the state by 2011. The provision for additional classrooms, drinking water, sanitation and toilet blocks, new gadgets for computer laboratory has been made in 104 government schools in the year 2009-10. Under '*Van Bandhu Scheme*, 43 Talukas of tribal areas have been covered and provided all infrastructural facilities required for beginning higher secondary classrooms of general stream and science stream. A similar scheme, "*Sagarkhedu Scheme*", covers 38 coastal area Talukas. The facility of secondary and higher secondary education has been made available in these areas by building new schools and developing other infrastructural facilities. The "*Nari Gaurav Scheme*" provides physical resources required by girls studying in high schools and higher secondary schools. It includes special prizes, scholarships, providing necessary medicines, sex education, distribution of bicycles, maintenance of the female teacher ratio, etc. which can empower women through education.

Education System Reforms

Introducing Semester System and Exam Reforms: The government of Gujarat has implemented semester system in IXth and XIth standards on pilot basis from 2010 to be upscaled to cover all schools from June 2011. Accordingly the syllabus of these standards have been divided into two semesters and the exams would also be held semester wise. The major change in examination system is introducing the multiple choice questions for testing. A 50 marks test will be taken on OMR sheets and the other 50 marks test will be descriptive. This will be implemented for the first time in the Xth standard board examination in March 2011. This will be further implemented in all standards in future. The Gujarat Secondary and Higher Secondary Education Board has withdrawn the tradition of declaring top ten students in the board exams and instead each student will get Percentile Rank in their mark sheets from the next year which will be helpful in reducing stress among the bright students and their parents as well. The passing standard in the board exams in Gujarat has been reduced to 33 per cent from 35 per cent to remove the system of awarding grace marks and the students getting less than 33 per cent will not be declared as "fail" but something like "Need to improve". These reforms, it is hoped would help the weak students to continue with positive attitude in the coming year.

Helpline for Board Exams: The students preparing for SSC and HSC examinations suffer from anxiety and stress especially when the exams are near. To make them free from such psychological pressure and confusions, and to guide and solve their problems GSHSEB has established a helpline with toll free number 1800-233-5500. As a result many students and other people will benefit every year. In 2010, it worked from 4th February to the last day of the exam and provided guidance in two shifts. Well known psychologists, principals and teachers were placed on the helpline to make this facility successful and effective. More than 10,000 students from all the districts of the state sought help through this helpline this year.

Curriculum

English Language Education: The government of Gujarat has revised its policy by making English compulsory (as a second language) in standard X, XI and XII in the last five years in all streams in phases. Furthermore, the government has prepared Supplementary Readers like Flamingo, Dolphin, Butterfly etc. containing a variety of contents for the students of secondary standards to provide quality exposure and to make English language learning interesting and joyful. These supplementary readers have also been included in the syllabus for evaluation purposes to ensure its reading among the students. The government has also introduced Oral Exams in English to balance the learning of all four skills in English namely LSRW. In addition, functional grammar and communicative approach have been adopted and the teachers have been trained to follow these in their day-to-day classroom work. Thus the scenario of English language teaching-learning has been reformed.

Upgrading of Curriculum and Preparing New Textbooks: A common 'CORE Curriculum' has been prepared for Science Stream in Standard XI and XII by COBSE at national level. Following this national level reform and NCF (National Curriculum Framework) prepared by NCERT, Gujarat Secondary and Higher Secondary Board has revised the syllabus of Maths and Science and accordingly new textbooks and workbooks for standard VIII to XII have been prepared by Gujarat State Board of School Textbook.

Faculty Development and Teaching-learning Process

The Secondary Teachers' Training Institution has recently organized several training programmes for capacity building of secondary and higher secondary teachers. A special training was held on School Management Software Programme (SMSP) for the principals and clerks. For the teachers of Maths, Non-formal Mathematics and model making programme was organized with the help of Dr. Vikram Sarabhai Community Science Center. The teachers were specially trained in the field of English Language Skills and use of digital content. All newly appointed teachers are trained to equip them with the current streams of knowledge and methodology. Quality enhancement programme are organized for the teachers of schools getting results less than 30 per cent.

ICT Integrated Blended Learning Design (iBLD): Government of Gujarat has decided to bring a paradigm shift in the teaching-learning process of secondary education by implementing iBLD designed and guided by Prof. Marmar Mukhopadhyay. iBLD has been designed to focus on Higher Order Thinking Skills (HOTs) with the teaching of the prescribed subjects. In order to facilitate this type of learning designs, the government of Gujarat has undertaken a project to develop e-content for all the secondary standards in subjects like Science, Maths, English and Social Sciences. The e-content will make the teacher's task of teaching the actual subject content easier and will save time for the activities to develop Higher Order Thinking Skills (HOTs). In the pilot project for iBLD, the GSHSEB has selected 60 principals and 600 teachers from the three districts namely Surat, Anand and Vadodara to train them to prepare iBLD for their respective subjects. The first phase of piloting has been recently completed. The implementation of this project in Gujarat will transform the teaching-learning process suitable to this ICT age.

Use of Satellite in Teaching-learning & Training with the Help of BISAG: Till February 2009, total 343 programmes on the subjects like Science and Technology, Maths and English were prepared and telecast by BISAG for 171 hours for the students of IX and X standard. Expert teachers provide subject and career guidance to the students in these programmes. In 2010,

33109 secondary and 6017 higher secondary teachers underwent “Karmayogi Training” through BISAG. This Karmayogi Training not only focus on the teaching-learning of the subjects but also includes the major issues like corporal punishment, school safety, sexual harassment, traffic problems etc. and projects in the field of education like cleanliness, research work, “Vache Gujarat” (A reading campaign), coaching for competitive exams etc. This training makes the teachers and principals well equipped every year to face new challenges and to work innovatively and more effectively.

Higher Education

In the context of challenges and advantages created by globalization, ICT has brought a paradigm shift in various fields of higher education in Gujarat. Relating the vision of Gujarat that is to make people healthy, educated and prosperous, Smt. Jayanti Ravi, IAS, Commissioner of Higher Education writes thus in her article “Education for Tomorrow—the Gujarat Way.”

> “A state committed to transform the quality of its citizens, realizes its importance that education in general and tertiary education in particular has in spearheading and initiating these changes”.

The emphasis here is not on changes in education system only but on changing the life of citizens. The three dimensions of Access, Achievement and Equity have uniquely formed the current frame of education including higher education.

Physical Resources

Digital laboratories with about 35 computers and necessary software have been set up in 216 colleges. The proposal to set up such laboratories in another 170 colleges is in pipeline. These labs have already received LCD projectors, headphones, Server computer and all other hardware facilities necessary for the use of ICT for learning purposes. The Education Department of the state is also going to help the colleges in setting up an audio-visual room in each college. This will promote and enhance use of ICT in teaching.

Knowledge Consortium of Gujarat has launched an initiative to strengthen the libraries of the colleges and to connect these with the libraries of other leading institutions of higher education. This initiative has a two fold plan that include: (i) strengthening the libraries with infrastructure, technology and access to learning resources, and (ii) capability building of human resources working in the libraries including strengthening teachers of academic programmes of library and information science. To make the classrooms of higher education more relevant and suitable to the needs of 21st century and to make the learning experiences more interactive and interesting, Knowledge Consortium of Gujarat has planned to facilitate the classrooms with the required designed furniture and teaching aids to the higher education classrooms of the state.

The Education Department is planning to prepare a repository of teaching learning materials and in that way to make the knowledge resources available at all levels across the subjects. The idea is to make it available to the remotest area of the state. The action plan is to create a database of teaching learning material in electronic form which may be accessed by all the teachers and students, whenever necessary.

Gujarat Commission for Educational Innovations: The government of Gujarat legislated and set up this commission to provide innovative inputs to the system of higher education. The major aim was "to demonstrate, inspire, nurture and encourage such innovations that lead to integral education". The commission concentrated on five great educationists and their innovations viz., Mahatma Gandhi, Rabindranath Tagore, Swami Dayanand Saraswati, Vivekanamda, Shri Aurobindo.

Specialized Universities: To encourage the specialized higher education in the needed areas, the government has set up specialized universities which include Forensic Science University, Raksha Shakti (Defense Study) University, Gujarat Technological University, Shree Somnath Sanskrit University, Children's University, Indian Institute of Teacher Education and Gujarat National Law University. The government has extended the legislation provisions to set up private universities in the state. As a result of all these efforts Gujarat has 40 universities and national level institutions of higher education in the system today. It has accelerated the access and opportunities in higher education immensely.

Knowledge Consortium of Gujarat (KCG): To strengthen the system of higher education, the government has established KCG the purpose of which is to "address the unique challenges and opportunities in higher education." It has provided a unique platform for academicians and stakeholders from all the universities and other institutions to deliberate, share and disseminate knowledge. This facilitates academic and administrative reforms in higher education in consonance with the changes in various dimensions of knowledge. The consortium also offers Knowledge Management Programme for Faculty (KMPF) to all the faculties of higher education in Gujarat. We will discuss it later in this paper. Most importantly, the KCG can involve models of integrated education that would facilitate the holistic development, a new consciousness and fraternity and prepare students to face the challenges of a globally competitive yet collaborative world and life.

Mission Mode Implementation Strategy: In order to empower the education system the State government is aiming towards:

- Structuring

- Training
- Benchmarking
- Monitoring
- Follow up and Re-strategizing

Following this strategy, the colleges across the state have been divided into 33 higher education districts. Each district is being mentored as well as monitored by two District Coordinators. The District Coordinators are a link between the office of Higher Education Commissioner and colleges. In addition, two professors from the university to which the colleges are affiliated are appointed as "Prabhai Professors". Colleges in each district have been further subdivided into Clusters. The Commissioner of Higher Education as well as Coordinators of various initiatives regularly interact with District coordinators by Video Conferencing as well as by live telecast through the sitcom channel of BISAG.

Academic and Administrative Audit: "The objective of AAA is to facilitate awareness among the colleges about the processes and systems that can ensure quality enhancement and realization of goals set in higher education." It works in close synchronization with NAAC and has identified Key Performance Indicators (KPI). It will assess each higher education institute through an alpha numeric grade, indicating both the grading (NAAC and AAA) ranging from A1 to E5. It will be preceded by an effort to address the issues that require intervention from the State at every institution level and will be an exercise in mentoring and handholding rather than inspection or monitoring. A mechanism will also be set-up in each institution to exhibit the achievements and success stories in the form of an annual 3-day festival involving activities like exhibition, seminars and cultural programmes for all the stakeholders including local community, University and State representatives, and parents. The cluster level, higher education district level and state level awards and incentives for the exceptional performances will also further enhance the spirit of the institution to work with excellence.

On Demand Online Examination: The plan is to set up about 180 testing centers for creating question banks, continuous evaluation, assigning credits/ grades, and building institutions of On Demand Online Examination. A comprehensive question bank is being prepared based upon Course objectives and Course outcome. The candidate will be evaluated at various levels of thinking skills with special emphasis on higher order thinking skills. Attempts are being made to have an On Demand Online Examination (ODOLE) based upon inputs from NIOS.

The Placement Cell—UDISHA: A separate placement cell for the university students has been established by the Education Department to increase the employability of the students. The cell tries to bridge the gap between job-seekers and job-providers. The cell creates a dynamic database of the graduate and post graduate students. Then it provides counseling as well as required information to fulfill human resource requirement in the job market. UDISHA reaches to all students through UDISHA Clubs that are being set up in all the colleges and departments in the State. Job fairs have been organized by inviting companies like Reliance HR Limited, Eureka Forbs Limited, Azure Knowledge Limited and TV9.

Choice Based Credit System (CBCS): From the year 2010-11, all the universities of Gujarat have adopted Choice Based Credit System (CBCS) for the PG courses while two of them, Saurashtra University and Sardar Patel University, have adopted it in the undergraduate courses also. In this system of curriculum, the students have the opportunities to choose their courses from a set of core courses, elective courses and foundation courses according to a prescribed distribution requirement. Here the core courses refer to their subjects of specialization while the electives refer to the inter-disciplinary courses to enhance their employability. Foundation courses will focus on soft skills mainly. Attempts are being made to impart vocational training as well as entrepreneurship to the students as a part of the programme.

Saptadhara: It is an initiative to promote overall development of students and to inculcate the cultural heritage of Gujarat and India. It facilitates the holistic development of the students and has widened the scope of the curriculum of higher education. The programme equip the students with what is now called "Multiple Intelligence" as it has been made mandatory for each student to participate in at least one of the seven streams of the intelligence. The seven streams are related to the following areas:

1. Literary Creative Club (Sarjanatmak Abhivyakti Dhara).
2. Fine Arts Club (Kaladhara).
3. Music and Dance Stream (Geetsangeet and Nrutya Dhara).
4. Knowledge Society (Gyandhara).
5. Theatre Art (Natyadhara).
6. Yoga, games and sports related activities (Khelkuddhara).
7. Community work and social service related activities (Saamudayik Seva Dhara).

Clubs and societies relate to each of the above mentioned areas in each college and students are mandated to choose at least one of these areas to learn and express at their best in these fields. The events on these areas are regularly organized at the college, University, zonal and State level where individuals and teams participate and winners are promoted to the next level. A total 1892 students from 33 academic districts across the state participated at zonal level competitions. The state level "Saptadhara" event was celebrated on a grand scale at Sardar Patel University, V V Nagar from 27th to 30th January 2010.

Content Development: Efforts have been initiated to produce good quality textbooks for the higher education curricula with the help of experts from other parts of the country and world. This is being done primarily by University Textbook Board. Under the ICT mission Sakshat, e content is also being created by academic experts from various colleges and universities through the Knowledge Consortium.

Faculty Development and Teaching-Learning Process

Karmayogi Training and Capacity Building: With a view to enable teachers, administrators and librarians to deal with the challenges of higher education, the government periodically organizes Karmayogi Training for the lecturers and principals of the colleges to make them aware about necessary changes, challenges and recent trends pertaining to research, teaching methodology, use of modern teaching aids, examination system etc. Knowledge Consortium of Gujarat has now identified several target groups for the purpose of training and capacity building. The major aim of the training is to create enlightened teachers through enhancing their skills, knowledge, attitude and perspectives of teaching-learning, understanding of their role as a teacher.

Knowledge Management Programme for Faculties: This programme has been designed to equip faculties with basic skills of communication, information technology and functional English. The major aim is to familiarize the faculties with knowledge available at global level. The knowledge of English language with computer skills helps the learners to be more efficient and competent to face everyday challenges. Under this programme, 30 key master trainers were trained at H.M. Patel Institute of English Training & Research, Vidyanagar for a day. These resource persons will train the other faculties of Gujarat. 70 lecturers were trained at SPIPA on 10-11th April. Now around 1300 lecturers of the state will undergo training for ICT, CBCS and Value education and Teaching Methodology.

SCOPE and Language Laboratory Courses: The acronym SCOPE stands for Society for the Creation of Opportunities through Proficiency in English. SCOPE conducts different level part time courses run by the centers spread all over Gujarat having collaboration with Cambridge University for exams and certification which is considered valid additional qualification for many government jobs as well. This initiative was planned to make the students efficient users of English. In order to add the ICT component in teaching-learning of the English language, the government began to offer Language Lab Courses through Dr. Babasaheb Ambedkar Open University after establishing Language Laboratory in more than 250 colleges. The lecturers of these colleges were also trained by the government to run these courses. More than 1 Lac students have benefitted from both of these courses till today which is a new beginning in teaching-learning of any language.

Networking of Research Institutions and Publications of Research Journals and Newsletter: Through this initiative Knowledge Consortium of Gujarat aims to establish connections with research scholars and faculties in different universities and to expand the scope of research activities and initiatives. KCG also aims to establish a common platform, for assessing books, journals and other academic materials for development and enlightenment of students, researchers and readers. In order to promote and strengthen the research, the higher education department of the state is coming up with the publication of eight journals pertaining to the eight major areas like Science and Technologies, Humanities, Social Sciences, Languages and Translation Studies, Law, Education, Commerce and Management and Interdisciplinary Studies. The department is also publishing a bimonthly newsletter "Vidya". The newsletter is focused on the current trends and developments in higher education in the state as well as country.

Conclusion

The big picture that emerges from this discussion of educational reforms shows that the state has achieved not only quantitative expansion but also qualitative improvement in all three sectors of education through increase in total number of institution, its infrastructural facilities and gross enrolment ratio on the one hand and emphasizing grading and accreditation of educational institutions on the other. The aim has been to provide maximum opportunity to each learner for comprehensive and sustainable development, and the focus has been on English language education and use of ICT at all levels. Activity Based Learning (ABL) and Continuous Comprehensive Evaluation are also upcoming innovations to support the enhancement of teaching-learning processes.

The overview in the preceding sections shows that certain areas need special attention in future planning. It is necessary to coordinate the various activities in primary, secondary and higher education sectors so as to make them complementary and more effective in their endeavour. It is equally necessary to develop a unified vision of teacher's role in education and to institutionalize professional development of the teachers at all levels.

We have tried to present the scenario of educational reforms in Gujarat on the basis of the information available to us. There may be many other significant movements and undercurrents in the field of education in Gujarat that remain to be taken note of here. To conclude we can say that education in Gujarat is passing through thorough transformational reforms at all levels.

Note

1. http://www.swarnimgujarat.org/about_golden_gujarat.aspx

References and Bibliography

AIU. 1997. *Handbook of Distance Education,* New Delhi: AIU.

Aradhya, N. and Kashyap, A. 2006. *The 'Fundamental' Right to Education in India,* Center for the Child and the Law, National Law School of India University, Bangalore.

Araneda, H. 2010. *Diversification of Post-Secondary Education to Expand Access and Improve Relevance: The Chilean Case.* A study sponsored by IIEP, Paris, IIEP, mimeo.

Asian Development Bank. 2012. *Shadow Education: Private Supplementary Tutoring and Its Implications for Policy Makers in Asia, Metro Manila: ADB.*

Aspiring Minds. (2013. Report on National Employability of Graduates, 2013. accessed on: http://www.aspiringminds.in/researchcell/whitepapers/national_employability_report_graduates_2013.html

Aspiring Minds. 2010. National Employability Study: IT/ITeS Sector (http://www.aspiringminds.in)

Assié-Lumumba, N'dri T. 2006. *Higher Education Reforms in Africa: Crisis Reforms and Transformation*. Dakar: Impremerie Saint Paul.

Atcharena, David and Lavinia Gasperini, (Coordinators and Editors). 2003. *Education and Rural Development: Towards New Policy Responses*. Rome: FAO / Paris: UNESCO /New Delhi: Rawat Books.

Bajpai, N. 2003. *India: Towards the Millennium Development Goals*, Background Paper, Human Development Report.

Banathy, Bela H. 1991. *Systems Design of Education: A Journey to Create the Future.* Englewoods Cliffs, Educational Technology Publications.

Barkley, E.F., Cross, K.P., and Major, C.H. 2005. *Collaborative Learning Techniques: A Handbook for College Faculty*. San Francisco: Jossey-Bass.

Bennett, T., Deluca, D., and Bruns, D. 1997. Putting Inclusion into Practice: Perspectives of Teachers and Parents. *Exceptional Children,* 64. http://en.wikipedia.org/wiki/Inclusive_education

Berge Zane L. and Susan. Mrozowski. 2001. Review of Research in Distance Education 1990 to 1999, *The American Journal of Distance Education*, 15(3), 5-19.

Berrien K.1985. *General and Social Systems.* New Brunswick: Rutgers University Press.

Besley, Timothy, and Robin Burgess. 2002. The Political Economy of Government Responsiveness: Theory and Evidence from India, *The Quarterly Journal of Economics*, Vol. 117, No. 4, 1415-1451.

Besley, Timothy, and Robin Burgess, 2003, Halving Global Poverty, *Journal of Economic Perspectives*, Vol. 17, No. 3, 3-22.

Bhalla, Veena, 2005. International Students at Indian Universities, *International Higher Education*, 41 Fall 2005.

Bhola, H.S. 1989. The CLER Model of Innovation Diffusion, Planned Change and Development: A Conceptual Update and Applications. *Knowledge in Society: The International Journal of Knowledge Transfer,* Vol. 1, No. 4, Winter 1988-89, pp. 56-66.

Bhola, H.S. 1992, "A Model of Evaluation Planning, Implementation and Management: Toward a 'Culture of Information' within Organizations," *International Review of Education*, 38(2): 103-115, 1992.

Bhola, H.S. 1994. The CLER Model: Thinking Through Change. *Nursing Management*, 25, 5, May 1994, 59-63.

Bhola, H.S. 1999a. Equivalent Curriculum Development as Situated Discourse: A Case in the Context of Adult Education in Namibia, *Curriculum Inquiry* (Blackwell/ OISE Journal), 29:4 (1999), 459-484.

Bhola, H.S. 1999b. World Trends and Issues in Adult Education on the Eve of the Twenty-first Century, *International Review of Education,* 44(5/6): 485-506.

Bhola, H.S. 2000. "A Policy Analysis of Adult Education in India: Across the Two National Policy Reviews of 1968 and 1986." In C.J. Daswani and S.Y. Shah (Eds.), *Adult Education in India: Selected Papers* (pp.47-65). New Delhi: UNESCO.

Bhola, H.S. 2002. A Model and Method of Evaluative Accounts: Development Impact of the National Literacy Mission (NLM) of India. *Studies in Educational Evaluation*, 28: 273-296.

Bhola, H.S. 2003, "Policy: A Holistic Perspective," *Journal of Educational Planning and Administration*. Volume XVII, No. 1, pp. 85-104.

Bhola, H.S. 2003a. Adult and Lifelong Education for Sustainable Development in India: Great Achievements; Greater Expectations, *International Journal of Adult and Lifelong Education*. Vol.1, No. 2, September 2003, 5-19.

Bhola, H.S. 2003b. "Policy: A Holistic Perspective," *Journal of Educational Planning and Administration*, January 2003, Volume XVII, No. 1, pp. 85-104.

Bhola, H.S. 2004a. Adult Education for Poverty Reduction: Political Economy Analysis in Systems Theory Perspective. *Indian Journal of Adult Education,* 65(12), 5-14.

Bhola, H.S. 2004b. Policy Implementation: Planning and Actualization. *Journal of Educational Planning and Administration*. Volume XVIII No. 3, (July 2004), pp. 295-312.

Bhola, H.S. 2005. Adult Education and Adult Learning: Between Poverty Reduction and Wealth Production, *International Journal of Adult and Lifelong Education*. Vol. 3, No. 1, April 2005. pp 52-70.

Bhola, H.S. 2006a, Access to Education: A Global Perspective. In: Akpovire Oduaran and H.S. Bhola, editors). In: *Widening Access to Education as Social Justice: Essays in Honour of Michael Omolewa* (pp. 44-68). Berlin, Heidelberg, New York: Springer/UNESCO/UIE.

Bhola, H.S. 2006b, Adult and Lifelong Education for Poverty Reduction: A Critical Analysis of Contexts and Conditions. *International Review of Education*, Vol. 52 (3-4): 231-246.

Bhola, H.S. 2007a, Adult Education in India after Independence: A Critical Historical Account (Pages 78-93), In: Mukhopadhyay, Marmar and Parhar, Madhu (eds.). *Education in India: Dynamics of Development*. New Delhi: Shipra Publications.

Bhola, H.S. 2007b. Capacity Building for Three Simultaneous Economies: Seeking Poverty Eradication for Sustainable Development in India. *Manpower Journal* (Quarterly Journal of the Institute of Applied Manpower Research). Vol. XLII, No. 1 (January-March 2007), pp. 1-18.

Bhola, H.S. 2009. Literacy, In Marcia J. Bates, and Mary Niles Maack (Eds). *Encyclopedia of Library and Information Sciences*, 3rd Edition, New York / London, U.K.: Taylor and Francis, January 2009.

Bhola, H.S. 2010b, Designing and Delivering Adult Education: Within the Quadrangle of Commitment, Capacity, Character and Communication, *Indian Journal of Adult Education* (Special Anniversary Issue), October-December, 2010, Vol. 71, No. 4, pp. 5-19.

Bhola, H.S. 2011a. "Reform of Adult Education in India," A paper presented (in absentia) at the *International Conference IEPT 2011: Indian Education: The Positive Turmoil*, organized by Educational Technology and Management Conference, at India Habitat Center, New Delhi, February 7-9, 2011.

Bhola, H.S. 2011b. Essentiality of a Policy Framework for Promoting Literacy, Adult Education and Lifelong Education, presented at the International Conference on Women's Literacy for Inclusion and Sustainability, organized by UN for the E-9 member States and hosted by the Government of India, September 8-10, 2011, New Delhi, India. [The paper is to be included in the Conference Compendium to be published by the Ministry of Education)].

Bhola, H.S. and Sofia Valdivielso Gomez, 2008, *Signposts to Literacy for Sustainable Development.* [Two Complementary Studies by the joint winners of the 2004-2005 International Award for Literacy Research.] Hamburg: UNESCO Institute for Lifelong Learning (UIL). [Available also in French and Spanish Translations]

Bhushan, S. 2005a. Foreign Education Providers in India, NIEPA, New Delhi.

Bhushan, S. 2005b. Foreign Universities in India: Market-Driven New Directions, *International Higher Education*, 41 Fall 2005

Bhushan. S. 2005c. Measures for Enhancing Competitiveness of Higher Education, *University News*, Vol. 43 No. 5.

Biswal, K. 2011. *Secondary Education in India: Development Policies, Programmes and Challenges.* Paper presented at the "International Seminar on Indian Education: The Positive Turmoil" organized in New Delhi from February 7-9, 2011 by ETMA.

Bowe, Frank. 2005. *Making Inclusion Work.* Merrill Education/Prentice Hall. http://en.wikipedia.org/wiki/Inclusive_education

Bray, M. 2009. *Confronting the Shadow Education System: What Government Policies for What Private Tutoring*, Paris: IIEP.

Braybrooke, D. and Lindblom, C.E. 1963. *A Strategy of Decision: Policy Evaluation as a Social Process*. New York: Free press.

Bressoux, P. 1996. The Effects of Teachers' Training on Pupil's Achievement: The Case of Elementary Schools in France. *School Effectiveness and School Improvement,* 7(3), 252-279.

Briseid, Ole and Caillods, Francoise. 2004. *Trends in Secondary Education in*

Industrialized Countries: Are They Relevant for African Countries? UNESCO: IIEP, Paris, France.

Buchberger, F., Campos, B. P., Kallos, D. and Stephenson, J. (Eds.). 2000. Green Paper on Teacher Education in Europe: High Quality Teacher Education for High Quality Education and Training. Umea: TNTEE.

Burbules, N.C. and C.A. Torres. 2000. *Globalization and Education: Critical Perspectives*. New York: Routledge.

CABE. 2005. Report of the CABE Committee: Universalization of Secondary Education, accessed on: http://www.teindia.nic.in/files/reports/ccr/cabe/use.pdf

Caillods, Francoise and Grauwe, Anton de. 2006. *Capacity Development in Educational Planning and Management: IIEP's Experience*. Document for International Working Group on Education; Rome, 12-14 June, IIEP, Paris.

Calvert, J. 1995. "Mapping Knowledge in Distance Education" In Sewart, David (ed.) *One World Many Voices: Quality in Open and Distance Learning* VI. Birmingham, ICDE, pp 384-8.

Carl Dahlman and Anjula Utz. 2005. *India and the Knowledge Economy Leveraging Strengths and Opportunities*, World Bank Finance and Private Sector Development Unit South Asia Region and the World Bank Institute

Cheney, Gretchen Rhines; Ruzzi, Betsy Brown and Muralidharan, Karthik. 2005. *A Profile of the Indian Education System*. Paper prepared for the New Commission on Skills of the American Workforce, national Centre on Education and the Economy.

CHEPS. 2009. *The First Decade of Working on the European Higher Education Area: The Bologna Process Independent Assessment, Volume 1 Detailed Assessment Report*. Bucharest: Centre for Higher Education Policy Studies and Institute of Education.

Chugh, Sunita. 2008. Achieving Universalization of Elementary Education in Slum areas: Problems and Issues, *Journal of Indian Education*, Number 4, February 2008.

Chugh, Sunita. 2009. Social Justice and Urban Educational Planning: An Examination of Free Seats in Private Schools, *Perspectives in Education*, Vol. 25, No. 1, 2009.

Clark, B. 1998. *Entrepreneurial Universities: Organizational Pathways of Transition*. Paris: International Association of Universities.

Clignet, R. 1968. The Legacy of Assimilation in West Africa Educational Systems. Its Meaning and Ambiguities. *Comparative Education Review,* 12, 57-68.

D'Costa. 2003. Uneven and Combined Development: Understanding India's Software Exports, *World Development* 31:1, pp. 211-226.

Das, G. 2004. Missing in Action, *The Times of India*, 25th September 2004.

Das, G. 2004. Stop Bullying Children, *The Times of India*, 11th January 2004.

Das, Subrat and Mishra, Yamini. 2006. Women's Component Plan and Gender Budgeting in India: Still a Long Way to Go!, *YOJANA*, Vol. 50, October 2006, http://www.cbgaindia.org

Dash, M. 2000. *Education in India: Problems and Perspectives*, Atlantic Publishers, New Delhi.

Dent, M. 2007. Symposium on Changing Modes of Governance in Public Sector Organizations: Action and Rhetoric. *Public Administration*, 85(1), pp. 1-8.

Desai, Armaity, S. 2009. Catalyzing Higher Education and School Education Linkages, in Mukhopadhyay, Marmar (Ed.) *Quality School Education for All*, New Delhi: ETMA.

Dhar, A. 2010. Education is a Fundamental Right Now, *The Hindu*, April 1.

Distance Education Council, *Open Universities in India,* New Delhi: IGNOU, 1995.

Duraisamy, P. 2002. Changes in Returns to Education in India, 1983-94: By Gender, Age-cohort and Location. *Economics of Education Review*, Vol. 21, No. 6, December 2002, pp. 609-22(14).

Dutta, B.B. 2014. Nehru to Modi: End of Nehruvian Republic, *South Asia Politics*, 13(1). July.

Dutta, S.C. 1986. *History of Adult Education in India*. New Delhi: Indian Adult Education Association.

Ellan, A. 1999. *Poverty and Disability: A Survey of the Literature*, Washington: The World Bank.

EY, FICCI, Planning Commission. 2012. Higher Education in India: Twelfth Five Year Plan (2012–2017) and beyond, FICCI Higher Education Summit 2012, accessed on: http://www.ey.com/Publication/vwLUAssets/Higher_ Education_in_ India/$File/EY-FICC_Higher_Education_Report_Nov12.pdf

Fagerlind, I. and Stromqvist, G. (Eds.). 2004. *Reforming Higher Education in Nordic Countries*, Paris, IIEP/UNESCO.

Fan, Shenggen, Peter Hazell, and Sukhadeo Thorat. 2000. Government Spending, Growth and Poverty in India, *American Journal of Agricultural Economics*, Vol. 82, No. 4, (November 2000), pp. 1038-1051.

Farzam, Arbab. 1994. *Lectures on Bahá'í Inspired Curricula.* Florida, USA: Palabra Publications.

Feenstra, R.C. and Hanson, G.H. 1999. Productivity Measurement and Impact of Trade and Technology on Wages: Estimates for the US, 1972-1990. *Quarterly Journal of Economics,* (Vol. 114, No. 3, pp. 907-940).

Feldman, Robert S. 2008. *Understanding Psychology*, (8th Edition), Retrieved from http://en.wikipedia.org/wiki/Inclusive_education

FICCI and EY. 2009. Making the Indian Higher Education System Future Ready, Higher Education Summit Report 2009.

Flood R.L. and Carson E. 1988. *Dealing with Complexity. An Introduction to the Theory and Application of Systems Science.* New York, Plenum Press.

Foster, P. 1966. The Vocational School Fallacy in Development Planning, In Anderson, C.A. and Bowman, M.S. (Eds.). *Education and Economic Development,* Aldine Publishing Co.

Foundation Ruhi. 2005. *Spirit of Faith.* Columbia, Florida, USA: Palabra Publications.

Franciosi, Robert J. 2004. *The Rise and Fall of the American Public School: The Political Economy of Public Education in the Twentieth Century.* New York: Praeger.

Fullan, M. 1991. *The New Meaning of Educational Change*. New York: Teachers College Press.

Fulton, Oliver (Ed.). 1981. Access *to Higher Education*, Surrey: The Society for Research into Higher Education at the University of Guilford.

Gehringer, E.F., 2000. Strategies and Mechanisms for Electronic Peer Review, http://serc.carleton.edu/introgeo/peerreview/references.html

Gill, S.S. 2005. Profit and Education Do Go, *The Indian Express*, 8th November 2005.

Ginsburg, Mark B. (Ed). 1991. *Understanding Educational Reform in Global Context: Economy, Ideology and the State*. New York: Garland.

Glyn, Andrews. 2006. *Capitalism Unleashed: Finance, Globalization and Welfare.* Oxford, New York: Oxford University Press.

Godbole, M. 2001. Elementary Education as a Fundamental Right: The issues, *Economic and Political Weekly*, 15 December, pp. 4609-4613.

Goggin, M. L., Bowman, A.O., Lester, J. P., and O'Toole, L. J. 1990. *Implementation Theory and Practice: Toward a third generation.* Glenview, IL: Scott Foresman.

Gold, B.A. 1999. "Punctuated Legitimacy: A Theory of Educational Change". In: *Teachers College Record*, 101(2), 192-219.

Goldsmith, Stephen. 2010. *The Power of Social Innovation: How Civic Entrepreneurs Ignite Community Networks for Good.* New York: Jossey-Bass (An Imprint of Wiley).

Gore, J., Williams. C., and Ladwig, J. 2006. Pedagogy and Teacher Induction: A Critical Moment in Professional Learning. *The New Educator.*

Government of Gujarat, Department of Education. 2010. Success Story, Gandhinagar: Govt. of Gujarat Publication.

Government of Gujarat, Department of Higher Education. 2010. *Glimpses of Higher Education in Gujarat,* Gandhinagar.

Government of India, Ministry of Education and Culture, 1950. *The Report of the University Education Commission*: Vol. I",

Government of India, Ministry of Education. 1966. *Report of the Education Commission 1964-66: Education and National Development.* New Delhi: Ministry of Education.

Government of India, Ministry of Education. 1986. *National Policy on Education,* New Delhi.

Government of India, MHRD, 1990. *Report of the Committee for the Review of National Policy on Education,* 1986

Government of India, MHRD. 1992. National Policy on Education, 1986 (Revised 1992), New Delhi.

Government of India. MHRD. 1992. Programme of Action on the National Education Policy, New Delhi.

Government of India, MHRD, 2000. *Sarva Shiksha Abhiyan* Accessed from: http://www.educationforallinindia.com/page119.html

Government of India, MHRD. 2000. *Sarva Shiksha Abhiyan A Programme for Universal Elementary Education; Framework for Implementation*, Ministry of Human Resources Development, Government of India, New Delhi. Available at: http://www.education.nic.in/ssa/ssa_1.asp

Government of India, Ministry of Law, Justice and Company Affairs. 2000. *Constitution of India* (As on January 2000), New Delhi.

Government of India, Ministry of Home Affairs. 2001. *Census of India. 2001,* New Delhi, Registrar General India (2001),

Government of India, MHRD. 2004. *Annual Report 2004-05*. Sarva Siksha Abhiyan, New Delhi. http://www.education.nic.in/Annualreport2004-05

Government of India, MHRD. 2004. *Annual Report 2004-05*. KGBV. New Delhi. http://www.education.nic.in/Annualreport2004-05

Government of India, MHRD. 2005. Sarva Shiksha Abhiyan: A Programme for Universal Elementary Education, New Delhi.

Government of India, MHRD. 2005. CABE Committee Report on Gender and Common Schools, 2005.

Government of India. 2005. Report of the Central Advisory Board on Education (CABE) Committee on Universalization of Secondary Education, accessed on www.education.nic.

Government of India. 2005a. Report of the CABE Committee on Free and Compulsory Education Bill and Other Issues Related to Elementary Education, June 2005. accessed on www.education.nic

Government of India, Planning Commission. 2008. *Eleventh Five Year Plan, 2007-12, Vol. II Social Sector.* New Delhi: Oxford University Press. Accessible at: http://planningcommission.nic.in/plans/planre/fiveyr/11th/II_v2/11th_vol2.pdf

Government of India. MHRD. 2009. Education for All Mid-Decade Assessment: Reaching the Unreached India, NUEPA, New Delhi

Government of India, MHRD. 2009. *Framework for Implementation of the Rashtriya Madhyamik Shiksha Abhiyan*. Department of School Education and Literacy, New Delhi.

Government of India, MHRD. 2009. Centrally Sponsored Scheme SAAKSHAR BHARAT. New Delhi: Accessible at: http://www.education.nic.in/Elementary/SaaksharBharat.pdf.

Government of India, MHRD. 2010. *Annual Report* 2009-10.

Government of India, MHRD. 2010. General Progress Card of Saakshar Bharat During the Year, September 09 to August 10. New Delhi: National Literacy Mission.

Government of India, MHRD, SSA. 2010. National Programme for Education of Girls at Elementary Level (NPEGEL), accessed on: http://ssa.nic.in/girls-education/npegel.

Government of India, Planning Commission. 2002. *Report of the Committee on "India: Vision 2020,"* New Delhi.

Government of India, Planning Commission. 2010. Mid-Term Appraisal of the XI Plan, New Delhi.

Government of India, Planning Commission. 2012. *Eleventh Five Year Plan.* New Delhi. Accessed from http://planningcommission.nic.in/plans/planrel/fiveyr/11th/11_v2/11th_vol2.pdf

Government of India, Planning Commission. 2012. *Twelfth Five Year Plan.* New Delhi. Accessed from http://planningcommission.nic.in/plans/planrel/12thplan/pdf/vol_3.pdf

Government of India, Planning Commission (several years). First to Eleventh Five-Year Plan (1951-56 to 2007-12) Vol. II, Thematic Issues and Sectoral Programmes, New Delhi, India.

Government of India. MHRD. (Various Years). *Selected Educational Statistics*, Department of Education, Planning, Monitoring and Statistics division.

Government of India, MHRD (Various Years). *Analysis of Budgeted Expenditure on Education*. Department of Higher Education, Planning, Monitoring and Statistics Bureau, New Delhi.

Government of India, MHRD (Various Years). *Selected Educational Statistics*. Department of Higher Education, New Delhi.

Government of India, MHRD. (Various Years). *Selected Educational Statistics*, 2000-01 to 2007-08.

Govinda R. and Biswal K. 2007. Access to Elementary Education in India: Identifying Issues, Gaps and Priorities, *CREATE-NUEPA*, New Delhi, mimeo.

Govinda, R. (Ed.). 2002. *India Education Report,* Oxford University Press, New Delhi.

Govinda, R. and Bandyopadhyay, M. 2010. Changing Framework of Local Governance and Community Participation in Elementary Education in India, *CREATE Research*, Monograph 35 Delhi/Sussex: CREATE.

Govinda, R. and Bandyopadhyay, M. 2007. Access to Elementary Education in India: Country Analytical Review. *Falmer: CREATE.*

Griliches, Z. 2000. *R&D, Education, and Productivity: A Retrospective.* Massachusetts: Harvard University Press.

Haddad, W.D. (with Demsky, T.). 1994. *The Dynamics of Education Policy Making: Case Studies of Burkina Faso, Jordan, Peru and Thailand.* Washington DC: World Bank.

Harvey, L. and Green, D. 1993. *Defining Quality Assessment in Higher Education.* 10(3), pp. 134-138.

Herreid, C.F. 1998. "Sorting potatoes for Miss Bonner: Bringing order to Case-Study Methodology through a Classification Scheme. *Journal of College Science Teaching* 27(4): 236–239.

Holmberg, B. 2000. Status and Trends of Distance Education Research, (retrieved from, http://www.eden.bme.hu/contents/r-net/r-net.html

Holsinger, Donald B. and Cowell, Richard N. 2000. *Positioning Secondary Education in Developing Countries*. UNESCO: IIEP, Paris.

Honig, Meredith I. 2004. Where's the "Up" in Bottom-Up Reform? *Educational Policy*, Vol. 18, No. 4, September.

Huba, M.E. and Freed, J.E. (2000), Learner Centred Assessment in College Campuses: Shifting the focus from teaching to learning, Needham, MA: Allyn and Bacon Heights

IGNOU, Academic Programmes on Offer 2014-15, IGNOU New Delhi

Inter-American Development Bank. 2007. *Reforming Primary and Secondary Education in Latin America and the Caribbean.* Washington, D.C.

Jayaram, N. 2004. Higher Education in India: Massification and Change, in Altbach Philip G. and Umakoshi Toru, (Eds.). 2004. *Asian Universities Historical Perspectives and Contemporary Challenges*, The John Hopkins University Press, Baltimore 2004.

Jean-Paul Sartre. 2001. (First published in French, 1964), *Colonialism and Neocolonialism*, London and New York: Routledge.]

Jegede, Olugbemiro. 1994. Distance Education Research Priorities for Australia: A study of the opinions of Distance Educators and Practitioners, *Journal of Distance Education*, 15(2), 234-253.

Jensen, Pollock Karen. 2004. *Glimmerings of Hope.* Florida, USA: Development Learning Press.

Jha, P. and Parvati, P. 2010. Right to Education Act 2009: Critical Gaps and Challenges, *Economic and Political Weekly*, Vol. XLV, No. 13, pp. 20-23.

Jhang, Z.J., Correspondence Education in People's University of China, in Mukhopadhyay, M. and Parhar, M. (Eds), *Open and Distance Education,* New Delhi: Jawahar Publishers and Distributors

Johnson, D.W. and Johnson, R.T. 1989. Introduction to Cooperative Learning: An Overview of Cooperative Learning, http://www.co-operation.org/home/introduction-to-cooperative-learning/

Kabir, Humayun. 1955. Secondary Education in India: An Overview. *Journal of Educational Sociology*, Vol. 28, No. 5, pp. 194-199.

Kapur, D. and Mehta, P.R. 2004. *Indian Higher Education Reform: From Half-Baked Socialism to Half-Baked Capitalism*, CID Working paper No. 108 September 2004.

Kaul, L. 1997. Open and Distance Education: Trend Report, In *Fifth Survey of Research in Education,* New Delhi: NCERT.

Kingdon, G.G. 2007. *The progress of school education in India.* http://www.gprg.org/

Kishore, N and Saxena, K. 1997. Quality Control in Management Education through Distance Education, in Mukhopadhyay, M. and Parhar, M. (Eds), *Open and Distance Education,* New Delhi: Jawahar Publishers and Distributors, 1997.

Kitaev, I. 2004. University funding by the central Russian Government: where the ends meet? In M. Shattock (Ed.), *Entrepreneurialism and the transformation of Russian* universities. Paris: IIEP-UNESCO, pp.36-57.

Koble, M. A. and Bunker, E.L. 1997. Trends in research and practice: An examination of *The American Journal of Distance Education* 1987-1995, *American Journal of Distance Education*, 11(2).

Kulkarni, P. 2010. Right to Education Act Faces Financial Hurdles, *Education Master*, March 25,

Kumar, Virendra. 1976. *Committees and Commissions in India, 1947-54*, New Delhi: Concept.

Lee, Y., Driscoll, M.P., and Nelson, D.W. 2004. The past, present and future of research in distance education: Results of a content analysis, *American Journal of Distance Education*, 18(4).

Leuze, K., Martens, K., Rusconi, A. 2007. "New Arenas of Education Governance—The Impact of International Organizations and Markets on Education Policy Making". In: K. Martens, A. Rusconi, and K. Leuze (Eds.), *New Arenas of Education Governance—The Impact of International Organizations and Markets on Education Policy*. New York: Palgrave Mcmillan, pp. 3-16.

Levy, D. 2006. "The Unanticipated Explosion: Private Higher Education's Global Surge". In: *Comparative Education* Review, 50(2), 218-40.

Levine, A. (2006). Educating School Teachers. The Education Schools Project. Accessed from: http://www.edschools.org/pdf/

Lewin, K. and F. Caillods. 2001. *Financing Secondary Education in Developing Countries: Strategies for Sustainable Growth*. UNESCO: International Institute for Educational Planning, France.

Lewin, Keith. 2008. *Beyond Primary Education: Challenges and Approaches to Expanding Learning Opportunities in Africa.* Working Document 1.2.03, Association for the Development of education in Africa.

Lewin, Keith. 2008. *Four Decades of Educational Planning: Retrospect and Prospect.* Paper presented at "Directions in Educational Planning: a Symposium to Honour the work of Francoise Caillods," July 3-4, IIEP, Paris.

Lewin, Keith. 2008. *Secondary Education in India: Managing Expansion with Affordable Costs.* Policy Guidance Note for MHRD, GOI, New Delhi.

Little, Angela W. 2010. Access to Elementary Education in India: Politics, Policies and Progress, *CREATE PATHWAYS TO ACCESS,* Research Monograph No. 44.

Loacker, G. Cromwell, and O'Brien, K. 1986. Assessment in Higher Education: To Serve the Learner, In C. Adelman (Ed), *Assessment in American Higher Education*, Washington: US Department of Education.

Lockheed, Marlaine, Verspoor, Adriaan, *et al.* 1991. *Improving the Quality of Primary Education.* New York, Oxford University Press for the World Bank.

Longworth, Norman. 2006. *Learning Cities, Learning Regions, Learning Communities: Lifelong Learning and Local Government.* London and New York: Routledge / Taylor & Francis Group. 230 pages. ISBN 10 0-415-37175-9 (pbk),

Lynch, J. 1994. *Provision for Children with Special Educational Needs in the Asia Region.* World Bank Technical Paper Number 261. Washington: The World Bank.

Martens, K., Rusconi, A., and Leuze, K. (Eds.). 2007. *New Arenas of Education Governance: The Impact of International Organizations and Markets on Educational Policy Making.* New York: Palgrave MacMillan.

Martin, M. and Antony, S. 2007. External Quality Assurance in Higher Education: Making Choices. *Fundamentals of Educational Planning*, No. 85. Paris: IIEP-UNESCO.

Mclendon, M.K., Hearn, J.C. 2009. "Viewing Recent US Governance Reform Whole: 'Decentralization' in a Distinctive Context". In: J. Huisman (Ed.), *Internatioanl Perspectives on the Governance of Higher Education: Alternative Frameworks for Coordination.* New York: Routledge, pp. 161-181.

McMahon, W.W. 1993. *An efficiency-based Management Information System.* Paris: UNESCO.

Mehrotra, Santosh (Ed). 2005. *The Economics of Elementary Education in India: The Challenge of Public Finance, Private Provision and Household Costs,* Sage, New Delhi.

Mehta, Arun. *Analytical Report for Various Years, NUEPA*

Mehta, B.C. and Kapoor, K. 2010. Implementing Right to Education Act, *Mainstream*, Vol. XLVIII, No. 10.

Mehta, V.R. 2003. The Killing of Higher Education, UGC Golden Jubilee Lecture Series, 2002-03

Mingat, Alain, and Jee-Peng Tan. 1996. *The Full Social Returns to Education: Estimates Based on Countries' Economic Growth Performance.* Working Paper. The World Bank, Washington, D.C.

Mishra, Sanjaya. 1997. A critical analysis of periodical literature in distance education, *Indian Journal of Open Learning*, 6(1 and 2).

Mishra, Sanjaya. 2002. Ten years of Indian Journal of Open Learning, *Indian Journal of Open Learning*, 11(2) 279-290.

Naidu, S. 2004. Researching distance education and e-learning, Paper presented at the National Workshop on Research Methodology for Distance and Online Learning, Feb. 14-15, New Delhi, IGNOU.

Mohammadbhai, G. 2008. *The Effects of Massification on Higher Education in Africa.* Accra: Association of African Universities.

Mohanty, J. 2002. *Primary and Elementary Education*, Deep &Deep Publications, New Delhi.

MSJE. 2011. The Rights of Persons with Disabilities Bill, 2011 (As submitted to MSJE Presented by Committee appointed by Ministry of Social Justice and Empowerment Government of India, 30 June 2011. http://en.wikipedia.org/wiki/Inclusive_education

Muley, V. and Phutela, R. 1980. Correspondence Education in India, New Delhi: UGC, (mimeo).

Mukhopadhyay, Marmar and Philips, Susan. 1994. Open Schooling: Selected Case Studies, Vancouver: COL.

Mukhopadhyay, M. 1995. National Open School: An Unfolding Institution, in Anzalone, S. (ed). *Multi-Channel Learning: Connecting All to Education,* Washington, D.C.: EDC, 1995.

Mukhopadhyay, Marmar. 1996. In-service Education of Primary Teachers through Distance Education: National Action Plan, New Delhi: UNESCO, 1996.

Mukhopadhyay, M. 1996. Sustainable Human Resource Development through Media and Distance Education, New Delhi: UNESCO, 1996.

Mukhopadhyay, Marmar. 1997. Distance Education: Social Relevance and Quality, in Mukhopadhyay, Marmar. and Parhar, M. (Eds), *Open and Distance Education,* New Delhi: Jawahar Publishers and Distributors.

Mukhopadhyay, Marmar. 1997. Distance Education: Social Relevance and Quality, in Mukhopadhyay, Marmar and Parhar, M.(eds). *Open and Distance Education,* New Delhi: Jawahar Publishers and Distributors.

Mukhopadhyay, Marmar. 1998. Teacher Education and Distance Education: The Artificial Controversy, in Buch, P.M. and Dave, J. (comp.) *Contemporary Thoughts on Education,* Baroda: SERD, 1998.

Mukhopadhyay, Marmar. 1999. School Education, in Mukhopadhyay, M. and *et al.* (eds), *Indian Education: Development Since Independence,* New Delhi: Vikas.

Mukhopadhyay, Marmar. 2001. Secondary Education: The Challenge Ahead, in Mukhopadhyay, Marmar and Narula, M. (Eds), *Secondary Education: The Challenge Ahead*, New Delhi: NIEPA.

Mukhopadhyay, Marmar and Narula, M. (Ed). 2002. *Secondary Education: The Challenges Ahead*, New Delhi: NIEPA, 2002.

Mukhopadhyay, Marmar (Ed).2004. Secondary Education in India: Emerging Demands, (Unpublished paper), New Delhi: NIEPA.

Mukhopadhyay, Marmar. 2004. Quality Assurance in Teaching Learning Process in Higher Education, Address at the UGC sponsored Conference on Quality in Higher Education, Ramakrishna Mission Vidyamandira, Belur, 2004

Mukhopadhyay, Marmar. 2004. Secondary Education in India: Emerging Demands, (Unpublished m/s circulated to the members of the CABE Committee on USE), NIEPA: New Delhi.

Mukhopadhyay, Marmar. 2005. *Total Quality Management in Education*, New Delhi: Sage.

Mukhopadhyay, Marmar. 2007. Indian Education since Independence, in Mukhopadhyay, Marmar and Parhar, Madhu (eds), *Indian Education: Dynamics of Development*, New Delhi: Shipra.

Mukhopadhyay, Marmar. 2007. Secondary Education: Victim of Perennial Neglect, in Mukhopadhyay, Marmar and Parhar, Madhu (eds), *Indian Education: Dynamics of Development*, New Delhi: Shipra.

Mukhopadhyay, Marmar. 2013. Education for Rural Transformation: A Case of Udang Forum, Stockholm: Stockholm University. (accessed on: http://www.edu.su.se/polopoly_fs/1.156577.1385371477!/menu/standard/file/ERT%20Volume% 201.pdf

Mukhopadhyay, Sudesh. 2001. *Case studies on Inclusive Education and Quality Improvement*, Paper Presented in the Regional Workshop on Building National Capacity for Quality Improvement of Primary Schools, UNESCO sponsored, Hiroshima, Japan,

Mukhopadhyay Sudesh and Singh, Renu. 2008. *Access to Education for the Disabled: A Case Study of India*, NUEPA, New Delhi (Mimeo).

Muley, V. and Phutela, R. 1980. *Correspondence Education in India*, New Delhi: UGC, 1980 (mimeo).

NAAC. 2007. *Quality Indicators for Teacher Education*. Bangalore.

Narula, Manju. 2010. Mainstreaming the Marginalised: Indian Initiatives, *International Journal of Education Economics and Development, Vol. 1, No. 3, 2010.*

Natarajan. R. 2004. Private Initiatives in Higher Education: Roles of Privatization in Professional Education, In Powar, K. B. and Johar, K. L. 2004. *Private Initiatives in Higher Education*, New Delhi: Sneh Prakashan.

National Centre for Promotion of Employment for Disabled People (NCPEDP). 2005. Journey towards Promotion of Inclusive Education (Mimeo).

NCERT, *All-India Educational Survey (various years)*. New Delhi.

NCERT. 2005. National Curriculum Framework. New Delhi.

NCTE. 2010. *National Curriculum Framework for Teacher Education, Towards Preparing Professional and Humane Teacher*". New Delhi.

Neave, G. and van Vught, F. 1991. *Prometheus Bound: The Changing Relationship between Government and Higher Education in Western Europe, 1986–1988.* Oxford: Pergamon.

Neave, G. 1988. The Evaluative State Reconsidered. In: *European Journal of Education*, 33(3), 265-284.

Nitst. 2010. *Right to Education Act, India: The Challenges Ahead,* accessed on http://www.indiastudychannel.com/resources/111415-Right-Education-Act-India-The-Challenges.aspx

NSSO. 2010. *Education in India: 2007-08—Participation and Expenditure*. 64th Round (July 2007-June 2008), Ministry of Statistics and Programme Implementation, GOI, New Delhi.

Nuna, Anita and Agrawal, Poonam. 2011. Post Independence Indian Perspective on Girls, *Education Dialogue April-June, 2011,* Volume 12 No. 4

O'Meara, Patrick, Mehlinger, Howard & Krain, Matthew (Eds.). 2000. *Globalization and the Challenges of the New Century: A Reader*. Bloomington and Indianapolis, IN: Indiana University Press.

OECD. 2005. *Teachers Matter: Attracting, Developing and Retaining Effective Teachers*. Paris, available at http://www.oedc.org/edu/teacherpolicy.

OECD. 2000. *Knowledge Management in the Learning Society: Education and Skills*. Paris: OECD.

Orkwis, R., and McLane, K. 1998. A Curriculum Every Student can Use: Design Principles for Student Access. ERIC/OSEP Topical Brief No. ED423654. Reston, VA: ERIC OSEP Special Project. [http://en.wikipedia.org/wiki/Universal_Design_for_Learning]

Panda, Santosh. 1992. Distance Education Research in India: Stock-Taking, Concerns and Prospects, *Distance Education*, 5(2).

Parhar, M. 1997. Distance Education in Inservice Education of Teachers: An Overview of the Developing World, in Mukhopadhyay, M. and Parhar, M. (eds), *Open and Distance Education,* New Delhi: Jawahar Publishers and Distributors.

Parhar, M. 1998. Human Resource Development in Open and Distance Education, *University News,* 36 (52), Dec. 28.

Parhar, M. 1998. Application of Educational Technology in Adult Education, Paper Presented at the *Second Asia Regional Literacy Forum,* New Delhi, 9-13 February,

Parhar, M. 1998. Universalization of Elementary Education: Evolving State Will, Editorial in *IASE Bulletin,* New Delhi: JMI, March,

Parhar, M. 1998. Open Schooling: International Scenario, *Media and Technology for Human Resource Development*, 10(1 and 2)

Parhar, M. 2003. Trends in Contemporary Research in Open and Distance Education, *Media and Technology for Human Resource Development*, AIAET, Vol. 14, No. 3 and 4.

Parson, C. and Fidler, B. 2005. A New Theory of Educational Change—Punctuated Equilibrium: The Case of the Internationalization of Higher Education Institutions. *British Journal of Educational Studies*, 53(4), pp. 447-465.

Pascale, R. and Athos, A. 1981. *The Art of Japanese Management*, London: Penguin Books.

Pass, S., Riccomini, P.J., and Switzer. D.M. 2005. A Case Study Documenting Experience and its Impact in the Classroom. *International Journal of Social Education,* 19(2), 88-101.

Patel, I.G. 1993. Higher Education and Development. In A. Ransom, S. M. Khoo and V. Sellvaratnam (Eds.), *Improving Higher Education in Developing Countries*. Washington DC: World Bank, pp.45-56.

Paul, Lample. 2000. *Creating a New Mind.* Florida, USA: Palabra Publications.

Paul, Lample. 2008. *Revelation and Social Reality*. Florida, USA: Palabra Publications.

Peters, S. *et al.* 2005. A Disability Rights in Education Model for Evaluating Inclusive Education. *International Journal of Inclusive Education*, Volume 9 No. 2, p142.

Peters, T. and Waterman, R. 1982. *In Search of Excellence*, New York, London: Harper & Row.

Philip O'Keefe. 2007. *People with Disabilities in India: From Commitments to Outcomes,* The World Bank, 2007

Phillips, David and Kimberly Ochs. 2004. *Educational Policy Borrowing: Historical Perspectives.* Oxford, U.K.: Symposium Books.

Probe Team. 1999. *Public Report on Basic Education in India*, Oxford University Press, New Delhi.

Bray, T.M. and Lykins, C.R. 2012. Shadow education: Private Supplementary Tutoring and its Implications for Policy Makers in Asia. Metro Manila, Philippines: Asian Development Bank.

Psacharopoulos, G. 1994. Returns to Investment in Education: A Global Update. In: *World Development*, *22*, pp.1325-1343.

Rajput, J.S. *et al.* 2001. *Experiences in School Education*, New Delhi: NCERT

Ramachandran, V. 2009. Right to Education Act: A Comment, *Economic and Political Weekly*, Vol. XLIV, No. 28, pp. 155-157.

Ramachandran, V., Kameshwari, J. and Aarti, S. 2003. Through the Life Cycle of Children: Factors Determining Successful Primary School Completion, *Economic and Political Weekly*, Vol. XXXVIII, No. 47. November.

Rani, P. Geetha. 2007. *Secondary Education in India: Development and Performance*. Paper presented at the 43rd Annual Conference of the Indian Econometric Society, IIT, Mumbai, 5-7 January.

Rasiel, Ethan M. and Friga, Paul N. 2001. *The McKinsey Mind: Understanding and Implementing the Problem solving Tools and Management Techniques of the World's Top Strategic Consulting Firm*, McGraw Hill, 2001

Reisz Mathew. 2008. Diversity Challenge, *Times Higher Education*. Accessible at: www.timeshighereducation.co.uk

Rekkedal, Torstein. 1993. Recent Research in Distance Education, *Open Learning*, 8 (1).

Roberts, T.S. 2004. *Online Collaborative Learning in Higher Education*, Hershey, PA: Information Science.

Rose, D.H. and Meyer, A. 2002. *Teaching Every Student in the Digital Age: Universal Design for Learning* Alexandria, VA: ASCD [http://en.wikipedia.org/wiki/Universal_Design_for_Learning]

Rourke, L. and Szabo, M. 2002. A Content Analysis of the Journal of Distance Education 1986-2001, *Journal of Distance Education*, 17(1).

Sabatier, P.A. 2007. *Theories of the Policy Process* (2nd ed.). Boulder: Westview Press.

Sadgopal, A. 2008. Misconceiving Fundamentals, Dismantling Rights, *Tehelka,* 14th June, 2008, pp. 44-45, New Delhi.

Sahoo P.K., *Higher Education at a Distance,* New Delhi: Sanchar, 1994.

Sahoo P.K., *Open Learning System,* New Delhi: Uppal, 1994.

Sahoo, P.K. Research in Distance Education, in Mukhopadhyay, M. and others (eds), *Educational Technology: Yearbook 1988,* New Delhi: AIAET, 1989.

Sahoo, P.K. 1997. In Mukhopadhyay, Marmar and Parhar, M. (Eds.). Open and Distance Education, New Delhi: Jawahar Publishers and Distributors.

Saldanha, Denzil. 2010. *Civil Society Processes and the State, The BGVS and the Literacy Campaigns*. New Delhi: Rawat Publications.

Salmi, J. 2009. *The Challenges of Establishing World-class Universities*. Washington DC: World Bank.

Sapon-Shevin, Mara. 2010. *Because We can Change the World: A Practical Guide to Building Cooperative, Inclusive Classroom Communities.* California: Corwin, p. 163.

Scriven, Bruce. 1991. Ten years of Distance Education, *Distance Education*, 12(1).

Semel, Susan F., Alan R. Sandovnick, and Peter W. Cookson, Jr., (Eds.). 1992.

International Handbook of Educational Reform, New York/London: Greenwood Press.

Sen, Amartya. 2009. *Idea of Justice.* Boston: Belknap Press of Harvard University Press.

Shaeffer, Sheldon, 2006. *Rethinking Secondary Education: Opportunities and Challenges in Asia.* UNESCO Asia and Pacific Regional Bureau for education, Bangkok.

Shah, A.M. 2005. Higher Education and Research: Roots of Mediocrity, *Economic Political Weekly*, -XL No. 22-23, May 28, 2005.

Shah, P. 2002. Liberalise the Education Sector, *The Economic Times*,18th July, 2002.

Sharma, Kavita, A. 2003. 50 Years of University Grants Commission, UGC 2003

Sharma, Shalendra D. 2002. *The Development of Democracy in India.* Boulder, CO: Lynne Rienner.

Shattock, M. 2004. "Introduction". In: M. Shattock (Ed.), *Entrepreneurialism and The Transformation of Russian Universities.* Paris: IIEP-UNESCO, pp.27-36.

Sherman, J. and Nedza A. 1990. Distance Education Research-Areas of Interest, *Research in Distance Education*, Page 14.

Srivastava, Manjulika. 2012. Open Universities: India's Answer to Challenges in Higher Education, New Delhi: Vikas Publishing House Pvt. Ltd.

Srivastava, Manjulika and Ramegowda N. S. 2006. Profile of Distance Learners in Garg *et al.* (Ed), *Four Decades of Distance Education in India*, Viva Books Pvt. Ltd. New Delhi.

Shubhi, V. 2009. Poor Quality Education in Government Schools, *The Views paper*, July 3.

Singh Gurminder. 2011. Elementary Education for Girls in India, *Journal of Educational Planning and Administration,* Vol. XXV, No.3.

Singh, Amrik. 2004. *Fifty Years of Higher Education in India: The Role of the University Grants Commission,* Sage Publications, New Delhi, 2004.

Sinha, A., Kishore, D. and Hashmi, J.N., *Interactive Communication for Distance Education.* Ahmedabad: DECU, ISRO, 1994.

Slantcheva, S. and Levy, D.C. 2007. "Introduction". In: S. Slantcheva and D. Levy (Eds.), *Private Higher Education in Post-Communist Europe: In Search of Legitimacy.* New York: Palgrave Mcmillan, pp. 1-23

Smith, M.K. *et al.* 2009. Why peer discussion improves student performance on in-class concept questions. *Science*, 323(5910), 122-124.

Stiglitz, Joseph E. 2002. *Globalization and its Discontents.* New York: W.W. Norton.

Sunder, S. 2010. *Higher education reforms in India.* Yale University (Mimeo).

Supreme Court of India. 2002. Judgment: Writ Petition (Civil) No. 607 of 1992, *T.M.A. Pai Foundation and Others Vs. State of Karnataka and Others,* SC, New Delhi, 8 SCC 481.

Supreme Court of India. 2005. Judgment: Writ Petition (Civil) No 19 of 2004 Prof. Yashpal vs. State of Chhattisgarh and others, New Delhi.

Supreme Court of India. 2003. Judgment: Writ Petition (Civil) No. 350 of 1993, *Islamic Academy of Education and Another Versus State of Karnataka and Others,* SC, New Delhi, 6 SCC 697.

Takwale, Ram. G. 2003. Challenges and Opportunities of Globalisation for Higher

Education in India—Alternatives through e-Education. UGC Golden Jubilee Lecture Series. UGC, New Delhi.

The copyright (Amendment Act, 2012, no. 27 of 2012, An Act further to Amend the Copyright Act, 1957, and June 2012

THE ECONOMIST. 2010. Banyan: The Elusive Fruit of Inclusive Growth —The tricky search for forms of economic growth that will offer opportunity and protection to everyone. May 15th–21st, 2010, p.50).

Tilak, J.B.G. 1999. Investment in Human Capital in India: An Inter-State Analysis of Stock and Flow of Human Capital, *Journal of Indian School of Political Economy*, Vol. XI, No.1, pp.39-75.

Tilak, J.B.G. 2001. *Building Human Capital: What Others Can Learn.* World Bank Institute Working Paper, World Bank, Washington, D.C.

Tilak, J.B.G. 2004. Free and Compulsory Education: Legislative Intervention, *Economic and Political Weekly*, February 14, 2004

Tilak, J. B. G. 2004. Absence of Policy and Perspective in Higher Education, *Economic and Political Weekly*, May 22, 2004

Tilak, J.B.G. 2005. *Post-Elementary Education, Poverty and Development in India.* Working Paper Series, No.6, Centre of African Studies, University of Edinburgh, U.K.

Tilak, J.B.G. 2010. The foreign educational institutions bill: a critique. *Economic and Political Weekly*, *XLV* (19), 12-15.

Tryggvason, Marja-Terttu. 2009. Why is Finnish teacher education successful? Some goals Finnish teacher educators have for their teaching, *European Journal of Teacher Education,* 32: 4, 369 —382

Tushman, M.L. and Romanelli, E. 1985. Organizational evolution: A metamorphosis model of convergence and reorientation. *Research in Organizational Behaviour*, *7*, 171-222.

UGC. (Year not mentioned). Growth of ODL System, http://www.ugc.ac.in/deb/pdf/growthDEB.pdf

UIS. 2010. *Global education digest 2009: comparing education statistics across the world.* Montreal: UIS.

UIS/OECD. 2003. *Financing education—Investments and returns: Analysis of the World Education Indicators* 2002 Edition. Paris: UNESCO/OECD.

UNDP. 2010. *The Real Wealth of Nations: Pathways to Human Development.* Human Development Report 2010, available at http://hdr.undp.org.

UNESCO. 2003. Literacy as Freedom. A UNESCO Round Table . Paris: UNESCO.

UNESCO. 2004. *EFA Global Monitoring Report 2005: Education for all—The quality imperative.* Paris: UNESCO.

UNESCO. 2008. *Global Monitoring Report*, UNESCO Publication.

UNESCO. 2009. Policy Guidelines on Inclusion in Education. UNESCO: Paris. http://unesdoc.unesco.org/images/0017/001778/177849e.pdf

UNESCO. 2010. *Reaching the Marginalized.* EFA Global Monitoring Report 2010, available at http://www.unesco.org/publishing.

United Nations. 1948. *Universal Declaration of Human Rights* (New York: UN, 1948); and UN, *International Conference on Population and Development Programme of Action* (New York: UN, 1994): para. 4.18.

United Nations. 1995. *Platform of Action, Fourth World Conference on Women,*

Beijing, China, 4-15 September 1995 (New York: UN, 1996): para. 69; and UN, *The Beijing Declaration* (New York: UN, 1996): paras. 13, 14, and 17

United Nations. 2000. The *Millennium Development Goals.* New York.

United Nations. 2002. *United Nations Literacy Decade: Education for All; International Plan of Action; Implementation of General Assembly Resolution 56/116. Report of the Secretary-General.* New York: United Nations; and UNESCO. 2003.

United Nations. 2003. Millennium Development Goals: About the Goals, accessed at www.developmentgoals.org/About_the_goals.htm

University Grants Commission. 2004. Annual *Report 2003-04,* New Delhi.

University Grants Commission. *Annual Reports* (Various Years), UGC, New Delhi.

Varghese, N.V. (Ed.). 2009a. *Higher Education Reforms: Institutional Restructuring in Asia.* Paris: IIEP-UNESCO.

Varghese, N.V. 2009b. *Institutional Restructuring in Higher Education within the Commonwealth of Independent States.* IIEP Research papers, Paris: IIEP-UNESCO.

Varghese, N.V. 2010. *Running to standstill: Higher Education in a Period of Global economic crisis.* Paris: IIEP-UNESCO.

Varghese, N.V. 2011. Drivers of reforms in higher education, In Adamson, Bob; Nixon, Jon and Feng, Su (eds.) *The Reorientation of Higher Education: Compliance and Defiance*, Springer for the university of Hong Kong (published in 2013).

Weatherley, R. and Lipsky, M. 1977. Street-level Bureaucrats and Institutional Innovation: Implementing Special-education Reform. *Harvard Educational Review*, 47(2), 171-197.

Wenzel, Thomas, 2000. Cooperative Student Activities as Learning Devices. *Analytical Chemistry,* 72, pp. 293A-296A

Wheelen, Thomas L. and Hunger, J. David, 2004. *Strategic Management and Business Policy*, 9th Edition, 2004, Pearson Prentice Hall

Wikipedia. wikipedia.org/wiki/communitcations_in_India, 2012, January 28,

Wood, A. and Mayer, J. 1999. *Africa's Export Structure in a Comparative Perspective.* Institute of Development Studies, University of Sussex.

Wood, B.D. and Waterman, R.W. 1994. *Bureaucratic Dynamics*. Boulder, CO: Westview Press.

Working Group for International Cooperation in Skill Development. 2008. *Post-Primary Education and Skill Development.* Paper No. 12, NORRAG, Geneva, available at http://www.norrag.org/wg.

World Bank. 1986. *Financing Education in Developing Countries: An Exploration of Policy Options*. Washington DC: World Bank.

World Bank. 2002a. *Constructing Knowledge Societies: New Challenges for Tertiary Education*. Washington DC: World Bank.

World Bank. 2002b. *Globalization, Growth and Poverty: Building an Inclusive World Economy*. New York: Oxford University Press.

World Bank. 2003. *Lifelong Learning in the Global Knowledge Economy: Challenges for Developing Countries,* World Bank Washington DC

World Bank. 2003. *Secondary Education in India.* Report No. 2, Discussion Paper, South Asia Human Development Sector, Delhi.

World Bank. 2005. *Expanding Opportunities and Building Competencies for Young People: A New Agenda for Secondary Education.* World Bank, Washington DC

World Bank. 2008. *Accelerating Catch-up: Tertiary Education for Growth in Sub-Saharan Africa.* Washington DC: World Bank.

World Bank. 2009. *Secondary Education in India: Universalizing Opportunity.* Human Development Unit, South Asia Region, Delhi.

World Bank. 2010. *Financing Higher Education in Africa.* Washington DC: World Bank.

World Bank. 2012. Knowledge Assessment Methodology. http://www.worldbank.org/kam

Zawacki-Richter, O. 2009. Research areas in Distance Education: A Delphi Study. *International Review of Research in Open and Distance Learning,* 10 (3).

Websites

www.azimpremzifoundation.org
www.edu.nic.in
www.edudialogue.in
www.indiavision2020.org
www.itu.int/wsis
www.ssa.nic.in
www.unesco.org
www.worlib.org/vol17no1/singh_v17n1.shtml
http://www.ncert.nic.in/new_ncert/ncert/rightside/links/pdf/focus_group/executive_summary.pdf
http://www.swarnimgujarat.org/about_golden_gujarat.aspx
www.ioe.ac.uk/study/MMAINC)
http://indiatoday.intoday.in/story/State+board+exams+marred+by+rampant+cheating/1/88997.html
http://mhrd.gov.in/sites/upload_files/mhrd/files/Report-english_0.pdf
http://www.cbse.nic.in/circulars/cir39-2009.pdf
http://www.cobse.org/result2005.pdf

Contributors

Bhola, Prof. H.S. Professor Emeritus, Indiana University, Bloomington, Indiana, USA.

Bhushan, Prof. Sudhanshu, Head, Department of Higher Education, NUEPA, New Delhi.

Biswal, Prof. K. Professor, Department of School & Nonformal Education, NUEPA, New Delhi.

Chugh, Dr. Sunita, Assistant Professor, Department of School & Nonformal Education, NUEPA, New Delhi.

Das, Prof. S.K., Dean (Academic), NIMS University, Jaipur.

Jadeja, Prof. R.P., Director of H M Patel Institute of English Training and Research, Vallabh Vidyanagar, Anand, Gujarat.

Joshi, Dr. Nishant, Assistant Professor, H.M. Patel Institute of English Training and Research, Vallabh Vidyanagar, Anand, Gujarat.

Mehta, Prof. Arun C., Head, Department of Educational Management Information Systems, NUEPA, New Delhi.

Merchant, Dr. A.K., Visiting Faculty at Centre for Cultural Resources and Training, and Senior Faculty at the Sai International Centre for Human Values, New Delhi.

Mukhopadhyay, Prof. Marmar, Chairman, Educational Technology and Management Academy, Gurgaon.

Mukhopadhyay, Prof. Sudesh, Chairperson, Rehabilitation Council of India, New Delhi.

Narula, Dr. Manju, Assistant Professor, Department of Educational Administration, NUEPA, New Delhi.

Parhar, Prof. Madhu, Professor, Staff Training and Research Institute of Distance Education, IGNOU, New Delhi.

Shamsu, Dr. Shakila, Deputy Director, Planning and Development Division, IGNOU, New Delhi.

Singh, Dr. Sweta, Assistant Professor, Department of Education, Lady Irwin College, New Delhi.

Singh, Dr. Sumanjeet, Assistant Professor, Ramjas College, University of Delhi, Delhi.

Srivastava, Prof. Gauri, Head, Department of Women's Education, NCERT, New Delhi.

Sungoh, Prof. Sherwin M., Department of Education, NEHU, Shillong.

Taj, Prof. Haseen, Department of Education, Bangalore University, Bangalore.

Varghese, Prof. N.V., Director, Centre for Policy Research in Higher Education, NUEPA, New Delhi.

Verma, Dr. Snehlata, Assistant Professor, Lovely Institute of Education, Lovely Professional University, Phagwara, Punjab.

Index